AF607859

Morphosyntactic Alternations in English

Functional and Cognitive Perspectives

Functional Linguistics
Series Editor: Robin Fawcett, Cardiff University
Guest editor, this volume: Christopher S. Butler

This series publishes monographs that seek to understand the nature of language by exploring one or other of various cognitive models or in terms of the communicative use of language. It concentrates on studies that are in, or on the borders of, various functional theories of language.

Published:

Functional Dimensions of Ape-Human Discourse
Edited by James D. Benson and William S. Greaves

System and Corpus: Exploring Connections
Edited by Geoff Thompson and Susan Hunston

Meaningful Arrangement: Exploring the Syntactic Description of Texts
Edward McDonald

Explorations in Stylistics
Andrew Goatly

From Language to Multimodality: New Developments in the Study of Ideational Meaning
Edited by Carys Jones and Eija Ventola

Text Type and Texture
Edited by Geoff Thompson and Gail Forey

An Introduction to the Grammar of Old English: A Systemic Functional Approach
Michael Cummings

Forthcoming:

Systemic Functional Perspectives of Japanese: Descriptions and Applications
Edited by Elizabeth Thomson and William Armour

The Texture of Casual Conversation: A Multidimensional Interpretation
Diana Slade

A Multimodal Approach to Classroom Discourse
Kay O'Halloran

Reading Visual Narratives: Inter-image Analysis of Children's Picture Books
Clare Painter

Voices Around the World – Recent Studies in Systemic Phonology
Volume 1: Focus on the English Language
Edited by Wendy L. Bowcher and Bradley A. Smith

Morphosyntactic Alternations in English

Functional and Cognitive Perspectives

Edited by
Pilar Guerrero Medina

SHEFFIELD OAKVILLE

Published by Equinox Publishing Ltd.

UK: Unit S3, Kelham House, 3, Lancaster Street, Sheffield S3 8AF
USA: DBBC, 28 Main Street, Oakville, CT 06779

www.equinoxpub.com

First published 2011

British Library Cataloguing-in-Publication Data
A catalogue record for this book is available from the British Library.

ISBN-13 978 1 84553 744 9 (hardback)

Library of Congress Cataloging-in-Publication Data

Morphosyntactic alternations in English: functional and cognitive perspectives / edited by Pilar Guerrero Medina.
p. cm.
Includes bibliographical references and index.
ISBN 978-1-84553-744-9
1. English language—Verb. 2. English language—Grammar. I. Guerrero Medina, Pilar. PE1271.M67 2010
425'.6—dc22
2010026351

Typeset by S.J.I. Service, New Delhi
Printed and bound in Great Britain by Lightning Source, Milton Keynes, UK

Contents

About the Contributors

Antonio Barcelona is Full Professor of English Language and Linguistics in the Department of English and German Philology at the University of Córdoba, Spain. His research has covered such areas as the pragmatic motivation of syntax (especially constituent order), conceptual metaphor and metonymy and cognitive linguistics in general. His early published work (from 1976 until about 1993) was concerned with the pragmatic motivation of certain constituent order structures in English and Spanish: inversion, theme/topic selection, various types of raising, existential-presentative and other presentative constructions, converses, passive and others. Since 1986 his publications have focused on the clarification of the cognitive-linguistic notions of metaphor and metonymy and on their interaction, on the role of these two cognitive mechanisms in various types of cognitive models and grammatical structures, and most recently, on the role of conceptual metonymy in cognition and in linguistic meaning and form. Among his many international publications in these areas: the edited book *Metaphor and Metonymy at the Crossroads: A cognitive perspective* (Mouton de Gruyter, 2000), and articles like "Metaphorical models of romantic love in *Romeo and Juliet*" (*Journal of Pragmatics* 25 (1995), 667–688), "The case for a metonymic basis of pragmatic inferencing: Evidence from jokes and funny anecdotes" (in K. Panther and L. Thornburg (eds) (2003) *Metonymy and Pragmatic Inferencing*, John Benjamins, 81–102), "Metonymy behind grammar: The motivation of the seemingly 'irregular' grammatical behavior of English paragon names" (in G. Radden and K. Panther (eds) (2004) *Studies in Linguistic Motivation*. Mouton de Gruyter, 357–374), or "The role of metonymy in meaning at discourse level: A case study" (in G. Radden, K. Koepcke, T. Berg and P. Siemund (eds) (2007) *Aspects of Meaning Construction*. John Benjamins, 51–75). One of his most recent publications is the co-edited book (with Klaus-Uwe Panther and Linda Thornburg), *Metonymy and Metaphor in Grammar* (John Benjamins, 2009). E-mail: antonio.barcelona@uco.es

Hans C. Boas is Associate Professor of Germanic Linguistics in the Department of Germanic Studies and the Department of Linguistics at the University of Texas at Austin. Before going to Austin, he was a postdoctoral researcher with the FrameNet project at the International Computer Science Institute and a research fellow in the Department of Linguistics at the University of California at Berkeley, funded by the Deutscher Akademischer Austauschdienst ("German Academic Exchange Service"). Prior to that, he studied law and linguistics at the Georg-August-Universität Göttingen, Germany. He received both his MA and Ph.D. in the Linguistics Department at the University of North Carolina at Chapel Hill. His research comprises three main areas: 1. Construction Grammar and Frame Semantics; 2. Computational Lexicography; and 3. Language documentation, language contact, and language death. His publications include *A Constructional Approach to Resultatives* (CSLI publication, 2003), *Grammatical Constructions: Back to the roots* (co-edited with Mirjam Fried, John Benjamins, 2005), *Contrastive Studies and Valency* (co-edited with Petra Steiner and Stefan Schierholz, Peter Lang, 2006), *Multilingual FrameNets in Computational Lexicography: Methods and applications* (Mouton de Gruyter, 2009), and *The Life and Death of Texas German* (Duke University Press, 2009). In 2001, he founded the Texas German Dialect Project to document, archive, and analyse the remnants of Texas German, a critically endangered dialect spoken in the Lone Star State since the 1830s. Recordings of interviews (including transcriptions and translations) with more than 350 speakers of Texas German can be accessed at http://www.tgdp.org E-mail: hcb@mail.utexas.edu

Kristin Davidse is Professor of English Linguistics at KU Leuven, the Catholic University of Leuven, Belgium. She has an MA in Germanic Languages (1981) from the University of Leuven. She is also an alumna of the University of Sydney, where she was introduced to Systemic Functional Linguistics by M. A. K. Halliday and Jim Martin and was awarded an MA in Applied Linguistics (1985). Halliday supervised, together with Emma Vorlat, her Ph.D. in Linguistics on the Categories of Experiential Grammar, awarded by the University of Leuven in 1991. In that year she was given a permanent appointment at the Leuven Linguistics Department. As a follow-up to her doctorate, she published mainly about the semantics of English constructions such as "ergative" and middle constructions, existential and copular clauses and ditransitives, branching out later to such topics as clefts, reported speech and tag questions. In recent years, she has also turned her attention to the grammar of the English noun phrase, and to phenomena of emergent grammar and grammaticalization in the NP. On these topics she has published in international journals such as *Cognitive Linguistics, English Language and Linguistics, Folia Linguistica, Journal of Historical Pragmatics, Linguistics, Text and Talk, Transactions of the Philological Society* and *WORD*, and an article in *Journal of Pragmatics* is forthcoming. She has also contributed to about fifteen internationally distributed volumes. A special focus of attention in her research has always been the pairing of form and meaning, whereby form is understood broadly as encompassing both syntagmatic and paradigmatic patterning, and syntactic as well as collocational patterning, including lexical selection restrictions and semantic prosody. She has supervised ten finished doctorates, all of which have been published or accepted for publication (six with Mouton). She has supervised four four-year projects awarded by the Research Foundation Flanders (FWO) and the Research Council of KU Leuven. She is currently coordinating the work package on nominal modification of the Interuniversity Attraction Poles project P6/44, Grammaticalization and (Inter)subjectification, coordinated by Johan Van der Auwera. She co-founded and for ten years co-edited the journal *Functions of Language*, and has co-edited books on functional grammar, the nominative and accusative, and grammaticalization. E-mail: kristin.davidse@arts.kuleuven.be

Casilda García de la Maza is Lecturer in English Language and Linguistics in the Department of English and German Philology, Translation and Interpreting at the University of the Basque Country, Spain, where she has taught courses in English Language, English Phonetics, the History of the English Language, Translation English-Spanish and, more recently, English for Specific Purposes. In 2005 she obtained her Ph.D. from the University of Cambridge (United Kingdom) for her thesis entitled *The Grammar, Semantics and Productivity of the English Middle Construction*. She has mainly carried out research in the area of English syntax and, more precisely, on issues of argument structure, verb valency and the syntax-semantics-pragmatics interface. Among her most recent publications are the articles: "A lexical approach to the derivation of the English middle construction" (*Cambridge Occasional Papers in Linguistics* 1 (2004), 127–145) and "Intransitivity, ergatives and middles" (*Estudios Ingleses de la Universidad Complutense* 16 (2008), 31–50). Her current research interests include ongoing change and variation in English, language use and degrees of acceptability, as well as the use and development of multimedia language learning tools in the ESP classroom. E-mail: casilda.garcia@ehu.es

Daniel García Velasco is Lecturer in English Linguistics at the University of Oviedo, Spain. His research interests centre on English lexicology and syntax from a functional perspective. He is an active researcher in Simon Dik's Functional Grammar and its successor Functional Discourse Grammar and has contributed to the development of the theory in different areas. In 2003, he published *Funcionalismo y lingüística: La Gramática Funcional de S. C. Dik* (University of Oviedo Press), an exhaustive critical presentation of the model in Spanish. In 2002, together with Kees Hengeveld he published "Do we need predicate frames?" (in R. M. Usón and M. J. Pérez Quintero (eds), *New Perspectives on Argument Structure in Functional Grammar*, Mouton de Gruyter, 95–123) in which the authors propose to separate lexemes from the frames in which they appear in the lexicon and dispense with the notion of "predicate frame". More recently, he has proposed a new approach to lexical semantics with significant consequences for the organization of the lexicon in Functional Discourse Grammar ("Lexical competence and Functional Discourse Grammar". *Alfa: Revista de Lingüística* 51 (2007), 165–187). The advantages of this proposal have been examined in two recent articles on the process of conversion ("Conversion in English and its implications for Functional Discourse Grammar", *Lingua* 119 (2009), 1164–1185) and on the creation of neologisms from proper nouns in the English language ("Innovative coinage: its place in the grammar", in C. S. Butler and J. Martín Arista (eds) (2009) *Deconstructing Constructions*, John Benjamins, 3–23). He has also co-edited the volume *The Noun Phrase in Functional Discourse Grammar* (2008, Mouton de Gruyter), together with Jan Rijkhoff. This book contains a contribution by Daniel García Velasco ("Functional Discourse Grammar and extraction from (complex) noun phrases"), in which the author offers a pragmatic-based approach to displacement. E-mail: danielg@uniovi.es

Francisco Gonzálvez-García is Lecturer in English Language and Linguistics in the Department of English and German Philology at the University of Almería, Spain. His research interests centre on the areas of syntax, semantics, pragmatics and discourse analysis, as well as on functionalist and constructivist approaches. His early work, deriving from his Ph.D. received at the University of Bologna (Royal Spanish College) for his thesis entitled *The Syntax-semantics Interface in Complex-transitive Complementation in Contemporary English*, was geared towards an eclectic approach to the syntactic analysis and semantico-pragmatic import of verbless complement clauses in English. This synthesizing analysis is outlined in "A modality view of predicate selection in small clauses" (*Texas Linguistic Forum* 38 (1997), 101–119). Over the last few years, he has published a number of articles focusing on argument structure in English and Spanish from a constructionist standpoint. His most recent publications include: with Christopher S. Butler, "Mapping functional-cognitive space" (*Annual Review of Cognitive Linguistics* 4 (2006), 39–96), a fine-grained comparison of 11 functionalist, cognitivist and/or constructionist models in terms of a list of 36 features; "Passives without actives: evidence from verbless complement clauses in Spanish" (*Constructions SV1-5* (2006), 1–65), a Goldbergian analysis of passive verbless configurations in Spanish as constructions in their own right; "'Saved by the reflexive': Evidence from coercion via reflexives in verbless complement clauses in English and Spanish" (*Annual Review of Cognitive Linguistics* 5 (2007), 193–238), an analysis of coercion via reflexive pronouns in secondary predication in English and Spanish; "Measuring out reflexivity in secondary predication in English and Spanish: Evidence from *verba cogitandi* in English and Spanish" (in C. S. Butler and J. Martín Arista (eds) (2009) *Deconstructing Constructions,* John Benjamins, 101–145), a constructionist analysis of the reflexivity continuum, and "The family of object-related depictives in English and Spanish: Towards a usage-based, constructionist analysis" (*Language Sciences* 31 (2009), 663–723), a Goldbergian analysis of object-related depictives in English in Spanish. E-mail: fgonza@ual.es

Stefan Th. Gries is Full Professor of Linguistics at the University of California, Santa Barbara. He earned his MA and Ph.D. degrees at the University of Hamburg (1998/2000), after which he held positions at the Department of Business Communication and Information Science of the University of Southern Denmark at Sønderborg (1998–2005), and in the Psychology Department of the Max Planck Institute for Evolutionary Anthropology in Leipzig. (He also was a Visiting Professor at the 2007 LSA Linguistic Institute at Stanford University.) Methodologically, Gries is a quantitative corpus linguist at the intersection of corpus linguistics and computational linguistics, who uses a variety of different statistical methods to investigate linguistic topics such as morpho-phonology, syntax, the syntax-lexis interface, semantics as well as first and second language acquisition and overall corpus-linguistic methodology. Occasionally, he also uses experimental methods (acceptability judgements, sentence completion, priming, self-paced reading times, and sorting tasks). Much of his recent work involves the open source software R (programming language). Theoretically, he is a cognitively-oriented linguist (with an interest in Construction Grammar) in the wider sense of seeking explanations in terms of cognitive processes. Gries has published three books – one research monograph, an introduction to statistics with R for linguists (in German and in English), and a book on corpus linguistics with R. He has co-edited two volumes on corpora in cognitive linguistics and one on corpus linguistics. He has published articles in a variety of journals, such as *Cognitive Linguistics, Annual Review of Cognitive Linguistics, International Journal of Corpus Linguistics, Corpora, Literary and Linguistic Computing, Journal of Quantitative Linguistics, Journal of Psycholinguistic Research, The Mental Lexicon,* and others. He is founding editor in chief of the international peer-reviewed journal *Corpus Linguistics and Linguistic Theory,* associate editor of *Cognitive Linguistics,* and performs editorial functions for *Constructions and Frames, Language and Cognition,* and *CogniTextes.* E-mail: stgries@linguistics.ucsb.edu

Pilar Guerrero Medina is Lecturer in English Grammar at the University of Córdoba, Spain. She has mainly conducted her research within a functionalist framework, focusing on the relationship between lexis and grammar on the one hand, and grammar and discourse on the other. Over the past decade, she has published articles on a range of topics, including transitivity in grammar and discourse, grammatical and lexical aspect and Object assignment. Among her earlier publications, framed within the Functional Grammar (FG) theory of Simon C. Dik, are: "A prototype approach to transitivity: its implications for the FG typology of SoAs" (in H. Olbertz, K. Hengeveld and J. Sánchez (eds) (1998) *The Structure of the Lexicon in Functional Grammar,* John Benjamins, 215–232) and "Reconsidering aspectuality: interrelations between grammatical and lexical aspect" (*Working Papers in Functional Grammar* 75 (2001), 1–11). More recently, the grammar-discourse interface has been explored in two of her articles: "Cardinal transitivity in foregrounded discourse. A contrastive study in English and Spanish" (in C. S. Butler, M. A. Gómez-González and S. M. Doval (eds) (2005) *The Dynamics of Language Use: Functional and contrastive perspectives,* John Benjamins, 349–369) and "A discourse-based approach to English de-transitivization: middle vs passive" (in P. Guerrero Medina and E. Martínez Jurado (eds) (2006) *Where Grammar Meets Discourse: Functional and cognitive perspectives,* University of Córdoba, 133–150). One of her latest publications is the article "Semantic and pragmatic constraints on the English *get*-passive" (in C. S. Butler and J. Martín Arista (eds) (2009) *Deconstructing Constructions,* John Benjamins, 271–294), where she incorporates insights from the Goldbergian version of Construction Grammar. E-mail: ff1gumep@uco.es

J. Lachlan Mackenzie is Honorary Professor of Functional Linguistics at VU University Amsterdam, Netherlands and a Researcher at the Instituto de Linguística Teórica e Computacional (ILTEC) in Lisbon, Portugal. His major research interest is in developing the theory of Functional Discourse Grammar (FDG) and on applying FDG in the analysis of Western European Languages. He is an editor of the journal *Functions of Language* and is Research Manager of the SCIMITAR group based in Santiago de Compostela, Spain. Born in Scotland, he holds an MA in Modern Languages from the University of Aberdeen and a Ph.D. in Linguistics from the

University of Edinburgh. He made his career in Amsterdam, Netherlands, specializing in the theory of Functional Grammar (FG) developed by the late Simon C. Dik. A major emphasis of his work in FG was on nominalizations, culminating in "English nominalizations in the layered model of the sentence", in B. Devriendt, L. Goossens and J. van der Auwera (eds) (1996) *Complex Structures: A functionalist perspective,* Mouton de Gruyter, 325–355. His work in FDG has focused on the analysis of fragmentary utterances and on the relation between the grammatical model and psycholinguistic findings: "First things first: Towards an Incremental Functional Grammar" (*Acta Linguistica Hafniensia* 32 (2000), 23–44) and "Functional Discourse Grammar and language production" (in J. L. Mackenzie and M. A. Gómez-González (eds) (2004), *A New Architecture for Functional Grammar,* Mouton de Gruyter, 179–195). In 2008 Kees Hengeveld and he published *Functional Discourse Grammar* with Oxford University Press. Other books from recent years are *Principles and Pitfalls of English Grammar* (Coutinho, 2002), *A New Architecture for Functional Grammar* (Mouton de Gruyter, 2004, co-edited), *Crucial Readings in Functional Grammar* (Mouton de Gruyter, 2005, co-edited), *Studies in Functional Discourse Grammar* (Peter Lang, 2005, co-edited), *Languages and Cultures in Contrast and Comparison* (John Benjamins, 2008, co-edited), *Writing in English: A guide for advanced learners* (UTB, 2008, co-authored), *Current Trends in Contrastive Linguistics* (John Benjamins, 2008, co-edited) and *Effective Writing in English: A sourcebook* (Coutinho, 2009, co-authored). E-mail: lachlan_mackenzie@hotmail.com Website: www.lachlanmackenzie.com

Ricardo Mairal Usón has been Full Professor of English Language and Linguistics in the Department of Modern Languages at the Spanish National Distance-Learning University (UNED) since 2002. His main areas of research interest are the architecture of the English lexicon, the representation of lexical knowledge, linguistic universals and the interactions between lexical semantics, syntax and morphology with particular reference to theoretical models, both formal and functional. He has been the head of various research projects funded by the Spanish Ministry of Education and the Regional Government of Madrid and has additionally participated in other projects that deal with various aspects of language research such as terminology, the compilation of lexical representations and linking mechanisms in Old English, natural language processing and the development of lexical databases for lexicography. He has co-authored or co-edited a number of books including: *Nuevas perspectivas en Gramática Funcional* (Ariel, 1999), *Constructing a Lexicon* *of English Verbs* (Mouton de Gruyter, 1999), *New Perspectives on Argument Structure in Functional Grammar* (Mouton de Gruyter, 2002), *En torno a los universales lingüísticos* (Cambridge University Press, 2003), *Linguistic Universals* (Cambridge University Press, 2006). He has also published over fifty scholarly articles which have appeared in specialized national and international journals. He has served as a scientific committee member for several specialized journals, including *Cuadernos de Investigación Filológica, Atlantis, RESLA, Estudios Ingleses de la Universidad Complutense, Onomázein* and *Functions of Language.* He has done occasional review work for *Cognitive Linguistics* and *Language Sciences* and has also been a member of the advisory committee of various international conferences on Role and Reference Grammar. He has also lectured extensively as keynote speaker at national and international conferences on Applied and Theoretical Linguistics. He is one of the co-founders of the LEXICOM research group (www.lexicom.es). His recent research has concentrated on the design of a multilingual and multifunctional lexical conceptual knowledge base (www.fungramkb.com). E-mail: rmairal@flog.uned.es

Juana I. Marín-Arrese is Full Professor of English Linguistics in the Department of *Filología Inglesa I* (English Language and Linguistics) at the Universidad Complutense of Madrid. Her main research interests involve the fields of evidentiality and modality, with specific interest in cross-linguistic studies on the expression of stance and subjectivity and intersubjectivity in discourse. She has coordinated several research projects on these topics and has published extensively in various journals and collective volumes: *Perspectives on Evidentiality and Modality* (Editorial Complutense, 2004); *English Modality in Perspective: Genre analysis and contrastive studies* (Peter Lang, 2004); *Belgium Journal of English Language and Literatures* 5 (2007); *Modality in English: Theory and description* (Mouton de Gruyter, 2009); *Studies on English Modality: In honour of Frank R. Palmer* (Peter Lang, 2009). She has also carried out research on the middle domain, passive and impersonal constructions in Spanish and English. Articles on these topics have appeared in journals and books such as: *Journal of English Studies 1* (1999), *Conceptualization of Events in Newspaper Discourse: Mystification of agency and degree of implication in news reports* (UCM, 2002), *Cognitive Linguistics in Spain at the Turn of the Century, Vol. I: Grammar and Semantics* (AELCO and Universidad Autónoma de Madrid, 2003), *Trends in Cognitive Linguistics* (Peter Lang, 2009), *Inside the Learner's Mind: Cognitive Processing in Second Language Acquisition* (John Benjamins, 2010). Her research interests also include studies on metaphor and metonymy, and humour studies: *Language Sciences* 18 (1996) and *Intercultural Pragmatics* 5 (2008). E-mail: juana@filol.ucm.es

Javier Martín Arista has been Senior Lecturer in English at the University of La Rioja, Spain, since 1996. He has carried out post-doctoral research at the University of Sheffield (1996), Pennsylvania (1999), SUNY Buffalo (2000) and Amsterdam (2001) and has delivered lectures by invitation at several European and American universities, including Newcastle, Strathclyde, Sheffield Hallam, Queen Mary-London, Copenhagen, Odense and Toronto. He also delivered a plenary lecture at the 2004 International Conference of the Spanish Association for Applied Linguistics. Javier Martín Arista has edited several collective works and published numerous book chapters and articles in journals specializing in theoretical linguistics, English studies and diachronic studies. He is the leading researcher of the Research Group in Functional Grammars of the University of La Rioja and has been a member of the editorial board of Shakespeare Quarterly-WSB until 2004, and is currently a reviewer of *ATLANTIS, STVDIVM, Journal of English Studies, Revista de Lingüística y Lenguas Aplicadas, Revista Española de Lingüística Aplicada, Revista Canaria de Estudios Ingleses* and *The Open Applied Lingustics Journal.* Dr Martín Arista is also editor of *RæL-Revista Electrónica de Lingüística Aplicada*. Javier Martín Arista has been a reviewer of the National Agency for Evaluation and Planning since 1999 and was Pro-Vice-Chancellor (Research and Staff) of the University of La Rioja since 2001 until 2004. He was a member of the organizing committee of the 1997 International Conference of the Spanish Association for Applied Linguistics and the 2003 International Conference in Cognitive Linguistics, and was the main organizer of the 2002 International Conference in Role and Reference Grammar. Javier Martín Arista has recently edited, together with Christopher S. Butler, *Deconstructing Constructions* (John Benjamins, 2009). E-mail: javier.martin@unirioja.es

Amy C. Neale has a Ph.D. from Cardiff University, Wales, United Kingdom, where she worked with Robin Fawcett, Gordon Tucker, and a number of other scholars developing the Cardiff Grammar dialect of Systemic Functional Linguistics. Her research interests are Systemic Functional grammar as a tool for natural language generation, in particular the modelling of "Transitivity" for verb generation, and the use of corpora to provide evidence of language in use. Her Ph.D. thesis, *More Delicate TRANSITIVITY: Extending the PROCESS TYPE system networks for English* *to include full semantic classifications,* was concerned with the generation of verbs in a large computational grammar, and contributed to the semantic classification of verb senses. This research produced a database of over 5000 fully analysed verb senses (including, uniquely, a high proportion of multi-word verbs, and extended system networks for three major Process types in English). Amy Neale is also interested in the application of linguistic research to real world problems, and is currently based at the National Digital Research Centre in Ireland, where her work focuses on the commercialization of academic research. E-mail: amy.neale@gmail.com

Carmen Portero Muñoz is Lecturer in English Language and Linguistics in the Department of English and German Philology at the University of Córdoba, Spain. Her research is mainly focused on lexical and morphosyntactic issues following functional approaches. Her Ph.D. dissertation, *Intensification: Study of a classeme,* supports the idea that syntactic aspects can be predicted from semantic features. A historical revision on this type of syntactically relevant feature is made in "Syntagmatic relations and the interconnection syntax-lexicon" (*Atlantis* 9 (1997), 267–280). Publications within the Functional Grammar (FG) framework include: with Daniel García Velasco, "Understood objects in Functional Grammar" (*Working Papers in Functional Grammar* 76 (2002), 1–22), where the authors give an account of object omission in English within the context of the theory of FG; "Conditional sentences revisited" (*Babel* 10 (2001), 99–112), where she studies conditional sentences following the FG proposal for a layered structure of the clause; "English 'Noun + Noun' sequences: their place in Functional Discourse Grammar" (*Web Papers in Functional Grammar* 80 (2007), 1–24), where she explores the mechanisms to account for the creation and interpretation of primary "noun + noun" compounds within Functional Discourse Grammar. Carmen Portero has also worked within the Role and Reference Grammar (RRG) framework. The article "Derived nominalizations in -ee: an RRG-based semantic analysis" (*English Language and Linguistics* 7 (2003), 129–159) is a study on a semi-productive English word-formation process using the RRG theoretical framework. Over the last few years her research interest has extended to cognitive theory and she is currently working on the empirical study of conceptual metonymy in grammar, discourse and sign language, with the aim of creating a metonymy data base, as part of a project funded by the Spanish Ministry of Education and Innovation (FFI 2008-04585/FILO). E-mail: ff1pomuc@uco.es

Francisco José Ruiz de Mendoza Ibáñez is Full Professor of English Linguistics at the University of La Rioja, Spain. He is the author of *Introducción a la teoría cognitiva de la metonimia* (Método, 1999) and co-author of *Metonymy, Grammar, and Communication* (Comares, 2002) and *Teoría lingüística: Métodos, herramientas y paradigmas* (Ramón Areces and UNED, 2010). He is co-editor of the book *Cognitive Linguistics: Internal dynamics and interdisciplinary interaction* (Mouton de Gruyter, 2005) and of *Cognitive Linguistics: Current applications and future perspectives* (Mouton de Gruyter, 2006). Francisco Ruiz de Mendoza has published numerous articles and book chapters. Many have appeared in journals such as *Journal of Pragmatics, Language and Communication, Folia Linguistica, Italian Journal of Linguistics, Jezikoslovlje, LAUD-Essen,* and in book series such as *Cognitive Linguistics Research* (Mouton), *Topics in English Linguistics* (Mouton), *Pragmatics and Beyond* (John Benjamins), *Lodz Studies in Language* (Peter Lang). He has also been a keynote speaker in international conferences such as the International Contrastive Linguistics Conference (Santiago, 2005), Converging and Diverging Tendencies in Cognitive Linguistics (Dubrovnik, 2005, 2008), Perspectives on Metonymy (Lodz, 2005), the 10th International Cognitive Linguistics Conference (Krakow, 2007), the 7th International Conference on Researching and Applying Metaphor (Cáceres, 2008), and III Conference on Metaphor in Language and Thought (Fortaleza, 2008). He serves on the scientific board of a number of journals, among them *Jezikoslovlje, Estudios Ingleses de la Universidad Complutense, Revista Española de Lingüística Aplicada, Revue Romane,* and *Cognitive Linguistics.* He is the editor of the *Review of Cognitive Linguistics* (John Benjamins) and co-editor of the series *Applications of Cognitive Linguistics* (Mouton de Gruyter). He is the current president of the Spanish Association of Applied Linguistics and the founder and Head of the Research Center in the Applications of Language (CRAL, University of La Rioja). E-mail: francisco.ruizdemendoza@unirioja.es

Acknowledgements

I am most grateful to Christopher Butler, guest series editor for this volume, for his invaluable help in the editorial process, and for his sound and generous advice throughout the construction of this book. I should also like to thank Robin Fawcett and Janet Joyce and the two anonymous reviewers who evaluated the book proposal, for their acute comments and criticism. And I also wish to give my personal thanks to all the contributors to this volume, for their patience and for all the hard work they have put into their articles.

Furthermore, I should like to acknowledge the support of the Spanish Ministry of Education and Innovation through grants FFI 2008-04448/FILO and FFI 2008-04585/FILO.

Finally, permission to reproduce copyright material in this book is gratefully acknowledged as follows:

Figures 2.1 (p. 40) and **5.1** (p. 125) were published as Figure 2 (p. 13) in Kees Hengeveld and J. Lachlan Mackenzie, *Functional Discourse Grammar: A typologically-based theory of language structure,* Oxford University Press © Kees Hengeveld and J. Lachlan Mackenzie (2008). With kind permission of the authors.

Figures 4.3 (p. 91), **4.4** (p. 93) and **4.5** (p. 94) have been reproduced from Robin P. Fawcett, *The Functional Semantics Handbook: Analyzing English at the level of meaning* © Equinox Publishing Ltd (forthcoming, 2011). With kind permission of Equinox Publishing Ltd, London.

Figure 4.7 (p. 96) was published as Figure 4 (p. 36) in Robin P. Fawcett, *A Theory of Syntax for Systemic Functional Linguistics* © John Benjamins (2000). With kind permission of John Benjamins Publishing Company, Amsterdam/Philadelphia. www.benjamins.com

Figure 4.9 (p. 100) was published as Figure 21 (p. 137) in Robin P. Fawcett, *Cognitive Linguistics and Social Interaction: Towards an integrated model of a systemic functional grammar and the other components of a communicating mind* © Julius Groos Verlag, Heidelberg (1980). Although every effort has been made, we have been unable to trace the copyright holders of this figure, here reproduced in a simplified form. Apologies are offered for this omission.

The verb list on p. 184 has been reprinted by kind permission of the publisher from Beth Levin, *English Verb Classes and Alternations: A preliminary investigation* © The University of Chicago (1993).

Introduction

Pilar Guerrero Medina[a]

1 The idea behind this book

This book has its origins in a seminar held at the University of Córdoba (Spain) in April 2008 on the topic "Morphosyntactic alternations in English: Theoretical, descriptive and applied perspectives". Five of the articles in the present volume derive from papers delivered in that session, whose main aim was to explore the role of the traditional notion of alternation in contemporary linguistic theory.

The study of argument structure alternations has been approached from different perspectives in the formal and functional paradigms of linguistic analysis. Lexical semantic studies have stressed the "autonomy of lexical semantics" (Pinker 1989: 108), guided by the assumption that "the behaviour of a verb, particularly with respect to the expression an interpretation of its arguments, is to a large extent determined by its meaning" (Levin 1993: 1). Functionalist and cognitivist non-derivational approaches, on the contrary, have placed a greater emphasis on the interaction between the lexical properties of the verb and the meaning of constructions, also accounting for the discourse-pragmatic and semantic motivations of "alternating" constructions such as *She broke the window/The window broke* or *He sprayed wall with the paint/He sprayed the paint on the wall* (see e.g. Givón 2001: chapter 13).

As Gries and Stefanowitsch (2004: 97–98) rightly observe, pairs of "semantically more-or-less equivalent expressions", like the above-mentioned, have played a significant role in the development of both formal and functional linguistics and continue to be a central topic in contemporary grammatical and psycholinguistic investigations. However, as stated by Davidse (this volume) "the general confidence in the usefulness of alternations to linguistic analysis was dealt a severe blow" (p. 12) within the context of recent constructional approaches to language, where

a Pilar Guerrero Medina is Lecturer in English Grammar at the University of Córdoba, Spain. E-mail: ff1gumep@uco.es traditional categories such as the "dative" construction or the "locative alternation" were argued to "under-represent the generalizations that exist" (Goldberg 2002: 328). One of the specific questions this book aims is to address is precisely whether the notion of "alternation" (with a "basic" and "derived" member) is at all valid or whether we should, as Goldberg suggests, look beyond alternations in the Levin sense.

As a whole, articles in this collection explore the discourse-pragmatic, semantic, morphological and syntactic factors involved in English morphosyntactic alternations within a wide range of contemporary theoretical approaches, ranging from structural-functionalist models such as Functional Discourse Grammar (FDG) or Systemic Functional Linguistics (SFL) to more cognitively-oriented approaches such as Goldberg's Construction Grammar or Fillmore's Frame Semantics. This attempt to explore the notion of alternation from different angles, will hopefully contribute to a better understanding of the phenomena traditionally subsumed under the rubric of *morphosyntactic alternation*, also showing that is "possible and useful to compare descriptive observations made within different frameworks" (Davidse 1998: 106).

The volume is organized in two main parts. Part I brings together four papers of a more theoretical orientation, which focus on the notion of alternation and/or verb classification, also providing descriptive evidence for the grammatical approaches to language where they are couched. Part II consists of ten specific studies of particular alternations.

2 Theoretically-oriented approaches to the issue of morphosyntactic alternations (Part I)

In the first article in the volume, Kristin Davidse takes issue with Goldberg's position in her 2002 article, where she advocated that the "robust generalizations" in the domain of argument-structure relations are "surface generalizations" (2002: 333). In contrast to Goldberg, Davidse emphasizes the heuristic potential of verb-specific alternations and defends the position that they are relevant both to verb meaning and the semantics of constructions. The descriptive heuristics that can be derived from Davidse's argument, set in the structural-functional tradition of Gleason and Halliday, is illustrated with two alternation-based case studies of the subclassification of ditransitive verbs and of the semantic elucidation of ergative intransitives.

The paper by Lachlan Mackenzie puts forward an innovative analysis of alternations within the framework of FDG (Hengeveld and Mackenzie 2008). The author analyses the implications of recent work on priming in dialogue for a re-interpretation of FDG as a dialogic model, "in which there is a balance between the creativity of the individual speaker and her participation in a mutually aligned interaction" (p. 47). The notion of morphosyntactic alternation is claimed to be applicable only when there is connectedness without a corresponding semantic or pragmatic effect between the alternants. Examination of an extract from the Michigan Corpus of Academic Spoken English reveals how this relatedness becomes visible in dialogue in the operation of priming.

In the article by Francisco Ruiz de Mendoza and Ricardo Mairal Usón, set within the framework of the Lexical-Constructional Model (LCM), the authors argue that syntactic alternation is a natural consequence of *lexical-constructional subsumption*, a cognitive fusion process regulated by a number of constraints that are either internal or external to the process. The mechanism of subsumption is illustrated with an inspection of the way in which the external principles of high-level metonymy and metaphor apply in the explanation of related alternations, such as the causative/inchoative and middle, on the one hand, and the caused-motion and resultative, on the other. This account allows the authors to offer a more detailed description of the notion of *constructional coercion*, which is now seen "in terms of the ability of lexical structure to be construed from different perspectives that will license its integration into constructional structure" (p. 79).

Amy Neale's contribution is located within the approach to TRANSITIVITY developed within the Cardiff Grammar (CG) version of systemic theory. Building on the Systemic Functional notions of "Process", "system network" and "delicacy" and extending the semantic classification of verb senses, she provides an alternative approach to Levin's (1993) for modelling paradigmatic relations between verb senses. After outlining how verbal alternations such as the "dative alternation" can be handled by the CG through the lexicogrammar, the article deals in more detail with alternating constructions which involve different Participant Role configurations, positing that they demonstrate a change in the verb sense conveyed and should be thus treated as examples of "near equivalences".

3 Studies of specific alternations (Part II)

The ten articles in Part II of the volume have been grouped into two main sections, according to the type of alternation considered.

3.1 Transitivity alternations involving a change in the configuration of semantic roles

The four papers in this section are centrally concerned with three classical instances of "transitivity alternations" (Levin 1993: 25): the causative/inchoative alternation (e.g. *Janet broke the cup/The cup broke*), the middle alternation (e.g. *The butcher cuts the meat/The meat cuts easily*) and the conative alternation (e.g. *Paula hit the fence/Paula hit at the fence*).[1]

Daniel García Velasco's contribution offers an FDG approach to the causative/inchoative alternation, showing that a proper account of this alternation (in English and other languages) should pay attention to the way in which events are conceptually constructed by speakers. The author explores the extent to which FDG can handle this alternation more adequately than Classical Functional Grammar. The introduction of a Conceptual component, including those aspects of cognition which are relevant for the immediate communicative intention, and the separation of lexemes from the frames in which they occur, are presented as relevant aspects of the FDG model to account for this process.

Juana Marín-Arrese's paper deals with the codification of facilitative and spontaneous linguistic types in English and Spanish. The author revisits the characterizing features of inchoative and middle constructions from a cognitive linguistic perspective. Marín-Arrese argues for a non-derivational analysis of these constructions, based on the notions of construal and profiling. A "fuzzy middle area" is posited between the two constructions, which accounts for instances of "blends" and other non-prototypical constructions.

The article by Casilda García de la Maza focuses on the semantics of English middles and "pseudo-middles" (e.g. *The subsequent article almost writes itself/This new sofa seats four*). The English middle is characterized as having a clear constructional meaning, which can be seen as a compositional function of the meaning of the subject in combination with the verb and the adverb. The author highlights the lexicalization process that some middles are undergoing, which is indicative of the semantic idiosyncrasy of the construction.

In the last contribution of this section, Pilar Guerrero Medina aims to explore the connection between the English conative construction and what is regarded as an "antipassive" in the functional-typological literature, drawing on corpus data with a sample of verbs from Levin's (1993) semantic classes of *Contact by Impact, Breaking, Cutting* and *Ingesting.* It is here argued that a constructionist approach of the English conative alternation along the lines of Goldberg (1995) is in principle superior to a lexically-based one. However, in the author's view, the Goldbergian approach still provides an incomplete picture of the problem, and she furthers claims that the semantic and discourse-pragmatic properties of the conative construction would be better captured under Cooreman's (1994) definition of the antipassive.

3.2 Alternations involving a change in the morphosyntactic expression and/or placement of arguments

The six studies in this section are concerned with other types of alternative realizations in the grammar of English, which do not affect the transitivity of the verb and which do not necessarily apply at the clause level.

The contribution by Hans Boas offers an alternative frame-semantic approach to the various syntactic alternations which Levin (1993) claims to occur with her class of *build* verbs. The author shows that not all members of this class exhibit identical alternating behaviour, arguing (as is also the case in Neale's article in Part I of this volume) that Levin's definitions of verb classes are too coarse-grained. It is then claimed that differences in syntactic behaviour are best accounted for in terms of the different polysemy networks of senses associated with each verb. Adopting ideas from Fillmore's (1982) Frame Semantics, Boas proposes that each sense of a verb is best characterized by referencing the semantic frame(s) that it evokes.

Stefan Gries's paper studies the early acquisition of the constituent order alternation of English verb-particle constructions such as *He gave back the bottle* vs. *He gave the bottle back,* where the choice between these two constructions has been shown to be determined by a large number of linguistic and psycholinguistic determinants. On the basis of data from the CHILDES set of corpora, the article investigates several hundred constructions from three children, with the aim of determining to what extent previously-studied syntactic and semantic factors, as well as new phonological and frequency variables that have received little attention, may affect early particle placement. Gries also discusses lexically specific preferences for particular verb-particle constructions and examines to what degree data from different children may be conflated.

The article by Francisco Gonzálvez-García focuses on the non-equivalence of predicative complement alternations with a phrasal and infinitival realization after *seem*-type verbs in English and Spanish (e.g. *He seems (to be) angry/Parece (estar) enfadado*). Through analysis of data from corpora and other sources, the author argues for a unified constructionist account of the semantico-pragmatic and information structure restrictions which impinge upon the alternation of predicative complements in the *subjective-attributive* construction with *seem*-type verbs and their Spanish counterparts. Gonzálvez-García then proposes that this unitary analysis can also be applied to the *evaluative subjective-transitive* construction with *consider*-type verbs in both languages, as both constructions display a number of similarities which affect not only the core constructional meaning but also the semantico-pragmatic profile of the construction's components.

The paper by Antonio Barcelona Sánchez argues for the role of conceptual metonymy as a crucial motivating factor in some instances of the three main types of morphosyntactic alternations which, in the author's view, can be discerned: (i) the conventional pairing of a basic form with more than one basic constructional meaning; (ii) the conventional pairing of a basic constructional meaning with more than one uninflected form; and (iii) the model-variant relationship of two constructions within the same network. Instances from the following morphosyntactic areas are discussed: suffixal derivation, conversion, abbreviatory lexical forms and ellipsis, and syntactic constructions.

The contribution by Carmen Portero Muñoz centres on the so-called "*Swarm*-alternation". As opposed to most traditional approaches which exclude verbal alternations from the realm of word-formation, the *Swarm*-alternation is here regarded as a case of conversion. Portero Muñoz favours a non-derivational account of this alternation and contends that the FDG framework may solve some of the shortcomings of former accounts of the process, given the separation of frames and lexemes postulated in the theory.

The final article in the collection, by Javier Martín Arista, is centrally concerned with morphological alternations as recurrent pairings of meaning and form. Martín Arista deals with *zero alternation* in Old English (OE) as comprising two phenomena involving an irregular association (or *mismatch*) between form and meaning: zero derivation and the empty morph. The author proposes a typology of affixless derivation in OE that distinguishes zero derivation and conversion, and shows that zero derivation and redundant derivation with empty morphs are related phenomena if word-formation is considered in its syntagmatic and paradigmatic dimensions.

Notes

1. Some of the alternations which become the object of discussion in this section have been treated under the rubric of "voice" alternations (Klaiman 1991: 45). The term "middle voice", for instance, has been applied to the English alternation *Max is cooking the rice* vs *The rice is cooking*, where no particular morphological marking is involved. (Cf. Klaiman 1991: 45). Other scholars advocate the use of the term "diathesis" as a universal semantico-syntactic category, as opposed to the (non-universal) morphological notion of "voice" (Khrakovsky 1979: 291; Martínez Vázquez 1998: 28). Levin herself speaks of "diathesis alternations", defined as "alternations in the expressions of arguments, sometimes accompanied by changes of meaning" (1993: 2).

References

Davidse, K. (1998) On transitivity and ergativity in English, or on the need for dialogue between schools. In J. van der Auwera and J. Vershueren (eds) *English as a Human Language* 95–108. München: Lincom Europa.

Davidse, K. (this volume) Alternations as a heuristic to verb meaning and the semantics of constructions.

Fillmore, C. J. (1982) Frame semantics. In Linguistic Society of Korea (ed.) *Linguistics in the Morning Calm* 111–138. Seoul: Hanshin.

Givón, T. (2001) *Syntax: An introduction. Vol II.* Amsterdam: Benjamins.

Goldberg, A. E. (1995) *Constructions: A construction grammar approach to argument structure.* Chicago, IL: University of Chicago Press.

Goldberg, A. E. (2002) Surface generalizations: An alternative to alternations. *Cognitive Linguistics* 13(4): 327–356.

Gries, S. and Stefanowitsch, A. (2004) Extending collostructional analysis: A corpus-based perspective on alternations. *International Journal of Corpus Linguistics* 9(1): 97–129.

Hengeveld, K. and Mackenzie, J. L. (2008) *Functional Discourse Grammar: A typologically-based theory of language structure.* Oxford: Oxford University Press.

Khrakovsky, V. S. (1979) Diathesis. *Acta Linguistica Academiae Scientarum Hungaricae* 29: 289–307.

Klaiman, M. H. (1991) *Grammatical Voice.* Cambridge: Cambridge University Press.

Levin, B. (1993) *English Verb Classes and Alternations: A preliminary investigation.* Chicago, IL: University of Chicago Press.

Martínez Váquez, M. (1998) *Diátesis: Alternancias oracionales en la lengua inglesa.* Huelva: University of Huelva.

Pinker, S. (1989) *Learnability and Cognition: The acquisition of argument structure.* Cambridge, MA: The MIT Press.

Part I

Theoretically-oriented approaches to the issue of morphosyntactic alternations

1 Alternations as a heuristic to verb meaning and the semantics of constructions*

Kristin Davidse[a]

1 Introduction

It is probably fair to state, following criticisms uttered already by Firth (1964), that modern linguistics has neglected the paradigmatic at the expense of the syntagmatic. While this is less the case for the smaller linguistic units studied in phonology and morphology, this observation does hold for the study of grammar. The form-aspect of clause grammar, for instance, has mostly been restricted to its syntagmatic organization. Approaches which assume some sort of motivated relation between form and meaning have generally located the meaning-construing power of clause grammar in its syntagmatic organization. Linguists according meaning-making power to paradigmatic networks of constructions such as Whorf (1956), Gleason (1966), Halliday (1967, 1968, 1985), Levin (1993) and Van den Eynde (1995)[1] form a minority in the linguistic tradition.

The tide seemed to turn somewhat when Levin's invaluable reference work *English Verb Classes and Alternations* (1993) drew attention to the heuristic potential of alternations in a way that resonated with large groups within the linguistic community. This influential book made a strong case that diathesis alternations of verbs "probe for linguistically pertinent aspects of verb meaning" (Levin 1993: 1) and allow the analyst to draw up linguistically-based, rather than intuition-based, classifications of lexical verbs.

However, in Goldberg's (2002) programmatic article "Surface generalizations: An alternative to alternations", the use of alternations in linguistic analysis came in for criticism. The article defended the position that alternations do not shed any light on the meaning of verb-argument

a Kristin Davidse is Professor of English Linguistics at KU Leuven, the Catholic University of Leuven, Belgium. E-mail: kristin.davidse@arts.kuleuven.be relations. As Goldberg (2002: 329) put it, "relying on explicit or implicit reference to a possible alternative paraphrase" in the analysis of argument structure patterns "puts blinders on, and limits a theory's ability to state the full extent of the relevant generalizations". According to Goldberg, verb-argument relations are located in the *syntagmatic* "surface patterns", which should be considered on their own terms: "the surface formal and semantic/pragmatic generalizations in this domain are captured by argument structure constructions" (Goldberg 2002: 327). "The robust generalizations are surface generalizations" (2002: 333). The use of alternations in verb classification was not explicitly discussed in this article. Even though in the conclusion it was recognized that "the essentially structuralist observation that the semantic interpretation of one linguistic construct tends to be affected by the existence of possible alternatives, receives empirical support from a number of studies" (2002: 349), the general confidence in the usefulness of alternations to linguistic analysis was dealt a severe blow.

In this article, I will reconsider the heuristic potential of verb-specific alternations and defend the position that, with some clarifications and caveats, they can be shown to be semantically relevant *both* to verb meaning and to the semantics of constructions. This position will be developed with reference to Whorf's (1956) thinking about cryptotypes and reactances, Gleason's (1966) concepts of enation and agnation, applied in Halliday's (1967, 1968) descriptions of transitivity, Van den Eynde's (1995) reflections on verb-specific and verb-general alternations, and of course Levin's (1993) work on alternations and verb classes. The descriptive heuristics that can be derived from this body of work will be illustrated with applications in the general areas of ditransitive and ergative intransitive constructions in English, which I explored in earlier work (Davidse 1998, 2002).

The article is structured as follows. §2 focuses on the notion of verb-specific alternations, or Levin's diathesis alternations, and their analytical reach. §3 homes in on the issue of linguistically motivated, rather than intuition-based, classifications of lexical verbs, taking ditransitive verbs as a case. §4 complements the notion of disambiguation traditionally associated with alternations with that of subclassification, arguing that most verb-specific alternations reveal similarities and differences between finer subtypes of the main transitivity types of constructions. §5 deals with the relevance of alternations to the semantics of (subtypes of) constructions and focuses on ergative intransitives.

2 Verb-specific alternations

Goldberg's (2002: *passim*) use of "rough paraphrase" to refer to alternation reveals a perception among its critics that alternations are formed in an unsystematic and nontechnical way. In this section, I want to dispel that perception by specifying the view assumed here on alternations in general and on verb-specific alternations in particular. I will also situate this view theoretically. While recognizing the important contributions made by the lexical school of Government and Binding, my own understanding of alternations is embedded in the structural-functional tradition of Gleason and Halliday.

2.1 Gleason on agnation and enation

Theorizing from the structural-functional angle on alternations was pioneered by Gleason (1966). He (1966: 195) stressed that the language system is not simply an inventory of **syntagmatic** structures, but also crucially involves the **paradigmatic** relations between structures. The latter, Gleason (1966: 195) held, constitute "an additional set of relationships that grammar must describe [...] at least as large and diverse" as the syntagmatic patterns. He (1966: 196) immediately added that his plea to study the relations between structures was not meant in a transformational or derivational sense,[2] but was aimed at revealing inherent formal and semantic properties of examples.

To refer to the relations **between** structures, Gleason (1966: 199) proposed the technical term **agnation**, a metaphor from kinship relations. He defined agnation as the relation of systematic and regular grammatical *variation* existing between examples whose main lexical elements are identical. For instance:

(1) (a) The man saw a stranger.
(b) A stranger was seen by the man.

As a complementary notion, he put forward **enation**, the relation of structural **identity** obtaining between examples which have an identical structure relating members from identical grammatical classes but contain different lexical items. For instance:

(1) (a) The man saw a stranger.
(2) (a) The dean heard a dog.

Enation and agnation are two mutually defining notions. On the one hand, the systematicity of an agnation pattern should be confirmed by enate examples displaying the same agnation relation, such as the passives corresponding to (1a) and (2a).

(1) (b) A stranger was seen by the man.
(2) (b) A dog was heard by the dean.

On the other hand, for examples to be enate, they should have identical sets of agnates. In this context, Gleason pointed out that if examples shared some agnates but not all, they could be **partially enate**.

The definition of structural identity in terms of shared agnation, entailed that structural **ambiguity** could be detected by the non-sharing of agnates. For instance, despite the superficial similarity in surface structure between

(1) (a) The man saw a stranger.
(3) (a) The man seemed a stranger.

These two sentences are not enate, as shown by their different agnate relations (Gleason 1966: 203).

(1) (b) A stranger was seen by the man.
(c) *The man saw to be a stranger.

(3) (b) *A stranger was seemed by the man.
(c) The man seemed to be a stranger.

Gleason also noted the relevance of agnation to the semantics of a construction. As he observed (1966: 213), a more explicit agnate construction is often felt to reveal the meaning of the related construction. For instance, *an automatic lathe operator* 'means' *an operator of automatic lathes*, not **an operator of lathes that is automatic*. Likewise the possibility of adding *to be* to *seem* in (3c) reveals the copular import of (3a), in terms of which it contrasts with (1a), for which no copular agnate (1c) is available.

Some further reflection on Gleason's thinking about the use of agnation in linguistic analysis seems in order at this point. Reference to alternates has been used on an ad hoc basis by most linguistic schools, but its more systematic application is found only, with different accents, in some specific schools such as the lexicalist school within Government and Binding and the Hallidayan functional tradition. The most important point of controversy between those advocating and those rejecting paradigmatic variants as a systematic heuristic in linguistic description seems to revolve around what counts as *formal evidence*. In a Gleasonian perspective, formal evidence is not restricted to observable characteristics of the syntagm in question, but also includes the syntagm's systematic relations to its agnates.

Or to put it in more mainstream terms, it includes the "syntactic behaviour" (Levin 1993: 4) of the syntagm – both of its parts and of the whole syntagm (cf. Haas 1954).

The next question is then what the observed possible and impossible agnates, are evidence of. The case Gleason made explicitly was that they may reveal ambiguity in case of "apparent" structural identity, as with examples (1) and (3). While theoretically recognizing partial enation, Gleason did not pursue the question of the status of examples that share some agnates but not others. This is an issue to which we will return in §4.

Given the much greater currency of the terms "alternation/alternates" in comparison with "agnation/agnates", I will henceforth also use the more common "alternations", but without implying any notions of derivational directionality.

2.2 Verb-general versus verb-specific alternations

Schøsler (2010: 26) nicely summarizes Van den Eynde's view of grammar in the following statement: "Grammar is organized in closed sets of alternations, i.e. in paradigms, which are language specific packages of expression and content". Crucial to this view of grammar is the distinction made by Van den Eynde (1995) between **verb-specific** and **verb-general** alternations.

On the one hand, all clauses allow for paradigmatic variants which are **not dependent on the lexical verb** used in them. Examples of these are anteposition of non-subjects and interrogative inversion – alternations which are generally available to clauses with internal constituent structure. These alternations are very regular and Van den Eynde refers to them as "dispositives". Drawing an analogy between grammar and morphology, he likens them to flexion. If we look at verb-general alternations of clauses from the perspective of functional frameworks such as Halliday (1985) and Dik (1997), they appear as options within mood and theme/information structure systems. Formation of basic clause types (such as declarative, interrogative, imperative) and theme/information variants (e.g. variation of the linear modification order) are by and large not dependent on the verbs used in clauses.

By contrast, other clausal variants are **dependent on the lexical verb** and are as a consequence much less regular. Pursuing his analogy with morphology, Van den Eynde compares them to derivations. They are in both functional and formal frameworks the variants associated with verb-argument structures. Levin (1993: 2) refers to them as "diathesis alternations – alternations in the expression of arguments, sometimes accompanied by changes of meaning". Investigation of clausal variants specifically sanctioned or disallowed by the verb can, therefore, according to Van den Eynde (1995) and Levin (1993: 1), be used as a descriptive heuristic to "probe for linguistically pertinent aspects of verb meaning" and to draw up linguistically-based, rather than intuition-based, classifications of lexical verbs.

This entails that only verb-specific alternations are relevant to (differences in) verb meaning and that only verb-specific alternations should be considered with a view to verb classification. In turn, this requires more theoretical reflection and discussion on which alternations are dependent on verb meaning and which are motivated by variation within the mood and theme/information systems of clause grammar. A well-known moot point in this area is whether alternations involving two non-agent arguments, such as the dative and locative alternations, are verb-specific (cf. Levin 1993: 45f) or belong mainly to the realm of variation in topicality, as argued by Givón (1979). Goldberg (2002) makes her case against alternations precisely with reference mainly to the ditransitive and locative alternations. She (2002: 337ff) rightly observes that no explanation referring to verb meaning has been found yet for why, for instance, verbs such as *load* and *spray* manifest the locative alternation, and others such as *put* or *cover* not. This point was confirmed by Laffut's (2006) extensive corpus-based study of the locative alternation.

(4) (a) Pat loaded the wagon with the hay. (Goldberg 2002: 337)
(b) Pat loaded the hay onto the wagon.

(5) (a) Pat put the hay on the wagon. (Goldberg 2002: 337)
(b) *Pat put the wagon with hay.

However, according to Givón (1979: 161) such alternations involving variation between nominally and prepositionally realized participants are motivated by discourse pressures. They allow variation in the relative topicality of these two participants, with the nominally coded participant being the more topical one. While the complex question of the nature of these alternations is beyond the scope of this article, it can be remarked that at least some of the evidence which Goldberg (2002: 330–332) adduces in favour of surface generalizations of verb-argument relations are general dispositives, e.g. interrogatives, pronominalization of final argument, etc. rather than verb-specific alternations.

3 Alternations as a heuristic to verb meaning and verb classes

3.1 Alternations and verb classes: Levin (1993)

In this section, we will see that the type of verb classification envisaged by Levin (1993) on the basis of diathesis alternations does not eschew "broader generalizations" about constructions, as Goldberg (2002: 335) suggests, in that it has a layered structure with more general and more delicate subclassifications.

A very general class such as that of transitive verbs, for instance, can be further subclassified into groupings which share some features but differ in terms of others. Levin illustrates this with the verbs *break, cut, hit* and *touch* (1993: 6). They all have in common that they are transitive, taking two arguments (1993: 6). In functional and cognitive frameworks, the passive alternation has been put forward as an index of transitivity (Halliday 1985: 151–153; Rice 1987). Clauses with two nominals that have a marked passive or none at all, such as (6a) and (7a) respectively,[3] have reduced transitivity.

(6) (a) Fortunately, you can climb most mountains the pretty way.
(b) Fortunately, most mountains can be climbed the pretty way [...] (CB)

(7) (a) [...] his Toyota blew a fuse. (CB)
(b) *A fuse was blown by his Toyota.

Beyond their shared general transitivity, these verbs differ in crucial meaning components, which are sensitive to diathesis alternations. In the first place, *cut, hit* and *touch,* but not *break,* license the body-part possessor ascension alternation: the possessed body part may be expressed either as the object of the verb or in a prepositional phrase (Levin 1993: 7):

(8) (a) Mary cut/touched/hit Bill's arm. (Levin 1993: 7)
(b) Mary cut/touched/hit Bill on the arm.

(9) (a) Janet broke Bill's finger. (Levin 1993: 7)
(b) *Janet broke Bill on the finger.

According to Levin (1993: 8), this alternation presupposes contact with the patient as an inherent semantic component. The first three verbs express actions involving contact, but not the event of *breaking,* which can also be brought about indirectly without contact.

Second, *cut* and *hit* allow the conative alternation, illustrated in (10), but the other verbs not. The conative construction (10b) expresses repeated direction of action onto a patient without "entailment that the action denoted by the verb was completed" (1993: 6).

(10) (a) Margaret cut the bread. (Levin 1993: 6)
(b) Margaret cut at the bread.

It presupposes contact as well as motion as inherent components of the verb, which is the case with *cut* and *hit* only.

Next, *cut* and *break* are differentiated from *hit* and *touch* in that only the former allow the middle alternation, illustrated in (11).

(11) (a) Janet broke the vase. (Levin 1993: 6)
(b) Crystal vases break easily.

The middle construction expresses that the subject lends itself to the action expressed by the verb, and, according to Levin (1993: 8–9), entails a change of state of the affected. That only *cut* and *break* contain this semantic component is also reflected by the fact that only they allow construction of resultative deverbal nominals, *a cut/break*, describing the effect of the action on the patient. With the other verbs, deverbal nominals, *a hit/touch*, refer to the action itself.

Finally, *break* differs from *cut*, and the other verbs, in being the only one to license the causative/inchoative or "ergative" alternation, as illustrated in (12).

(12) (a) The window broke. (Levin 1993: 9)
(b) The little boy broke the window.

Levin's explanation of this is that only *break* is a verb of pure change of state "without specifying how this change comes about" (1993: 9). Levin and Rappaport Hovav (1995: 103–104) add to this that the eventualities described by *break* allow natural forces, instruments or agents as causers of the change of state, whereas *cut*, *hit* and *touch* require agents.

Corresponding to each verb are other verbs that have the same possible and impossible alternations. Levin calls these the *break*, *cut*, *hit* and *touch* verbs (Levin 1993: 7). The shared syntactic behaviour of their members reflects the fact that they resemble and differ from each other according to the subclassification and crossclassification of semantic components just discussed.

3.2 Alternations and the subclassification of ditransitive verbs

In this section, we will contrast a non-alternation based classification with an alternation-based one. Ditransitive verbs impose themselves as a case, as the semantic relevance of alternations to ditransitives was questioned in Goldberg (2002).

3.2.1 Green's classification

In *Semantics and Syntactic Regularity*, Green (1974: 80) offered what she called an "informal semantic characterization" of ditransitive verbs alternating both with a prepositional *to*-phrase and a *for*-phrase. In the classification she used features such as direct/indirect, accompanied/unaccompanied and physical/non-physical transfer of DO to IO. In these terms it is a carefully developed and semantically revealing classification, which strongly influenced later work by, amongst others, Pinker (1989)[4] and Goldberg (1995). It is summarized below:

> *To*-class 1: "*bring*" class: direct and accompanied physical transfer of an object from an agent to the IO, e.g. *bring, take, carry, drag, hand, haul, pass, pull, push*
> *To*-class 2: "*give*" class: direct, unaccompanied and not necessarily physical transfer of an object to the IO, e.g. *give, advance, award, cede, concede, entrust, feed, lend*
> *To*-class 3: "*send*" class: unaccompanied physical transfer of object to IO, e.g. *send, float, fling, hurl, lower, mail, pitch, push, relay, roll, ship, shove, slide, throw, toss*
> *To*-class 4: alternating "communication verb" class, e.g. *radio, wire, cable, telegraph, telephone, shout, gesture, relay, mail, tell, cite, preach, quote, read, write*
> *To*-class 5: verbs of "future having" of DO by IO, e.g. *promise, guarantee, owe, permit, offer, grant, assign, bequeath, leave, allot*
> *For*-class 1: verbs denoting intentional creative acts (open class), e.g. *make, cook, boil, roast, sew, knit, paint, draw*
> *For*-class 2: verbs denoting activities involving selection, e.g. *buy, purchase, find, get, choose, pick out, gather, save, leave*
> *For*-class 3: verbs denoting performances, e.g. *sing, chant, recite, play, dance*
> *For*-class 4: verbs of obtaining, e.g. *earn, gain, win*
> *For*-class 5: verbs denoting acts intended to be symbolic of the subject's devotion to the IO, e.g. *capture, kill, sacrifice, take*

Green (1974: 80) herself pointed out that these classes did not display complete syntactic coherence. On an introspective basis, she had checked the verbs' behaviour with regard to the following constructions: IO passive, DO passive, IO-deletion, DO-deletion, preposing of IO. That is, she had brought in paradigmatic variants as a second step, not as the basis of the classification. None of the proposed semantic classes are characterized by a consistent set of alternations.

Looking more closely at the syntactic variants, we can note that preposing of IO is a verb-general alternate (Van den Eynde 1995), more specifically, a textual alternate (Halliday 1985), which is generally available for ditransitive verbs and thus uninformative with regard to finer semantic differences between them. The passive and deletion tests, then, are verb-specific alternates and it is these that do not apply systematically within the proposed semantic classes. For instance, some verbs in the "give" class such as *pay* and *feed* allow for DO-deletion, as illustrated by the following attested examples:

(13) [...] workers pay the lawyers if the case is lost [...] (CB)

(14) [...] he fed the colourful fish [...](CB)

while others such as *advance* and *award* do not:

(15) *They advanced the customers.

(16) *They awarded the winners.

Likewise, with some verbs of *to*-classes 1, 2 and 3, the IO is always understood, even if not expressed (*bring, pass, give, loan, sell*), and with others not (*haul, drag, pull, push*).

3.2.2 Towards an alternation-based classification

The aim of this section is to explore whether the availability or impossibility of alternations with ditransitive verbs will allow us to subclassify them in a meaningful way. There is no clarity yet in the literature whether alternations changing the relative ordering of DO and IO should be studied as textually motivated or verb-specific alternations. Therefore I concentrated on alternations that are clearly dependent on verb semantics, viz. ones relating to the obligatoriness and inherency of the two non-agentive participants,[5] which I will refer to as the Dative and Patient role. I drew up a list of 135 ditransitive verbs which included most of the verbs contained in Green's classes (see §3.2.1 above) and some extra ones such as *command, pledge, prove, admit, announce, address* (for a complete list, see Appendix I).[6]

For these verbs, I investigated whether or not they allow for what Green referred to as DO-deletion and IO-deletion, by verifying whether the following alternations were possible:

(i) active with Dative/Complement only, as in

(17) "Don't tell them yet," he advises. (CB)

(ii) active with Patient/Complement only, as in

(18) Goss told the truth. (CB)

As a further reflex of non-obligatoriness of the Patient, I also checked the possibility of

(iii) Dative as Subject of passive participle, as in

(19) However, there were differences according to the age at which they had been told of their conception, with those told during adulthood more likely to report feeling confused, shocked, upset, relieved, numb and angry.
http://www.physorg.com/news134642980.html
Accessed on 05/05/2010.

The (im)possibility of these alternations with each verb was decided on the basis of grammaticality judgements in clear cases, but, when in doubt, by consulting the COBUILD corpus or the Internet. After the results had been noted for each verb, I investigated groupings of possible and impossible alternates.

This identified the following alternation-based subclasses which focus on the obligatoriness and inherency of the participants:

1. Those for which Dative and Patient are always obligatory
e.g. *attribute, ascribe, accord, impute, grant, bequeath, leave, entrust, award, deny, deal.*

2. Those for which constructions with both only Dative and only Patient are possible (but with these roles inherently implied when not expressed)
e.g. *charge, pay, serve, feed, give; cable, phone, e-mail, telegraph, (tele)phone, radio, wire; ask, explain, show, advise, teach, tell, write, read, sing; permit, allow, refuse, forgive, excuse, pardon, confess, promise, address.*

3. Those for which Patient is non-obligatory (but always implied)
e.g. *reproach, address.*

4a. Those for which Dative is non-obligatory (but implied when not expressed)
e.g. *book, send, keep*; many verbal processes: *advocate, suggest, propose, prescribe, declare, issue, recommend.*

4b. Those for which Dative is non-obligatory (and not implied when not expressed)
e.g. *bring, fling, throw, hurl, haul, drag, cast, shove;* most *for*-ditransitive verbs such as *create, bake, embroider, prepare, gather, clear; find, choose, fix, steal, select.*

Despite having been neglected in the literature, class 1 constitutes a clearly recognizable group of verbs with obvious semantic homogeneity. They are in essence processes of "attribution" – attribution of qualities, states, authorship, ownership, etc. The verbs foreground the component of establishing a possessive relation – alienable or inalienable – between Dative and Patient. In this respect, these **obligatorily ditransitive** verbs can be argued to be the most protypical instances of "causation of a possessive relation", generally held to be the core meaning of ditransitive constructions (e.g. Fawcett 1987; Goldberg 1995).

It has often been claimed that Datives, not Patients, are the omissible element with ditransitive verbs (see e.g. Wierzbicka 1988: 361). This case study shows that this is the main trend: ditransitive verbs which can occur without explicit Dative do form the biggest class (class 4). But it is not the whole picture. There are two exceptions to this general trend.

First, there is a considerable subgroup, class 2, which allows, as well as for Dative-omission, also for Patient-omission. Each of these roles is inherently implied when not expressed, as illustrated for Patient-omission by (13) and (14) above. In other words, whereas class 1 is characterized by obligatory **inclusion** of both Dative and Patient in all constructions, class 2 is typified by the possible **omission** of either Dative or Patient. It is by virtue of their ability to occur with Dative only that they distinguish themselves most from the majority of ditransitive verbs. The way I would interpret this is that the Dative is not a "secondary graft" onto what is basically an Agent-Patient causal chain but constitutes an extension of the action, which is, so to speak, a valid alternative to the Patient. We can think of the action chains expressed by these verbs as being "two-pronged": the act may be extended either to Dative or Patient, without requiring explicit coding of a third participant.

A further alternate is associated with class 2, but it applies to a **part** of class 2 only. This is the passive participle construction in which the Dative functions as Head, e.g. *those told, those served, those promised.* This alternate applies to a neat subgroup of class 2, viz. *cable, (tele)phone, e-mail, telegraph, radio, wire; tell, address, ask, teach, advise promise, excuse, pardon, forgive, refuse; serve, feed, charge, pay.* Semantically, this alternate seems to be related to the clausal variant without Patient (examples 13–14) but one could hypothesize that it singles out those verbs in which the Dative is truly an extension equal to the Patient. We could perhaps think of this subgroup as **equi-ditransitive** verbs: they permit, equally naturally, Patient- and Dative-headed participles: *the students/the classes taught, the sinners/the sins pardoned, the guests/the dinners served.*

There is a second, minor, exception to the general trend of Dative-omissibility, viz. a very small class of ditransitive verbs, class 3, that can occur with Dative, not Patient, only, instantiated in my data by *reproach* and *address*. With these two verbs, a Patient is implied when it is not expressed.

Class 4 contains verbs which *can* be used ditransitively, but which also occur without Dative. These form, as already noted, the majority of ditransitive verbs. A further distinction can be made here between those that imply a Dative, even when it is not expressed (class 4a) and those for which the Dative is implied, when not expressed (class 4b). Thus, *They send their love* implies a receiver the love is sent to, and *He booked a seat* implies a beneficiary the seat is booked for. In contrast, *He was carrying a suitcase* and *He found a seat* do not imply a Dative.

We can conclude this case study by noting that verb-specific alternations do identify (sub)classes of verbs, but that a distinction has to be made between alternations that are diagnostics of general subclasses and minor alternations associated with smaller, more irregular subclasses. With ditransitive verbs, alternations hinging on Dative- and Patient-omissibility have such general diagnostic value relating to the obligatoriness and inherence of Dative and Patient. The Dative + passive participle alternation, by contrast, identifies a subset of the ditransitive verbs allowing for both Dative- and Patient-omissibility.

4 Alternations and the disambiguation/ subclassification of identical surface syntagms

When authors such as Gleason (1966) and Van den Eynde (1995) discuss the use to which alternations can be put in the structural analysis of examples, they discuss only **disambiguation** explicitly. For instance, as we saw in §2.2, Gleason argues that with (1a) *The man saw a stranger* and (3a) *The man seemed a stranger* the different alternates (examples 1b–c and 3b–c above) show these two examples to have only apparent structural identity. In this particular case, there seems little doubt that this is a standard case of constructional ambiguity, i.e. "a single surface form having unrelated meanings" (Goldberg 2002: 335). Van den Eynde likewise brings verb-specific alternates to bear on identical surface structures to detect ambiguity. As he (1995: 119) puts it, "The meaning determining unit is not the construction itself, but the **network** it is part of". In according different readings to ambiguous structures, the language user "projects" the different alternation sets behind each reading (Van den Eynde 1995: 118).

However, it is important to point out that verb-specific alternations may also reveal different subtypes of a more general construction type, rather than instances of unrelated constructions. Analogous with the complex subclassification of verb meanings (see §3.1), alternations can be used as a heuristic for the subclassification of constructions. In this section, I will discuss an early study in Halliday (1968), in which the semantics of subtypes of constructions are elucidated with reference to shared and different alternations.

In "Notes on transitivity and theme", Halliday (1968: 196) distinguished two subtypes of transitive constructions, which he referred to as the "goal-directed" and "descriptive" subtypes. The former, e.g. *John hit the ball,* is analysed by Halliday in terms of the process-participant configuration Actor – Process – Goal, the latter, e.g. *John marched the soldiers,* as Initiator – Process – Actor. The two subtypes share general alternates, argued to be indicators of transitivity, such as the passive (Halliday 1985: 151–153; Rice 1987) and clefts with *do to* relating the two participants.

Paradigm I:

(20) (a) John marched the prisoners.
(b) The prisoners were marched by John.
(c) What John did to the prisoners was march them.

Paradigm II:

(21) (a) John hit the ball.
(b) The ball was hit by John.
(c) What John did to the ball was hit it.

In his argumentation for subclassifying them as distinct types of transitive, Halliday (1968: 196) brings in alternates such as the intransitive, cleft with proform *do* relating verb and second participant, and analytical causative.

(20) (d) John made the prisoners march.
(e) The prisoners marched.
(f) What the prisoners did was march.
(g) What John made the prisoners do was hit.

(21) (d) *John made the ball hit.
(e) *The ball hit.
(f) *What the ball did was hit.
(g) *What John did the ball do was march.

These distinct sets of alternations are exploited as a heuristic to **interpret** the semantic difference between (20a) and (21a). The alternations in Paradigm I show *the prisoners* to be "doers", or actors. They can appear as Actor of an intransitive clause, and in clefts their relation to the verb can be expressed with the proform *do*. The more specific model of transitivity involved in (20a) is one of causation, as shown by alternates (20d) and (20g), which contain analytical causation with *make*. By contrast, the corresponding impossible alternates in Paradigm II show *the books* not to be "doers", but rather mere "undergoers", i.e. Goals. The transitivity model here is not one of causation of intransitives, as shown by the impossibility of (21g), but of goal-directed action.

Like Van den Eynde, Halliday projects the distinct alternation networks behind the two transitive subtypes, but to interpret the finer semantic distinctions between them, not to "disambiguate" them. It is also not the case that Halliday assigns exactly the same semantics, the same relations between process and participants, to the alternates within one set. He recognizes that the different alternates, in their turn, have specific formal and semantic properties characterizing them as individual constructions. For instance, while the *soldiers* in the intransitive in (20e) are ordinary Actors in control of their marching, they are what he calls "enforced" Actors in the transitive alternates, such as (20a). The introduction of an Initiator into the typically intransitive constellation suppresses the features of control and initiative force normally associated with actors marching. Typical fillers of the enforced Actor role are subjugated humans or animals. For instance, *soldiers* can be *marched* and *horses* can be *trotted* (Davidse and Geyskens 1998).

In conclusion, differences in verb-specific alternates often do not show examples to be instances of different constructions, but they can be used as revealing heuristics of subtypes of the general transitivity types (intransitive, transitive, ditransitive, complextransitive). Goldberg (2002: 338) rightly pointed out that structures with different alternates are not always ambiguous, but she seems to throw out the baby with the bathwater, when she dismisses verb-specific alternates as "rough paraphrases" that "put[s] blinders on [...] and limit[s] a theory's ability to state the full extent of the relevant [surface] generalizations" (2002: 329). Not getting the heuristic mileage out of differences in verb-specific alternates is equally a case of putting on blinders.

5 Alternations and the semantics of constructions

This section further explores the suggestions for using alternations as a heuristic to the semantics of subtypes of constructions. It will focus on the distinction between "pure" intransitives versus ergative intransitives.

I begin this section with Whorf's little remembered discussion of English intransitives in the context of his definition of cryptotypes. It is common knowledge that cryptotypes refer to covert grammatical categories, but what is less well known is that Whorf operationalized their covertness in terms of paradigmatic variants, which are intrinsically only there *in absentia.* Cryptotypes are submerged meanings shown only as an influence (Whorf 1956: 105), or to use the metaphor from chemistry which Whorf introduced as a semi-technical term, as a **reactance** (1956: 89). A reactance is the interaction between the meaning of the cryptotype and the meaning of certain values in other systems of the grammar such as voice, causation, tense, aspect and nominalization. Such semantic interactions are revealed by the possibility or impossibility of alternates realizing values from specific grammatical systems, which, as noted by Gleason (1966: 213) may make semantic features of the cryptotype explicit, or may show up their absence. Reactances thus constitute the "configurative" (1956: 80) paradigmatic realization of the category, which has to be related to its syntagmatic realization to have a good basis for a truly meaningful characterization. In this context, Whorf (1956) noted that

> In English, intransitive verbs form a covert category marked by lack of the passive participle and the passive and causative voices; we cannot substitute a verb of this class (e.g. "go, lie, sit, rise, gleam, sleep, arrive, appear, rejoice") into such sentences as "It was cooked, It was being cooked, I had it cooked to order". (89)

He suggested that a significant characterization could be arrived at only if the intransitive in English was investigated as the cryptotypical category it really is, and if the aspects of its meaning were pushed to consciousness that bar it from being passivized or causativized (*I went, *I am being gone, *They went me*).

Smith (1970: 107) proposed that intransitive clauses with verbs such as *laugh* and *play* depict actions that "can be controlled only by the person engaging in it". However, as correctly pointed out by Levin and Rappaport Hovav (1995: 91), some intransitive verbs such as *blush* and *stumble,* which cannot be causativized, describe uncontrollable actions. For this reason, I have characterized the semantics of intransitive clauses as depicting actions, both voluntary and involuntary, which can have only one energy source (Davidse 1991: 108). The energy source of an action or event is defined by Langacker (1991: 283) as the entity in which the energy required for the action or event originates. This notion is just as applicable to voluntary as to involuntary actors. The specification that in intransitive clauses no other energy source is involved reflects the impossibility of the causative/inchoative alternation, with these clauses, e.g. **John blushed Mary.*

Whereas ordinary intransitives do not causativize, English has a subtype of intransitive that does have a transitive as systematic alternate, as illustrated by:

(22) (a) [...] the string broke. (CB)
(b) [...] he broke a string (...) (CB)

(23) (a) [...] word spread of Chris's fascinating collection. (CB)
(b) [...] how to spread the word about the service or product provided. (CB)

(24) (a) [...] steel beams [...] had begun to corrode. (CB)
(b) [...] it may corrode the case. (CB)

In the literature this alternation has been referred to as the "ergative" alternation. In that the subject of the intransitive corresponds to the object of the transitive, examples such as (22)–(24) have ergative alignment, comparable to the subject of the intransitive and the object of the transitive being coded by the absolutive in ergative case marking systems. The intransitives manifesting this alternation have, accordingly, been referred to as ergative intransitives (e.g. Keyser and Roeper 1984). Obviously, some distinctive meaning components of clauses such as (22a), (23a) and (24a) license this alternation by which they distinguish themselves from ordinary intransitives.

There is a tradition of long standing in English linguistics on what semantic features of an intransitive are revealed by the ergative alternation. It started with the descriptive grammarians of the first half of the twentieth century, and has continued in both Government and Binding and functionalist work. These elucidations have consistently referred to its specific voice and quasi-reflexive value.

To interpret the specific semantic value of the pair *roll the stone – the stone rolls*, Jespersen (1927: 332f) pointed out a similarity between *the stone rolls* and the passive. He (1927: 336) noted that "*the stone rolls* is nearly the same thing as *the stone is rolled*, though in the former case, the stone is thought of as somehow causing its own movement while in the latter case some other agent is more or less clearly present in the mind of the speaker." Here already we find the thought, which we re-encounter in much later work, that the contrast between the pure and ergative intransitive is one of self, or internal, causation versus external causation. Jespersen viewed the passive flavour of "change and move" intransitives as one of the links in the long chain of developments in English by which active forms have acquired (quasi-)passive meaning (1927: 350).

Curme (1931: 437f) also viewed the increased tendency in present-day English to use transitive verbs without an object as a general voice phenomenon. According to him, this tendency which has grown over many centuries has led to three peculiar uses of the intransitive:

1. intransitives which predicate "an act pure and simple of some particular person or thing" (1931: 437), e.g. *The turkey is roasting nicely, The bread baked too long*;
2. intransitives with reflexive force for which Modern German and other languages tend to use reflexive forms (1931: 438f), e.g. *The door suddenly opened, The thick fog lifted*;
3. intransitives with passive force (1931: 440f), e.g. *This cloth has worn (has been worn) thin, My hat blew (was blown) into the river.*

The three subtypes can be interpreted as constituting a gradient from more active to more passive. Still, the basic development is towards a passive meaning:

> Since many of the new intransitives, [...], as well as many old intransitives, represent something as naturally developing or accidentally entering into a new state, or as having the power or fitness to enter it, consequently as affected or capable of being affected, they acquire passive force, so that now passive force is often associated with intransitive form. (Curme, 1931: 440)

These early treatments influenced later work. For instance, Halliday (1967, 1968) refers to Curme, and Levin and Rappaport Hovav (1995: 91) follow Jespersen in characterizing intransitive verbs as internally caused and ergative verbs as externally caused: "Unlike internally caused verbs, externally caused verbs by their very nature *imply* the existence of an 'external cause'". The external cause can, for Levin and Rappaport Hovav (1995: 92) also be coreferential with the undergoer itself, as in (25), in which *by itself* means "without outside help".

(25) The vase broke <u>by itself.</u> (Levin and Rappaport Hovav (1995: 92)

Arguably, the term "external causation" is not optimal for a notion also including self-causation.

While there are many sharp insights in all these discussions of ergative intransitive clauses, they should, in my view, be further nuanced with reference to other alternations. More specifically, the alternate constructions expressing self-instigation have to be investigated, i.e. the reflexive and the *(all) by itself* construction. This should happen in an empirical data-based way, as both these constructions have been cited in what seem "metalinguistic", rather than naturally occurring, examples, such as *The vase broke by itself* and *The door opened itself.* In fact, the *by itself* construction is very infrequent with ergatively used verbs in the COBUILD corpus (about eight cases), whilst in Heerman's (2000) corpus-based study of English reflexives, ergative reflexives accounted for only 3%. Of the attested *by itself* examples, one was only a "virtual" example, as indicated by *as if,*

(26) It's as if the rock has moved <u>by itself</u>. (CB)

and others occurred in contexts invoking ghosts or magic, e.g.

(27) "Even though we have plenty of ghosts, I have never felt anything other than utterly relaxed here," she says. (...) Acording to Dwina, there is a water bowl in the prayer room that fills up <u>by itself</u> (...), bolts across a massive iron door which close by <u>themselves</u>, and the sound of someone winding clocks in the Great Hall. (CB)

The three examples in which *by itself* was used to depict spontaneously occurring eventualities all alternated with reflexives, e.g.

(28) (a) it [a wound] would probably close up <u>by itself</u> [...] (CB)
(b) it would probably close itself up

It thus appears that the ergative reflexive is the only alternate that we have to reckon with.

To typify the semantics of ergative intransitive clauses, I propose that a distinction has to be made between those that alternate with reflexives and those that do not (Davidse 2002: 170). This distinction is strongly rooted in lexical selection restrictions attaching to the subjects of ergative intransitive clauses. The relation between subject and ergative intransitive verb contains, as suggested by Curme (1931: 440), both active and passive elements, which may be foregrounded in different proportions by the semantics and pragmatics of specific examples. The main cut in this continuum is marked by the opposition between ergative intransitive clauses that reflexivize and ones that do not. With the former, there is a **more active** component to the relation between subject and verb, which is actualized in reflexives (which express "self-instigation"). Lexically, these subjects fall within the class of **potents** (Pederson 1991: 63). Ergative intransitive clauses that are not reflexivizable have a **more passive** relation between verb and subject. The subject entity can never be construed as self-instigator; it is not potent enough – it is merely **inclined**, or predisposed, to the process in question.

Classes of entities capable of self-instigation in English include animates, human collectives, and potent inanimates. The class of **animates** is illustrated in:

(29) "I dropped outta school. I met friends. I started to [...]" He stopped himself, his choppy words disjointed. (CB)

Collectives include institutions, companies, geographical units, etc., whose instigational power stems from the humans that are metonymically associated with them, as in

(30) Lombardi's survey of curial opinion revealed that with its bureaucratic stick-in-the-mud habits the Curia would be incapable of reforming itself. (CB)

The class of **potents**, is defined by Pederson (1991: 63*)* as "a stage of such an extension where the animacy criterion for the use of the reflexive has been weakened, but only to the point where the subject must still be potent in some conceptualizable or metaphorical sense". Potents include machines (example 31) as well as other entities with some form of internal activation mechanism. From various perspectives certain entities can be construed as capable of self-instigation. Examples (32), (33) and (34) evoke the perspectives of physics, biology and chemistry respectively.

(31) Powered by rechargeable battery pack [...] each 5" unit switches itself off automatically when not is use. (CB)

(32) Where it had been was only a great heap of yellow-gold rubble that [...] flattened and sifted itself into a mere stretch of ochreous dust. (CB)

(33) Sun damage is reversible and skin will heal itself. (CB)

(34) If they take the paper down the tip [...] it will eventually break itself down. (CB)

The lexical fillers of the subject of ergative intransitives that do not reflexivize are less potent and have a more passive relation to the process. For lack of a better term, I refer to them as **inclinees**. "Inclinees" are basically – physical or abstract – items, which, at first sight, might be thought of as immobile and unchanging. However, they have a certain likelihood of being involved in physical and chemical processes as well as more abstract changes and fluctuations. This inclination is directly linked to specific properties of them. For instance, related to their shape or mechanistic properties, certain entities may be disposed to a particular form of instigatable motion: *wheels turn, doors open, barrels roll, logs float,* etc. Likewise, depending on their internal composition, substances may be inclined to – or threatened by – specific chemical processes with natural causes: *ice melts, hair bleaches, steel corrodes,* etc. Humans and animates may be construed as consisting of matter subjected to natural laws, e.g. *men age.*

Another class of typical subjects of ergative intransitives is that of fragile objects in relation to the typical mishaps that may befall them: *glass chips, paint fades, skin flakes,* etc. In our world view, many phenomena are viewed as being given to fluctuation and change, such as weather and economic phenomena: *water freezes, air pressure decreases,* and similarly *wages* may *freeze* and *currencies increase.* Then, there are also objects which, with the right human manipulation, manifest certain types of predictable, desired behaviour. For instance, certain foods can be construed as inclined to the specific changes they are made to manifest in various processes of food preparation: *stews* may be *simmering, eggs boiling,* etc. Likewise, the very design of bombs and explosives makes them inclined to explode, e.g. *mines detonate.* Inclination is thus not only a matter of natural composition but also of conscious human design. Finally, it should not be forgotten that entities may for rhetorical or ideological purposes be construed as naturally inclined to certain processes to downplay the responsibility of controlling humans in these events, e.g. *The prices of all houses inflate at approximately the same rate* (CB).

Ergative intransitives that alternate with reflexives, then, are characterized by a "voice vagueness": they are **vague** between the features "self-instigated" and "externally instigated". An example such as *The wound will heal* is synonymous neither with the reflexive **The wound will heal itself,* which expresses self-instigation, nor with *Ointment will heal the wound,* which includes an external instigator. Rather, it is left open whether self-instigation or external instigation is involved.

The point about the vagueness of ergatives can be illustrated with the verb *unify,* whose development of an ergative intransitive use can be traced back rather precisely to a specific historical context. In the 1987 edition of *Collins COBUILD English Language Dictionary* (CCELD),[7] it is treated as a transitive verb. No ergative intransitive use had been attested up to that time.[8] By contrast, in the 1995 *Collins COBUILD English Dictionary* (CCED),[9] an ergative subsense is included, which is illustrated with the following examples of the ergative alternation:

(35) (a) Helmut Kohl completed the task of unifying thriving West Germany with the old communist state of East Germany.
(b) Mr Major said his main job will be to unify the Conservative Party.
(c) (...) the benefits of unifying with the West.
(d) The plan has been for the rival armies to demobilize, to unify, and then to hold elections to decide who rules.

In other words, *unify* had detransitivized (see García Velasco, this volume)[10] in certain contexts of use in the period between the two editions of the Dictionary. Investigation of the COBUILD corpus showed that the emergence of the ergative use of *unify* was strongly associated with the unification of the two Germanies, after the fall of the Berlin Wall in 1989. After this it quickly gained currency in other political contexts. It is not hard to think of the ideological motivation behind this change in the use of *unify*. The intransitive use creates an ideologically convenient vagueness, leaving it open whether external forces were involved or whether the two Germanies unified themselves. Because humans are metonymically associated with states, a reflexive explicitly expressing self-instigation is a possible alternate here.

To ergative intransitives that do not alternate with reflexives and alternate with transitives only, the point applies that they always hint at the existence of an external instigator. For this subset (but only this subset), Levin and Rappaport's (1995: 92) observation that the verbs "by their very nature imply the existence of an 'external cause'" seems true to me. As they further explain for the verb *break*, "Something breaks because of the existence of an external cause; something does not break solely because of its own properties (although it is true that an entity must have certain properties in order for it to be breakable)" (1995: 92). However, the actual contexts in which such ergative intransitive clauses are used support the implication of an external instigator to differing degrees. Some contexts barely hint at an external instigator and replacing the intransitive verb by a transitive one, even in the passive form, would be rather forced. The differing degrees to which an external instigator is implied can, in principle, be further investigated by corpus study, quantifying the relative proportions of transitive to intransitive uses and comparing the selection restrictions on the participants in these two constructions. Olivier (2000: 43–44), for instance, found that *break*, in its ergative subsense of something "snapping" (CCELD: 164) less strongly implied an external instigator than the ergative subsense of something "separating into pieces, often because it has been hit or dropped" (CCED: 193). Ergative intransitives that do not reflexivize are hence also characterized by a certain vagueness which pertains to the strength with which an external instigator is implied.

6 Conclusion

In this article we have seen that throughout the history of modern linguistics a strain of linguists can be found such as Whorf and Gleason who hold that the semantics of constructions cannot be adequately captured without bringing in the constructions they systematically alternate with and the ones they crucially do not alternate with. There is also a tradition of researchers concerned with the classification of verb meanings, such as Levin and Van den Eynde, who have argued that verb-specific alternations can form the basis for a lexicogrammatically motivated classification in which components of verb meaning and syntactic behaviour dovetail. These notions were – directly and indirectly – criticized by Goldberg (2002), who spoke out against bringing alternations to bear on the study of verb-argument relations and advocated surface generalizations based only on the formal and semantic similarities of syntagmatic structures and the properties of individual verbs.

In this article I set out to reaffirm the heuristic usefulness of verb-specific alternations, with some clarifications and caveats, to verb classification and the semantics of constructions. I recapitulated the main arguments given in the literature why alternations are revealing of verb meaning and hence of verb classification (§2 and §3.1) and of the semantics of constructions (§4 and §5). I complemented this with alternation-based case studies of the subclassification of ditransitive verbs (§3.2) and of the semantics of ergative intransitive clauses (§5).

The results offer, I hope, a nuanced picture of what alternation-based research can achieve in these two areas at the present state of knowledge. The classification of ditransitive verbs on the basis of deletability of Dative and Patient revealed two things that had tended to be neglected so far. First, it revealed the existence of an important class for which both Dative and Patient are obligatory and which hence prototypically expresses the "causation of possession" associated with ditransitives. Second, it showed, against claims that ditransitive verbs basically code Agent-Patient relations onto which a Dative may be grafted, that various subclasses strongly profile Agent-Dative action chains.

For the semantic elucidation of ergative intransitives taking into account their characteristic alternations there is a long tradition of research, the main thrust of which is that ergative intransitives are externally caused. I proposed that they form a cryptotypical subclass of intransitives. Purely intransitive clauses, which do not allow for transitive and reflexive alternates, represent the Actor as the sole energy source of the action. Ergative intransitive clauses, by contrast, systematically allow for transitive alternates, while a subset also allows for reflexive ones. The semantics of the latter were characterized as vague with regard to whether the event was externally or self-instigated. Ergative intransitives that do not alternate with reflexives were argued to imply an external instigator to varying degrees. The distinction between these two subsets of ergative intransitives was further elaborated in terms of different lexical selection restrictions on their subjects.

This article thus recommends renewed study of alternations both on the theoretical and the descriptive level. Theoretically, a number of distinctions should be clarified: that between verb-specific alternations and more general variation in the systems of mood and theme/information, and also that between verb-specific alternations which are diagnostic of wide-ranging lexicogrammatical distinctions and minor ones correlating with smaller subclasses. Descriptively, new case studies should be carried out and ways devised of studying alternations as much as possible on the basis of corpus data.

Notes

* My particular thanks go to Pilar Guerrero Medina and Chris Butler for their very careful and helpful reading of an earlier draft. I also gratefully acknowledge the support of grant no. HUM2007-60706/FILO of the Spanish Ministry of Education and Science and the European Regional Development Fund.

1. Of these authors, Halliday and Van den Eynde were trained within the Firthian tradition. It can also be noted that the work of these theorists of alternation further influenced other authors, such as McGregor (1997), in which, following Gleason and Halliday, verb-specific alternations (or "agnates") are accorded an important place in the analysis of the relation between process and participants, and Kirchmeier-Andersen and Schøsler (1997) and Schøsler (forthcoming), which develop insights from Van den Eynde.
2. Gleason (1966: 196) stated his primary interest in the inherent properties of the language system rather than in "moves" through it — as he characterized transformations — with the following metaphor: "A trip is not part of a highway system, though only the highway system makes it possible."
3. All examples followed by (CB) are from the COBUILD corpus; they were extracted from *Wordbanks* via remote log-in and are reproduced here with the permission of HarperCollins.

4. Pinker's (1989) classification compares with Green's as follows. Her *to*-classes 1, 2, 3, 4 and 5 correspond to his ditransitive classes 4, 1, 3–2, 6–7 and 5 respectively. Her *for*-classes 1 and 2 correspond to his ditransitive classes 8 and 9, while her *for*-classes 3, 4 and 5 are not covered by his classification.
5. Following the Hallidayan tradition, the nominal complements of verbs are referred to as participants, or participant roles, rather than as arguments.
6. This case study is an expanded version of that presented in Davidse (1998).
7. *Collins COBUILD English Language Dictionary* (1987). Ed. J. McH. Sinclair. London: HarperCollins.
8. It should be recalled here that the COBUILD dictionaries were created from scratch on the basis of study of concordances for every entry. They systematically label verb senses manifesting the ergative alternation in the corpus data as V-erg.
9. *Collins COBUILD English Dictionary* (1995). Ed. J. McH. Sinclair. London: HarperCollins.
10. As rightly stressed by García Velasco (this volume), English verbs stand out by their diachronic flexibility, offering cases both of transitive verbs detransitivizing and intransitive ones developing causative uses.

References

Curme, G. O. (1931) *Syntax.* New York: Heath.

Davidse, K. (1998) Agnates, verb classes and the meaning of construals: The case of ditransitivity in English. *Leuven Contributions in Linguistics and Philology* 87(3–4): 281–313.

Davidse, K. (2002) English reflexive constructions as a test case for distinct Agent-Patient models. In K. Davidse and B. Lamiroy (eds) *The Nominative & Accusative and their Counterparts* 187–230. Amsterdam: Benjamins. [Case and grammatical relations across languages 4.]

Davidse, K. and Geyskens, S. (1998) *Have you walked the dog yet?* The ergative causativization of intransitives. *WORD* 49(2): 155–180.

Dik, S. (1997) *The Theory of Functional Grammar, Part 2: Complex and derived constructions.* (Second revised edition.) Ed. K. Hengeveld. Berlin: Mouton de Gruyter.

Fawcett, R. P. (1987) The semantics of clause and verb in English. In M. A. K. Halliday and R. P. Fawcett (eds) *New Developments in Systemic Linguistics, Vol. I: Theory and description* 130–183. London: Pinter.

Firth, J. R. (1964) *The Tongues of Men and Speech.* London: Oxford University Press.

García Velasco, D. (this volume) The causative/inchoative alternation in Functional Discourse Grammar.

Givón, T. (1979) *On Understanding Grammar.* New York: Academic Press.

Gleason, H. A. (1966) *Linguistics and English Grammar.* New York: Holt, Reinhart and Winston.

Goldberg, A. E. (1995) *Constructions: A construction grammar approach to argument structure.* Chicago, IL: University of Chicago Press.

Goldberg, A. E. (2002) Surface generalizations: An alternative to alternations. *Cognitive Linguistics* 13(4): 327–356.

Green, G. (1974) *Semantics and Syntactic Regularity.* Bloomington, IN: Indiana University Press.

Haas, W. (1954) On defining linguistic units. *Transactions of the Philological Society* 54–84.

Halliday, M. A. K. (1967) Notes on transitivity and theme in English 1. *Journal of Linguistics* 3(1): 37–81.

Halliday, M. A. K. (1968) Notes on transitivity and theme in English 3. *Journal of Linguistics* 4(2):179–215.

Halliday, M. A. K. (1985) An *Introduction to Functional Grammar.* London: Arnold.

Heerman, C. (2000) *Reflexives as They Manifest Themselves: A corpus-based typology of English reflexives.* MA Thesis. Dept. of Linguistics, University of Leuven.

Jespersen, O. (1927) *A Modern English Grammar on Historical Principles. Part III.* London: George Allen and Unwin.

Keyser, S. J. and Roeper, T. (1984) On the middle and ergative constructions in English. *Linguistic Inquiry* 15(2): 381–416.

Laffut, A. (2006) *Three-participant Constructions in English: A functional-cognitive approach to causative relations.* Amsterdam: Benjamins [Studies in Language Companion Series 79].

Langacker, R. (1991) *Foundations of Cognitive Grammar, Vol. II: Descriptive Application.* Stanford, CA: Stanford University Press.

Levin, B. (1993) *English Verb Classes and Alternations: A preliminary investigation.* Chicago, IL: University of Chicago Press.

Levin, B. and Rappaport Hovav, M. (1995) *Unaccusativity: At the syntax-lexical semantics interface.* Cambridge, MA: The MIT Press.

Olivier, T. (2000) *An Empirical Analysis of Ergative Verbs: A study of the COBUILD-approach.* M.A. Thesis. Dept. of Linguistics, University of Leuven.

Pederson, E. (1991) *Subtle Semantics: Universals in the polysemy of reflexive and causative constructions.* Ph.D. Thesis. Dept. of Linguistics, University of California at Berkeley.

Pinker, S. (1989) *Learnability and Cognition: The acquisition of argument structure.* Cambridge, MA: The MIT Press.

Rice, S. (1987) Towards a transitive prototype: Evidence from some atypical English passives. In J. Aske, N. Beery, L. Michaelis and H. Filip (eds) *Proceedings of the Thirteenth Annual Meeting of the Berkeley Linguistics Society* 422–434. Berkeley, CA: Berkeley Linguistics Society.

Schøsler, L. (2010) Organization and reorganization of a constructional paradigm. The case of dative two-argument constructions from Latin to Modern French. *Acta Linguistica Hafniensia* 42: 26–45.

Smith, C. S. (1970) Jespersen's "move and change" class and causative verbs in English. In M. A. Jazayery, E. C. Polomé and W. Winter (eds) *Linguistic and Literary Studies in Honor of Archibald A. Hill, Vol. 2: Descriptive linguistics* 101–109. The Hague: Mouton.

Van den Eynde, K. (1995) Methodological reflections on descriptive linguistics. Knud Togeby's principles and the pronominal approach. In L. Schøsler and M. Talbot (eds) *Studies in Valency* 111–131. Odense: Odense University Press.

Whorf, B. L. (1956) *Language, Thought and Reality: Selected writings of Benjamin Lee Whorf.* J. Carroll (ed.) Cambridge, MA: The MIT Press.

Wierzbicka, A. (1988) *The Semantics of Grammar.* Amsterdam: Benjamins. [Studies in Language Companion Series 18].

Appendix 1: Ditransitive verbs studied in §3.2.2

Verbs included in Green's (1976: 210–214) classification:

administer, bring, deliver, hand, pass, take, advance, award, bring, bring up, bring down, cede, entrust, feed, give, lease, lend, loan, pay, sell, serve, fling, send, ship, shove, toss, throw, admit, announce, cable, cite, confess, convey, declare, describe, e-mail, explain, mail, narrate, recount, reveal, phone, preach, prescribe, quote, radio, read, show, suggest, telegraph, telephone, whisper, wire, write, accord, allot, allow, assign, choose, delegate, grant, leave, bequeath, pay, permit, promise; bake, boil, build, cook, draw, knit, make, paint, pour, roast, sew, buy, choose, find, get, keep, leave, select, steal, kill, sing

Verbs not included in Green's classification:

address, advise, advocate, affirm, ask, assert, attribute, book, charge, command, confirm, concede, deal, deliver, deny, dispute, distribute, excuse, forgive, introduce, issue, pardon, pledge, predict, prescribe, prove, propose, recommend, refuse, relate, reproach, reserve, reveal, report, scatter, strew, teach, volunteer; clear, cost, dance, fix, peel, prepare, gather, order, save, spare

2 The study of alternations in a dialogic Functional Discourse Grammar*

J. Lachlan Mackenzie[a]

1 Introduction

Functional Discourse Grammar (FDG; Hengeveld and Mackenzie 2008) is a model of grammar that arose in the first decade of this century. To a considerable extent, it is a continuation and expansion of Functional Grammar (FG; Dik 1978, 1989, 1997) by linguists who formerly situated their work within that model. Many of the detailed representational techniques first elaborated in FG are retained in FDG, as is the former's strong commitment to typological adequacy, by which is meant the desire to give a neutral account of all types of language. However, FDG has a number of distinctive characteristics that mark it off from its predecessor. The most prominent of these are: (a) the objective of accounting for all types of grammatical unit by taking the Discourse Act as the primary object of description; (b) an expansion of the model to encompass four levels of analysis, each with its own internal layering; and (c) an architecture that is designed to give substance to the notion of cognitive adequacy, a notion to which FG paid little more than lip service (cf. Mackenzie subm.; Butler 2008, 2009). The present article will be couched in the general framework of FDG, employing a revised model that aims to reflect the use of language in dialogue.

It will accordingly begin with an overview of FDG (§2), which will explore its potential as a framework for understanding alternations. A confrontation of the model with recent developments in the psycholinguistics of dialogue will lead to various proposals to rethink FDG

a J. Lachlan Mackenzie is Honorary Professor of Functional Linguistics at VU University Amsterdam, Netherlands and a Researcher at the Instituto de Linguística Teórica e Computacional (ILTEC) in Lisbon, Portugal. E-mail: lachlan_mackenzie@hotmail.com Website: www.lachlanmackenzie.com

as a dialogic model (§3). The next section (§4) will discuss the study of alternations in psycholinguistics, leading – in the light of FDG – to a clearer understanding of the notion of "morphosyntactic alternation". The final major section (§5) will turn to the analysis of some data drawn from the Michigan Corpus of Academic Spoken English, which will exemplify some of the issues facing the grammarian working with alternations.

2 Functional Discourse Grammar

The model of FDG took form during a series of discussions, workshops and conferences held in the early years of this century. The new architecture (first set out in Mackenzie and Gómez-González 2004) not only expands the existing framework but also places it in a broader context, interpreting FDG as the grammatical component of an overall model of verbal interaction that also comprises conceptual, contextual and articulatory components. Like any grammatical model, FDG seeks to correlate meaning and form. An unusual but essential feature is that the meaning of a Discourse Act is shown as a pair of complementary representations, one pragmatic and the other semantic. What counts as a valid representation at each of these levels, as they are called, is determined by the process of **formulation**. The internal structuring of the two levels, the interpersonal level and the representational level, is governed by the same principles, namely hierarchical layering and the restriction of variables by operators and modifiers. The linguistic form used to express the Discourse Act is accounted for by the other major process in the grammar, **encoding**, which deals with the conversion of the contents of the interpersonal and representational levels into morphosyntactic and phonological form. Like formulation, encoding is language-specific: universal properties of meaning and form (if there are any) are deduced from empirical research rather than being postulated *a priori*.

The model of FDG as presented in Hengeveld and Mackenzie (2008, 2010) is shown in Figure 2.1. The ovals represent processes, while the rectangles show the levels. The boxes on the left-hand side of the grammatical component contain the primitives, i.e.: (a) the structures permitted by the language under analysis for formulation (frames) and encoding (templates); (b) the forms available to the grammar at each level (lexemes, grammatical morphemes, suppletive forms); and (c) the operators that apply at the various layers of analysis within the distinct levels. It will be immediately noticeable that the arrows point from the intention

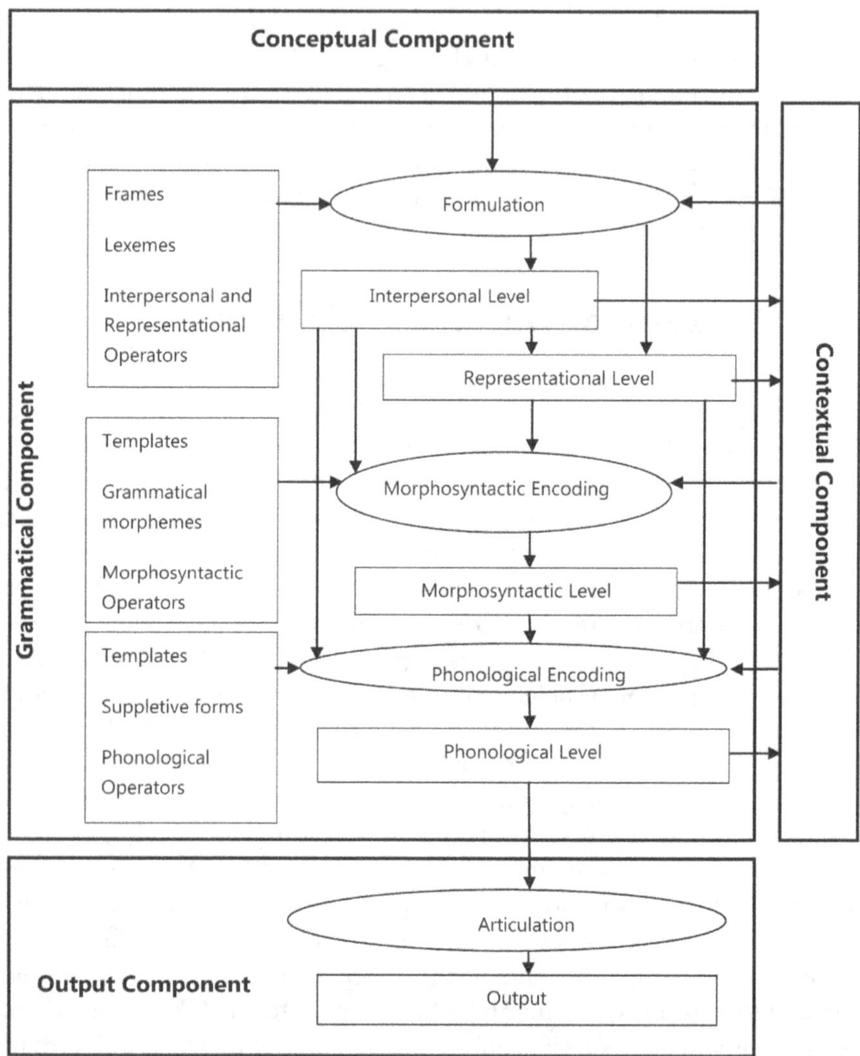

Figure 2.1. Layout of FDG

formulated in the conceptual component through formulation and encoding to articulation. This is in keeping with the aim of FDG, to "mirror [...] the language production process in individual speakers" (Hengeveld 2004: 267), a point to which I shall return.

The layout of FDG allows linguistic phenomena to be described and distinguished with a considerable degree of precision. This is made possible by a methodology that requires distinctions to be made once only in the grammar, namely at the place where they are relevant. Other approaches to grammar have tended to overload the (morpho)syntax with distinctions that are either pragmatic or semantic (see also Jackendoff 2007: 35–38 for critique of such "syntactocentric" architectures). One need only think of such notions as Topic Phrase, Focus Phrase and Force Phrase (Rizzi 1997). The pragmatic functions Topic and Focus as well as illocutionary force are indeed essential to an understanding of the structure of Discourse Acts, but should be (and in FDG are) located at the interpersonal level of analysis, with consequences in encoding. Another example would be Van Valin and LaPolla's (1997: 26–33) incorporation into their syntax of a Core corresponding to the main predicate and its arguments. In FDG there is no such entity at the morphosyntactic level, since the distinction is already made at the representational level, where the configurational property (Hengeveld and Mackenzie 2008: 181–215) consists of the predicate and its arguments.

As a functional model, FDG is set up to ensure that most of what happens in encoding, both morphosyntactic and phonological, is functionally motivated. In other words, encoding serves to operationalize distinctions that are made at the interpersonal and representational levels. Nevertheless, each language may have additional, functionally neutral requirements that encoding must also take into consideration: the choice between head-modifier vs. modifier-head ordering, for example, does not follow from anything at the formulation levels, but is determined at the morphosyntactic level. Encoding thus reacts to a-functional principles internal to the morphosyntactic level while chiefly finding forms of expression that are motivated by principles that do reflect functionality such as **iconicity** (precedence in form reflecting precedence in meaning), **domain integrity** (pragmatic and semantic units being preferentially realized as morphosyntactic units) **and scope-to-precedence mapping,** whereby the scope relations that strongly characterize the inner structuring of the formulation levels are mirrored in the relative ordering of formal units. For detail on the working of these functional principles, see Hengeveld and Mackenzie (2008).

The fundamental organizing principle for the internal structuring of the interpersonal and representational levels is hierarchy: at the interpersonal level, for example, the highest layer in the hierarchy, the Move, contains one or more Discourse Acts, which lie within its scope. In turn, each Discourse Act may contain and scope over Illocutions, etc., and so on, down to the lowest layer, that of subacts; the representational level has a similarly hierarchical structure. However, both levels also recognize the possibility of multiple units occurring at the same hierarchical layer. These units, termed **equipollent**, are found at the interpersonal level in the form of multiple subacts within the communicated content, and at the representational level in the form of multiple units (lexical properties, individuals, etc.) within the configurational property. The encoding of such equipollent units involves the additional principle of **alignment**, a term borrowed from language typology. Individual constructions are classified accordingly as they display interpersonal, representational or morphosyntactic alignment and entire language systems may be typologized as displaying a preponderance of one or another type of alignment. On this basis, Hengeveld and Mackenzie (2008: 317–326) classify the dominant constructions in Tagalog as being attributable to interpersonal alignment, those in Acehnese to representational alignment and those in Kham to morphosyntactic alignment. In constructions/languages with interpersonal or representational alignment, the morphosyntax of the constructions/languages in question are faithful reflections of the pragmatic or semantic organization, respectively, of the Discourse Act. Morphosyntactic alignment means that the morphosyntax imposes its own principles of organization, overruling both pragmatic and semantic considerations. Where a language attributes great importance to subject and/or object (or another "privileged syntactic argument", see Butler subm.), allowing these to mask pragmatic or semantic notions, that language will be said to have (predominantly) morphosyntactic alignment.

Analogously, it should be possible to provide a similar typology of alternations within the theory of FDG. The notion of alternation has had a long history in linguistics, originating in phonology and morphology, where it is closely associated with the notion of a minimal pair. Discovering the phonological system of a language initially involves working with pairs of forms that – ideally – differ only minimally in one segment of sound or tone; where that minimal difference correlates with a meaning difference, this is strong evidence for a phonemic contrast. Similarly, in morphology, a contrast between single phonemes or phonemic units that correlates with a difference in meaning or use is evidence for the presence of two distinct morphemes (e.g. different case-suffixes). The common features of an alternation are thus: (a) the comparison of two forms that are largely identical; (b) the identification of the difference between the two forms as being significant for the structure of the level at which the difference applies; and (c) an appeal to meaning difference as the arbiter of the reality of difference. The last feature means that if there is no meaning difference, the conclusion will be that there is no alternation, but merely a pair of allophones/allomorphs.

The alternations that are central to the present volume apply to larger units than phonemes or morphemes, namely morphosyntactic units, typically clauses, but in principle any kind of Discourse Act. Here, too, the clauses being compared (explicitly or implicitly) are identical except for the formal characteristics that are inherent to the alternation. The identification of alternations is, again, essential for our understanding of the structure of morphosyntax: after all, it is through the manipulation of alternations that linguists have argued for constituent structure. Whether or not the alternation is always associated with a meaning difference, however, is a matter of one's theoretical stance; as Barcelona Sánchez (this volume) rightly points out, for a cognitive/constructionist linguist it is a fundamental assumption that every alternation correlates with some meaning difference, no matter how subtle.

As mentioned above, meaning is operationalized in FDG as formulation, the translation of conceptual material into a pair of representations, one pragmatic and the other semantic. In accordance with this distinction, we can label those alternations that are attributable to the former as interpersonal-level alternations and those that reflect semantic oppositions as representational-level alternations. In this way, the presence of pragmatic and semantic motivations for the alternations observed in morphosyntax (or indeed in phonology) makes it possible to determine the internal composition of the interpersonal and representational levels in each language, since only those pragmatic and semantic distinctions that have morphosyntactic (or phonological) consequences are in FDG posited for the grammar of the language under analysis.

To make this more concrete, let us consider what FDG regards as interpersonal-level and what as representational-level alternations. The following pairs of discourse acts from English all involve alternations (minimally different forms distinguished by a regular meaning difference):

(1) (a) Bad driving caused the accident.
    (b) It was bad driving that caused the accident.

(2) (a) Lucia sat reading in the garden.
    (b) Lucia sat reading in a garden.

(3) (a) The vandal sprayed the artwork with paint.
    (b) The vandal sprayed paint on the artwork.

(4) (a) Global warming is melting the icecap.
    (b) The icecap is melting.

In (1) and (2) we see interpersonal-level alternations, where the distinction between the alternants reflects various differences in the interaction between speaker and hearer. In FDG, the distinction between the non-cleft (1a) and cleft (1b) version of a clause is the result of differential assignments of pragmatic functions to subacts within the communicated content. The alternation of the definite and indefinite article in (2a) and (2b) is associated with different choices of operator on the respective subact. In a language lacking the cleft construction (see Gundel 2008 for discussion of Spanish as a language disfavouring clefting) or definite/indefinite articles (e.g. Russian) there will be no alternations directly parallel to those in (1) and (2) and the interpersonal level of those languages will be correspondingly different.

In (3) and (4) we see representational-level alternations, where the difference between the alternants is a matter of semantics, quite independent of communicative use. In (3) the "locative alternation" (Levin 1993: 2), with the familiar holistic and partitive readings, the analysis at the representational level will differ, with the *artwork* being Undergoer and Locative and the *paint* Locative and Undergoer respectively within the configurational property associated with the lexical property *spray*. In (4), we find an alternation between a causative and an inchoative use of *melt*. This follows from distinct quantitative valencies of the lexical property *melt*, with Actor and Undergoer arguments in (4a) and a single Undergoer argument in (4b); for further discussion in an FDG framework see García Velasco and Hengeveld (2002).

The study of examples such as (1) to (4) suggests that minimal differences between morphosyntactic forms of the type analysed will have a strong tendency to correlate with distinctions that can be drawn at either the interpersonal or the representational level. Some may, indeed, flow from differences at both levels: thus a cleft construction of the type illustrated in (1b) arguably results not only from the assignment of pragmatic functions at the interpersonal level but also from the presence of a structure at the representational level that involves attributing the causation of the accident to bad driving. In many contexts, similarly, the use of (4a) or (4b) will be associated with different assignments of Topic and Focus to the three subacts that compose the communicative content of the discourse acts in question. The question that remains to be addressed is whether there are, from this point of view, any alternations that may be regarded as a matter of the morphosyntactic level, i.e. alternations that do not flow from distinct choices in formulation. To answer this question, we need to place FDG in a wider context.

3 FDG from the perspective of dialogue

The current architecture of FDG, as was pointed out in the discussion of Figure 2.1 above, is strongly oriented to an understanding of linguistic forms as deriving from the activity of an individual speaker. In addition, each of these forms is assumed to have the same origin (or "derivational history", in generative parlance): it is an entirely novel creation resulting from the development of a communicative intention in the conceptual component which triggers formulation, then encoding and finally articulation. This individual-creative assumption is, however, impossible to square with results that have been emerging from both the linguistic study of language use and psycholinguistic investigations into interaction.

In seeking to be "cognitively adequate", a theory such as FDG is committed to bear in mind (at the very least) the findings of contemporary psycholinguistics.[1] In Hengeveld and Mackenzie's (2008: 1–2) words, "a model of grammar will be more effective the more its organization resembles language processing *in the individual*" (my emphasis, JLM). In writing these words, they were echoing the trends and methodologies of the major psycholinguists of the 1980s and 1990s, who achieved remarkable advances in the study of individual language production (see Levelt 1989 and the overview in Bock and Levelt 1994). However, experts in language production have also been aware, in a tradition of research initiated by Bock (1986), that the production of utterances is subject to **priming**. In an experimental context, priming is manifest in the extent to which experimental subjects re-use linguistic material to which they have had prior exposure. One experiment, reported in Bock (1986), involved individuals describing pictured events after exposure to certain priming words, which were either phonologically or semantically related to target words describing the events. A picture of lightning striking a church would be preceded by a prime such as *frightening* or *thunder*, or else by *search* or *worship*; the finding was that semantically related primes (*thunder* and *worship*) had a significant effect on the individuals' choice of grammatical subject, whereas phonologically related primes (*frightening* and *search*) did not. This kind of result was used to justify the separation of semantic and phonological processing in psycholinguistic models of language production and indeed confirms the FDG architecture in which the identification of the morphosyntactic subject "follows" formulation but "precedes" the operation of the phonological level.[2]

In more recent research, however, psycholinguists have taken the prevalence of priming effects to suggest that these reflect a deeper property of human verbal interaction, namely a powerful drive to imitate. This has been variously linked to the recent discovery of mirror neurons in macaques (and possibly humans, too; see Iacoboni 2008; Mukamel *et al.* 2010), but more specifically in language production research it has been interpreted as a matter of **interactive alignment** (Pickering and Garrod 2004). The force of the drive to imitate has also been discussed outside the context of psycholinguistic research by Tannen (2006: 97–100), who recognizes that there may be resistance to a view of language as "relatively imitative or prepatterned" since it "seems to push us towards automatism". However, she argues that there is a "balance between the individual and the social, the fixed and the free" and suggests that "speakers repeat, rephrase, and echo (or shadow) others' words in conversation without stopping to think, but rather as an automatic and spontaneous way of participating in conversation".

The notion of interactive alignment developed by Pickering and Garrod (2004) is fully compatible with Tannen's view, suggesting that language production involves a combination of creativity and automatic mutual adjustment – with the latter showing up in the priming effects observed in experiments. In order to understand this phenomenon, they abandon the tradition of associating language production with the individual (as in Levelt 1989) and focus on dialogue as the arena of verbal interaction. Their argument is based on the observation that speech, despite being produced under severe time constraints, is normally fluent and rapid. Turns typically follow each other with only a fraction of a second's delay and often overlap. Nevertheless, the mental processes underlying language production are highly complex: to give but one example, for every subact of reference, a calculation must be made of the amount of detail to be supplied (involving different amounts of specificity in formulation, showing up as zero through to a complex NP in encoding), and all this unconscious reckoning guzzles up processing space. Their overall prediction, then, is that conversation should be extremely taxing, but of course it is not; and the reason for this is that the communicator is not alone, but is collaborating in a joint effort (cf. Clark 1996). With the effort of communicating being shared in this way, verbal interaction becomes efficient for all participants in a dialogue and, in processing terms, cost-effective.

The evidence adduced by Pickering and Garrod comes from transcriptions of dialogues recorded in the psychology laboratory involving participants working together on a task. They concentrate, as psychologists, on how the data show the collaborators implicitly creating a joint model of the situation in which they find themselves, tacitly "agreeing on" terms with which to describe features of that situation. However, they stress

(2004: 174) that "dialogue transcripts are full of repeated linguistic elements and structures indicating alignment at various levels in addition to that of the situation model". This echoes results that are coming in from various quarters of linguistics, ranging from the observations of massive repetitiveness in corpora in Wang (2005) through the study of how constructions emerge as an entrenchment of repeated structures (Bybee 2006), and even to formal semantics, where Gargett *et al.* (2009) have modelled how conversationalists jointly construct both meaning and form.

A finding that emerges repeatedly from these research lines is that each speaker's production is affected as much by her own earlier utterances (**autopriming**) as by those of her conversation partners (**allopriming**). The arena of language production is therefore not just the individual speaker's cognitive and linguistic capacities but the dialogue in which she and her interlocutors are participating. The opportunity arises, then, to rethink FDG, which is committed to being a grammar that is part of and compatible with a wider theory of verbal interaction, as a dialogic rather than an individualistic model in which there is a balance between the creativity of the individual speaker and her participation in a mutually aligned interaction. A proposal for such a dialogic model is made in Mackenzie (subm.), as shown in Figure 2.2.

As will immediately be clear from a comparison of Figures 2.1 and 2.2, the architecture of FDG remains unchanged in the dialogic model: all four levels of analysis are retained, as are the components representing the individuals' conceptualization and articulation. The only change is that the contextual component, the status of which has so far remained rather unclear in discussions about FDG, is visualized as being shared by both participants. This is entirely in keeping with Pickering and Garrod's notion of the **implicit common ground** that arises in any interaction, defined simply as "the information that is shared between the interlocutors" (2004: 177). The dialogic contextual component thus becomes the conduit through which the participants in the dialogue (A and B) share aspects of all levels within the grammar; it is this sharing that makes mutual alignment possible.

In this dialogic model of FDG each level of Speaker A's grammatical apparatus has the potential to transfer some or all of its material to the corresponding formulator or encoder of Speaker B (and *vice versa*). This mimics the effect of priming. The result is that both formulation and encoding in each individual involved in a dialogue take on the task of balancing input from a variety of sources. Thus, as in orthodox FDG, formulation receives input from the conceptual component and from the inventory of frames, lexemes and operators; in the dialogic model, the

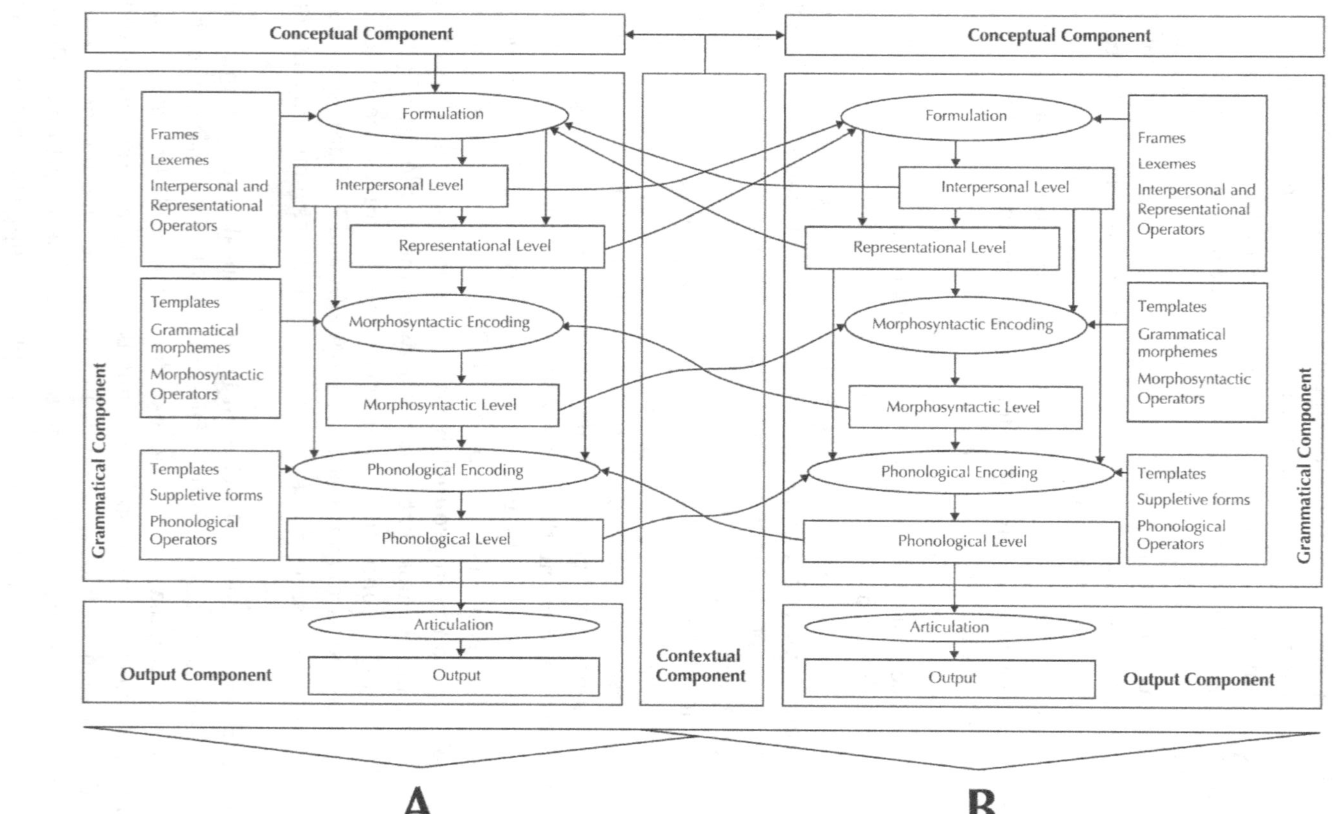

Figure 2.2. Layout of a dialogic FDG

contextual component additionally permits the content of the interlocutor's interpersonal and representational levels to become available to the formulation process. Similarly, an individual's morphosyntactic encoding combines input from: (a) her own interpersonal and representational levels; (b) her inventory of templates, morphemes and morphosyntactic operators; and (c) through the contextual component, the content of her interlocutor's morphosyntactic level; and analogously for phonological encoding.

The resultant architecture provides a framework for understanding and describing how the similarities between interlocutors' production arise through continual mutual and automatic alignment of each level of representation.[3] This interactive alignment serves to greatly reduce the complexity of language production and comprehension and the resultant model goes quite some way towards explaining the rapidity and fluency of dialogic speech and the phenomenon of shared utterances.

4 Morphosyntactic alternation in a dialogic FDG

Against this backdrop, let us now reconsider the phenomenon of morphosyntactic alternation in English within the dialogic model of FDG shown in Figure 2.2. Alternations have not only been the stock in trade of linguists for decades, but have also played a central role in psycholinguistics, and specifically in experimental studies of the phenomenon of priming in language production (Pickering and Ferreira 2008). Much of this work has focused on the phenomenon known as **structural priming**, the observation that experimental subjects will tend to re-use the structural, i.e. morphosyntactic, properties of a clause that functions as a prime.

In a succession of experiments carried out in the 20 years after the appearance of Bock (1986), which launched this strand of research, it was shown that particular meaning-form correlations display priming effects. Thus the experience of being exposed to a prime in the active or the passive voice was shown to have a significant effect on experimental subjects' subsequent description of images that could have been described with either construction, and similar effects were found for primes corresponding to either of the alternative forms for expressing the recipient in English (as Np or Prepp – the "dative alternation"). In our terms, since these alternatives follow from different configurations at the interpersonal and/or representational levels, the priming would affect the speaker's formulation, with knock-on effects on encoding. Just such a semantic effect was found by Chang *et al.* (2003) for the above-mentioned *spray*-alternation, see (3) above. Although both (3a) and (3b) have the morphosyntactic structure [Np V Np Prepp], *spray-on* primed other *spray-on* descriptions and *spray-with* primed *spray-with* descriptions. This was taken as further evidence for the involvement of meaning-form correlations in priming (cf. Goldberg and Bencini 2005 for discussion).

The question accordingly arose whether there was also evidence for purely structural priming, i.e. instances where a clause structure could prime an identical or sufficiently similar structure without any involvement of meaning, i.e. where the two forms encode totally different interpersonal or representational configurations. This was essentially the question underlying Bock and Loebell (1990), working with clause pairs such as those in (5a) and (5b):

(5) (a) The wealthy widow drove her Mercedes to the church.
(b) The wealthy widow gave her Mercedes to the church.

Here the interpersonal configuration is held constant but there are significant differences at the representational level, namely between the lexical items *drive* and *give* and between the Locative semantic function of *to the church* in (5a) and the Recipient function of *to the church* in (5b). The difference is reflected in the acceptability of (6b) as against the unacceptability of (6a):

(6) (a) *The wealthy widow drove the church her Mercedes.
(b) The wealthy widow gave the church her Mercedes.

Although they are semantically distinct, the two clauses in (5) have the same morphosyntactic structure, shown in the FDG formalization in (7):

(7) $(\mathrm{Cl}_1$: $[\mathrm{Np}_1\ \mathrm{Vw}_1\ \mathrm{Np}_2\ [\mathrm{to}\ \mathrm{Np}_3]_{\mathrm{Prepp1}}]\ (\mathrm{Cl}_1))$

Now, as Bock and Loebell (1990) demonstrate, where there is an alternative between a Prepp dative and an Np dative (as seen in (5b) and (6b) respectively) the locative form in (5a) primes the Prepp alternant. However, from an FDG viewpoint, one might question whether the semantic functions are indeed distinct at the representational level. After all, both are L(ocative) in Hengeveld and Mackenzie (2008: 197), with the grammaticality difference between (6a) and (6b) being attributable to the semantic status of *the church* as (l_i) in (5a)/(6a) and (x_i) in (5b)/(6b).[4] Similar doubts about this kind of example, from the perspective of Construction Grammar, are expressed by Goldberg and Bercini (2005: 12).

A more striking example from Bock and Loebell (1990) is seen in (8):

(8) (a) The 747 was landing by the control tower.
(b) The 747 was alerted by the control tower.

Here it is clear that there are major differences at the representational level. Whereas *land* in (8a) is a one-place property with an Undergoer argument, *alert* in (8b) is a two-place property, with an Actor and an Undergoer. *By the control tower* is a Locative modifier in (8a), but in (8b) it is an Actor argument. The preposition *by* in (8a) is a lexical item, but corresponds to a semantic function (Actor) in (8b). In other words, there is no generalizable semantic relation between (8a) and (8b). Nevertheless, both clauses have the same morphosyntactic structure shown in (9):

(9) (Cl_1: [Np_1 [Vw Vw]$_{Vp1}$ [by Np_2]$_{Prepp1}$] (Cl_1))

Bock and Loebell found that experimental subjects exposed to structures like (8a) were more likely to produce clauses like (8b) than their active equivalents (i.e. *The control tower alerted the 747*). This example therefore gives a *prima facie* indication of the existence of alternations that have cognitive reality (as is evidenced by the priming effect) but which are based purely on similarity in the outcome of the encoding process. This conclusion has been challenged for these data by Bencini *et al.* (unpubl.), however, who replicated Bock and Loebell's results but found that the presence of the preposition *by* in (9) is essential: "locatives without *by* showed no priming". Nevertheless, the point remains that semantically unrelated clauses of the form shown in (9) are capable of priming each other.

The examples we have seen share many lexical items, but it has been known since Bock (1986) that priming is observed even when the prime and the subsequent target share no lexical items at all, although the presence of shared lexical material unsurprisingly does induce stronger priming effects. In other words, a structure totally unspecified for lexemes or function words, such as (10):

(10) (Cl_1: [Np_1 Vp_1 $Prepp_1$] (Cl_1))

is capable of priming another clause with the same structure. This means that the clauses found in (11), all of which have the same morphosyntactic structure without any similarity of meaning, are potentially capable of priming one another:

(11) (a) The moon has set in the west.
(b) A man should rely on his friends.
(c) These arguments were refuted by several scholars.

The suggestion I wish to make is, accordingly, that pairs like those in (8) above and lexically unrelated but morphosyntactically parallel clauses as in (11) should be recognized as morphosyntactic alternants. Because they are not related semantically but only have a coincidental similarity, they cannot be regarded as representational-level alternations; and since there is also no relatedness in the distribution of pragmatic functions, interpersonal-level alternation is also not relevant. Yet psycholinguistic evidence has compelled us to recognize that they do group together cognitively: hence the proposal to recognize these as morphosyntactic alternations.

The existence of truly morphosyntactic alternations means that in a dialogic FDG both formulation and morphosyntactic encoding will be affected by the structures created at the interpersonal/representational levels and the morphosyntactic level, respectively, of the interlocutor.[5] The contextual component will thus be both a storehouse of each speaker's structures at all three levels which can influence and facilitate her own later formulation and encoding (autopriming) and also a conduit for the interlocutor's structures at all three levels to impact on her formulation and encoding (allopriming). This is fully in line with Luka and Barsalou's (2005) finding that priming is a matter of both production and comprehension.

5 Multiple explanations for morphosyntactic alternations in a dialogue fragment

Investigations of priming originated in psycholinguistics and call for further rigorous testing in the laboratory. In the context of this volume, the question arises how grammarians oriented to the dialogic nature of human communication can react to this work in their studies of alternations. In recent work in corpus linguistics, considerable evidence has been advanced for the claim that language users' choice of alternants is indeed significantly affected by exposure to earlier tokens. Gries (2005), applying multivariate analysis to alternations in the ICE-GB corpus, was able to show that the priming effects found for ditransitive and for verb-particle constructions can also be detected in the corpus. His work also provides evidence for the boost that lexical effects give to structural priming. Each verb is shown to have its own collocational and constructional preferences (which he refers to as "collostructional") that affect priming in verb-specific ways (see also Gries, this volume). Szmrecsanyi (2005) adopts a generally similar approach, using corpus data that includes dialogic material. He also finds that significant "persistence effects", in his terms, exist in morphosyntax, with regard to the choice between analytic and synthetic comparatives, the placement of verb particles and the selection of future markers. He also finds evidence for an effect of textual distance (with closer primes having more target effects) and for differences between autopriming and allopriming (the former having stronger effects).

The results of this corpus work, added to those emerging from psycholinguistic research, suggest that the revised architecture of FDG proposed in Figure 2.2 is capable of showing the pathways of relevant effects on interlocutors' interactive use of their grammatical competence. Yet the fact that the effects are statistical rather than categorical also poses challenges to the qualitative analytical work of the functional grammarian. The central task for a grammarian who is committed to understanding the motivations behind alternative linguistic structures (alternations) becomes much more complex, because, when confronted with a particular data fragment, s/he cannot be sure that it has been used in response to functional pressures since it might be simply a repetition of an earlier formulation (which itself may have been primed by an earlier occurrence, and so on into infinite regress).

In order to exemplify this and to clarify the issues, we will consider (12) below, which is a segment of dialogue taken from the MICASE corpus that was developed at the English Language Institute of the University of Michigan and has been made available online for research purposes at http://quod.lib.umich.edu/m/micase/. The extract comes from the subcorpus of discussions between students and their advisers about their selection of courses. Bold letters (in the on-line corpus shown in orange) indicate embedded backchannels while italic letters (shown in blue in the on-line corpus) indicate overlaps of turns; an underscore indicates a pause. "L-S-and-A" stands for Letters, Sciences and the Arts. Extract (12) consists of 8 turns, 4 by each participant; the turns have been numbered 1–4 for each participant.

(12) ADVISER [1]: well as an L-S-and-A student even if you don't major in L-S _ in in organizational studies you may take up to twelve credits, [STUDENT: *anywhere*] *in the* Business School which is four course _ you know you could take it four _ up to twelve credits in any school outside of *L-S-and-A,* [STUDENT: *okay*] but if you wanted to do Business School you could take all twelve of your credits, [STUDENT: **uhuh**] at the Business School *and that's that's*

STUDENT [1]: *i've taken like* engineering already, *so that's one*
ADVISER [2]: *and then you* can take three classes and still get _ you have to have a hundred and eight L-S-and-A credits, [STUDENT: **mhm**] and a hundred and twenty credits total to graduate so if you wanted to take *more*
STUDENT [2]: *but _ if _ a double major* would take me like how many years to graduate like um?
ADVISER [3]: um, it depends on what you want your double major to be *if you, want to b-*
STUDENT [3]: *what do you suggest? i mean i want* one to be economics for sure i want to do something
ADVISER [4]: so you know you want _ if you wanted to econ-economics, and organizational studies you could certainly do that
STUDENT [4]: and organizational studies? i could do both?

It will be immediately clear that in this extract, which is not untypical of the dialogue corpus from which it has been taken nor of dialogue in general, there is a large amount of repetition. We see extensive evidence of presumably unconscious recycling, with both speakers re-using their own and the other's formulations and encodings. Consider in particular the following four occurrences of repetition:

i) There are 6 occurrences of *if*-Clauses, initially in real and later in hypothetical conditionals, 5 of them occupying initial position within the linguistic expression in which they occur.
ii) With 7 occurrences in total, the lexical verb *take* is found to persist in clauses with – to use the self-explanatory FDG formalism – the patterns (Cl_1: [Np_1 Vp_1 Np_2 $Prepp_1$] (Cl_1)), (Cl_1: [Np_1 Vp_1 Np_2] (Cl_1)) or (Cl_1: [Np_1 Vp_1 Np_2 Np_3] (Cl_1)). The semantics varies according to circumstances: *take* has an individual (x_1) second argument in the sense "earn (credits)", a state-of-affairs (e_1) second argument in the sense "select (a course)" or a time (t_1) second argument in the sense "last (a period of time)".
iii) There are 8 occurrences of the verb *want* in the related patterns (Cl_1: [Np_1 Vp_1 Vp_2 Np_2] (Cl_1)) and (Cl_1: [Np_1 Vp_1 Np_2 Vp_2] (Cl_1)), as in *You wanted to do Business School* and (*what*) *you want your double major to be.*
iv) After an initial occurrence in the adviser's first turn, we find 3 further occurrences of the non-finite verb *do* in the (Cl_1: [Vp_1 Np_1] (Cl_1)) pattern, in the 3 final turns.

From the perspective of priming, then, we may posit that the language production of the two speakers is subject to both autopriming and allopriming. Table 2.1 shows the distribution of these four instances of priming across the dialogue.

It is clear from Table 2.1 that there is no turn without priming (of at least one of the four instances identified), and that the occurrences of

Table 2.1. Distribution of four chains of structural priming in (12)

Turn	*Number of occurrences*			
Adviser [1]	2	3	2	1
Student [1]		1		
Adviser [2]	1	2		
Student [2]	1	1		
Adviser [3]	1		2	
Student [3]			2	1
Adviser [4]	1		2	1
Student [4]				1
	if	*take*	*want*	*do*

priming tend to cluster around adjacent turns. It is also clear that there is a mixture of autopriming and allopriming, with all of the phenomena being shared by both speakers. This supports the idea that priming is a property of the dialogue mediated through the implicit common ground (or in terms of a dialogic FDG, the shared contextual component). This encourages us to understand that the distinction between autopriming and allopriming must ultimately be rather blurred: who is to say whether the adviser's use of *take* in her second turn is autoprimed (by Adviser [1]) or alloprimed (by Student [1])?

Having observed these apparent instances of the persistence of lexical and syntactic phenomena in dialogue, we must recognize that the four phenomena can just as plausibly be understood as attributable to functional factors. After all, the presence of conditional clauses is highly likely in any discussion of possible course options for a student (the hypothesis) and of the repercussions of taking any of those options (the consequence). Analogously, the two meanings associated with *take* and their associated morphosyntactic patterns are anything but unusual in a counselling session about courses to be selected ("to be taken") with particular durations ("taking a certain amount of time"). Third, since the identification of suitable courses must also take the student's personal ambitions and intentions into account, we may expect there to be many occurrences of *want* with an infinitive complement clause as in *want to do Business School* or *want my major to be economics*. Finally, since the discussion is about future actions by the student, we may predict that non-finite *do* will frequently occur after desiderative and modal verbs as in *want to do, could do*, etc. In these respects, then, the effect of priming and functionality work together. Methodologically, however, this raises the possibility that the grammarians analysing a dialogue such as (12) could concentrate on one of the two explanatory factors at the expense of the other.[6] Nevertheless, a complete description of the grammatical properties would be incomplete without due consideration of both priming and functional effects, as becomes apparent from an examination of various dysfluencies and dysfunctionalities in the transcript.

As pointed out above, priming effects are capable of overriding the mapping of formulation to encoding. This may also be seen in (12). Thus, the false-start *if* in Student [2] may well have been triggered by the high activation of initial *if*-clauses (three having occurred in the Adviser's first two interventions). In the same turn, when the student does produce a full linguistic expression, the question phrase *how many years* is, despite being in Focus, is not placed initially, but in the position associated with Np_3 in the (Cl_1: [Np_1 Vp_1 Np_2 Np_3] (Cl_1)) pattern that has been primed by six earlier occurrences in the Student and the Adviser's speech: it is thus not just the lexical item but the entire morphosyntactic template that is primed. In Adviser [4], we find the dysfluent sequence *wanted to econ-economics*, which is explicable as resulting from the priming effect of the *want* plus infinitive complement found in six previous utterances (across both speakers). Here, then are three aspects of the dialogue that arguably show priming effects interfering with or indeed overruling the grammatical processes within the individual.

It needs to be pointed out that the dialogue transcribed in (12) also comprises sections in which there is little or no evidence of priming. The beginning of the Adviser's turn [1], *as an L-S-and-A student even if you don't major in L-S _ in in organizational studies you may take up to twelve credits* does contain an error-hesitation-repair sequence that may be attributed to autopriming (specifically by the earlier mention of *L-S-and-A*); nevertheless, the remainder is fully accountable for as encoding a succession of three Discourse Acts with the rhetorical functions Orientation (*as an L-S-and-A student*), Dependent Act (*even if you don't major in organizational studies*) and Nuclear Act (*you may take up to twelve credits*) respectively. In Adviser [2], as well, with regard to the sequence *you have to have a hundred and eight L-S-and-A credits and a hundred and twenty credits total to graduate* we see that where the adviser draws on her expert knowledge and the sense of dialogue is less pronounced, there is much less evidence of priming.

Our examination of the passage in (12) has shown that in a dialogic FDG of the type shown in Figure 2.2, the various levels of grammar do not merely operate to formulate and encode the individual speaker's conceptualizations (as in orthodox FDG) but also are fully involved in re-using formulations and encodings that have occurred earlier in the dialogue and remain activated. The transcription shows examples of priming effects running parallel to the standard functional procedures, with unconscious recycling of representations at each level of analysis. Effects often ascribed to cohesion such as "syntactic parallelism" or "lexical repetition", which were taken to support the functional coherence of the dialogue, are here re-interpreted as arising from an unconscious alignment in the context of a dialogic grammar. We have also seen passages in which priming seems hardly to impinge at all upon the speaker's production, when the speaker is "quoting" from her own body of expert knowledge which has been learned and stored prior to the conversation. Finally, we have observed some examples of priming that interfere with the regular relationships between formulation and encoding: where this impedes communication, for example where the hearer is unlikely to interpret the speaker's communicative intentions, this will typically cause the speaker to repair and normalize the expression.

The discussion has presupposed the notion of morphosyntactic alternation. If we consider the seven instances of the verb *take* in (12), we find the clausal structures shown in (13):

(13) (a) you may take up to twelve credits in the Business School
(b) you could take it four _ up to twelve credits in any school outside of L S and A
(c) you could take all twelve of your credits at the Business School
(d) i've taken like engineering already
(e) then you can take three classes
(f) if you wanted to take more
(g) a double major would take me like how many years to graduate

(13a-c), (13d-f) and (13g) all differ at the representational level, in corresponding to different concepts ("earn", "select" and "last" respectively), with corresponding differences at the morphosyntactic level. Nevertheless, the evidence from the dialogue transcript that they enter into a priming relation suggests that although they are semantically distinct there is relatedness at the morphosyntactic level.

6 Conclusion

The purpose of this article has been to consider some implications of recent work on alternations in psycholinguistics and corpus linguistics for Functional Discourse Grammar, a model of language that makes pretensions to cognitive adequacy. In response to a re-orientation of grammatical theory to language as a truly interactive rather than individual tool for communication, a revised model of FDG has been proposed that takes account of the impact of priming on both formulation and encoding. This model has been used to reconsider the matter of alternations. Most alternations examined in the literature to date have been associated with regular differences in meaning, either pragmatic or semantic, or both; in FDG, these will follow from distinct formulations. However, where there is connectedness without any corresponding semantic effect, we may talk of a truly morphosyntactic alternation, to be dealt with in FDG as a matter of encoding. The connectedness in question, we have claimed, is visible in dialogue in the operation of priming, which becomes most evident where its effects override functionality and lead to (usually temporary) dysfluencies.

Notes

* This work was supported by a grant from the Spanish Ministry of Science and Innovation (HUM2007-62220, PI: M. A. Gómez-González).

1. The aim of attaining "cognitive adequacy" follows from the wish to participate in interdisciplinary ventures. As Bornkessel-Schlesewsky and Schlesewsky (2009: 299) point out, "if a theory does not seek to be 'psychologically adequate' [...] it needn't – and shouldn't – concern itself with processing facts".
2. For an overview of research into language production priming from its inception to the present day, see Pickering and Ferreira (2008).
3. The reader will have noticed an unfortunate terminological clash: the notion of alignment borrowed from Pickering and Garrod (2004) is orthogonal to the notion of alignment that applies within individualistic FDG.
4. In FDG the variable (l_1) indicates the semantic category "location" and (x_1) the semantic category "individual". See Hengeveld and Mackenzie (2008: 130–132).
5. The possibility of phonological priming will not be considered here.
6. A reviewer points out that a delicate register- or genre-based study of the frequencies of particular lexemes and/or structures might permit us to tease apart the truly functional factors. In this context, it should be conceded that the ubiquity of dialogic priming has recently been challenged by Healey *et al.* (to appear) on the basis of corpus analysis. Their results suggest that "genre [...] significantly alters the likelihood that people will produce similar syntactic constructions"; in other words, we are most likely to adopt one another's forms if we are using the same "style".

References

Barcelona Sánchez, A. (this volume) Metonymy-motivated morphosyntactic alternations.

Bencini, G. L. M., Bock, K. and Goldberg, A. E. (unpublished) How abstract is grammar? Evidence from structural priming in language production.

Bock, K. (1986) Syntactic persistence in language production. *Cognitive Psychology* 18(3): 355–387.

Bock, K. and Levelt, W. J. M. (1994) Language production: Grammatical encoding. In M. A. Gernsbacher (ed.) *Handbook of Psycholinguistics* 945–984. San Diego, CA: Academic Press.

Bock, K. and Loebell, H. (1990) Framing sentences. *Cognition* 35(1): 1–39.

Bornkessel-Schlesewsky, I. and Schlesewsky, M. (2009) *Processing Syntax and Morphology: A neurocognitive perspective.* Oxford: Oxford University Press.

Butler, C. S. (2008) Cognitive adequacy in structural-functional theories of language. *Language Sciences* 30(1): 1–30.

Butler, C. S. (2009) Criteria of adequacy in functional linguistics. *Folia Linguistica* 43(1): 1–66.

Butler, C. S. (submitted) Syntactic functions in Functional Discourse Grammar and Role and Reference Grammar: An evaluative comparison. *Language Sciences.*

Bybee, J. (2006) From usage to grammar: The mind's response to repetition. *Language* 82(4): 711–732.

Chang, F., Bock, K. and Goldberg, A. (2003) Can thematic roles leave traces of their places? *Cognition* 90(1): 29–49.

Clark, H. H. (1996) *Using Language.* Chicago, IL: University of Chicago Press.

Dik, S. C. (1978) *Functional Grammar.* Amsterdam: North-Holland.

Dik, S. C. (1989) *The Theory of Functional Grammar.* Dordrecht: Foris.

Dik, S. C. (1997) *The Theory of Functional Grammar.* 2 vols. (Second revised edition.) Ed. K. Hengeveld. Berlin: Mouton de Gruyter.

García Velasco, D. and Hengeveld, K. (2002) Do we need predicate frames? In R. Mairal Usón and M. J. Pérez Quintero (eds) *New Perspectives on Argument Structure in Functional Grammar* 95–123. Berlin: Mouton de Gruyter.

Gargett, A., Gregoromichelaki, E., Kempson, R., Purver, M. and Sato, Y. (2009) Grammar resources for modelling dialogue dynamically. *Cognitive Neurodynamics* 3(4): 347–363.

Goldberg, A. E. and Bencini, G. L. M. (2005) Support from language processing for a constructional approach to grammar. In A. Tyler, M. Takada, Y. Kim and D. Marinova (eds) *Language in Use: Cognitive and discourse perspectives on language and language learning* 3–18. Washington, DC: Georgetown University Press.

Gries, S. Th. (2005) Syntactic priming: A corpus-based approach. *Journal of Psycholinguistic Research* 34(4): 365–399.

Gries, S. Th. (this volume) Acquiring particle placement in English: A corpus-based perspective.

Gundel, J. K. (2008) Contrastive perspectives on cleft sentences. In M. A. Gómez-González, J. L. Mackenzie and E. M. González Álvarez (eds) *Language and Cultures in Contrast and Comparison* 69–87. Amsterdam: Benjamins. [Pragmatics and Beyond New Series 175].

Healey, P. G. T., Howes, C. and Purver, M. (to appear) Does structural priming occur in ordinary conversation? Retrieved on 15 January 2010 from http://www.sfb833.uni-tuebingen.de/wb/media/LE2010_abstracts/HealeyHowesPurver.pdf.

Hengeveld, K. (2004) Epilogue. In J. L. Mackenzie and M. A. Gómez-González (eds) *A New Architecture for Functional Grammar* 365–378. Berlin: Mouton de Gruyter. [Functional Grammar Series 24].

Hengeveld, K. and Mackenzie, J. L. (2008) *Functional Discourse Grammar: A typologically-based theory of language structure.* Oxford: Oxford University Press.

Hengeveld, K. and Mackenzie, J. L. (2010) Functional Discourse Grammar. In B. Heine and H. Narrog (eds) *Oxford Handbook of Linguistic Analysis* 367–400. Oxford: Oxford University Press.

Iacoboni, M. (2008) *Mirroring People: The new science of how we connect with others.* New York: Farrar, Straus, and Giroux.

Jackendoff, R. (2007) *Language, Consciousness, Culture.* Cambridge, MA: The MIT Press.

Levelt, W. J. M. (1989) *Speaking: From intention to articulation.* Cambridge, MA: The MIT Press.

Levin, B. (1993) *English Verb Classes and Alternations: A preliminary investigation.* Chicago, IL: University of Chicago Press.

Luka, B. and Barsalou, L. W. (2005) Structural facilitation: Mere exposure effects of grammatical acceptability as evidence for syntactic priming in comprehension. *Journal of Memory and Language* 52(3): 436–459.

Mackenzie, J. L. (submitted) Cognitive adequacy in a dialogic Functional Discourse Grammar. *Language Sciences.*

Mackenzie, J. L. and Gómez-González, M. A. (eds) (2004) *A New Architecture for Functional Grammar.* Berlin: Mouton de Gruyter. [Functional Grammar Series 24].

Mukamel, R., Ekstrom, A. D., Kaplan, J., Iacoboni, M. and Fried, I. (2010) Single-neuron responses in humans during execution and observation of actions. *Current Biology* 20(8): 1–7.

Pickering, M. J. and Ferreira, V. S. (2008) Structural priming: A critical review. *Psychological Bulletin* 134(3): 427–459.

Pickering, M. J. and Garrod, S. (2004) Toward a mechanistic psychology of dialogue. *Behavioral and Brain Sciences* 27(2): 169–226.

Rizzi, L. (1997) The fine structure of the left periphery. In L. Haegeman (ed.) *Elements of Grammar: Handbook of generative syntax* 281–337. Dordrecht: Kluwer.

Szmrecsanyi, B. (2005) Language users as creatures of habit: A corpus-based analysis of persistence in spoken English. *Corpus Linguistics and Linguistic Theory* 1(1): 113–150.

Tannen, D. (2006) *Talking Voices: Repetition, dialogue, and imagery in conversational discourse.* (Second edition.) Cambridge: Cambridge University Press.

Van Valin, R. D., Jr. and LaPolla, R. J. (1997) *Syntax: Structure, meaning and function.* Cambridge: Cambridge University Press.

Wang, S.-P. (2005) Corpus-based approaches and discourse analysis in relation to reduplication and repetition. *Journal of Pragmatics* 37(4): 505–540.

3 Constraints on syntactic alternation: Lexical-constructional subsumption in the Lexical-Constructional Model*

Francisco J. Ruiz de Mendoza Ibáñez[a] **and Ricardo Mairal Usón**[b]

1 Introduction

The **Lexical-Constructional Model** (LCM; Ruiz de Mendoza and Mairal 2008; Mairal and Ruiz de Mendoza 2009; cf. Butler 2009) is a broad meaning construction model of language that provides meaning characterizations at the levels of argument structure (level 1), pragmatic implication (level 2), illocution (level 3) and discourse (level 4). Although essentially focused on meaning construction, the LCM contains logical structure variables that are bound to other kinds of conceptual structure that can be projected into syntactic representations. As a result of this feature, linguistic representation in the LCM can be discussed in terms of form-meaning pairings of the kind proposed in the various versions of **Construction Grammar** (CxG; cf. Gonzálvez-García and Butler 2006).

But the LCM differs significantly from other constructionist accounts. One of the crucial differences is that the LCM provides a unified account of meaning construction where all conceptual integration operations are explicitly constrained. Thus, a central goal of the LCM is to determine the range of possibilities available for language users to communicate by

a Francisco José Ruiz de Mendoza Ibáñez is Full Professor of English Linguistics at the University of La Rioja, Spain. E-mail: francisco.ruizdemendoza@unirioja.es

b Ricardo Mairal Usón is Full Professor of English Language at the Spanish National Distance-Learning University (UNED). E-mail: rmairal@flog.uned.es combining degrees of inferential and non-inferential activity in building meaning representations within each of the four levels specified above and in incorporating conceptual structure from one level into the next. Whether conceptual integration occurs at one level or across levels, the process is constrained by a number of licensing or blocking factors.

At the level of argument structure, with which the present article is concerned, the LCM studies the way in which lexical predicates take part in argument structure constructions of the kind discussed by Goldberg (1995) in her version of CxG. However, while the Goldbergian approach focuses its attention on the conditions that argument constructions impose on lexical meaning for a lexical predicate to be a candidate for incorporation into a given construction, the LCM sees lexical-constructional integration as a cognitive process that is constrained by a number of principles that are internal (e.g. conceptual consistency) and external (e.g. high-level metaphor and metonymy) to the process itself. The external principles will be our focus of attention in this contribution.

The study of lexical-constructional integration has consequences for the phenomenon that has become known by the name of **syntactic alternations** in formal and functional accounts of language. Syntactic alternations are generally understood to be formal variants in the expression of arguments that verbs may participate in (Levin 1993: 2). Classical cases of such variants are the **causative/inchoative** alternation (e.g. *The wind opened the door/The door opened*), the **dative** alternation (e.g. *He gave the book to Mary/He gave Mary the book*), and the **locative** alternation (e.g. *He loaded the truck with the hay/He loaded the hay onto the truck*). The members of an alternation are assumed to express basically the same meaning and their syntactic properties are taken to be a matter of lexical knowledge. For example, the dative alternation, as illustrated by *John sent a package to Peter/John sent Peter a package* is not operational if the receiver is not animate (e.g. *John sent a package to Madrid/*John sent Madrid a package*).

In CxG, what Levin considers a syntactic alternation of the same verb is understood as two connected, though different, constructions (cf. Iwata 2008). As a result, the notion of alternation is epiphenomenal, i.e. a consequence of more powerful postulates called **surface generalizations** (Goldberg 2002). Such generalizations are constructed by looking into a single surface argument structure form rather than into other hypothetically related forms. For example, in this perspective, it is postulated that the configuration [NP/SUBJ [VP/PRED NP/OBJ1 NPOBJ2]], known as the **dative construction**, implies the notion of "giving". This underlying notion is the reason why **John sent Madrid a package* is not possible, since the construction necessitates a giver, an object and a receiver that becomes the possessor of the object, but *Madrid* is literally a destination of the object and not its possessor. The correct constructional choice in this case is the **caused-motion** construction (*John sent a package to Madrid*), which here is not used to express the idea of "giving". However, the caused-motion construction, which basically consists of a causer of motion, an object of motion and a destination of motion, can be used to convey a transfer of possession, as in *John sent a package to Peter* above. In constructionist approaches, it is assumed that in cases like this, the construction directly profiles the *designatum* of the prepositional phrase as the destination of motion and that the sense of "giving" can be activated by implication provided that the destination is an entity that can possess an object, since once an object reaches a person, it falls within that person's sphere of control.

The LCM takes sides with the epiphenomenal view of alternations, but differs from other constructionist models in the way in which it deals with the integration of lexical structure into constructional characterizations. Goldberg's CxG generally assumes that lexical-constructional integration (so-called **fusion**) is merely a question of conceptual consistency regulated by the **Semantic Coherence** and **Correspondence Principles** (Goldberg 1995, 2002, 2006). The former makes fusion possible if the participant role of the verb and the argument role of the construction are compatible. The latter principle, which can be overridden in a number of ways (Goldberg 2006), arranges the alignment of coded lexical structure and its discourse function in such a way that profiled participant roles receive discourse prominence. The LCM takes for granted the general discourse prominence tendency of the Correspondence Principle, which identifies level 4 activity, but assigns no special role to this principle as a constraining factor in lexical-constructional integration at the level of argument structure. However, it does take into account semantic coherence as a level 1 constraining factor and fleshes out the specific ways in which such coherence is achieved when it does not happen by itself. In other words, the LCM formulates specific conditions for lexical-constructional integration to be possible (i.e. licensed) in cases in which it is not naturally so.

In order to explore the nature of such integration conditions it is first necessary to introduce some of the explanatory tools that we will be using, especially the notion of **cognitive model**, drawn from **Cognitive Linguistics** (Lakoff 1987) and the levels of genericity at which the notion is operational (Ruiz de Mendoza and Mairal 2007), which we will study in §2. Then, in §3, we will address some of the advantages and shortcomings of the standard approach to lexical-constructional integration in Goldberg's

CxG. Finally, §4 will discuss some cases of lexical-constructional integration that apparently violate the Semantic Coherence Principle but that are licensed by constraints that are external to this process. In so doing, our account will flesh out the notion of **constructional coercion**, a phenomenon whereby lexical structure becomes adapted to constructional requirements (Michaelis 2003).

2 Cognitive models and generic-level conceptual structure

Conceptual structure is the result of the activity of one or more organizing principles. Among such principles Lakoff (1987) has distinguished **propositional structure**, **image schemas**, **metaphor**, and **metonymy**. Propositional structure (or predicate-argument relationships), which is essential in setting up networks of connections among concepts, gives rise to **frames** (cf. Fillmore 2003). Metaphor is a **conceptual mapping** (a set of correspondences) across relevant portions of frames or conceptual domains where the elements and structure of one domain, called the **source**, allows us to understand and reason about elements and structure of another domain, called the **target**. For example, we use our knowledge about war to talk about people debating in terms of enemies facing each other, gaining or losing ground, and winning or losing. Metonymy is also defined as a conceptual mapping, but it differs from metaphor in two respects: first, the mapping is internal to a conceptual domain while in metaphor the mapping takes place between two separate domains; second, in metonymy the source stands for the target whereas in metaphor the target is seen in terms of the structure and logic of the source (cf. Barcelona 2002, for discussion). For example, the container stands for its contents in *He drank bottle after bottle*. Finally, image schemas (Johnson 1987) are topological knowledge structures that arise from our interaction with the world, such as the notions of CONTAINER, PATH, and MOTION (see also Hampe 2005; Peña 2008). They are often used to construct metaphors. For example, *She fell into a depression* combines the path, motion and container schemas to talk about a change of state: the person that undergoes the change of state is seen as a moving object; the change of state is seen as a change of location; the resulting state is the destination of motion where there is a container whose internal conditions affect the person negatively.

On the basis of preliminary work in Panther and Thornburg (2000), Ruiz de Mendoza and Pérez (2001) and Ruiz de Mendoza and Peña (2008) have developed the notion of **high-level metonymy**. A high-level metonymy is one that makes use of generic-level conceptual structure, which can have consequences for grammar. An example is GENERIC FOR SPECIFIC, which applies in the interpretation of the generic verbal predicate *do* in *She'll do* ("wash") *the dishes and I'll do* ("clean") *the carpets.* It is true that the collocational structure of *do* is broad and it has become conventionalized to some extent (e.g. *Do your homework, your job, etc.*), but cases like *do the dishes/the carpets/the floor*, etc., need some inferential activity associated with the context. In such cases "do" is metonymic for the more specific activity.

Another example of high-level metonymy is provided by constructions that make use of a verb expressing the speaker's attitude (e.g. *enjoy, want, miss*) or (ingressive, progressive, eggresive) phasal aspect (e.g. *begin, continue, finish*) followed by a typically non-actional noun phrase, as in *He began/enjoyed the beer.* Depending on the situation we may have varied interpretations: "He began/enjoyed drinking/bottling/selling, etc., the beer". Again, there is a high-level metonymic operation supplying the inferential schema for the process: AN OBJECT FOR AN ACTION (IN WHICH THE OBJECT IS INVOLVED). This explanation is complementary of the one given by Jackendoff (1997), who discusses similar examples as cases of **enriched composition**. Jackendoff argues that the hearer is faced with the incompatibility of a verb (e.g. *begin, enjoy*) that selects for an action that is complemented by an NP denoting an entity. The incompatibility is solved by looking into the world knowledge structure of the complement for an extension of it that matches the complementation requirement of the verb. In our view, which follows the explanation given in Ruiz de Mendoza and Pérez (2001: 340), expressions like *enjoy/begin a beer* present the hearer with a case of conceptual incongruity (people enjoy and begin "doing something" but not "something") which can be sorted out by means of a metonymy. In essence, this solution is not any different from the solution that we apply when faced with the conceptual incongruity of saying that a person has drunk "a container" instead of its liquid content. The only difference between the two kinds of metonymy is to be found in the level at which they are operational. While OBJECT FOR ACTION (just like GENERIC FOR SPECIFIC discussed above) has grammatical consequences (it affects the complementation pattern of verbs), CONTAINER FOR CONTENTS works at the lexical level (e.g. "bottle" stands for the "alcoholic beverage in the bottle").

Other cases of high-level conceptual incongruity with grammatical consequences call for a solution based on metaphor. A few such cases have already been identified in the literature, although their implications for grammar have largely gone unnoticed. This is the case of ACTIONS ARE TRANSFERS (e.g. *They gave the thug a big beating*) and STATES ARE LOCATIONS (e.g. *She has a lot of fear*), discussed by Lakoff (1993) as involving image-schematic thinking. However, in our view, the first metaphor also underlies the conversion of a verb into an idiomatic phrase and the second metaphor involves the use of one grammatical construction (a standard transitive construction) to express meaning that is canonically associated with another construction (a predicative construction with *be*-support as in *She is full of fear*). A more complex case is provided by metaphors that underlie changes in the transitivity type of a sentence (cf. Ruiz de Mendoza and Mairal 2007). Thus, it is possible to see general causation in terms of caused motion, as in *She sent me into despair* ('She caused me to feel despair') or to see actions that have no directly affected object in terms of an action with a directly affected object, as in *The audience laughed the actor off the stage*. In this sentence, the internal psychological reaction of the actor that causes him to leave the stage is interpreted in terms of external physical causation (cf. *They pushed him off the stage*). There are even more interesting cases. For example, in *He drank himself into a stupor* the originally intransitive predicate "drink" (denoting an activity) is seen as if it were a transitive structure of the actor-object kind. Finally, consider the use of *love* in *She loved him back into life*. "Love" is what Halliday and Matthiessen (2004) consider a mental process predicate and it has two associated roles, a sensor and an object of sensing or phenomenon. Here, the sensor is treated as if it were the causer of an action and the phenomenon as the object of such an action.

The examples that we have examined are suggestive of the important role of high-level metaphor and metonymy in grammar. In what follows, we will argue that this role is in fact one of constraining the process of integrating lexical characterizations into constructions and that understanding the nature of these two high-level phenomena is essential to account for constructional coercion over lexical structure.

3 Syntactic alternations: lexical projection or constructional coercion?

Syntactic alternations, which may be accompanied by changes in meaning, often result from the properties that verbs belonging to the same lexical class have in common. For example, while *break* verbs may take part in the causative/inchoative alternation (e.g. *The child broke/smashed/shattered, etc., the window* vs. *The window broke/smashed/shattered, etc.*), *destroy* verbs, which are to some extent similar in meaning to *break* verbs, do not participate in the same alternation: *The enemy destroyed the city/*The city destroyed.* In this view, syntactic alternations are a question of the *projection* of lexical structure into syntax (Levin and Rappaport Hovav 2005).

It has been pointed out that the change of syntactic behavior of a verb is somehow constrained by its potential to become adapted or not to eventive frames (e.g. the inchoative use of *open* in *The door opened* is facilitated by the eventive frame information that entities can be opened spontaneously; cf. García-Velasco, this volume). However, the possibility or impossibility of making an inchoative use of a typically causative verb has to do with other factors too. A case in point is *kill,* which has a causative component but cannot be used in an inchoative pattern: *The cat killed the mouse/*The mouse killed.* This is easy to explain since English has a lexical item *die,* which codes exactly the same meaning that would be ascribed to the impossible inchoative use. A more difficult case is the inchoative use of the verb *handle* in *The car won't handle without the proper shock package,* since *handle* has no clear causative component (*People handle the car* can hardly be paraphrased as "people cause the car to be driven"). The reason for this use lies outside a projectionist account since it goes beyond the meaning structure coded in the verbal predicate and its associated syntactic configuration. We will come to similar examples below.

In a different view of alternations, these are the result of constructional coercion over lexical structure. This is the position recently taken by Goldberg (2006), following work by Michaelis (2003). As was mentioned above, Goldberg's CxG postulates that some syntactic configurations have their own cognitive status and are thus stored in the mind as such. This claim can be easily illustrated by a now classical example from Goldberg (1995). The verb *sneeze* is intransitive (*Mary sneezed*); however, it can be used transitively with a causative sense, as in *She sneezed the napkin off the table,* if caused-motion is implied and a destination of motion is made explicit (cf. **She sneezed the napkin*). According to Goldberg, since the caused-motion sense is not an inherent part of the meaning of *sneeze,* it is not unreasonable to postulate that it derives from an independent source. The independent source is an abstract semantic characterization containing elements such as "cause", "move" and "destination"' (X CAUSES Y TO MOVE Z), which are paired to corresponding elements in syntactic structure [SUBJ [V OBJ OBL]]. There are other such predicates that are not intrinsically caused-motion predicates but can be used with a caused-motion sense. We may consider *allow* in *She allowed me into the room* and *help* in *He helped me into the car*. These predicates have little in common, which further argues in favor of the idea that caused-motion is an independent conceptual construct to which verbal predicates can be ascribed under certain conditions.

In the Goldbergian approach, the ascription of a verbal predicate to a construction is sometimes assumed to coerce the meaning structure of the verbal predicate in such a way that it can be accommodated into the construction. It is thus through coercion that the verb *sneeze is* forced to take a second argument that is the object of motion caused by the subject argument. Usually, accounts of coercion look for regularities in lexical structure that explain the conditions under which a given lexical item or a class of items is sensitive to being used with a certain construction. *Sneeze* can thus be part of the caused-motion construction since sneezing involves air forcefully set in motion, which can consequently affect an object that is movable in such a way.

However, accounting for the integration of verbal predicates into the caused-motion construction in this way is not fully satisfactory. For example, *The audience laughed the actor off the stage* involves physical motion caused by an emotional reaction. However, unlike in the case of *sneeze*, there is not a material causer of motion, but simply an induction to self-instigated motion. In turn, in *They stared me into silence* motion is not even literal, but figurative, used to indicate a change of state. This second example is interesting: it uses the caused-motion construction with a resultative meaning, while the resultative construction, which uses an adjective as a secondary predication of the object of a transitive verb denoting a dynamic, controlled action (e.g. *The blacksmith hammered the metal flat*), is not possible: **They stared me silent.* However, if the verb designates a non-dynamic, controlled state of affairs, the adjectival predication is possible: *They kept me silent.* The complexity of the situation calls for a refinement of the standard account in terms of coercion. In the case of *sneeze* coercion results in the introduction of a causative element into its lexical structure; but verbs like *laugh* and *stare* need to introduce not only the causative element, but also the whole force-dynamics image schema involving motion. The distance of the latter from verbs that do not need coercion, such as *push* or *blow* is even greater, which leads us to wonder where the limits to coercion are to be found. For there are limits, as witnessed by the impossibility of using some verbs with the caused-motion construction: **He described/apologized/owned me into the room.* A plausible solution will be given in §4 below.

In any event, our discussion so far has revealed inadequacies in both projectionist and constructionist accounts of syntactic alternations. The former cannot deal with cases of expanded or reduced lexical structure on a systematic basis (cf. Boas 2008; Iwata 2008, for similar criticism). The latter can complement projectionist explanations by taking into consideration the properties of constructional characterizations as a way to account for how lexical structure is modified. However, the constructionist account needs to look beyond degrees of conceptual compatibility between lexical predicates and constructions in order to set limits to so-called constructional coercion. In the following sections we will discuss some of the principles that play a role in this process. These principles, which are a central feature of the LCM, tie in with our previous description of high-level cognitive models.

4 Subsumption phenomena

Consider the sentence *Fate brought my parents together*, which makes use of a high-level characterization, the caused-motion construction, whose semantic part consists of a causer of motion, an object of motion and a destination of motion. It typically requires a verbal predicate that is compatible with this structure. *Bring* is such a predicate: the bringer is a causer of motion, the object brought is the object of motion, and there is a destination of motion that coincides with the causer's destination of motion. In realizing the constructional elements, *bring* supplies the idea of the "bringer" as a controller of the process and the destination of motion of the object. In the caused-motion construction the destination element is often used to express result. This is so because of what in Cognitive Linguistics has been identified as a **conflation** of concepts. Conflation happens when two concepts identify events that tend to co-occur in our everyday experience (Lakoff and Johnson 1999). Since reaching a destination is the result of the action of moving along a path, it is only natural that the two concepts become difficult to distinguish in our minds and that we use each of them to stand for the other. In our example, the resultative notion of "being together" is understood metaphorically in terms of reaching the end of two paths that converge.

4.1 Metaphoric and metonymic constraints on subsumption

The process that we have just described is one of **lexical-constructional subsumption**. The conceptual structure of *bring*, which is image-schematic, is incorporated, together with its argument structure, into the caused-motion construction and its corresponding argument structure, as specified below:

[**bring**' (fate, parents, LOC)] CAUSE [BECOME **be-LOC**' (parents, together)]

In this example, there is a perfect match between the quantitative and qualitative aspects of the argument structure of the caused-motion construction and the verb *bring*. However, such a perfect match is not invariably the case. Consider the verb *wink* in *She winked me into her bedroom*. It has two arguments: one is an actor and the other is the goal of the activity. Syntactically, the goal argument is realized through a prepositional phrase with *at* (cf. *She winked at me* but **She winked me*) and a third argument is impossible. Evidently, the configuration [NP/SUBJ, VP/PRED, NP/OBJ, PP/OBL] is not directly derivable from the lexical structure of *wink* but has to be attributed to the incorporation of *wink* into the caused-motion construction. With the incorporation, the lexical configuration of *wink* changes its form in two ways: first, the oblique object realized by a PP is converted into a direct object realized by an NP; second, a new argument realized by a PP indicating motion is added. From a conceptual perspective, the verb *wink*, which typically governs a **non-effectual** object, i.e. an object that does not experience the action in terms of physical impact having a physical effect on it, now governs an **effectual** object, i.e. one that does experience the action in terms of physical impact. In CxG it is assumed that modifications like these are a consequence of coercion of the construction over the verb.

A consequence of this assumption is the goal that constructionists generally share of identifying verb categories that can be adapted to given constructions. However, such identification only provides a very partial solution to the problem of lexical-constructional integration. For example, Goldberg (1995) notes that the verbs *convince, persuade, instruct* and *encourage* do not appear in the caused-motion construction: **Sam convinced/persuaded/instructed/encouraged him into the room*. However, other semantically related verbs such as *frighten, coax* and *lure* do appear: *The ghost frightened Peter out of the room; The siren lured the sailor onto the rocks; She coaxed him into the room*. Goldberg argues that the verbs in the former set, but not those in the latter set, entail that the entity denoted by the direct object makes a cognitive decision that mediates between the causing event and the entailed motion. For this reason, it is possible to use these verbs in a caused-motion sense without making direct use of the caused-motion construction, as in *Sam convinced/persuaded/instructed/encouraged him to go into the room*, where the syntactic object of the finite verb is, from a semantic perspective, the willful agent of motion. However, as noted by Peña (2009), this constraint does not apply in cases of figurative motion: *He persuaded me into staying with him; My wife convinced me into selling my art to the public; Their uncle instructed them into the banking business; His father encouraged him into a musical career*. Peña (2009) suggests that the constraint does not apply in cases of figurative motion because in them the cognitive decision has been made in the process of being persuaded/convinced, etc. But Peña herself admits that there is corpus evidence of these verbs being used with literal caused motion, as in the sentence *The scent of lemons persuaded her into the right room*. Peña dismisses examples like this as marginal, but even if marginal in terms of frequency, they are possible and their feasibility has to be explained. What is more, together with the cases of figurative motion, the marginal examples pose an important problem for Goldberg's formulation of the constraint and cast doubts on the reliability of the methodology of exclusively looking into verb classes when attempting to solve the problem of the ability of lexical items to take part in a given construction.

Now, let us return to the problem of formulating a constraint that excludes examples like **Sam persuaded me into the room* but not others like *Sam persuaded me into business* and *The scent of lemons persuaded her into the right room*. We believe that the key to the problem is found in the strongly resultative character of the caused-motion construction, which can be contrasted with the greater focus on the process of the object + infinitive construction. This difference is substantiated by the ease with which it is possible to omit the expression of the destination of motion in the latter (cf. *Sam persuaded me to go*) but not in the former (*#The scent of lemons persuaded her*). Interestingly enough, the caused-motion construction is used figuratively to express result (Ruiz de Mendoza and Luzondo 2010): *The child broke the vase into a thousand pieces*; *The blacksmith hammered the metal into the shape of a bird*; *She drove me into despair*. So, when the whole predication – not just the verb – focuses on the result of an action rather than the process, then the caused-motion construction can be used; if the focus is on the process, then other constructions, such as the object + infinitive construction, are preferred. Verbs such as *persuade/convince/encourage*, etc., tend to focus on the process except when there are either contextual or textual clues that override this default assumption. Thus, in the sentence *The scent of lemons persuaded her into the right room,* the use of the adjective *right* is very significant: it emphasizes the idea that the protagonist, who was led by the scent of the lemons, made the correct choice thereby highlighting the destination of motion. The same implication is hardly derived from #*The scent of lemons persuaded her into the room,* where the choice element is absent. In *Sam persuaded me into business* the focus is also on the result (the speaker goes into business), in contrast to *Sam persuaded me to go into business,* which focuses on the process of the speaker doing whatever it was necessary to become a business person.

What we are here suggesting is not that verb class features should be ignored, but that, when it comes to lexical-constructional interaction, verb classes cannot be constructed on an *ad hoc* basis as apparently needed by the construction. Verb classes do exist and they play a significant role in meaning construction, but they exist independently, as shown by a whole tradition of work that includes Faber and Mairal's (1999) analysis of verb classes and Boas's (2008) study of lexical semantics within the context of CxG approaches to language. This means that a class of lexical items, or part of a class, may have features that will create conditions for a perfect match with a construction. A clear example is provided by *break* and *destroy* in connection to the causative/inchoative alternation. The two verbs are very similar in semantic terms: one can define *break* informally as "act in such a way that an entity will become not whole" (e.g. *The child broke the vase into pieces*), and *destroy* as "act in such a way that an entity will become extremely damaged or cease to exist". Since there is a resultative element in both characterizations that specifies some loss of functionality and/or integrity through damage, one might be tempted to think that the two verbs can take part in the same constructions. This is not the case. While *break* can be used in both the causative and inchoative constructions, *destroy* can only be used causatively: *We broke/destroyed the vase*; *The vase broke/*destroyed.* The reason for this difference in constructional behavior lies in the fact that *break* belongs to the class of change-of-state verbs, whereas *destroy* involves cessation of existence. The relevance of class ascription for participation in the inchoative construction is revealed by the possibility and impossibility of the following examples: *The glass broke/cracked/shattered*; **The window destroyed/smashed*; **The building demolished/destructed; *The plague exterminated/eradicated.* The impossible examples are cases of cessation of existence verbs, which, unlike change of state verbs, cannot take the inchoative form.

We have thus shown that lexical classes have their own theoretical status and some (or all) of their properties may facilitate or impede the subsumption of their members into a given construction. But the situation is still more complex. Let us compare the inchoative and **middle** constructions, which, as described in the literature, are semantically and formally very close to each other (cf. Marín-Arrese, this volume). Contrast *This door won't open easily* and *These clothes don't wash well.* Both sentences contain an evaluative element (expressed by the adverbs *easily* and *well*) that draws our attention. But while the evaluative element is clearly optional in the first sentence, this is not so in the second: *This door won't open*; *#These clothes don't wash.* One explanation of these data would make a distinction between the inchoative and the middle constructions. The former, which is not inherently evaluative but can accept evaluative elements, would have the function of helping us to report on a causal state of affairs where the identity of the causer is not an issue. The function of the latter, which is evaluative, would be to assess some aspect of a causal state of affairs where the identity of the causer is also immaterial. Both constructions would subtly differ from passivized causatives (e.g. *The door was opened [by the wind]*; *The clothes were not washed with care [by your employee]*) in the treatment of the relationship between the agent-causer and the affected entity. In the passivized causative, the agent-causer is schematized to a large extent but it is not regarded as immaterial; in the inchoative and middle constructions, although the agent-causer is conceptually present on the basis of world knowledge, its importance is played down to such an extent that the action is presented as if it were a process. It is for this reason that the subject of the inchoative and middle constructions is often perceived as having a special "enabling" function with certain agent-like quality (cf. Radden and Dirven 2007). In our view, this agent-like quality of the subject of inchoative and middle constructions facilitates the fusion of either of these constructions with the instrument-subject construction: *This soap washes white clothes better* (cf. *With this soap, white clothes wash better*); *One hand will open the door (easily)* (cf. *The door will open (easily) with one hand*). Fusion with the instrument-subject construction, however, is not possible in the case of passives: **This soap is washed white clothes better*; **One hand will be opened the door (easily).* In the LCM we postulate constructional fusion at the same level, while subsumption occurs at different levels. Same-level fusion is also a constrained process. In the case of the inchoative and middle constructions, the agent-like quality of the constructions is what licenses fusion with the instrument-subject construction, which endows the instrument with agent-like qualities (e.g. *A ball broke the window*), just as the inchoative and middle constructions do with the semantic object.

The explanation given so far, however, misses two important points. First, it assumes that the difference between the inchoative and middle constructions lies in the optionality or non-optionality of the evaluative component. However, we can take an inchoative sentence like *The door won't open* and with a little modification of the subject – which realizes the affected object – make the evaluative component more necessary: *A deadbolted door doesn't open easily/#A deadbolted door doesn't open.* Conversely, we can eliminate the evaluative element of some middle sentences, as in *These clothes won't wash!*, but not of all middles: **This soap washes.* All these facts point to a unified treatment of the inchoative and middle constructions and consequently to postulating a single causative/middle alternation where the middle alternate can be evaluative or not depending on factors that go beyond the semantic properties of the verbal predicate into those of the whole predication. Second, our explanation has not looked into the factors that motivate the causative/inchoative (or middle) alternation. Why can we construe actions in such a way that the affected object is seen as if it were the causer as much as the affected object? From a syntactic perspective this process requires the intransitivization of the verb and giving the object subject status. From a semantic perspective, since we prototypically associate subjects with agents, it would seem natural that this syntactic mechanism can have the effect of endowing the semantic object with agent-like qualities. However, the semantic object of a passive sentence, which has become a syntactic subject, does not experience the same resemanticization process. This difference is very important: while passive sentences may take an agentive complement (e.g. *The window was opened by the wind*), there is no such a possibility for inchoative and middle sentences (e.g. **The window opened by the wind*). This means that the agentivity "load" of the subject in a passive is much smaller than in an inchoative or middle, probably because, as has been discussed in the abundant literature on passives, passivization is a matter of sentence perspective where the semantic object acquires not the function of an agent – as is generally the case with the inchoative and middle – but of a thematic or given element about which the rest of the predication will supply some new information, including information about who or what carried out the action. This information has to be completely omitted from formal expression in the inchoative and middle construction, which is why the true agent of the action can only be retrieved through inferential activity when we make use of these sentence forms. In other words, when the verb is intransitivized and the object (or other predication elements, such as the instrument) is realized as the syntactic subject, the semantic effect is one of presenting a causal action as if it were a non-causal process. We have used "as if" intentionally to indicate that the semantic consequence is a figurative one. From a formal perspective we are presented with a process, which, on the grounds of inference, stands for a causal action. Semantically, a process only has one role, an undergoer. A causal action typically has an agent (or causer), an object (which is an experiencer or undergoer), and an instrument. In the case of inchoative and middle constructions, where an action is figuratively treated as a process, the process becomes a subdomain of the action for which it stands. So we first have a high-level metaphorical operation (ACTIONS ARE PROCESSES), which is the pre-requisite for another high-level operation, a metonymic one, whereby the figurative process stands for the action (PROCESS FOR ACTION).

This combination of high-level metaphor and metonymy acts as a **co-licensing factor**, together with conceptual coherence and lexical class membership, for the ascription of verbal predicates to the inchoative and middle constructions. We have already seen some of the conditions for verbs to take part in the inchoative and middle constructions. For example, we have noted that cessation of existence predicates cannot take part in these constructions, probably because they involve radical action and a radical outcome, which makes it difficult to present these predicates (metaphorically) as an agent-less process and to make this process stand (metonymically) for the causal action which they actually denote. Thus, while we may easily think of windows opening or glasses breaking, as it were, by themselves, it is hardly possible to think of cities getting destroyed or buildings getting demolished by themselves. These conditions are internal to lexical-constructional subsumption, since they have to do with the conceptual structure of lexical items and constructions, while high-level metaphor and metonymy are external to the process, since they involve operations across such conceptual structures.

The importance of taking into account the activity of high-level metaphor and metonymy should not be underestimated. This is particularly true of extended uses of the middle construction where there is no causative element, as in *My new car handles better than the old one*, and to others where there is not even an evaluative element as in *This item ships to the US and Europe only*. The verbs *handle* (e.g. *He handles the car well*) and *ship* (e.g. *We shipped the goods*) do not involve a change of state but simply express a controlled action. This means that, in the absence of a lexical-class co-licensing factor, their ability to participate in the middle construction hinges exclusively on whether external high-level metaphoric and/or metonymic activity is possible. And it *is* possible. The actions of handling a car, in the first example, and of shipping goods, in the second example, are both construed as if they happened without the intervention of an agent. The ACTIONS ARE PROCESSES metaphor does not require a causal agent that triggers off a change of state.

4.2 Metaphoric and metonymic complexes

Our account can be refined still further. Above, we have argued that the middle construction is essentially an inchoative construction that adds an evaluative component. Now, as discussed in Ruiz de Mendoza and Mairal (2007) and Ruiz de Mendoza and Peña (2008), the middle evaluative construction can be of two kinds: it may evaluate the process, as in *The bolted door did not open easily,* or the result, as in *The clothes were too dirty and didn't wash well.* The difference between these two variants of the middle construction is evidenced by the impossibility of paraphrasing the result-oriented version (cf. **It wasn't well to wash the clothes*) in the same way as the process-oriented one (cf. *It was not easy to open the bolted door*). This difference has to be captured by our analysis, which is possible if we postulate a double metonymic shift for the cases of middle evaluative constructions from process to action to the result of the action (PROCESS FOR ACTION FOR RESULT). In the case of the result-oriented variant the resultative element is given conceptual prominence; in the case of the process-oriented variant, it is the process that is highlighted (cf. Marín-Arrese, this volume, for a similar treatment in terms of profile-base relationships). In this view, inchoative constructions, which lack the evaluative component, are grounded in the single metonymy PROCESS FOR ACTION.

There are also cases of double metaphor. Consider the following triple alternation: *He beat me silent/He beat me into silence/He beat silence into me.* The first example of the alternation is a case of the so-called **resultative** construction, which typically expresses the result of an effectual action, i.e. an action that has physical impact on an object. But it is also possible to express resultative meaning through a figurative use of the caused-motion construction, as evidenced by the second and third examples. A reasonable explanation of why the caused-motion construction can be used to express resultative meaning is found in experiential conflation. The caused-motion construction, at its semantic pole, contains a causer of motion, an object of motion, and a destination of motion, which is – and thus conflates with – the result of motion. In the case of the verbal predicate *beat,* we have a beater, which is an **effector** (i.e. the agent of an effectual action), an object of beating, which is an **effectee**, and a result of the effectual action (the object is beaten). The caused-motion construction supplies adequate metaphorical correlates for each of these three elements: the causer of motion maps onto the effector, the object of motion onto the effectee, and the destination of motion onto the result. In its application to the sentence *He beat me into silence,* the action of beating the speaker is seen metaphorically as having physical impact on the speaker and moving him into a different figurative location, which maps onto the speaker being caused to change into a different state (i.e. from talking to being silent). In fact, on a more refined level of analysis, what we have here is a **metaphorical complex** based on the incorporation of a subsidiary metaphor, A CHANGE OF STATE IS A CHANGE OF LOCATION, into the architecture of the main metaphor, AN EFFECTUAL ACTION IS CAUSED MOTION (see Table 3.1). The subsidiary metaphor is activated as a requirement of the target domain, which contains a change of state specification. Not all uses of effectual action predicates contain such a specification (e.g. *He hit the wall, He beat me*).

The metaphorical complex that results from understanding an effectual action involving a change of state as if it were caused motion involving a change of location becomes a licensing factor for the subsumption of the verbal predicate *beat* into the caused motion construction. Non-effectual predicates (e.g. *own, describe, handle*) cannot be subsumed into the construction, nor can effectual predicates that contain in their semantic characterization a specification of the kind of result that they give rise to (e.g. *kill* "cause to become not alive").

The third example of the alternation, *He beat silence into me,* introduces a different case of metaphorical licensing of lexical-constructional subsumption. In this example, the object of motion does not map onto the effectee but onto the new state that the effectee is going to acquire by virtue of the state being figuratively caused to move into the effectee. This is a high-level metaphorical complex with two source domains that map onto the same target. One source, as in the previous example, is caused motion; the other source is the notion of possession, as construed in the

Table 3.1. Single-source high-level metaphorical complex

SOURCE (CAUSED MOTION)	TARGET (EFFECTUAL ACTION)
Causer of motion	Effector
Object of motion	Effectee
Source (change of location)	**Target (change of state)**
Source of motion	Initial state
Destination of motion	Resultant state

Table 3.2. Double-source high-level metaphorical complex

Source (caused motion)	*Target*	*Source (possession)*
Causer of motion	Effector ("he")	
Causing motion	Effecting ("caused to acquire")	
Destination of motion	Effectee ("me")	New possessor of an object
Object of caused-motion (moving object)	New property ("silence")	
	Resultant state ("acquiring the new property of silence")	Gaining possession of an object
Manner of causing motion	Manner of effecting ("beating")	

metaphor ACQUIRING A PROPERTY IS RECEIVING A MOVING OBJECT. By being figuratively forced into the effectee, "silence" becomes the effectee's property (see Table 3.2).

5 Conclusion

This article has discussed syntactic alternations as epiphenomenal to constrained lexical-constructional integration or subsumption processes. The LCM has provided us with the theoretical machinery to do so through its recognition of the role of high-level metaphor and high-level metonymy as constraining factors on such processes, to be added to the principles of conceptual consistency that have been identified in the Goldbergian formulation of CxG. We have studied different ways in which simple and complex cases of high-level metaphor and metonymy apply in the explanation of alternations involving the related inchoative and middle constructions, on the one hand, and the likewise related caused-motion and resultative constructions, on the other hand. This account has allowed us to refine previous accounts of lexical-constructional interaction by fleshing out the still not sufficiently constrained notion of constructional coercion, which is now seen in terms of the ability of lexical structure to be construed from different perspectives that will license its integration into constructional structure.

Notes

* Financial support for this research has been provided by the Spanish Ministry of Science and Innovation, grants HUM2007-65755, FFI2008-05035-C02-01. Additional support has been provided by the Chinese Ministry of Education, Humanities and Social Sciences Project 09YJA740022. We are grateful to Francisco Gonzálvez (University of Almería), Pilar Guerrero (University of Córdoba) and Christopher S. Butler (Swansea University) for useful comments on a preliminary version of this paper. We take full responsibility for any remaining misconception.

References

Barcelona, A. (2002) Clarifying and applying the notions of metaphor and metonymy within Cognitive Linguistics: An update. In R. Dirven and R. Pörings (eds) *Metaphor and Metonymy in Comparison and Contrast* 207–277. Berlin: Mouton de Gruyter.

Boas, H. C. (2008) Determining the structure of lexical entries and grammatical constructions in Construction Grammar. *Annual Review of Cognitive Linguistics* 6: 113–144.

Butler, C. S. (2009) The Lexical Constructional Model: Genesis, strengths and challenges. In C. S. Butler and J. Martín Arista (eds) *Deconstructing Constructions* 117–152. Amsterdam: Benjamins.

Faber, P. and Mairal Usón, R. (1999) *Constructing a Lexicon of English Verbs.* Berlin: Mouton de Gruyter.

Fillmore, C. J. (2003) Double-decker definitions: The role of frames in meaning explanations. *Sign Language Studies* 3(3): 263–295.

García Velasco, D. (this volume) The causative/inchoative alternation in Functional Discourse Grammar.

Goldberg, A. E. (1995) *Constructions: A construction grammar approach to argument structure.* Chicago, IL: University of Chicago Press.

Goldberg, A. E. (2002) Surface generalizations: An alternative to alternations. *Cognitive Linguistics* 13(4): 327–356.

Goldberg, A. E. (2005) Argument Realization. The role of constructions, lexical semantics and discourse factors. In J.-O. Östman, and M. Fried (eds) *Construction Grammars: Cognitive grounding and theoretical extensions* 17–43. Amsterdam: Benjamins.

Goldberg, A. E. (2006) *Constructions at Work: The nature of generalization in language.* Oxford: Oxford University Press.

Gonzálvez-García, F. and Butler, C. S. (2006) Mapping functional-cognitive space. *Annual Review of Cognitive Linguistics* 4: 39–96.

Halliday, M. A. K. and Matthiessen, C. M. I. M. (2004) *An Introduction to Functional Grammar* (Third edition). London: Hodder Arnold.

Hampe. B. (2005) Image schemas in Cognitive Linguistics: Introduction. In B. Hampe (ed.) *From Perception to Meaning: Image schemas in Cognitive Linguistics* 1–12. Berlin: Mouton de Gruyter.

Iwata, S. (2008) *Locative Alternation: A lexical-constructional approach*. Amsterdam. Benjamins.

Jackendoff, R. (1997) *The Architecture of the Language Faculty*. Cambridge, MA: The MIT Press.

Johnson, M. (1987) *The Body in the Mind: The bodily basis of meaning, imagination, and reason.* Chicago, IL: University of Chicago Press.

Lakoff, G. (1987) *Women, Fire, and Dangerous Things: What our categories reveal about the mind.* Chicago, IL: University of Chicago Press.

Lakoff, G. (1993) The contemporary theory of metaphor. In A. Ortony (ed.) *Metaphor and Thought* 202–251 (Second edition). Cambridge, MA: Cambridge University Press.

Lakoff, G. and Johnson, M. (1999) *Philosophy in the Flesh: The embodied mind and its challenges to Western Thought.* Chicago, IL: University of Chicago Press.

Levin, B. and M. Rappaport Hovav (2005) *Argument Realization.* Cambridge: Cambridge University Press.

Levin, B. (1993) *English Verb Classes and Alternations: A preliminary investigation.* Chicago, IL: University of Chicago Press.

Mairal Usón, R. and Ruiz de Mendoza Ibáñez, F. J. (2009) Levels of description and explanation in meaning construction. In C. S. Butler and J. Martín Arista (eds) *Deconstructing Constructions* 153–198. Amsterdam: Benjamins.

Marín-Arrese, J. I. (this volume) Spontaneous and facilitative events revisited.

Michaelis, L. A. (2003). Word meaning, sentence meaning, and syntactic meaning. In H. Cuyckens, R. Dirven and J. Taylor (eds) *Cognitive Approaches to Lexical Semantics* 163–209. Berlin: Mouton de Gruyter.

Panther, K.-U. and Thornburg, L. (2000) The EFFECT FOR CAUSE metonymy in English grammar. In A. Barcelona (ed.) *Metaphor and Metonymy at the Crossroads: A cognitive perspective* 215–232. Berlin: Mouton de Gruyter.

Peña Cervel, M. S. (2008) Dependency systems for image-schematic patterns in a usage-based approach to language. *Journal of Pragmatics* 40: 1041–1066.

Peña Cervel, M. S. (2009). Constraints on subsumption in the caused-motion construction. *Language Sciences* 31: 740–765.

Radden, G. and Dirven, R. (2007) *Cognitive English Grammar: The simple sentence.* Amsterdam: Benjamins.

Ruiz de Mendoza Ibáñez, F. J. and Mairal Usón, R. (2007) High-level metaphor and metonymy in meaning construction. In G. Radden, K.-M. Köpcke, T. Berg and P. Siemund (eds) *Aspects of Meaning Construction* 33–51. Amsterdam: Benjamins.

Ruiz de Mendoza Ibáñez, F. J. and Mairal Usón, R. (2008) Levels of description and constraining factors in meaning construction: An introduction to the Lexical Constructional Model. *Folia Linguistica* 42(2): 355–400.

Ruiz de Mendoza Ibáñez, F. J. and Luzondo Oyón, A. (2010) Lexical-constructional subsumption in resultative constructions in English. In M. Brdar, M. Zic Fuchs, I. Raffaelli, M.-M. Stanojevic and N. Tudjman Vukovic (eds) *Cognitive Linguistics: Between universality and variation.* Cambridge: Cambridge Scholars Publishing; vol. in prep.

Ruiz de Mendoza Ibáñez, F. J. and Pérez Hernández, L. (2001) Metonymy and the grammar: motivation, constraints, and interaction. *Language and Communication* 21: 321–357.

Ruiz de Mendoza Ibáñez, F. J. and Peña Cervel, M. S. (2008) Grammatical metonymy within the "action" frame in English and Spanish. In M. A. Gómez González, J. L. Mackenzie and E. M. González Álvarez (eds) *Current Trends in Contrastive Linguistics: Functional and cognitive perspectives* 251–280. Amsterdam: Benjamins.

4 Alternation and Participant Role: A contribution from a Systemic Functional Grammar

Amy Neale[a]

1 Introduction

Levin's (1993) detailed investigation of the syntactic and semantic properties of English verbs proposes that lexical entries for verbs must "incorporate a representation of verb meaning and [...] allow the meanings of verbs to be properly associated with the syntactic expressions of their arguments" (1993: 1). In contrast with Levin's lexicon-based approach, this paper will consider the occurrence of verbal alternation and alternating verbal argument structures from the standpoint of developing an extendable system of TRANSITIVITY with the explicit purpose of Natural Language Generation.

A goal of the Systemic Functional approach to language is to put into practice fully semantic system networks that are able to generate both syntactic structure and lexical items on a single continuum, or "lexicogrammar" where "lexis can be defined as 'most delicate grammar'. The exit to lexis would then be closed and all exponents ranged in systems" (Halliday 1961: 267).

The examination of alternating verb behaviour provides an opportunity to demonstrate how the system network can generate lexicogrammatical output. Through the TRANSITIVITY system network one can establish meaning clustering at points along a cline of "delicacy": at a very broad level where groups of verbs with the same Process type and Participant Role configuration are meaning-related in respect of the changes they

a Amy C. Neale has a Ph.D. from Cardiff University, Wales, United Kingdom, where she worked with Robin Fawcett, Gordon Tucker, and a number of other scholars developing the Cardiff Grammar dialect of Systemic Functional Linguistics. E-mail: amy.neale@gmail.com bring about in the world; through to a narrow – or "delicate" – level, where the penultimate systems to the realization of lexical items provide fine-grained semantic distinctions. In this way, Systemic Functional Linguistics provides the means to not merely link syntactic and semantic properties but to conflate them in a system.

With this proposal as our starting point, this paper will separate Levin's alternations into two types:

1. Alternations which are concerned with the placing of arguments, and the covert or overt expression of these arguments in the clause.
2. Alternations whose expression involves different Participant Role configurations.

The discussion presented is located within the approach to TRANSITIVITY developed within the Cardiff Grammar (CG) framework. CG is a model of language that finds its basis in Systemic Functional Linguistics (SFL), and has grown from the work of a number of scholars at Cardiff University and beyond. The tenets of this branch of SFL theory originate from the ideas first presented by Fawcett (1973/1981; 1980). As we shall see, the CG framework enables one to consider the generation of verb senses and their associated arguments, and the generalization of alternations by taking Process type and Participant Role configurations as the starting point for developing the system networks for TRANSITIVITY.

This paper demonstrates how type 1 above can be handled by the CG through the functions/operations that enable the system network, but how, in type 2 above the meaning differences conveyed are large enough to suggest that different verb senses are involved. Such verb senses involve different inherent semantic roles, or Participant Roles, and as such are generated through different choices in the system network. In this case I propose that this is not a verb alternation at all, but rather a "near equivalence" of two separate verb senses.

Based on the developments in CG from Fawcett (1980) to the present, the approach presented here takes its lead from Neale (2003), the main aim of which was to generate a very wide range of types of Process for a large computational grammar by providing delicate system networks for the part of the grammar that generates the Main Verb in the clause. A related aim of this work was to contribute to the theory by building on the concepts of "Process", "system network" and "delicacy" and extending the semantic classification of verb senses. This systemic lens provides an alternative approach to Levin for modelling paradigmatic relations between verb senses. The two major outputs of Neale (2003) are a database of 5400 fully analysed verb senses,[1] and extended system networks for three major Process types in English. Both of these outputs are drawn on in this paper, and provide an evidence base for the CG theoretical-descriptive approach to verb alternation.

The Systemic Functional model of language has been attractive to researchers in the field of Natural Language Generation (NLG) because of the emphasis placed on the concept of **system**, and of **choice** within that system. SFL has been considered as particularly useful to NLG because of the attention paid not only to the grammar but to all the aspects required for language generation – that is, a **mind**. It is this potential within the theory that has been brought to bear on the work of Fawcett and those working with him to develop the CG branch of SFL. Fawcett (1980) sets out a combinatory approach that does not separate the cognitive from the interactional, and he proposes a "psychosociolinguistic" model. This approach has led to the exploration of how the model might be useful within the field of computational linguistics, and consequently led to the development of the COMMUNAL project.[2] Here we are particularly concerned with GENESYS:[3] the sentence generation component of COMMUNAL which consists of the system networks and realization rules of the lexicogrammar. An ambition of the CG framework is to develop fully semanticized system networks or, more specifically, to model the meaning potential of language to the point of "lexis as most delicate grammar" (Halliday 1961). In the case of the work being presented here, the focus is on the fully semanticized TRANSITIVITY system and the associated meanings that can be realized through this system.

The system of TRANSITIVITY enables us to refer to events, this type of "experiential" meaning being manifested in the clause in the Main Verb and its extensions which realize the "Process", and in the associated "Participant Roles". It is through the system of TRANSITIVITY that the semantic classification of verbs (Process types) and associated semantic roles in the Clause (Participant Roles) are realized. The Participant Role classification framework is now fully developed within CG, with a detailed and delicate system network for generating Participant Roles and a refined set of re-expression tests that can be applied to determine Participant Role type when analysing clauses. The elements that make up the CG Participant Role framework relate to the work of, for example, Fillmore (1968), Gruber (1965), Halliday (1967, 1968) and Lyons (1968). Despite being conducted in different linguistic frameworks, these works are all motivated to explore the semantic classification of verbs and the associated syntactic-semantic relationships and semantic roles in the clause. A key work in this regard is Halliday's (1970) paper "Language Structure and Language Function", where he first introduces the notion that the meaning potential of language is modelled by choices in a system network. Here he begins to consider the major Process types to be classifications in terms of semantic roles – or "Participant Roles/Functions" – providing overtly semantically defined labels for the roles.

Section 3 of this paper outlines how a semanticized system network can allow for type 1 above, followed by §4 which details how the CG approach allows for type 2 above, with an inspection of the causative/inchoative alternation. This detail will provide: (a) the argument for why the phenomenon that Levin describes as the causative/inchoative alternation is not recognized as an alternation in CG; and (b) a walk through the two sub-systems that generate the two different verb senses.

First, however, we shall consider the treatment of TRANSITIVITY in the CG, providing the context for both the theoretical approach to verbal alternation within the framework, and the motivation of natural language generation for modelling verbal alternation through the system network.

Specifically, §2 provides a guide to understanding how Participant Role configurations are inherently tied to Process type, and, therefore, meaning clustering.

2 TRANSITIVITY in the Cardiff Grammar

Halliday states that the TRANSITIVITY system allows for "constru(ing) the world of experience into a manageable set of process types" (Halliday 1994: 106), and Fawcett (1980) describes how in this experiential component of language:

> The referent situation that has been formulated by the performer's problem solver for transmission to the addressee is viewed as "process", and then the term "process" is to be interpreted in a sense that includes "relationships" and "states" as well as "actions" and "changes of relationship and state". (134)

In the current CG TRANSITIVITY network there are three main Process type categories – "action", "relational" and "mental" processes – plus three further categories of "influential", "event-relating", and the minor and referentially limited "environmental" processes. These initial features in the system network for TRANSITIVITY are provided in Table 4.1, and presented as a table rather than a system network because the percentages

Table 4.1. The initial features in the system network for Process Type and the frequency of occurrences of each type as recorded in the PTDB (Neale 2003: 148)

Process type	*Sub-Process type*
Action (54%)	One role (37%)
	Two role (63%)
Relational (31%)	Attributive (8%)
	Directional (49%)
	Locational (20%)
	Possessive (15%)
	Matching (8%)
Mental (10%)	Cognition (56%)
	Perception (16%)
	Emotion (28%)
Influential (2.6%)	
Event-relating (2.3%)	
Environmental (0.1%)	

included are not "probabilities" that occur in the system network,[4] but are the figures for the number of "types" found to occur in the Process Type Database (PTDB) (Neale 2003).

The following sub-sections will address each of these Process types; describing the meanings that each construes, and the system networks through which these meanings are realized. Each sub-section also includes the CG Participant Role labels associated with each Process type.[5]

2.1 "Action" Processes

What is now called the "action" Process network in CG continued for some time after Fawcett (1980) to be the "material" Process network, following Halliday's own terminology (see Halliday 1985, 1994; Halliday and Matthiessen 2004). In recent years Fawcett has returned to the description "action", recognizing that there are a large number of what might be termed "non-material action" Processes. There are many "social action" Processes that pass the requisite tests for Processes of this type but which do not involve material action.

More detail is provided on the action process network in §4.1, and so here we will simply present the initial system for action processes in Figure 4.1.

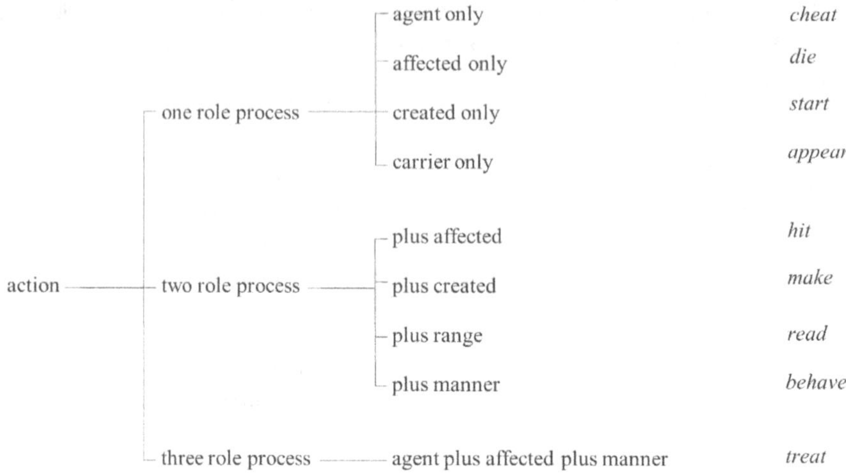

Figure 4.1. The current system network for action Processes in the Cardiff Grammar

The primary distinction in the system network is the number of Participant Roles that accompany the Process in the clause. This is a change in CG from that described in Fawcett (1980), and reflects the abandonment of the system that offers a choice between [agent-centred] and [affected-centred] Processes. This change is critical to the present discussion, and is detailed in §4.1, which illustrates how verb alternations which do not entail a change in Participant Roles can be realized and described in CG.

The processes which are realized through the "action" system network are those which Halliday and Matthiessen would describe as "processes of doing-&-happening" (2004: 179).

2.2 "Relational" Processes

Figure 4.2 depicts the CG "relational" Process system network which expands on Fawcett's early descriptions (1987), incorporating two new Process types of "directional" Processes and "matching" Processes.

Figure 4.2 also models the possible Participant Role configurations for all the "relational" Process types. All five semantic subclasses of Process type ("attributive", "locational", "directional", "possessive" and "matching") can take the same Participant Role configurations, and this generalization is captured with the left hand 'curly' bracket signifying simultaneity. The

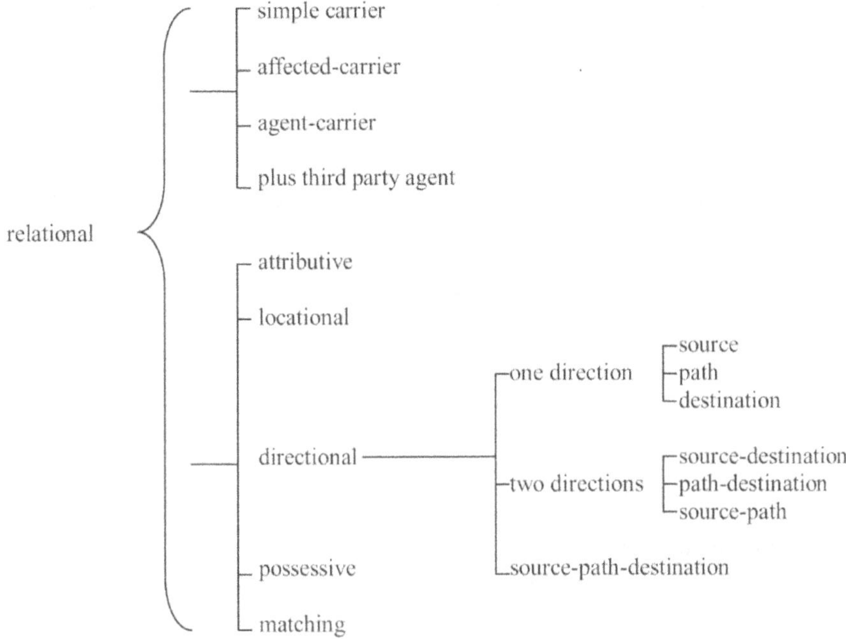

Figure 4.2. The current System Network for Relational Processes in the Cardiff Grammar

"relational" Process system also allows for the generation of compound roles to specify the precise semantic function of the role.

Particularly important is the combination of an Agent with the compound role of Affected-Carrier, which is central to the three role processes that can be generated through the "relational" system. In the network they are termed "third party agent" Processes, because a "third party" is introduced to what would otherwise be a two-role Process. This configuration facilitates the generation of "possessive" Processes such as (1):

(1) Belle gave Sebastian the key.

The CG classification of "attributive", "locational", "directional", "possessive" and "matching" "relational" Processes is based on the patterning of the Participant Roles that each can take. We will now briefly take each in turn to discover the types of meaning that can be realized through this portion of the system network.

In all the Participant Role patterns available to "attributive" Processes (i.e. simple carrier, compound carrier, or third party agent), the following verb senses are generated through this system:

(2) It (Ca) feels like (Pro)[6] cashmere (At).

(3) She (Af-Ca) broke out in (Pro) a rash (At).

(4) I (Ag-Ca) qualified as (Pro) a doctor (At).

(5) We (Ag) should elect (Pro) him (Af-Ca) Mayor (At).

The "attributive" section of the network also generates the high frequency verb sense "being".

The Processes generated through the "locational"[7] section of the network include the following examples:

(6) The church (Ca) sits (Pro) in the middle of the village (Loc).

(7) Her hands (Af-Ca) rested (Pro) on the table (Loc).

(8) Hoteliers (Ag-Ca) inhabit (Pro) the town (Loc).

(9) She (Ag) delivered (Pro) a blow (Af-Ca) to his stomach (Loc).

The Processes generated through the "directional" section of the network include the following examples, where the directional Participant Role will be either "Source" (So), "Path" (Pa), or "Destination" (Des).[8]

(10) The river (Ca) flows (Pro) into a lake (Des).

(11) The lift (Af-Ca) descended (Pro) one floor (Pa).

(12) The boy (Ag) crept (Pro) towards the bush (Des).

(13) The drum (Ag) brought (Pro) the men (Af-Ca) rushing to the village (Des).

The Processes generated through the "possessive" section of the network are concerned with both "having" and "lacking", with the following verb senses generated through this system:

(14) They (Ca) lack (Pro) the confidence (Pos).

(15) I've (Af-Ca) lost (Pro) the paper (Pos).

(16) She (Ag) bought (Pro) a dress (Pos).

(17) What (Pos) are you (Ag) giving (Pro) Rachel (Af-Ca)?

The final Process type in the "relational" Process system network is the new type, that of "matching",[9] with the following verb senses generated through this system:

(18) These shoes (Ca) go with (Pro) my coat (Mtch).

(19) He (Af-Ca) fell in with (Pro) a good crowd (Mtch).

(20) Carson (Ag) separated from (Pro) him (Mtch).

(21) Mr A (Ag) married (Pro) his daughter (Af-Ca) to a rich man (Mtch).

2.3 "Mental" Processes

The current "mental" Process system network is taken from Fawcett (forthcoming) and is as presented in Figure 4.3.

Different Participant Roles are associated with each "mental" Process type, and four separate single Participant Roles are offered to fulfil these different configurations: Emoter, Perceiver, Cognizant and Phenomenon. Perceiver and Cognizant also function as compound roles. All of these can occur with the fourth Participant Role of Phenomenon. This set of Participant Role configurations allows for a delicate semantic specification, in turn allowing for revealing analyses of the Process in a clause.

The first subsystem, of "emotion", leads to a choice between [emotive] and [desiderative]. In a Process of this type the Emoter will typically be a conscious participant and the Phenomenon may be an object or an event, as example (22) shows:

(22) Belle (Em) loved (Pro) her new shoes (Ph).

Alternatively, [phenomenon-oriented] can be chosen, allowing for Processes where the Phenomenon triggers a response, such as in example (23):

(23) He (Ph) disgusted (Pro) Simon (Em).

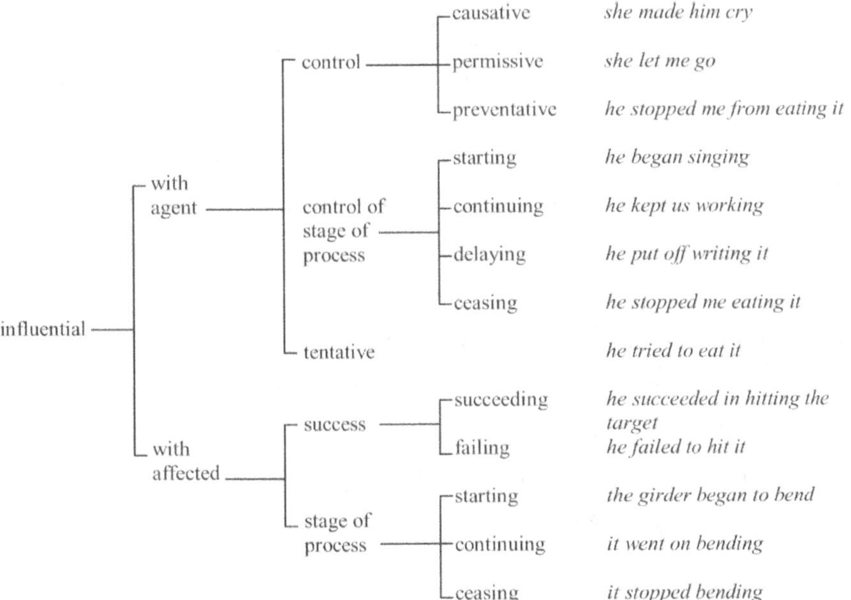

Figure 4.3. The major options in the "mental" part of the Cardiff Grammar TRANSITIVITY network (Fawcett, forthcoming, Chapter 2, Section 3.5)

The option [desiderative] involves the same Participant Role configuration as [emoter-oriented] (Em + Ph), and again the Emoter will typically be a conscious Participant. "Desiderative" Processes convey "the feeling of 'desiring' that some event will come about" (Fawcett, forthcoming, Chapter 2) and so the Phenomenon involved will be an event, which typically has not yet happened, as in Examples (24) and (25):

(24) Belle (Em) wishes (Pro) she had some new shoes (Ph).

(25) Belle (Em) wants (Pro) new shoes (Ph).

The second subsystem of "perception" generates Processes which pertain to the senses, for example *looking at, watching, listening, thinking, smelling,* etc., and as such they can be agentive and non-agentive, as with the difference between *looking at* versus *seeing,* and *listening to* versus *hearing.*

The CG "mental" Process system also models "three role" Processes of "perception", in which someone "causes someone to perceive something". The most obvious example of a "three role" "perception" Process is *showing,* as in (26) where the Participant Roles are Agent plus Affected-Perceiver plus Phenomenon:

(26) Belle (Ag) showed (Pro) Sebastian (Af-Perc) her clean windows (Ph).

The final subsystem for "cognition" Processes includes "communication" type Processes, where the Agent causes the Affected-Cognizant to *know/ come to know of* some Phenomenon, where the latter contains the speech item as in examples (27) and (28). "Cognition" Processes also include the high frequency Processes "knowing" and "remembering", as in (29) and (30); also "coming to know" Processes of (31) and (32); and Processes which involve actively going about "knowing", as in (33) and (34).

(27) Belle (Ag) asked (Pro) Sebastian (Af-Cog) if he loved her (Ph).

(28) She (Ag) told (Pro) him (Af-Cog) to go (Ph).

(29) I (Cog) know (Pro) this area (Ph).

(30) Sebastian (Cog) forgot (Pro) my birthday (Ph).

(31) I (Af-Cog) didn't realize (Pro) you two lived so close (Ph).

(32) We (Af-Cog) learned (Pro) that he had left (Ph).

(33) She (Ag-Cog) studied (Pro) French (Ph).

(34) We (Ag-Cog) will plan (Pro) a trip abroad (Ph).

2.4 "Influential" processes

Fawcett (forthcoming, Chapter 2, Section 3.7) has formulated the "influential" Process type to model a set of Processes that are not accounted

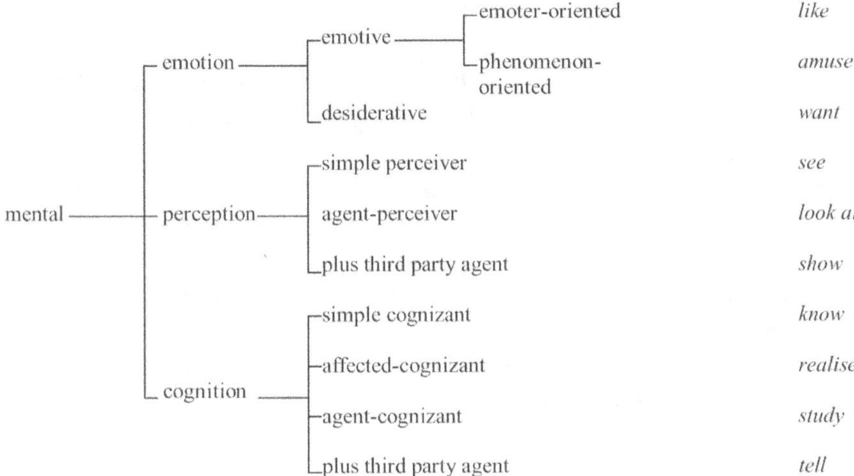

Figure 4.4. Some major options in the "influential" part of the TRANSITIVITY network (Fawcett, forthcoming, Chapter 2, Section 3.7)

for elsewhere in the TRANSITIVITY system. Processes of this type all include an embedded event in the matrix clause that is somehow "influenced" in one way or another by the Process. Figure 4.4 presents the initial choices in the system network.

There are 12 possible types of "influential" Process. The first choice is between those Processes whose first PR is an Agent and those Processes whose first PR is an Affected. This is an interesting distinction because it means that not all "influential" Processes are "causative" (or rather, "instigated" – i.e. they do not all involve an Agent). For example, in "succeeding" or "failing" in something, the typically first role is an Affected entity, as in Example (35):

(35) He (Af) failed (Pro) to hit it (Ph).

The second distinction between the 12 possible Processes is whether the typically second PR is a Created or a Range. The PR Created occurs in clauses where the embedded event did not exist until the "influence" occurred, as in Example (36):

(36) Belle (Ag) made (Pro) Sebastian cry (Cre).

The PR "Range" occurs where the embedded event extends for the same period of time as the matrix event, and therefore it cannot be affected by the matrix event. In the "influential" Process system network, the Range functions as the semantic label for the embedded event in an example such as (37):

(37) Belle (Ag) kept (Pro) Sebastian working (Ra).

2.5 "Event-relating" Processes

This new addition to the CG TRANSITIVITY system is described by Fawcett as "work in progress" which recognizes a Process type that is a relatively new phenomenon in the language. They are originally Processes whose meaning has been extended through metaphor to relate two events to each other. Fawcett proposes that these Processes should be analysed as a separate Process type, suggesting that "there is no longer any semantic connection with (their) historical origin" (Fawcett, forthcoming).

Figure 4.5 presents the full system network that Fawcett (forthcoming) proposes for this new Process type.

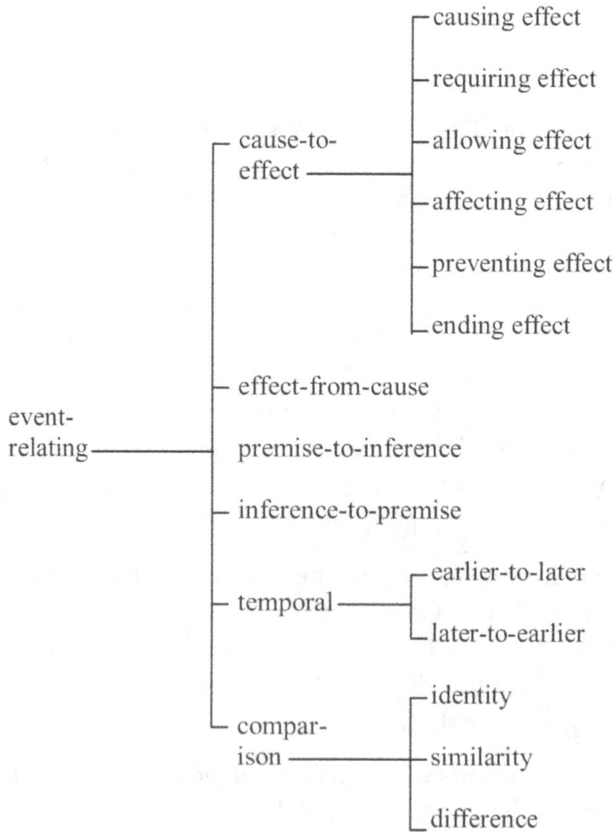

Figure 4.5. Some major options in the "event-relating" part of the TRANSITIVITY network. (Fawcett, forthcoming, Chapter 2, Section 3.8)

2.6 "Environmental" processes

Finally, the CG includes a system for recognizing a referentially limited Process type, but one that is necessary in a full model of language. This is the system for "environmental processes". These are not only frequent, especially in casual conversation, but are also constructed in a unique manner. Figure 4.6 demonstrates that there are two options in the system for environmental processes.

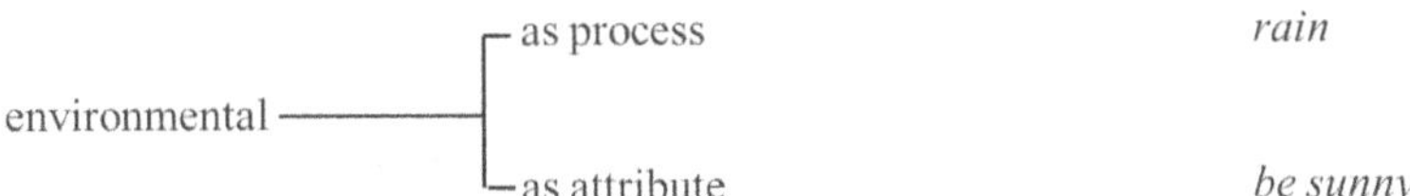

Figure 4.6. The system for Environmental Processes

Having addressed the main areas of TRANSITIVITY in the CG, we have seen that each Process type, with its meaning-related verb senses, is distinguishable according to its PR configurations and how, therefore, the notion in the system network of semantic features that reflect the names of the Participant Roles is significant alongside the classification of verb senses. This is critical to the CG approach to the types of verb alternations where the alternation changes the Participant Roles involved with the Process, as we will see in §4.1.

3 Verbal alternations and the Cardiff Grammar

In all verbal alternations, it is the Participant Role that undergoes some alternation; either the internal structure of the argument with which the PR conflates, or the placing of the PR in the clause, or the semantic role in the clause itself changes, and thus the PR inherent to the Process.

In a large number of cases, the CG provides a means to handle a diathesis alternation through the operations of the system network, as represented in GENESYS. In the case of verb senses where the alternation involves a change in either the positioning of the PR in the clause or the likelihood of the inherent PR occurring overtly in the clause, then this alternation type can be managed by the **probabilities** assigned to features in the network. One important feature of the CG approach to the modelling of language is that it is not grammaticality which is paramount but rather frequency of occurrence. The features in the system network have probabilities expressed in percentages which reflect the probability of one feature occurring in the system over another. In such cases, the PR configuration remains the same – i.e. the semantic roles inherent to the Process stay the same – but the realization of the arguments alters.

To illustrate, verbal alternations such as the "dative alternation", where the Process is "relational" of the type "possessive" such as (40a) and (40b), are handled in CG by operations such as the **realization rules** in the system network and **re-entry** into the network:

(40) (a) Bill (Ag) sold (Pro) a car (Pos) to Tom (Af-Ca).
(b) Bill (Ag) sold (Pro) Tom (Af-Ca) a car (Pos).

We will explore exactly how this is achieved after briefly considering the approach of language as **system**.

3.1 System network

The "system networks" are the modelling of Halliday's "meaning potential" (1970: 142). Meaning potential is the set of choices open to the language user, and the system network serves as the formalism for expressing choice, a pathway through which the meaning potential is instantiated.

Fawcett (2000: 36) illustrates how language can be viewed in this way in a diagram that includes "the four components that are essential for modelling any semiotic system".

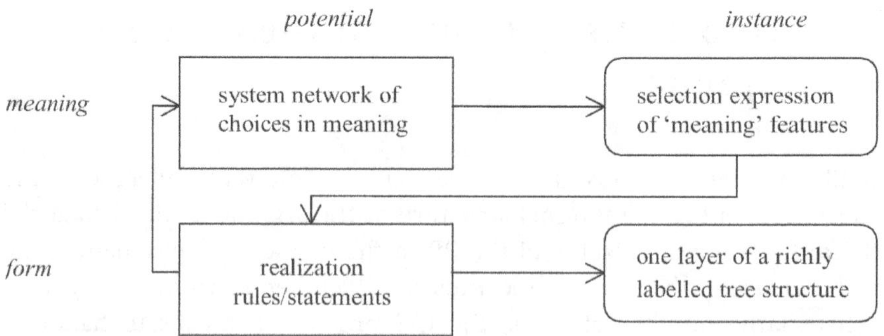

Figure 4.7. The main components of a systemic functional grammar (Fawcett 2000: 36)

By viewing language in this way, one is able to build a model in which all instances of language can be described and classified. Halliday (1994) summarizes by stating that:

> The system network is a theory about language as a resource for making meaning. Each system in the network represents a choice: not a conscious decision made in real time but a set of possible alternatives, like "statement/question" or "singular/plural". (xxvi)

The notion of system is central to both Systemic Functional theory and to the description in this paper. The system network is a means for modelling the paradigmatic and dependency relations between features in the language. These relations allow for choices that range from more general to more delicate features, producing an ever finer specification to the most delicate part of the system – and onwards in some cases to further specification of structure.

When all the possible choices on a particular pass through the network have been made, the features are collected into the "selection expression" which is an instance at the level of meaning. The grammar then inspects each selection expression to see if a realization rule is attached, which specifies the actual lexicogrammatical output for each lexical item. The function of these rules, in the words of Fawcett *et al.* (1993: 119), is to "specify how the somewhat abstract features that have been chosen in the networks come to be expressed as specific items, structures, and intonation or punctuation". If the system network is the meaning potential of language, the realization rules allow for the form potential.

To produce the appropriate output, the realization rule uses certain "realization operators" (Fawcett 1993: 131) which either build structures and produce descriptions OR predetermine, absolutely or probabilistically, the features to be chosen on subsequent journeys through the network. It is these operators which enable a fully dynamic system network rather than a flat taxonomy. In the case of verbal alternation, the "Re-entry" realization operator determines – through a next pass through the network – what type of structure will fill the Participant Role. The most detailed description of how these realization operators function is Fawcett *et al.* (1993), and the following description of Re-entry operators is based on this.

Typically the Participant Role we have generated (e.g. *Bill* in example (40a) above) will be filled with a nominal group. To generate the nominal group that will fill the Participant Role ("Agent" in this example) we need to re-enter the network and choose [thing]. The Re-entry operation will ensure that this happens, with the operator stating "for Agent re-enter at [thing]". Then, after re-entry and the selection of another set of features, the other types of operator would insert a nominal group and build its structure.[10]

A further rule or operator instantiated in CG is the "Same Pass" (SP) rule. This is an important part of the network as SP rules "make the networks very much richer and more sensitive to different environments, whether of register or immediate linguistic context [...] (SP rules have) important implications for the way in which we think about the nature of grammatical rules" (Fawcett and Tucker 2000: 2). The SP rules provide a choice at a point in the network which can alter the options available at a later stage in the network, thus making the system dynamic. Moreover, for our current purposes the SP rule allows us to generate certain verb alternations through the network.

Using Levin's "Understood Body-Part Object Alternation", we will take alternation (41) as an example:

(41) (a) I washed my hair.
(b) I washed.

This Transitivity Alternation example is a sub-set of the "Unexpressed Object Alternation", where "the subject of the transitive verb bears the same semantic relation to the verb as the subject of the intransitive use does. The intransitive variant in each of (the unexpressed object) alternations involves an unexpressed but understood object" (Levin 1993: 33). In this case, the understood object equates to the Participant Role inherent in the Process. In CG, the two Examples (41a) and (41b) represent the same verb sense, Process type and Participant Role configuration, of "action Process; material Process; two role plus affected", but the Affected Participant Role in (41b) is covert.

Let us refer to the appropriate section of the material action network in Figure 4.8 to understand how a SP rule can enable a verbal alternation.

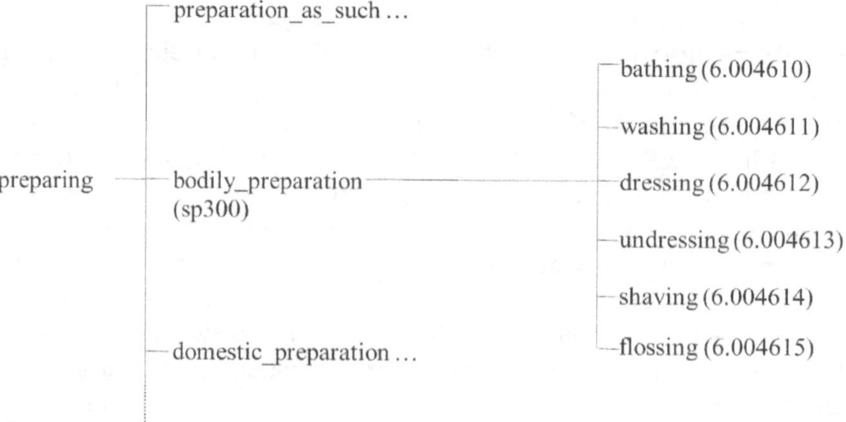

Figure 4.8. The system for [bodily preparation] with "same pass" rule

Figure 4.8 includes both realization rules (e.g. 6.004610, which specifies that the Main Verb will be expounded by the item *bath*) and an SP rule, on the feature [bodily preparation] where we find the rule (sp300). This rule states that the probabilities must be changed in the PARTICIPANT ROLE part of the network. The first reason for the SP rule on [bodily preparation] is that in these types of Process the probabilities for the realization of the Affected entity in the clause need to reflect a higher probability of this entity being changed from the default. This is to assign a higher probability to the likelihood of the Affected entity being covert, for Processes such as *washing, flossing,* etc.

Therefore, the same pass rule "sp300" changes the probabilities for the system [affected role type], which offers a choice between [affected unmarked], [affected sought], [affected relating out], [affected exclaimed at] and [affected covert], to increase the probability of [affected covert] being chosen in this system.

The second reason for having an SP rule on this item in the network is because there is a higher chance (than there is with other Process types) that the outcome will be a reflexive clause; the Affected being the same referent as the Agent, allowing for a change of probabilities assigned to reflect the "Understood Reflexive Object Alternation" associated with this group of verb senses. If [affected is other] is chosen, then the probabilities will remain the same. However, if [affected is self] is selected then the probabilities must be changed to allow for reflexivity.

4 Alternations involving changes in the Participant Role configuration

Having discussed the CG approach to handling verbal alternation through the system network, we now consider the examples of what others would view as alternations but which the CG considers as separate "near equivalences".

Consider examples (42) and (43):

(42) The glass broke.

(43) Sebastian broke the glass.

Levin (1993) would regard these as a "causative/inchoative alternation". In the (1980) CG TRANSITIVITY system, this alternation – or generalization between the two structures – is captured through the network as depicted in Figure 4.9, and described as follows.

Having made the choice [action process] in the system network, and on having reached the entry condition [affected-centred], the (1980) system led to **either** a possible "simple" Process, which would be a "one-role", "affected only" Process, **or** a [plus agent] Process, which would be a "two-role" Process. Either of these choices would lead to the same network for choice of Process type, with realizations of verb senses such as *change, break, cook, melt,* etc.

Fawcett's terms "agent-centred" and "affected-centred" were an attempt to provide more explicit labels for what are often called "ergative" and "transitive" clauses. Halliday (1967, 1985, 1994, and also Halliday and Matthiessen 2004) distinguish these two types by using different Participant Roles for each: transitive clauses involve Actors and Goals, and ergative clauses involve Agents and, by 1985, Mediums. Fawcett (1980) departs from the use of the terms transitive and ergative, and from the two sets of Participant Roles, and proposes a means for distinguishing the two types in which "the terms used [...] have the advantage of reflecting the fact that it is the 'centrality' of a particular inherent role in each process that determines its nature" (Fawcett 1980: 140).

As a result of detailed work on the modelling of verb senses in the system network carried out in Neale (2003), the current CG system network for TRANSITIVITY has abandoned this distinction, and models the

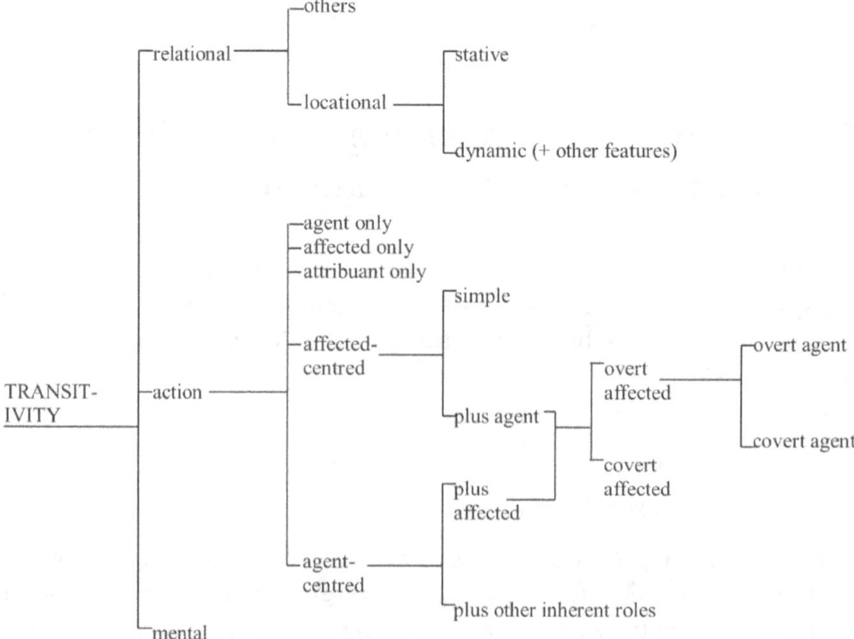

Figure 4.9. The TRANSITIVITY system network (Fawcett 1980: 137)

difference through other means. At the centre of the argument lies the distinction between a "one role" ergative example such as (42) and a "two role" ergative example such as (43).

I suggest that rather than requiring an alternation which enables us to generalize two realizations of this ergative verb sense, with two different associated patterns of Participant Roles, these examples illustrate different senses of the verb form *break*, and two separate Processes. In (42) an object changes its state into the state of being *broken*, while in (43) an agent either intentionally or unintentionally causes an object to change its state into the state of being broken. These two meanings are modelled successfully using the current CG framework for TRANSITIVITY, and §4.5 will reveal the way in which these two Processes are modelled in different places in the system network of TRANSITIVITY.

The question that must be addressed at this point is whether this approach loses an important generalization. My opinion is that it does not. The grammar still shows that the two senses of *break* share a single form, through the fact that they share the same realization rule in the system network for the purposes of language generation. Indeed, in some cases such a near equivalence is represented with a change in verb form:

(44) Belle died.

(45) Sebastian killed Belle.

The common ground between the two senses of *break* is similar to that between *die* and *kill*, *rise* and *raise*, etc. and it would be inconsistent to treat the two senses of *break* in a way that is different from the distinction between *die* and *kill*. Just as *kill* and *die* refer to related activities they are nonetheless recognized by Levin as separate senses, and so occur in separate verb classes.[11] Boas (this volume), although working with a Frame-Semantic model, also demonstrates that Levin's methodology "of using syntactic criteria to arrive at coherent semantic classes predictive of syntactic behaviour is problematic" (p. 230) and provides instead a semantically-based classification.

I would also suggest that a generalization which captures (42) and (43) proposes a norm (probably the "two role", causative example) and a transformation of that norm. Working within a framework motivated by the principles of Systemic Functional Linguistics entails that the aim is not to generate norms and transformations but to generate directly the most appropriate instance of language for a given context, based not only on form but also on function. A move away from a formal alternation such as this one is therefore in keeping with the SF approach to modelling language.

Davidse's (1992) paper, "Transitivity/ergativity: the Janus-headed grammar of actions and events", considers example (42) to be an "ergative middle", which is equivalent to the CG analysis of being "one role" "affected only". She states that "the ergative middle leaves it open whether the action was self-instigated or external" (1992: 114). This statement, in my view, supports not generalizing the two separate senses of *break* in the grammar. In the construction of the "one role" or "middle" type (42) (and more clearly in example (44)), there is no implied, recoverable "agent", and so this should not be modelled in the system. It is proposed here that the terminology used for introducing Participant Roles involved in "action" Processes provides us with a means for describing all meaning types, and while the use of the labels Agent and Affected for the functions/roles may colour the system to make it seem more causative – and therefore more ergative – the presence (overt or covert) or absence of these Participant Roles provides a useful means for analysing all types of "action" Process.

In Davidse and Geyskens (1998) paper, "The ergative causativization of intransitives", (shortened to "ECI"), they look at the introduction of the role "instigator" to the non-instigatable structure of the intransitive:

(46) The dog walked Intransitive

(47) He walked the dog ECI construction

Davidse and Geyskens highlight that this recognizes a pair that seems to be neither inergative-ergative nor intransitive-transitive, but "intransitive-ergative".

The CG analysis of this pair would be:

(46) (a) The dog walked (for exercise) [action process, agent only]

Or more probably:

(46) (b) The dog walks to the park [relational, directional process, two role]

(47) (a) He walked the dog (for exercise) [action process, agent plus affected]

Or more probably:

(47) (b) He walks the dog to the park [relational, directional process, three role]

This phenomenon is an argument for recognizing these two (or four) occurrences of *walking* as different senses generated through different parts of the system, and so for **not** using the generalization of the agent-centred/affected-centred distinction. Pushing out the semantically-oriented features to the most delicate point in the system network allows for a fine-grained approach which should logically allow for all kinds of extended meanings.

In Fawcett's (1980) TRANSITIVITY system network, on making the choice [affected-centred], the next system choice is between [simple] (i.e. "one role", "affected only") or [plus agent] (i.e. "two role"). However, in recognizing this ECI construction, Davidse and Geyskens highlight the fact that example (46) is not a "one role", "affected only" process, but an "agent only" process, in which *the dog* undertakes the action of *walking*. Thus, Davidse and Geyskens' study adds weight to the argument for not seeking to generalize by modelling an alternation that distinguishes between "agent-centred" and "affected-centred", but rather for distinguishing between "one role", "affected only" Processes; "one role", "agent only" Processes; and "two role", "agent plus affected" Processes.

The argument for abandoning the "agent-centred/affected-centred" distinction is a result of following through to a conclusion the notion that the distinction between transitive and ergative reflects the Participant Roles involved in the process. By classifying all the Participant Roles in the "action" Process system network as either Agent or Affected, or both, the CG framework has enough labels to indicate the degree of the causation.

4.1 A walk through the system networks for one role and two role action Processes, to generate examples (42) *break* and (43) *break*

To emphasize the context for dealing with these constructions as near equivalences rather than as alternations, we will return to the system network through which the verb senses are intended to be generated and I will present the places where these two verb senses occur within the CG system network for TRANSITIVITY. On entry into the TRANSITIVITY network, the first portion is as follows:

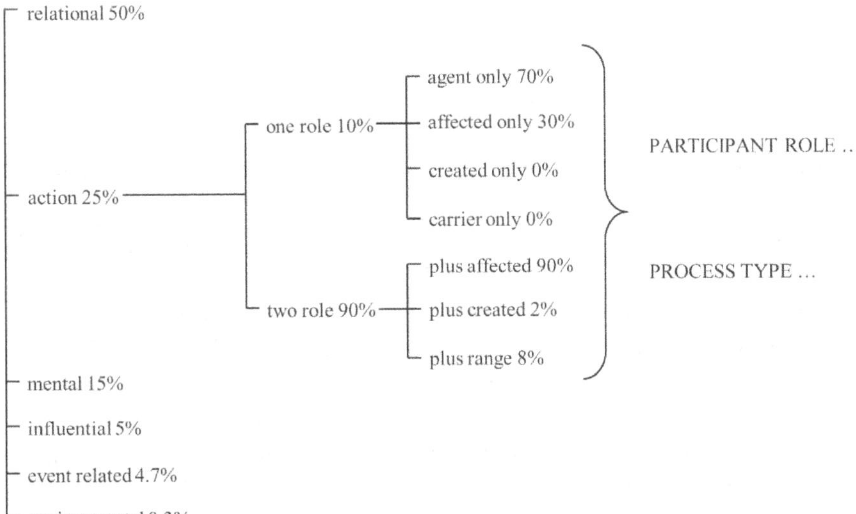

Figure 4.10. The initial portion of the TRANSITIVITY system network in the Cardiff Grammar

First, to generate the Process that will be expounded by the Main Verb *break* in example (42) we choose "action", "one role", "affected only". At this point there are simultaneous choices in the systems for PROCESS TYPE and PARTICIPANT ROLE. We will now enter the sub-network for the PROCESS TYPE choice. The initial section of the PROCESS TYPE network for "one role" Processes is as presented in Figure 4.11.

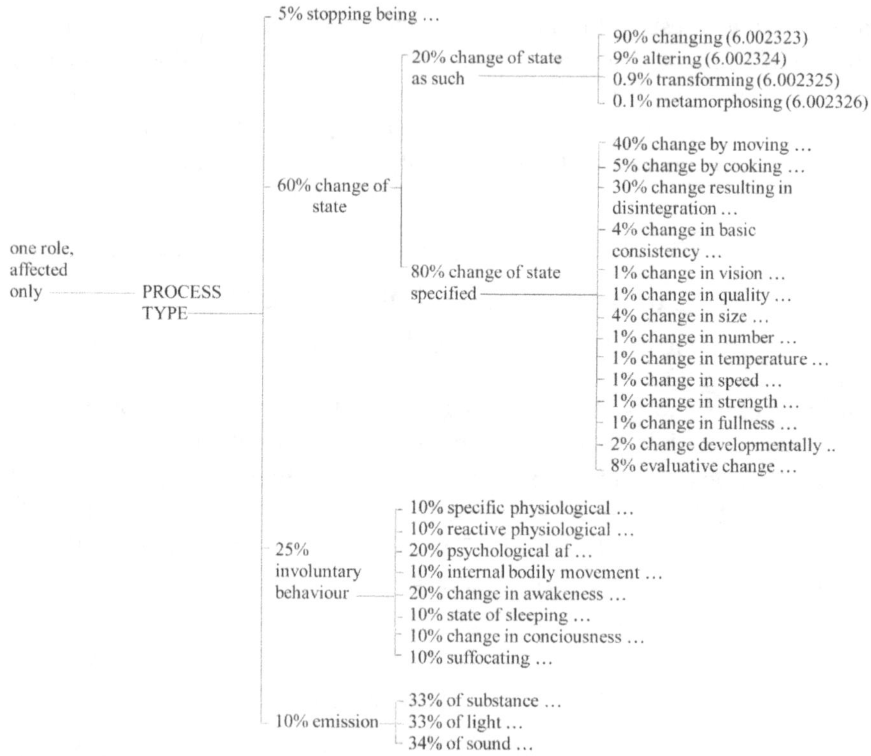

Figure 4.11. "One role", "affected only" PROCESS TYPE system network

To generate Example (42), we enter the "change of state" sub-network. This is a very broad category and includes a large number of verb senses. In Levin (1993) these verb forms all fit the behaviour of a "middle alternation" or a "causative/inchoative alternation". Within the "middle alternation" Levin recognizes verbs that behave in the "middle construction", which in traditional grammar are intransitive, or in CG is a "one role" and "affected only" Process. Within the "causative/inchoative alternation" Levin recognizes the "inchoative construction" which in the CG is also a "one role" and "affected only" Process, and is traditionally the one-role form of an ergative verb.

The basis for Levin's categorization is syntactic; her point of departure is "to arrive at a classification on purely syntactic grounds, with the hope that this classification would receive semantic support" (Levin 1985: 2). The objective here, however, is to build system networks that are semantic in their basis, but where the syntactic realizations are explicitly specified.

The "change of state" section involves a distinction between "change of state as such" verbs and "change of state specified". "Change of state as such" enables the super-ordinate Processes of change to be generated: *changing, altering, transforming,* and *metamorphosing.* In contrast, the feature "change of state specified" leads to further systems for choices between more semantically specific and therefore more delicate Processes of *change.*

To generate the verb sense for (42) we enter the further sub-network "change resulting in disintegration". The Processes generated through this system are of two types, defined by the degree of disintegration, and so the choice in the system is "total disintegration" and "non-total disintegration", as shown in Figure 4.12. This choice was designed to reflect a split between

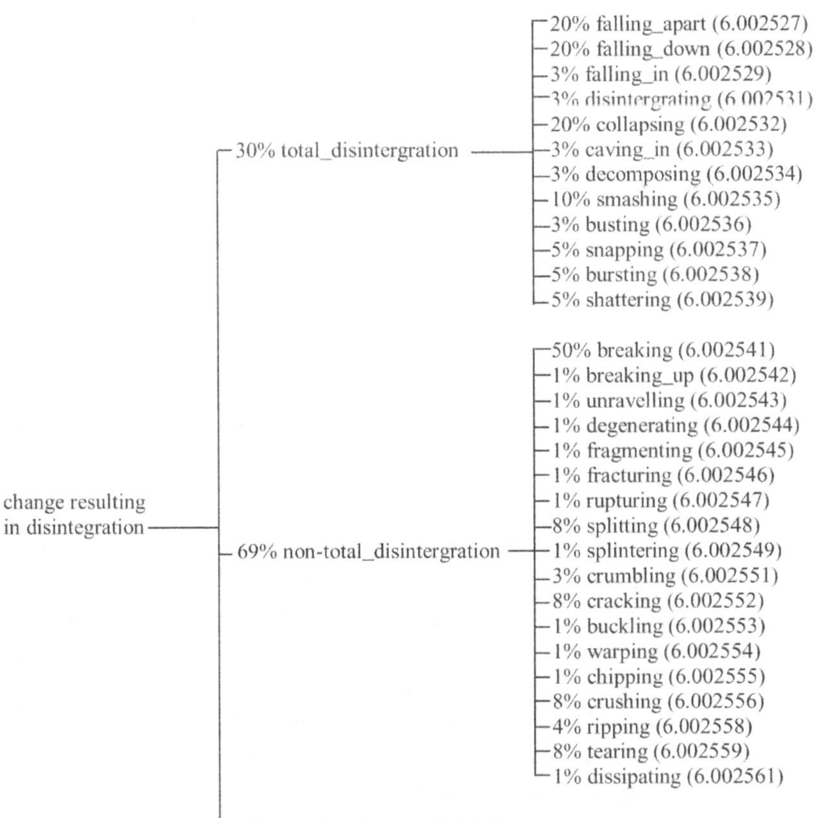

Figure 4.12. The system network for "change resulting in disintegration" Processes

two semantic types, and also between the functioning of the two types, with the "total disintegration" type verbs only functioning as "one role", "affected only" Processes, (these being *falling apart, disintegrating, collapsing, caving in* and *decomposing*), and the "non-total disintegration" type verbs generated both in this system and also in the "two role", "agent plus affected" system.

It is in this section of the system network, therefore, that we generate our Main Verb for Example (42).

To generate the Process that will be expounded by the Main Verb *break* in Example (43) we return to Figure 4.10, and choose "action", "two role", "agent plus affected".

Again, at this point there are simultaneous choices in the systems for PROCESS TYPE and PARTICIPANT ROLE. We will now enter the sub-network for the PROCESS TYPE choice. The initial system is presented in Figure 4.13.

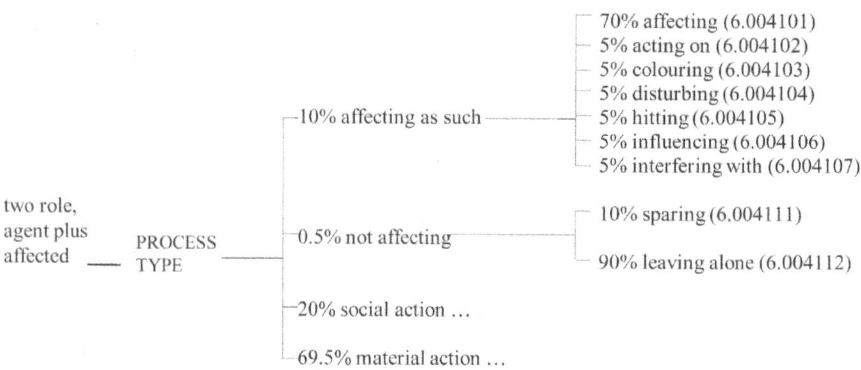

Figure 4.13. The initial system network for "two-role", "agent plus affected" Processes

To generate the Process for Example (43), we enter the "material action" section of the network. This is a very large group of verb senses and the initial system emerged from the grouping of Processes in this type into semantically coherent groups, with Figure 4.14 presenting the initial choices.

The sub-network that we must enter to generate the Process for Example (43) is "affecting by contact", which leads to numerous subsystems, the entry conditions to which are presented in Figure 4.15.

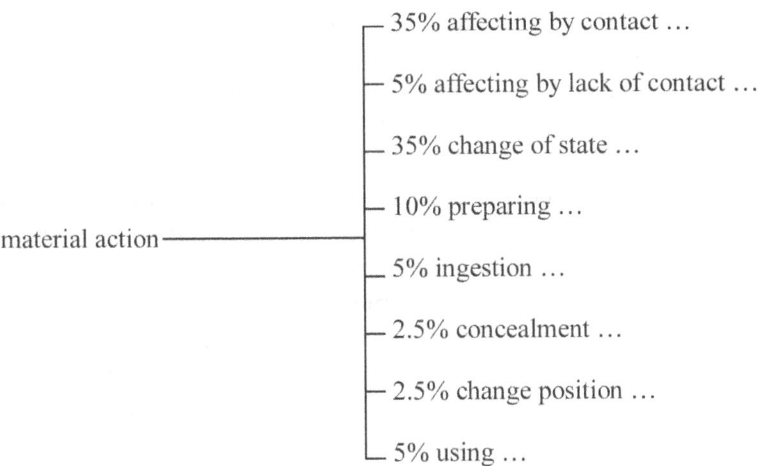

Figure 4.14. The initial choices in the system network for "material action"

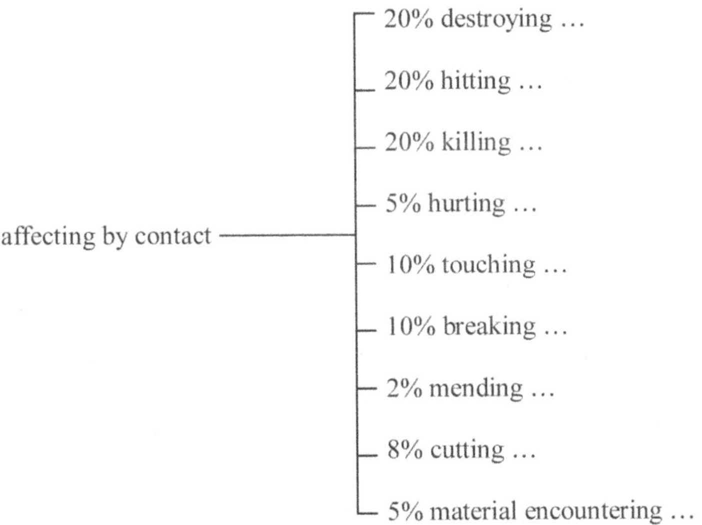

Figure 4.15. The system network for "affected by contact" Processes

We can compare the subcategories in this system with four of Levin's (1993) Verb Classes: *break* verbs, *cut* verbs, *touch* verbs and *hit* verbs. She recognizes these separate groups according to the different alternations they take, with these differences in behaviour indicating meaning differences. Her basic hypothesis can then be captured in a system network, as in Figure 4.15, with the subsystems representing her classes.

The subsystem for generating *destroying* verb senses contrasts with the "one role", "affected only" subsystem of "total disintegration/non-total disintegration", which we saw above, where it was noted that Processes of the type "total disintegration" can ONLY occur with one PR, whereas the Processes in the "non-total disintegration" system can occur with both a single PR sense ("affected only") and a two PR sense ("agent plus affected"). It is here, among the *destroying* Processes that we find the majority of two-role senses equivalent to the forms in the "non-total disintegration" system.

In the group of *destroying* verbs, many of the verb forms function with two separate PR configurations, whereas some verb forms can ONLY function with "two roles" of "agent plus affected". To illustrate the point, consider the verb *destroy*. This verb sense can only function as in (48) and not in (49). This Process necessarily requires an Agent to bring about the happening that is *destroying*.

(48) The wrong instructor can destroy your confidence.

(49) *The building destroyed.

There is, therefore, a mix of ergative and transitive verb senses that can be generated through this single subsystem, all of which have the PR configurations Agent plus Affected. The fact that some of these verbs occur only with two Participant Roles (such as *destroy*), while others occur with one or two (such as *explode*), is still reflected in the grammar through the fact that the features generating the two Process types share the same realization rule number.

Finally, we reach the subsystem for generating the semantic group of *breaking* type verbs, which includes the verb sense *break*. The verb form *break* here will have the same realization rule as the verb form *break* generated through the "one-role", "affected only" Process network; however it is generated through this network because it is a different verb sense.

5 Conclusions

A major concluding difference between Levin and the CG is that Levin's lexicon approach does not recognize different verb **senses**. While she recognizes a single verb form as behaving in different ways according to the alternations it can occur in, she does not explicitly state that a verb form behaves differently depending on its sense. For example, she places the verb form *open* in four different verb classes:

1. "Verbs of signs involving bodies' parts: crane verbs".
2. "Alternating verbs of change of state".
3. "Appear verbs".
4. "Verbs of spatial configuration".

Rather than recognizing the different senses a form might have, Levin proposes that the verb form has "extended meaning". She claims that "when a verb has more than one meaning, one of its meanings is basic and the others are systematically related to it, that is, they are instances of extended meaning" (1993: 22). I would posit that most of Levin's extended meanings are in fact separate senses and I propose that a systemic approach enables us to treat all verb senses as individual and unrelated items, where so-called alternating constructions (e.g. transitive versus intransitive) should not be generalized.

In this paper I have presented an approach to verbal alternation using a framework which views language (lexis and grammar) as system. Levin's premise that alternations guide us to both clusters of meaning related verbs, and the converse that "the behaviour of a verb, particularly with respect to the expression and interpretation of its arguments, is, to a large extent, determined by its meaning" (1993: 1) claims a strong link between form and meaning, and a paradigmatic approach. Such a link shares common ground with the SFL approach to form and meaning. However, I have sought to illustrate how the SFL approach goes further, providing not only paradigmatic relations through the system but also dependency relations between features in the language – a factor which any lexicon based approach will not capture.

It is only by taking a fully semanticized approach to language that the distinction between true alternations and near equivalences is possible, where semantic labels are provided for the functions in the clause (i.e. the Participant Roles), which then conflate with elements of structure.

Notes

1. This database, called the Process Type DataBase (PTDB), includes the most frequently occurring verb senses according to Francis *et al.* (1996) and, unlike any other study of this kind, a high proportion of multi-word verbs.
2. COMMUNAL stands for Convivial Man-Machine Understanding through Natural Language.
3. This aspect of the COMMUNAL system is called GENESYS because it GENErates SYStemically.

4. For choices to be made in a system network, there needs to be some basis on which to establish a reason for each choice. It has long been a guiding principle of SFG that choices should be based on evidence of usage, and that some "probability" of occurrence should be captured. We will visit the concept of "probability" in the system network presented in §3.
5. The full set of CG Participant Role abbreviations are as follows: Ag: "Agent"; Af: "Affected"; Ca: "Carrier"; At: "Attribute"; Ag-Ca: "Agent-Carrier"; Af-Ca: "Affected-Carrier"; Loc: "Location"; Pos: "Possessed"; Mtch: "Matchee"; Em: "Emoter"; Ph: "Phenomenon"; Af-Perc: "Affected-Perceiver"; Cog: "Cognizant"; Ag-Cog: "Agent-Cognizant"; Af-Cog: "Affected-Cognizant"; Ra: "Range".
6. "Process".
7. The introduction of separate "locational" and "directional" Process types is a recent addition to the CG "relational" Process system, again with the same Participant Role configurations available to both. It is interesting to note, however, that the probability for the Participant Role configuration that is likely to occur with "locational" and "directional" is different. Most "locational" Processes choose "simple carrier", and most "directional" Processes choose one of the other options.
8. "Source" gives information regarding where the direction originates; "Path" conveys where the movement takes place, and "Destination" conveys where the movement is directed.
9. For a full description of "matching" Processes, see Neale (2006).
10. It is because the realization rules work in this way that Tucker 2000 (13th EISFW, Glasgow, July 2000) has suggested that it is not in fact "lexis" that is most delicate grammar, but whatever it is that the realization rule states, as this happens at a more delicate point than the realization of lexis.
11. Levin includes *kill* in the "murder verbs" class (1993: 230), and *die* in the "verbs of disappearance" class (1993: 260).

References

Boas, H. C. (this volume) A frame-semantic approach to syntactic alternations: The case of *build* verbs.

Davidse, K. (1992) Transitivity/ergativity: The Janus-headed grammar of actions and events. In M. Davies and L. Ravelli (eds) *Advances in Systemic Linguistics: Recent theory and practice* 105–135. London: Pinter.

Davidse, K. and Geyskens, S. (1998) *Have you walked the dog yet?* The ergative causativization of intransitives. *Word* 48(2): 155–180.

Fawcett, R. P. (1973/1981) Generating a sentence in a systemic functional grammar. University College London. Reprinted in M. A. K. Halliday and J. R. Martin (eds) (1981) *Readings in Systemic Linguistics* 146–183. London: Batsford.

Fawcett, R. P. (1980) *Cognitive Linguistics and Social Interaction: Towards an integrated model of a systemic functional grammar and the other components of a communicating mind.* Heidelberg: Julius Groos Verlag and Exeter University.

Fawcett, R. P. (1987) The semantics of clause and verb for relational processes in English. In M. A. K. Halliday and R. P. Fawcett (eds) *New Developments in Systemic Linguistics, Vol. 1: Theory and description* 131–183. London: Frances Pinter.

Fawcett, R. P. (2000) *A Theory of Syntax for Systemic Functional Linguistics: Current issues in linguistic theory.* Amsterdam: Benjamins.

Fawcett, R. P. (2008) *Invitation to Systemic Functional Linguistics through the Cardiff Grammar: An extension and simplification of Halliday's Systemic Functional Grammar.* (Third edition). London: Equinox.

Fawcett, R. P. (forthcoming, 2011) *The Functional Semantics Handbook: Analysing English at the level of meaning.* London: Equinox.

Fawcett, R. P., Tucker, G. H. and Lin, Y. Q. (1993) How a systemic functional grammar works: the role of realization in realization. In H. Horacek and M. Zock (eds) *New Concepts in Natural Language Generation* 114–186. London: Pinter.

Fawcett, R. P. and Tucker, G. H. (2000) The system network and realization rules for meanings realized in the clause. *COMMUNAL Working Papers* 19. Cardiff: Computational Linguistics Unit, Cardiff University.

Fillmore, C. J. (1968) The case for case. In E. Bach and R. T. Harms (eds) *Universals in Linguistic Theory* 1–88. New York: Holt, Rinehart and Winston.

Francis, G., Hunston, S. and Manning, E. (1996) *Collins COBUILD Grammar Patterns 1: Verbs.* London: HarperCollins.

Gruber, J. (1965) *Studies in Lexical Relations.* Ph.D. dissertation. Cambridge, MA: MIT.

Halliday, M. A. K. (1961) Categories of the theory of grammar. *Word* 17(3): 241–292. Reprinted in part in Kress, G. (ed.) (1976) *Halliday: System and function in language.* Oxford: Oxford University Press.

Halliday, M. A. K. (1967) Notes on transitivity and theme in English: Part 1. *Journal of Linguistics* 3(1): 37–81.

Halliday, M. A. K. (1968) Notes on transitivity and theme in English: Part 3. *Journal of Linguistics* 4(2): 179–215.

Halliday, M. A. K. (1970) Language structure and language function. In J. Lyons (ed.) *New Horizons in Linguistics* 140–165. Middlesex: Penguin.

Halliday, M. A. K. (1985) *An Introduction to Functional Grammar.* London: Edward Arnold.

Halliday, M. A. K. (1994) *An Introduction to Functional Grammar.* (Second Edition.) London: Edward Arnold.

Halliday, M. A. K. and Matthiessen, C. M. I. M. (2004) *An Introduction to Functional Grammar.* (Third Edition.) London: Hodder Arnold.

Levin, B. (1985) Lexical semantics in review: An introduction. *Lexicon Project Working Papers* 1: 1–62. Center for Cognitive Science, Cambridge, MA: MIT.

Levin, B. (1993) *English Verb Classes and Alternations: A preliminary investigation.* Chicago, IL: University of Chicago Press.

Lyons, J. (1968) *Introduction to Theoretical Linguistics.* Cambridge: Cambridge University Press.

Neale, A. (2003) *More Delicate TRANSITIVITY: Extending the PROCESS TYPE system networks for English to include full semantic classifications.* Ph.D. thesis. School of English Communication and Philosophy, Cardiff University.

Neale, A. (2006) "Matching" corpus data and system networks: using corpora to modify and extend the system networks for TRANSITIVITY in English. In S. Hunston and G. Thompson (eds) 143–163 *System and Corpus: Exploring connections.* London: Equinox.

Part II

Studies of specific alternations

II.1 Transitivity alternations involving a change in the configuration of semantic roles

5 The causative/inchoative alternation in Functional Discourse Grammar*

Daniel García Velasco[a]

1 The causative/inchoative alternation: Relevant properties

The terminology **causative/inchoative alternation** refers to the alternative transitive and intransitive use of some verbs, as illustrated with the examples in (1):

(1) (a) John broke the window.
    (b) The window broke.

(1) illustrates the use of the verb *break* in two different syntactic patterns. (1a) is a transitive construction and (1b) an intransitive one. From a semantic point of view, the intransitive variant denotes a process which is undergone by the subject, whereas the transitive pattern refers to an action which is instigated by an agent. The semantic relationship between the two variants resides in the fact that the agent in the transitive *causes* the process introduced in the intransitive variant. An informal paraphrase for (1a) would thus be something like "John caused the window to become broken", whereas (1b) is roughly equivalent to "the window became broken". We see then that the transitive variant incorporates the meaning of the intransitive one plus a causality component, hence the name of the alternation.[1] Other verbs which participate in the alternation include *bake, close, cook, melt, move, roll, shatter, whiten,* and many others (see Levin 1993).

A first problem addressed by previous studies on the topic centres on the identification of a common property shared by all alternating verbs. Indeed, what these verbs seem to have in common is the fact that they

a Daniel García Velasco is Lecturer in English Linguistics at the University of Oviedo, Spain. E-mail: danielg@uniovi.es belong to a semantic class of **verbs of change**, originally named by Jespersen (1927: 332) verbs of "**move** and **change**", that is, they entail a change of location or physical/mental state (Kilby 1984). This excludes alternations such as the following (Levin and Rappaport Hovav 1994: 39):

(2) (a) The children played.
(b) *The parents played the children.
(cf. The parents made the children play)

(3) (a) The actor spoke.
(b) *The director spoke the actor.
(cf. The director made the actor speak)

In these examples, the subject participants are agents and so the intransitive verbs *play* and *speak* do not denote processes of movement or change undergone by the subject participant. Note that this restriction would also account for the impossibility of detransitivizing the verb *destroy*, which although closely related in meaning to alternating *break*, can only figure in transitive environments. According to Ruiz de Mendoza and Mairal (this volume), *destroy* really belongs to the class of verbs of "cessation of existence" and not to change of state.

However, Levin and Rappaport Hovav (1994) also note that in English there are intransitive verbs which denote changes of state and which cannot be transitivized either:

(4) (a) The cactus bloomed/blossomed/flowered early.
(b) *The warm weather bloomed/blossomed/flowered the cactus early.

(5) (a) The jewels glittered/sparkled.
(b) *The queen glittered/sparkled the jewels.

This, they claim, shows that the semantic restriction identified by Jespersen and others is not enough to account for the possibility of a verb to participate in the process.

A second theoretical problem is to establish the direction of the derivation, that is, to determine whether the transitive variant derives from the intransitive one or *vice versa*. The existence of a grammatical marker in one of the variants is typically taken as evidence of its derived nature. Consider the following examples from Spanish:

(6) (a) Juan abrió la puerta.
Juan open:PST;3SG the:F door
"Juan opened the door".

(b) La puerta se abrió.
The:F door REFL open:PST;3SG
"The door opened".

Just like its English counterpart, the Spanish verb *abrir* ("open") can both be used transitively (6a) and intransitively (6b). However, in its intransitive use, the reflexive marker *se* is added, which can be taken as an indicator of its derived status.

However, this criterion is difficult to apply in languages like English in which alternating verbs do not present a visible marker in any of the constructions. Van Valin and LaPolla (1997: 183) claim that "it seems that in English, there are fewer intransitive process verbs which do not undergo causativisation than there are causative verbs which do not undergo decausativisation". Therefore, it might possible to assume tentatively that English derives causatives from intransitive process verbs if we use absolute productivity as a criterion for the direction of the derivation. As Van Valin and LaPolla (1997) indicate, an advantage of this analysis can be seen in its predictiveness: if there is a morphological rule which derives causatives from intransitives, it is natural to expect that speakers should extend the process to verbs which would not normally admit a causative use. The following examples (adapted from Bowerman and Croft 2008: 281) illustrate errors produced by children in which intransitive verbs are used causatively:

(7) (a) He disappeared the green one. = "make it disappear"
(b) Can I glow him? = "make him glow"

It could thus be argued that children erroneously extend the use of the verbs *disappear* and *glow* until they learn that they cannot be used transitively. According to Van Valin and LaPolla (1997) this would argue for an intransitive to transitive derivation. Unfortunately, children seem to make similar mistakes in the opposite direction, as the following example also from Bowerman and Croft (2008: 281) shows:

(8) Bert knocked down. = "fell down"

Yet, Davidse (this volume) notes the case of the verb *unify* in English, originally used as a causative verb which subsequently detransitivized, as attested in corpus-based editions of the Collins COBUILD dictionaries. This development seems to be connected with the process of unification of the two Germanies which could thus be conveniently coded as something which had occurred by itself rather than through external intervention. That obviously means that the grammar of the English language should also allow for a morphological rule which creates intransitive process verbs from their causative uses.

Moreover, the criteria of morphological marking and productivity seem to offer controversial results on some occasions. In certain varieties of Spanish, the process verb *desaparecer* ("disappear"), typically used intransitively, can also be used with a causative reading in a transitive construction:

(9) Por eso nos persiguieron y nos quedamos.
By that:M we:ACC chase:PST;3PL and we.REFL stay:PST;3PL
Por eso nos desaparecieron a tres compañeras
By that:M we:DAT disappear:PST;3PL to three partner:F;PL

"That's why they chased us and we stayed. That's why they took three comrades from us."
http://www.aporrea.org/actualidad/n56819.html
Accessed on 20 January 2009.

(10) A: ¿Puede desaparecer una Isla?
Can:PRS;3S disappear:INF an:F island?
B: En México sí. Han desaparecido a la Isla
In Mexico yes. Have:PRS;3PL disappear:PTCP to the:F Island
Bermeja, ubicada a 100 millas al Norte
Bermeja, locate:PTCP at 100 mile:F;PL to-the North
de Yucatán y Campeche
of Yucatán and Campeche.
A: ¿Y quiénes la desaparecieron?
And who:PL it:F;ACC disappear:PST;3PL
B: En México los legisladores tienen este poder
In Mexico the: M;PL legislators have:PRS;3PL this:M power

"Can an island disappear?
In Mexico, it can. They have made the Island Bermeja disappear, which is located 100 miles to the North of Yucatán and Campeche.
And who made it disappear?
In Mexico, the legislators can do that."
http://publicalpha.com/isla-bermeja-como-recuperarla/
Accessed on 20 January 2009.

The examples in (9) and (10) show that there is an apparent contradiction between the criteria of morphological marking and productivity in determining the direction of the alternation. On the one hand, the Spanish language has a grammatical marker to indicate derived intransitivity, while at the same time the basically intransitive *desaparecer* seems to extend its use to a transitive construction. This might indicate that within the same language it is possible to find both directions in the derivation.

Indeed, Haspelmath (1993: 104) notes that the situation across languages is rather complex. In his study, he presents data of 31 alternating verbs, which he considers reasonable representatives of the causative/inchoative alternation, from a total of 21 languages. The different formal types attested in languages are summarized in Table 5.1.

Table 5.1. Haspelmath's (1993) classification of formal types in the causative/inchoative alternation

Formal types	*Direction of derivation*
Directed (one variant is derived from the other)	
Causative	transitive causative derived
Anticausative	intransitive inchoative derived
Non-directed (no variant is derived from the other)	
Labile	same verb is used in both variants
Equipollent	both forms are derived from the same stem
Suppletive	different verb roots for each use

Thus, English would illustrate a non-directed labile formal marking, whereas Spanish would fall within the category of anticausative formal marking. As Haspelmath notes, the causative/inchoative alternation shows a disparity between semantic derivation and formal marking across languages. The general principle of diagrammatic iconicity suggests that formal marking in a derived construction should be seen as the result of the addition of a semantic component which is not present in the underived form. In the present case, this would correspond to an inchoative-to-causative direction with causatives being formally marked; however, this is not universally reflected in languages. In his own words, "the typological survey in this paper shows that the hypothesized direction of semantic derivation is not matched by a uniform direction of formal derivation" (Haspelmath 1993: 89).

An interesting observation from Haspelmath's study is the fact that languages are not uniform in the type of formal marking they select and several types can be found in the same language. To cite a few examples, Swahili shows 11 anticausatives, 11 causatives plus eight equipollent alternations. English is unique in its strong preference for labile alternations (25 of the 31 verbs examined) a fact that Haspelmath attributes to the fact that the language shows "little morphology in general" (1993: 102). Romanian illustrates the other extreme in the sample as it shows 24 instances of anticausative alternation. In all, there are languages with a strong tendency for directed alternations, both causative and anticausative (Finnish, Turkish), and others for non-directed alternations (English, Japanese, Indonesian, Greek, etc.). From a theoretical perspective, then, this wide diversity in formal types should force grammar models to provide an equally generous technical apparatus to handle them.

Another interesting observation in Haspelmath's work relates to the formal expression of individual verbs across the languages in the sample. His hypothesis is that the anticausative variant should be favoured when the verb denotes an activity with a high probability of an outside force bringing about the event. This hypothesis is borne out by the data. For example, *break* is anticausative in 15 languages whereas *freeze* appears as causative in 12. He concludes that verbs can be "located on a scale of increasing likelihood of spontaneous occurrence" (1993: 105). To quote his words:

> Events that are more likely to occur spontaneously will be associated with a conceptual stereotype (or prototype) of a spontaneous event, and this will be expressed in a structurally unmarked way. On the other hand events that are more likely to occur through causation by an external agent will be associated with a stereotype of a caused event, so the caused event will be expressed in a structurally unmarked way. (Haspelmath, 1993: 107)

The crucial thing in Haspelmath's view is to assume "a broader view of the nature of 'semantic' properties" (1993: 106) which goes beyond the features identified in models of semantic decomposition and delves into conceptual meaning.

A similar conclusion is arrived at by Levin and Rappaport Hovav (1994) in their analysis of this construction. The authors assume that those intransitive verbs which participate in the alternation denote events which are **externally caused**, whereas those intransitive verbs which do not are **internally caused**. As noted by Davidse (this volume) these intuitions can be traced as far back as Jespersen's work at the beginning of the twentieth century. Levin and Rappaport Hovav explain them in the following way:

> With an intransitive verb denoting an internally caused eventuality, some property inherent to the argument of the verb is "responsible" for bringing about the eventuality. [...] In contrast to internally caused verbs, verbs which are externally caused inherently imply the existence of an external cause with immediate control over bringing about the eventuality denoted by the verb: an agent, an instrument, a natural force, or a circumstance. Thus something breaks because of the existence of some external cause; something does not break solely because of its own properties. Some of these verbs can be used intransitively without the expression of an external cause, but, even when no cause is specified, **our knowledge of the world** tells us that the eventuality these verbs denote could not have happened without an external cause. (1994: 49–50; emphasis mine, DGV)

In all, then, both Haspelmath and Levin and Rappaport Hovav agree that the relevant factor to understand the alternation is not the semantic properties of the participating verbs, but the patterns of experience and the speakers' perception of the general properties of the event denoted by the verb. This points to a conceptual rather than to a purely linguistic explanation for the process. Further evidence is provided by the fact that whether a particular verb admits the process seems to depend on the type of entity which plays the role of affected participant. Such is the case of the verb *clear* as the following examples show (Levin and Rappaport Hovav 1994: 65):

(11) (a) The men cleared the table/the sidewalk.
(b) *The table/the sidewalk cleared.

(12) (a) The wind cleared (up) the sky.
(b) The sky cleared (up).

The event in (11) cannot be understood without the intervention of a volitional agent hence the ungrammaticality of the transitive variant. This is not so in (12). This also explains why internally caused verbs such as verbs of emission cannot participate in the alternation:

(13) (a) *The jeweller sparkled the diamond.
(b) *Max glowed Jenny's face with excitement.
(c) *We buzzed the bee when we frightened it.

According to the authors, those transitive verbs which accept an intransitive variant denote an event which can occur without the intentional intervention of an agent. It is common, therefore, that these verbs may take Forces or Instruments as subjects:

(14) The wind/the key opened the door.

However, transitive verbs which require a volitional subject do not take part in the alternation:

(15) (a) *The candidate assassinated/murdered.
(b) *The letter wrote.
(c) *The house built.

As expected, they do not readily accept the presence of an Instrument or Force in subject position:

(16) (a) *The knife assassinated/murdered the candidate.
(b) *The pen wrote the letter.
(c) ??The crane built the house.

To sum up, we can see that the possibility of a verb to take part in the alternation is deeply related to the type of event denoted by that verb, which, in turn, is closely associated with our apprehension of the world around us. Also, Haspelmath's study clearly shows that there is no uniform characterization of participating verbs or the direction in the derivation across languages and, significantly, in the same language. Thus, a proper account of the alternation should be based not on its formal features but on its conceptual properties which are truly behind the possibility of a verb to participate in the two variants.

2 The causative alternation in classical Functional Grammar

Classical Functional Grammar (FG) assumes that the lexicon component is the starting site for the generation of linguistic expressions. Yet, the lexicon in FG contains not only lexemes but also those morphological rules by means of which it is possible to create new items in a productive way (i.e. derivational processes). These rules are called **Predicate Formation Rules** (PFR) in the theory. In FG lexemes appear in the lexicon in the form of **predicate frames**, structures which contain the number and type of arguments a lexical item takes. (17) is an example of a predicate frame:

(17) $give_V$ (x_1: <animate> $(x_1))_{Ag}$ $(x_2)_{Go}$ (x_3: <animate> $(x_3))_{Rec}$

As the representation in (17) shows, the verbal predicate *give* appears in a structure which defines the number and type of arguments it takes together with their semantic functions and selection restrictions. Thus, PFRs operate on these structures and create new predicate frames. The causative alternation is treated as a lexical alternation and thus a PFR is proposed for it. In particular, Kahrel (1985) proposes a rule which derives causatives from intransitives. Although the author is not explicit in its formulation, following the usual format in the theory, it might look like the following:

(18) INPUT: $pred_V$ $(x_1)_{Proc}$
OUTPUT: $pred_V$ $(x_1)_{Ag}$ $(x_2)_{Go}$
MEANING: x_1 causes the process undergone by x_2

Thus, the verb *sink* would appear in the lexicon in the intransitive frame (19a), which, after the application of the rule produces the frame in (19b):

(19) (a) $sink_V\ (x_1)_{Proc}$ "The boat sank".
(b) $sink_V\ (x_1)_{Ag}\ (x_2)_{Go}$ "The sailor sank the boat".

The causative meaning is therefore implicit in the rule itself and transmitted to the verb which participates in the alternation. However, Siewierska (1991: 28) proposes the following rule with the opposite direction in the derivation:

(20) INCHOATIVE FORMATION
INPUT: $pred_V\ (x_1)_{Ag}\ (x_2)_{Go}$
OUTPUT: $pred_V\ (x_2)_{Proc}$

It would thus seem that the theory is not able to capture the typological diversity found in Haspelmath's study. At most, FG can offer different rules for different languages but the PFR approach amounts to nothing but a formalization of the structural facts observed. Second, the semantic function change seems to me barely justifiable, and the pertinence of the semantic role Processed has also been criticized by several authors within the FG tradition (Schack-Rasmussen 1994: 44 and Siewierska 1991: 70). Actually, no analysis of this construction that I know of assumes the existence of a semantic function change by the affected entity.

But, maybe, the most important problem this analysis has to face is of a theory-internal nature. As noted above, the application of the process to individual verbs is restricted by the possibility of conceptualizing the denoted action as a process which can obtain spontaneously. Yet, it seems difficult for this to be included within a PFR as envisaged in the theory. FG requires that Predicate Formation Rules apply only to productive processes. The following quote illustrates Dik's concept of productivity:

> By a synchronically productive rule I mean a rule which can be formulated in terms of some open-ended class of input predicates. An open-ended class is a class the members of which need not be enumerated one by one, but may be characterized by **some general property** or several such properties. (1980: 26; emphasis mine, DGV)

The quote shows that the theory forces a search for some property which guarantees the grammatical cohesion of the verbs participating in the process. To identify such a property in this case seems to be an extremely difficult task, as Kahrel acknowledges:

> The precise characterisation of which predicates may be used in derived intransitive constructions, then, cannot be given in this paper; such a characterisation seems not possible within the framework of Functional

> Grammar, although this framework is able to describe the syntax of the several uses of the derived intransitive. (1985: 45)

The problem Kahrel faces is easy to understand. Unlike cognitive models, FG makes a strict division between linguistic and general knowledge to the extent that restrictions on the application of the rule are not naturally expressed in terms of conceptual features.

It seems difficult to envisage how such knowledge can be captured in terms of a general grammatical property as the theory demands. Given its conceptual nature, it seems to me that this construction can be handled in a much more natural way with an approach resting on the relevance of the conceptual level. Thus, as the author indicates, the theory can only hope to describe the syntax of the alternation, but it cannot point out accurately which verbs may and which verbs may not participate in the alternation. In the following section I will consider whether FDG has superseded FG in the analysis of this process.

3 Functional Discourse Grammar: Morphology and verbal alternations

The general organization of Functional Discourse Grammar (FDG), the most recent upshot of Dik's FG is presented in Figure 5.1. A complete overview of the theory is to be found in Hengeveld and Mackenzie (2008).

There are three important differences between FG (as presented in Dik 1997) and FDG. First, FDG presents a top-down orientation as it intends to model its internal architecture in such a way that it becomes compatible with well-established findings in the field of psycholinguistics. In particular, Levelt (1989) views linguistic behaviour as a process running from a communicative intention to actual speech generation. This is reflected in FDG in the priority given to the Interpersonal Level which takes care of coding the pragmatic aspects of the utterance. Second, and in accordance with this top-down organization, FDG takes the **Discourse Act** rather than the clause as the basic unit of linguistic description. Although FG was meant to be a theory of connected discourse, in actual practice it has mostly been restricted to the analysis of intrasentential units. This is avoided in FDG as a discourse act is defined as any linguistic expression which provides a complete contribution to ongoing discourse regardless of its particular structure. Thus, non-clausal units such as vocatives or phrases may be analysed as discourse acts.

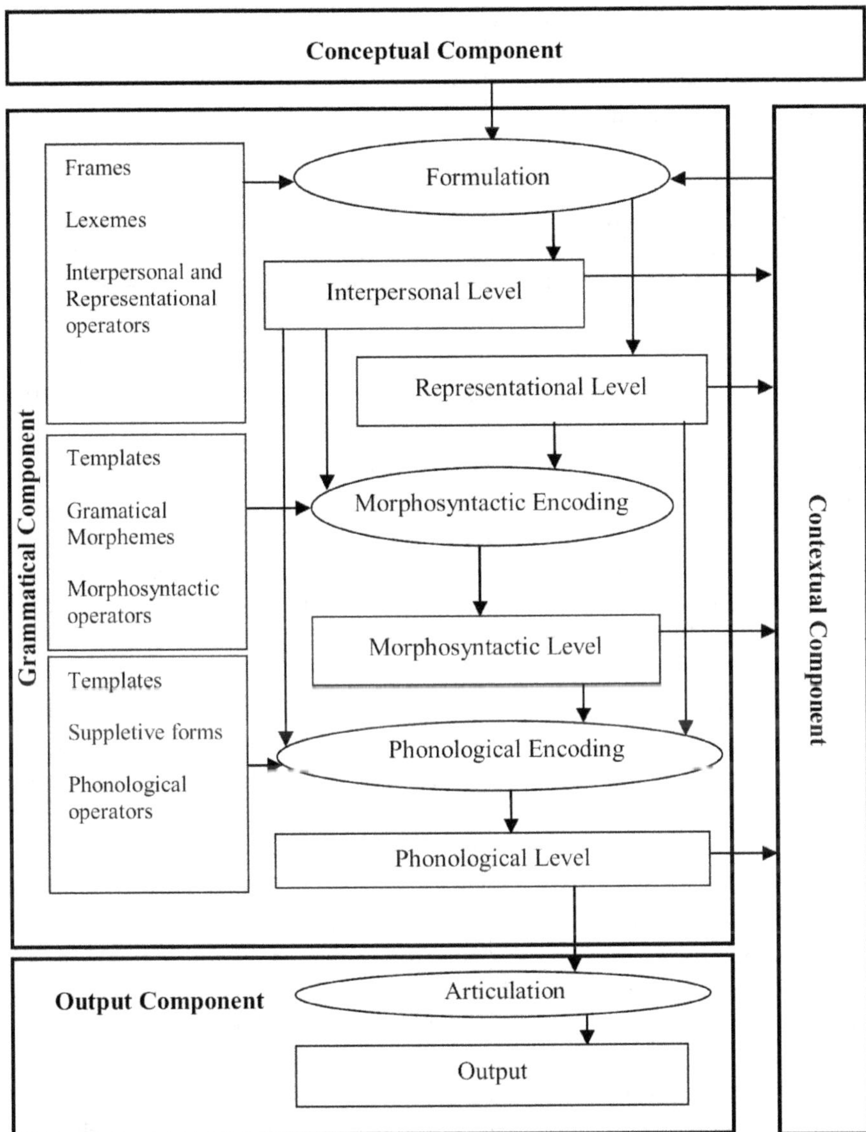

Figure 5.1. General layout of FDG (Hengeveld and Mackenzie 2008: 13)

A third important difference between FG and FDG is the introduction of a number of components adjacent to the grammar module. Hengeveld and Mackenzie (2008: 6) characterize FDG as the Grammatical Component of a wider theory of verbal interaction which also comprises a Conceptual, a Contextual and an Output component. The Conceptual component is described as follows:

> The Conceptual component is responsible for the development of both a communicative intention relevant for the current speech event and the associated conceptualizations with respect to relevant extra-linguistic events. (Hengeveld and Mackenzie, 2008: 6)

Hengeveld and Mackenzie do not go into the structure of the conceptual component, but they claim that it includes those aspects of cognition which are relevant for the immediate communicative intention. In §1, I assumed that the possibility of an alternating verb to be basically anticausative or causative relates to the speakers' ability to view the event it denotes as likely to occur spontaneously or not. I also accepted, following Haspelmath and also Levin and Rapapport Hovav, that this is a matter which depends on conceptual meaning or world knowledge. It thus seems adequate to assume that this choice is made in the conceptual component in FDG when a preverbal message is constructed.

Figure 5.1 also shows that FDG posits four levels of representation in the grammatical component: the Representational level, the Interpersonal level (both inherited from classical FG), as well as the Morphosyntactic level and the Phonological level. Finally, the ovals in the figure indicate stages in the procedure at which particular operations take place in the grammatical component. The process of **Formulation** translates a particular communicative intention into a pragmatic and a semantic representation at the Interpersonal and Representational Levels, respectively; the two **Encoding** stages indicate where morphosyntactic and phonological representations (in that order) are being generated. Each operation has its own set of primitives in the form of frames, templates and operators (among others). Although primitives are assumed to be language-specific (the lexemes of a language are perhaps the most obvious examples of language-specific primitives), FDG aims at discovering significant cross-linguistic generalizations and hierarchies, which can predict the number and type of frames and templates that a language employs on the basis of a limited set of parameters.

One aspect of the model which is of particular relevance here is the fact that lexemes are separated from the frames in which they occur and the classical notion of predicate frame is dispensed with. This proposal, which is to be found in García Velasco and Hengeveld (2002), was justified by the authors on psychological, pragmatic and typological grounds. In that paper, it was argued that lexemes are linked to **predication frames** through linking rules mediated by abstract meaning definitions (see Hengeveld and Mackenzie 2008: 207 for an update on predication frames).

An elaboration of this proposal is to be found in Butler (unpublished), who, on the basis of definition (21a), proposes the predication frame in (21b) for the lexeme *open* in its transitive use:

(21) (a) $[f_1$: [CAUSE (x_1) [BECOME **open'** $(x_2)]]]$
(b) $(\pi\ e_1: (f_1: [(f_2)\ (x_1)_{Ag}\ (x_2)_{Pat}]\ (f_1))\ (e_1))$

Significantly, García Velasco and Hengeveld (2002) made no claim as to whether the transitive variant is derived from the intransitive or the other way round, as the authors simply assume that the lexeme *open* is attached to two different definitions. Thus, the problem of directionality is not solved.

Hengeveld and Mackenzie (2008) update the representational level and the role of frames and lexemes in the theory. In their discussion on part-of-speech systems (2008: 217; 400), the authors draw a distinction between **lexeme classes**, a notion relevant at the Representational Level, and **word classes**, which are relevant at the Morphosyntactic Level. The distinction is needed, they argue, because there is not a one-to-one relation between the two classes. This is illustrated with the compound form *sword-swallower*, which is formed by the combination of a verbal and a nominal lexeme (Hengeveld and Mackenzie 2008: 217):

(22) $(x_i: (f_i: [(f_j: \text{swallow}_V\ (f_j))\ (x_i)_A\ (x_j: \text{-sword}_N\text{-}\ (x_j))_U]\ (f_i))\ (x_i))$

At the Morphosyntactic level, the compound is processed as a Noun and the affixal unit *er* is added.[2]

(23) $(Nw_i: [(Ns_j: \text{sword}\ (Ns_j))\ (Vs_j: \text{swallow}\ (Vs_j))\ (Aff_i: \text{er}\ (Aff_i))]\ (Nw_i))$

Another reason to distinguish lexemes from words is the fact that units which constitute just one lexeme at the Representational Level, may consist of several words at the Morphosyntactic Level. This is the case of idioms like *kick the bucket,* which are said to constitute just one semantic unit as its meaning is not constructed compositionally. Also, languages with a flexible part-of-speech system, that is, those languages which can systematically use the same lexeme for several syntactic functions (see e.g. Hengeveld and Rijkhoff 2005) are claimed to have no lexeme classes but they do have word classes. Finally, grammatical words are examples of units relevant at the morphosyntactic level with no corresponding lexeme at the representational level.

Given the distinction between words and lexemes, an obvious question which arises itself is the place of derivational morphology in the model. In line with the distinction between words and lexemes the authors defend a parallel distinction between morphological processes that produce words and those that produce lexemes. The former are characterized as "morphosyntactic processes that can be interpreted as means to adapt the class of a lexeme in such a way that the resulting word can be used appropriately in the grammatical environment in which it occurs" (Hengeveld and Mackenzie 2008: 218). In other words, word-forming processes merely adapt a lexeme to a different syntactic use by inserting it into a semantic slot "it was not designed to occupy" (2008: 229). Those processes which contribute aspects of meaning to the resulting unit are treated as instances of lexeme derivation. Hence, it might seem that the main reason to distinguish types of derivational processes is whether they contribute meaning to the new form. However, albeit indirectly, the authors also show that the formal impact of the process is crucial to understand its syntactic or semantic (representational) nature. Thus, they compare the formal differences in the causative/inchoative alternation between English and Turkish (Hengeveld and Mackenzie 2008: 403):

(24) Hasan kapı-yı kapa-dı
Hasan door-ACC close-PST
"Hasan closed the door."

(25) Kapı kapa-n-dı
door close-INTR-PST
"The door closed."

Following the formal criterion to establish the directionality of the process (see §1), the authors assume that the Turkish verb *kapa* is intrinsically transitive and is detransitivized by being inserted into an intransitive predication frame. The intransitive marker *n* would thus be the formal spell-out of such a process. Similarly, the derivation of causative verbs from adjectives in English is treated as a syntactic rather than as a lexical process and is assumed to result from the insertion of an adjectival lexeme into a transitive predication frame. Hengeveld and Mackenzie (2008: 413) offer the following example:

(26) They Americanized Belgium.

Seen this way, the affix *ize* is again the spell-out of the causativization process. However, there are several problems with both the criterion of semantic contribution and formal impact as used by Hengeveld and Mackenzie. First of all, derivational affixes do contribute meaning to the word they form. In fact, the causative component identified in the alternation is provided by the affixes *ize*, *ify* and *en* in many alternating verbs, which also license the presence of an agent or causer entity. In other cases, the meaning contribution of derivational affixes is so obvious to the native speaker that they can sometimes be used as lexemes themselves:

(27) I hate all *isms* and *ologies*.

If affixes such as *ism* and *ology* are mere spell-outs of syntactic processes it is surprising that speakers can attribute meaning to them and use them as common nouns. Also, derivational affixes usually produce semantic effects in the output forms; take, for example, the case of *-er*, which does not only denote individuals who can perform the verbal action, as would be expected if it were a mere inflectional marker, but, typically, those who do so professionally (*singer, writer*) or frequently (*drinker, reader*).

Note, furthermore, that assuming that derivational affixes are mere spell-outs of the insertion of lexemes in unusual syntactic frames would entail that a new frame would be needed for each affix. Thus, given the fact that affixation is a recursive process, a complex item such as *organizational*, which contains three suffixes, should be inserted in as many syntactic frames. This is a rather inefficient solution. It would thus seem more appropriate to include meaningful affixes in the set of primitives of the theory.

But apart from the theoretical problems, the relevance conferred on the formal impact is also inadequate. Hengeveld and Mackenzie's analysis would imply the establishment of a distinction in the treatment of directed and non-directed alternations, given the fact that only in the first case can one be sure of the direction of the alternation. The question is obviously how to treat non-directed alternations. Hengeveld and Mackenzie seem to suggest that labile verbs in English are both naturally transitive and intransitive. One is tempted to believe, then, that they would opt for each variant to have its own definition. While this is a possible solution, it is obviously inconsistent with the fact that both uses tend to be perceived by native speakers as variants of the same unit and, second, it does not capture the important generalization that many verbs in English have the same property.

Moreover, consider the problem this poses for the analysis of equipollent verbs. In this case, the same stem receives different affixes, one for each use. The affixes therefore cannot be seen as the result of the insertion of the stem in a slot it was not meant to occupy. One could argue that both forms should appear in the lexeme inventory, each associated with a corresponding definition, but then, the same problem as in labile alternations would obtain.

The solution to this puzzle, in my view, would entail the assumption that, as Haspelmath (1993: 90) claims, "variation in the direction of formal derivation can generally be seen as the manifestation of indeterminacy of the conceptual-semantic relation". In other words, the diversity of formal manifestations in the alternation is the consequence of the vagueness of lexical meaning. In García Velasco (2009) I argued that this meaning indeterminacy is behind the process of conversion in English, which I compared with the putative elasticity of lexemes in flexible languages (see Hengeveld 1992). Flexible languages such as Mundari are assumed to have no lexeme classes; thus, the same lexeme may be used predicatively or referentially as long as it is inserted in the required frame. In García Velasco (2009) I claimed that the same analysis can be provided for the process of conversion in English, which allows a given lexeme to be used in several functions. In that paper, I defended the view that conversion is different from affixation and should not be considered affixation without affixes (i.e. zero-derivation). As Bauer and Huddleston (2002: 1641) claim, in standard affixation different affixes produce diverse semantic effects on the input bases. As conversion also produces numerous distinct semantic effects on bases, we should accordingly assume the existence of numerous "zero-affixes" whose identification and description would be rather difficult, if possible at all. Furthermore, Plag (2003) and Lieber (2004) have noted that the semantic range exhibited by conversion to verbs in English is wider than that exhibited by the verb-forming suffixes *–ize* and *–ify*. This leads Lieber (2004: 94) to claim that "verbal conversion simply does not behave semantically like derivation with *–ize, –ify* or any other verb-forming affix".

Note that in García Velasco and Hengeveld's (2002) proposal, flexible lexemes in the languages that have them were inserted in predication frames as needed. This idea is also adopted in Hengeveld and Mackenzie (2008: 296), but with a significant difference: the addition of the Morphosyntactic Level now allows the insertion of flexible lexemes in a word template, as the language is assumed to have word classes, but to lack lexeme classes. Adapting my analysis of conversion in English to this new proposal, one could say that a lexeme such as *fine* (in its penalty sense) appears in the lexicon without a category label and can be inserted in a nominal or verbal template in morphosyntax. Thus, I would argue, English presents a mixed lexicon in which a significant number of lexemes show the same type of semantic flexibility which is rampant in languages of the Mundari type. In the following section I will try to extend this analysis to causative/inchoative pairs.

4 The causative/inchoative alternation as lexeme flexibility

English is particularly generous in the use of lexical items in functions which would correspond to distinct word classes in other languages. Thus, a lexical item such as *fax* can be used both as a noun as in *I received a document by fax*, or as a verb as in *He faxed me the document*, a process which has traditionally been known as conversion or zero-derivation in morphological theory. However, the status of verbal alternations has been subject to a certain degree of controversy among morphologists (Portero Muñoz, this volume). For those who view word-class shift as the essence of the process, this type does not really qualify as conversion (e.g. Bauer 1983; Bauer and Huddleston 2002). Quirk *et al.* (1985: 1563–1565) speak of **change of secondary word class**, a process which involves syntactic or semantic alternations within the same category and cite verbal transitivity alternations as an example. However, the issue is not entirely clear. Consider the following quote by Haspelmath:

> The English alternations are not usually discussed under the heading of morphology, but there is really no deep reason why they should not. Morphological operations need not be associated with a particular change in the pronunciation [...] When they are not, morphologists speak of conversion, and, while this term is mostly applied to uncoded word-class-changing operations, it could easily be transferred to uncoded valence-changing operations. (2002: 219)

If, as I argued in García Velasco (2009), conversion in English can be seen as an indication that English is moving towards a more flexible lexicon, it seems worth considering whether the causative/inchoative use of certain verbal lexemes is also an illustration of that process. As several authors have noted (Bauer 1983: 227; Vogel 2000: 266) the loss of morphological markers in the English language may be connected with the possibility of using lexemes in different functions. Vogel even goes as far as to suggest that Modern English has two overlapping part-of-speech systems, a flexible one and a rigid one, since the language still retains significant aspects of its inflectional morphology. Now, as mentioned earlier, Haspelmath also attributes the exceptional preference for labile alternations to the fact that English has little morphology in general. Significantly, languages with a flexible part-of-speech system show what Hengeveld and Rijkhoff (2005: 425) call **formal integrity**, that is, the lexemes of the language should "be formally independent of morphological material specific to a certain syntactic slot" and "are therefore not expected to show morphologically conditioned stem alternation". This is understandable, for if a lexeme is to be used in different syntactic functions it should not be morphologically restricted in its applicability to those different functions. Similarly, the authors argue that flexible word classes are not expected to show morphological or semantic subclasses since this again would restrict the potential applicability of lexemes to different functions. In particular, they argue that lexemes in Mundari cannot be subdivided into transitive or intransitive. In other words, it is possible to see non-directed alternations as connected with the flexibility of part of the English lexicon.

However, unlike fully flexible lexemes, causative/inchoative pairs can only function in predicative use and do not alter their denotation type. I would like to account for this difference by claiming that alternating lexemes such as *open* appear in the lexicon with an ontological label in their meaning definition (cf. Honselaar and Keizer 2009). They are inserted at the Representational Level in a transitive or intransitive predication frame and in a verbal word template at the Morphosyntactic Level. This would give us the possibilities shown in Table 5.2 for flexible lexemes and verbs with alternating valence.

Table 5.2. Alternating verbs and flexible lexemes

	Lexeme class	*Word Class*
Flexible lexemes	Contentive	Nominal/Verbal/Adjectival
Inchoative/causative	Event-denoting	Verbal

The difference between a flexible lexeme (contentive) and an alternating verb resides in their semantics. Whereas flexible lexemes present a rather vague meaning and, in particular, are not specified for the type of ontological category they designate, alternating verbs denote events whose basic meaning is fixed but they allow for differences in the number of participants they take and their semantic contribution. This entails that lexical meaning cannot be simply based on definitions constructed on the basis of a fixed number of necessary and sufficient features which all competent speakers of a language should possess, but on meaning specifications which can be adapted or restricted in a given context (see García Velasco 2007 for discussion). An elaboration of this idea is to be found in Allwood's (2003) notion of **meaning potential** (see also Evan's 2006 **semantic potential**). Allwood maintains that a word's meaning potential contains "all the information that the word has been used to convey either by a single individual or, on the social level, by the language community". The author argues that the interaction of the meaning potential with the linguistic and extralinguistic context determines which part of the meaning potential is activated. For example, the word *heavy* as used in *a heavy question* and *a heavy stone* receives different interpretations (difficult and weighty, respectively) on the basis of the conditions activated in its meaning potential by the modified nouns. Thus, one could argue that the insertion of a flexible lexeme in a predication frame is the first step in the process of restricting the item's meaning potential. Frames contain variables indicating the ontological category of the denoted entity, plus a number of argument positions and semantic functions. Thus, the event-denoting use of the item *fine* is accounted for once it is inserted in an eventive frame, whereas its thing-denoting use is tied to its insertion in a first-order entity frame. Causative/inchoative verbs follow a similar derivation, but since they are characterized in the lexicon as event-denoting items, they can only select for an eventive frame. As long as the event can be construed as occurring spontaneously or not, the event selected will be causative transitive, inchoative intransitive or both.

Thus, the lexical concept *open* might be linked to, at least, the following pieces of information:[3]

(28) *Open*:
  (a) Opening is an event.
  (b) By opening somebody allows entrance of something.
  (c) People open doors to enter buildings or rooms.
  (d) Entities can open spontaneously.
  etc.

Specification (a) guarantees that *open* is characterized in the lexicon as an event-denoting item, which will most naturally guide the selection of an eventive frame in the representational level. Speakers should also have an intuition about the number of participants typically involved in the bringing about of the event (28b–c). Finally, the event is characterized as likely to occur spontaneously, which accounts for its inchoative use. The fact that participants will be coded as agents, patients or processed entities is represented in the grammar of the relevant languages through the inventory of frames and need not be included in (28). All that is needed is a representation of the action of "opening" either in propositional format as in (28) or in referential format (i.e. images, 3D representations, etc.). As indicated by Haspelmath (1993) the existence of formal markers in causative or anticausative alternations will be a direct reflection of the possibility for a given event to be characterized as likely to occur spontaneously or not. This should be reflected in the meaning specifications of each lexeme, as shown in (28d).

5 Conclusion

In this article, I have shown that a proper account of the causative/inchoative alternation in English and other languages should pay crucial attention to the way events are conceptually constructed by speakers. I have also shown that the introduction of a conceptual component in FDG provides a natural locus to represent such a proposal. From a technical point of view, the separation of lexemes from frames and the introduction of morphosyntactic templates give a number of different possibilities to account for the relations between lexemes and the syntactic environments in which they occur. Following previous proposals of mine, I have argued that the causative/inchoative alternation should be seen as a consequence of the move towards a more flexible lexicon in the English language and alternating verbs as lexemes which can be inserted in transitive or intransitive frames if the meaning specifications in their lexical entries so permit.

Notes

* I would like to thank Chris Butler and Pilar Guerrero for useful comments on a previous version of this article. All errors that may remain in the text are my sole responsibility.

1. Alternatively, the name "ergative alternation" has also been employed to highlight the parallelism with languages with an ergative/absolutive case marking system (see Davidse, this volume).
2. A similar treatment is proposed for adverbs in *-ly* in the English language.
3. I would not like to claim that all the pieces of information that may be linked to the different actions and events of "opening" (see Evans 2009: 9ff. for discussion) belong in the meaning of the lexeme *open*. The fact that lexemes may point to a very complex body of general knowledge which may be activated in the production and comprehension of the expressions in which they are used does not mean that one cannot identify a central core meaning for a lexeme. Following Marconi (1997), I argued in García Velasco (2007) that central specifications are those perceived by speakers as constitutive of normal competence, and it is those that constitute the definition of a lexical item under a functional view of language.

References

Allwood, J. (2003) Meaning potentials and context: Some consequences for the analysis of variation in meaning. In H. Cuykens, R. Dirven and J. Taylor (eds) *Cognitive Approaches to Lexical Semantics* 9–65. Berlin: Mouton de Gruyter.

Bauer, L. (1983) *English Word-formation.* Cambridge: Cambridge University Press.

Bauer, L. and Huddleston, R. (2002) Lexical word-formation. In R. Huddleston and G. K. Pullum (eds) *The Cambridge Grammar of the English Language* 1621–1721. Cambridge: Cambridge University Press.

Bowerman, M. and Croft, W. (2008) The acquisition of the English causative alternation. In M. Bowerman and P. Brown (eds) *Crosslinguistic Perspectives on Argument Structure: Implications for learnability* 279–309. New York: Lawrence Erlbaum Associates.

Butler, C. S. (unpublished ms.) From conceptualisation to morphosyntax in a cognitively-adequate FDG: The role of predication frames.

Davidse, K. (this volume) Alternations as a heuristic to verb meaning and the semantics of constructions.

Dik, S. C. (1980) *Studies in Functional Grammar.* London. Academic Press.

Dik, S. C. (1997) *The Theory of Functional Grammar, Part I: The structure of the clause.* (Second revised edition.) Ed. K. Hengeveld. Berlin: Mouton de Gruyter.

Evans, V. (2009) *How Words Mean.* Oxford: Oxford University Press.

García Velasco, D. (2007) Lexical competence and Functional Discourse Grammar. *Alfa. Revista de Lingüística* 51(2): 165–187.

García Velasco, D. (2009) Conversion in English and its implications for Functional Discourse Grammar. *Lingua* 19: 1164–1185.

García Velasco, D. and Hengeveld, K. (2002) Do we need predicate frames? In R. Mairal Usón and M. J. Pérez Quintero (eds) *New Perspectives on Argument Structure in Functional Grammar* 95–123. Berlin: Mouton de Gruyter.

Haspelmath, M. (1993) More on the typology of the inchoative/causative verb alternations. In B. Comrie (ed.) *Causatives and Transitivity* 87–120. Amsterdam: Benjamins.

Haspelmath, M. (2002) *Understanding Morphology.* London: Arnold.

Hengeveld, K. (1992) Parts of speech. In M. Fortescue, P. Harder and L. Kristoffersen (eds) *Layered Structure and Reference in a Functional Perspective* 29–55. Amsterdam: Benjamins.

Hengeveld, K. and Rijkhoff, J. (2005) Mundari as a flexible language. *Linguistic Typology* 9: 406–431.

Hengeveld, K. and Mackenzie, J. L. (2008) *Functional Discourse Grammar.* Oxford: Oxford University Press.

Honselaar, W. and Keizer, E. (2009) A Functional Discourse Grammar account of set nouns in Dutch and its implications for lexicography. *International Journal of Lexicography* 22(4): 361–397.

Jespersen, O. (1927) *A Modern English Grammar on Historical Principles. Part III.* London: George Allen and Unwin.

Kahrel, P. (1985) Some aspects of derived intransitivity. *Working Papers in Functional Grammar* 4.

Kilby, D. (1984) *Descriptive Syntax and the English Verb.* London: Croom Helm.

Levelt, W. J. M. (1989) *Speaking: From intention to articulation.* Cambridge, MA: The MIT Press.

Levin, B. (1993) *English Verb Classes and Alternations: A preliminary investigation.* Chicago, IL: University of Chicago Press.

Levin, B. and Rappaport Hovav, M. (1994) A preliminary analysis of causative verbs in English. *Lingua* 92: 35–72.

Lieber, R. (2004) *Morphology and Lexical Semantics.* Cambridge: Cambridge University Press.

Marconi, D. (1997) *Lexical Competence.* Cambridge, MA: The MIT Press.

Plag, I. (2003) *Word-formation in English.* Cambridge: Cambridge University Press.

Portero Muñoz, C. (this volume) A Functional Discourse Grammar approach to the *Swarm*-alternation as a case of conversion.

Quirk, R., Greenbaum, S., Leech, G. and Svartvik, J. (1985) *A Comprehensive Grammar of the English Language.* London: Longman.

Ruiz de Mendoza Ibáñez, F. J. and Mairal Usón, R. (this volume) Constraints on syntactic alternation: Lexical-constructional subsumption in the Lexical-Constructional Model.

Schack-Rasmussen, L. (1994) Semantic functions in perspective – reconsidering meaning definitions. In E. Engberg-Pedersen, L. Falster Jacobsen and L. Schack Rasmussen (eds) *Function and Expression in Functional Grammar* 41–63. Berlin: Mouton de Gruyter.

Siewierska, A. (1991) *Functional Grammar.* London: Routledge.

Van Valin, R. D. and Lapolla, R. J. (1997) *Syntax: Structure, meaning and function.* Cambridge: Cambridge University Press.

Vogel, P. M. (2000) Grammaticalisation and part-of-speech systems. In P. M. Vogel and B. Comrie (eds) *Approaches to the Typology of Word Classes* 259–284. Berlin: Mouton de Gruyter.

6 Spontaneous and facilitative events revisited

Juana I. Marín-Arrese[a]

1 Introduction

Spontaneous and facilitative situation types (Kemmer 1993) are linguistically coded by thematic-subject constructions (Langacker 1991) – inchoative (*The vase broke*) and middle (*Crystal vases break easily*). The inchoative and the middle have been considered related but distinct constructions, differing syntactically and semantically (Keyser and Roeper 1984; Fagan 1992, *inter alia*). However, the difference between these constructions may be a matter of degree, as the existence of "blends" seems to point to (Davidse 1992). With regard to "blends" and other non-prototypical phenomena, this paper posits a fuzzy middle area involving the following features: distinctness of participants, source of energy input, degree of control of the *theme* participant,[1] and de-actualization (Marín-Arrese 2003).

The discussion in most of the literature has centred on the basic vs. derived nature of inchoative verbs and the direction of the derivation (Comrie 1981; Haspelmath 1993; Levin 1993; Levin and Rappaport Hovav 1995). The inchoative construction has commonly been assumed to derive from the transitive causative via deletion of the causing subevent (CAUSE operator + causer argument) (Grimshaw 1982). Non-derivational proposals tend to consider causative/inchoative verb pairs as distinct lexical items with related meanings (Næss 2007). This paper posits a non-derivational analysis, based on the notions of construal and profiling (Langacker 1991, 2000). It is also argued that the inchoative construction denotes an event that occurs spontaneously, though this does not preclude the construal of the event as involving some covert external cause, however abstract or

a Juana I. Marín-Arrese is Full Professor of English Linguistics at the Universidad Complutense of Madrid. E-mail: juana@filol.ucm.es schematic it may be (Langacker 1991; Marín-Arrese 2003; Næss 2007; Koontz-Garboden 2009).

In the case of the middle construction it has been claimed that the role of the external agent is irrelevant (van Oosten 1986). Following Langacker (1991), it will be here assumed that a "potential" and unspecified agent is definitely implied, since the construction evokes the way in which the efforts of this virtual agent are facilitated or hindered by the inherent properties of the thematic subject. The existence of middles with non-patient subjects and the occurrence of the middle construction with basic intransitives, where the subject designates a location or setting, will also be discussed (van Oosten 1986; Yoshimura 1998). It will be argued that these non-prototypical instances involve motivated extensions resulting from resemblance relations to the prototype (Marín-Arrese 2003).

This paper aims to: (a) examine the prototypical features of inchoative and middle constructions; (b) examine the relationship between inchoatives and middles, and explain the occurrence of blends of the two constructions; and (c) provide an explanation for the occurrence of the middle construction with instrument, means or locative entities as subjects, and of middles with inherently intransitive predicates.

The paper is organized as follows: §2 describes spontaneous and facilitative events in English and Spanish (Kemmer 1993, 1994); §3 examines the characterizing features of the inchoative and middle constructions, and also discusses non-prototypical middles; §4 presents a proposal for the prototypical characterization of the inchoative and middle and explains the meaning relations between these constructions, and with other constructions of reduced transitivity. The final section presents the concluding remarks.

2 Spontaneous and facilitative events and constructions of reduced transitivity

This section focuses on spontaneous and facilitative situation types, and briefly describes the role of the inchoative and middle constructions coding these types of events within the systems of transitivity and ergativity.

2.1 Spontaneous and facilitative situation types and the middle domain

Kemmer (1994: 206) argues that a crucial property of transitivity and middle semantics is that of the *relative distinguishability of participants*. She observes that a transitive event may be characterized schematically as a two-participant event involving an Initiator (an Agent or some other analogue) and an Endpoint participant (Patient or some analogous entity) in some asymmetric interaction or relation. Within the middle domain, the reflexive situation type evokes an event where the Initiating and Endpoint roles are filled by the same entity. The reflexive marker thus signals the fact that the two semantic roles are conflated in a single participant. The middle marker, according to Kemmer (1994: 207), has "the basic function of indicating that the two semantic roles of Initiator and Endpoint refer to a single holistic entity without conceptually distinguished aspects". Spontaneous events are semantically middle since the Endpoint participant may also be conceptualized as an Initiator. In the case of facilitative events, Kemmer (1993: 147) points out that "the Initiator status of the Patient, unlike in the case of spontaneous events, derives from the fact that the event is conceived of as proceeding from the Patient by virtue of an inherent characteristic of that entity which enables the event to take place".

Spontaneous events characteristically involve a change of state or location. Many of these events are *intrinsically spontaneous*, that is, they are construed as occurring without the direct initiation of an external cause, but rather as internally induced. This is the case of physiological processes (*die, morir/morirse*), change of position or location (*fall, caer/caerse*), events involving non-translational motion (*spin, girar*), visual perception (*shine, brillar*), existential change/denaturement (*appear, aparecer/aparecerse*). There are situations, however, which might be termed *non-intrinsically spontaneous events*, in that the theme participant is construed as exerting a certain degree of control over the change-of-state, but at the same time the event invokes some covert external cause (agent, instrument, natural force or circumstance). These involve physico-chemical changes (*freeze, congelarse*), events of partial or global disruption (*break, romperse*), and change of position or location (*sink, hundirse*), and psychological change (*sadden, entristecerse*) (for a detailed classification, see Kemmer 1993: 269–270) [my examples in Spanish].

Non-intrinsically spontaneous events are coded by the inchoative construction, as in (1a), and facilitative events are coded by the middle construction, as in (1b).

(1) (a) The vase broke.
(b) Wholemeal bread cuts easily.

In English, the same verb form is found in both the transitive construction (2a) and the inchoative (2b). Intrinsically spontaneous events (2c) are designated by the unmarked intransitive construction with "initially unaccusative" verbs (Perlmutter 1978).

(2) (a) John opened the door.
(b) The door opened.
(c) Snow fell on the roofs.

Spanish has a one-form middle system where the reflexive marker is morphologically identical to the middle marker (MM) *se*. The MM *se* is found in the inchoative construction designating non-intrinsically spontaneous events and the middle construction designating facilitative events, and also in related situation types such as the passive middle and the impersonal (Gómez Torrego 1992; Marín-Arrese 1993, 2003; Maldonado 1999).

(3) (a)

El	jarrón	*se*	rompió.
the	vase	MM	break.PST

"The vase broke".

(b)

El	pan	integral	*se*	corta	con	facilidad.
the	bread	whole	MM	cut.PRS	with	ease

"Wholemeal bread cuts easily".

Intrinsically spontaneous events tend to receive no marking, but they may take the MM *se*, in cases where they receive a force-dynamic construal (Maldonado 1988). Langacker (1991: 390–391) makes the point that the MM *se* "derives an energetic, thematic-subject verb in either of two ways: from a transitive stem, by defocusing the initial portions of an action chain [as in (3a)]; or from an intransitive stem, by imposing a force-dynamic interpretation on an event whose construal would otherwise be absolute", as in (4b).

(4) (a)

La	nieve	cayó	sobre	los	tejados.
the	snow	fall.PST	on	the	roofs

"The snow fell on the roofs".

(b)

El	niño	*se*	cayó	de	la	cuna.
the	little.boy	MM	fall.PST	of	the	cot

"The little boy fell from the cot".

The inchoative and the middle constructions differ from the transitive construction in the extent of their participant distinctiveness, that is, the conceptual distinction of entities into separate participants (agent vs. patient), or the relative salience of these entities with respect to each other and from their background (Langacker 1991; Kemmer 1993). This requirement of participant distinctness is similarly pointed out by Næss (2007), who argues for the need to describe distinctness in terms of the semantic specifications of the roles played by the participants in the event. The properties characterizing the semantic relation "agent" are Volitionality and Instigation, and that of the "patient" is Affectedness. A prototypical agent is thus defined in terms of the following feature configuration as [+VOL, +INST, –AFF], and a patient as [–VOL, –INST, +AFF]. However, as Næss (2007: 46) predicts, an argument may show other configurations of feature specifications, having a "mixed" role, and so "combine properties typically associated with agents and with patients". This is the case of the single (S) argument in the inchoative and middle constructions, which can be defined by the following feature specifications: S inchoative [–VOL, +INST, +AFF], S middle [–VOL, –INST(+FACIL), +AFF].

2.2 Event conception and transitivity alternations

The role of the inchoative and the middle constructions within the system of transitivity and intransitivity in English has been characterized by García de la Maza (2008: 39) in terms of the relationships between transitive and intransitive constructions available in the language and the types of verbs involved. Thus, "pure" transitive agentive verbs, such as the *cut*-class, may be found in the transitive construction (*Mary cut the bread*) and in the intransitive middle construction (*The bread cuts easily*). Unergative verbs, such as *laugh* or *walk* (Perlmutter 1978), are typically found in the unmarked intransitive construction (*The dog walks*), with a single agent argument, coding internally caused volitional events. A corresponding transitive causative construction is also available with a Causer argument as subject and a Causee/Actor as object (*I walk the dog*). Non-alternating unaccusatives, such as *appear, die, shine* (Perlmutter 1978), are only found in the unmarked intransitive construction (*The light glittered on the water*), coding intrinsically spontaneous events. Finally, alternating unaccusatives or "ergatives" are found in the transitive (*I broke the jar*), and in the intransitive inchoative construction (*The jar broke*), and also in the middle (*Crystal jars break easily*).

This characterization, however, does not account for the different participation of the *break*-class and *cut*-class of verbs (cf. Fillmore 1967) in constructions of reduced transitivity. Langacker (1991) observes that in explaining clause structure both a force-dynamic perspective and the notion of A/D organization must be taken into account, since each affords a relevant perspective on the conception of a complex event. These two distinct ways of describing the structure of our conception of events are: (a) the notion of an action chain, which is based on the billiard-ball cognitive model, where there is a transfer of energy from one object to another as they come into contact; and (b) the notion of A/D organization, which involves the distinction between conceptually autonomous (A) and conceptually dependent (D) event components, and where the conceptually autonomous thematic relationship constitutes the core of the event.

In a complex event involving causation, as Langacker (1991: 287) notes, A/D asymmetry among the components of the event is manifested in the possibility of conceptualizing the change-of-state component as occurring autonomously and designating it by means of an intransitive construction (b). In contrast, the causation component, in (c), is conceptually dependent and does not allow independent coding.

(5) (a) The wind caused the tree to fall over.
(b) The tree fell over.
(c) *The wind caused.

This fact leads to the conclusion that "what constitutes the innermost layer" of the conception of an event, the nucleus of an event, is "a comparatively simple, conceptually autonomous relationship involving just a single participant". Langacker (1991) refers to this relationship as a single-participant thematic relationship, and uses the term *theme* to refer schematically to the role of the single participant involved (see note 1).

There is thus a linguistic contrast between a conceptually autonomous event, and a complex event involving external causation. Langacker (1991: 290) notes that the intransitive verb stems in (6a) "incorporate both a change-of-state thematic relationship and a conception of the energy most immediately responsible for it", and that the transitive stems in (6b) arise when the conception of the thematic relationship "is expanded to include an input of energy that induces the change-of-state". Langacker (1991: 291) also notes that in cases where the thematic relationship occurs independently and corresponds to the full conception evoked by the verb, as in (6c), "its construal is *absolute*".

(6) (a) My balloon {burst/broke/popped}.
(b) Jason {burst/broke/popped} my balloon.
(c) The tree fell over.

In terms of A/D organization, the inchoative construction in (7a) below describes the conceptually autonomous nucleus of the event: a thematic relationship (T) in which a theme undergoes a change of state. This thematic relationship may be expanded to include a dependent layer of causation, in which an additional participant supplies the input of energy (E), as in (7b), which represents a higher-order structure (E_1(T)), and so on recursively: **(T) > (E_1(T)) > (E_2(E_1(T))) > (E_3(E_2(E_1(T)))) > ...** (Langacker 1991: 292).

(7) (a) The ice cracked. **(T)** (ice cracked)
(b) A rock cracked the ice. **(E_1(T))** (rock → (ice crack))
(c) A waiter cracked the ice with a rock. **(E_2(E_1(T)))** (waiter→(rock→(ice rack)))

From the perspective of an action chain model, the flow of energy proceeds "from the initial *energy source* [agent or cause] to the ultimate *energy sink* (i.e. the theme)" (Langacker 1991: 292). These alternative paths in the flow of energy have different starting points: in the case of the action chain, the head is the energy source (agent or cause), whereas in A/D alignment the thematic relationship (patient or theme) constitutes the starting point. There is thus, an inherent tension between these two paths, as Langacker (1991: 293) notes, and between the two cognitively salient starting point participants which "instantiate the archetypal roles of agent and patient".

From a functionalist perspective, Davidse (1998: 101–103) similarly argues for the distinction between a transitive and an ergative paradigm. The former represents an "action" model, where the nucleus is constituted by the "Actor-process unit", and where the action may extend onto a Goal participant in a transitive clause configuration ("transitive effective"), but where the Goal "does not co-participate in the action effected". The ergative paradigm is based on a "causation" model with a "Medium-process unit" as the nucleus, where the "Medium crucially co-participates" in the effective event ("ergative effective"), which is externally instigated by the Instigator participant. This distinction between the Goal and the Medium neatly accounts for the behaviour of the inchoative and middle constructions in selecting for the *break*-class and *cut*-class of verbs. On the basis of the above distinctions regarding the conception of events between an action chain model and A/D organization (Langacker 1991), and the transitive and ergative paradigms (Davidse 1998), a classification is proposed which captures the options and constraints on the verbs and constructions in these paradigms. The notations A, O, S are used to refer to participants

Table 6.1. Verbs and constructions in the transitivity and ergativity systems

Constructions	*Transitivity*	*Ergativity*
Transitive: A, O	*Mary cut the bread*	*I broke the jar.*
Inchoative: S(O)	**The bread cut*	*The jar broke.*
Middle: S(O)	*The bread cuts easily*	*The new door opens easily*
Intransitive: S(A) or S(O)	*The dog walks*	*The light glittered on the water.*
Absolutive: S(A)	*Mary is eating*	**Mary is breaking*
Causative: C_{er}, C_{ee}(A)	*I walk the dog*	**I glittered the light on the water.*

in two- and one-participant events respectively, not syntactic arguments, and C_{er} and C_{ee}(A) stand for Causer and Causee (Actor).

3 The inchoative and the middle constructions revisited

This section presents a characterization of the inchoative and the middle construction based on the notions of construal and profiling (Langacker 1991, 2000), and re-examines some of the features frequently attributed to these constructions.

3.1 Construal and profiling: Thematic-subject constructions

The meaning relation between the transitive and the inchoative or the middle construction may be explained in terms of profiling options. Langacker (2000: 6–7) notes that in addition to "the array of conceptual content" any expression invokes, it also "imposes a particular *profile*" on its conceptual *base*. When we designate all the event components of a complex transitive event, the complete action chain, the transfer of energy from agent (AG) to theme or mover (TH), is profiled, as in (8a). Example (8b) evokes the same action chain as its conceptual base, but profiles only the theme-instrument interaction (the profiling options for each sentence are signalled in bold) (adapted from Langacker 2000: 32).

(8) (a) Leona opened the door with this key.
(**AG** → **INSTR** → **TH**)

(b) This key opened the door.
(AG → **INSTR** → **TH**)

(c) The door opened suddenly.
(AG → INSTR → **TH**)

(d) This door opens easily.
(AG → INSTR → **TH** [>/<])

In the inchoative and the middle constructions, in (8c) and (8d), only the single-participant thematic relation is profiled. In the profiling of the middle, Langacker (1991: 334, Fig. 8.3) includes the specification of the hindrance (<) or facilitation (>) of the occurrence of the event due to the inherent characteristics of the theme.

As Langacker (1991: 334) notes, one might argue that any reference to an agent or cause component in the inchoative and the middle constructions is "extrinsic to the linguistic meaning of these expressions", as has been argued in derivational analyses of these constructions. However, he considers that it is "far more natural to suppose that these unprofiled participants are evoked (and figure in an expression's meaning) to varying degrees, depending on the example and the circumstances". In the middle and the inchoative, though the profile is limited to the thematic relation, the non-salient and unspecified agent is an unprofiled facet of the conceptual base, and is thus evoked. In the middle construction, Langacker (1991: 334) argues that "while the ease or difficulty of carrying out the action is attributed to inherent properties of the subject, it can only be assessed as easy or hard in relation to the capability of an actual or potential agent". Thus, the actual or potential "efforts of an unspecified agent are definitely implied", and the inherent characteristics of the thematic subject facilitates or hinders those efforts (Langacker 1991: 336). In the inchoative, however, "the implicit reference to an agent is non-salient and may be absent altogether (i.e. the construal of the profiled thematic process may be *absolute*)" (Langacker 1991: 336).

The difference in the evocation of agency or cause is brought out by the adverbs typically found in these constructions; while the middle accepts modifiers which evoke the efforts of an agent, the inchoative favours "pace" adverbials and those which foreground the feature of spontaneity of the event.

(9) (a) Dry mud scrapes off quite easily/effortlessly.
(b) The door opened slowly/suddenly/unexpectedly.

Under this account of the conception of complex events and the notion of profiling, the relation between the transitive and the inchoative or middle constructions in English does not require a derivational interpretation. These notions also explain in a natural way the effects observed in inchoative expressions which point to the presence of a cause component.

3.2 Spontaneous events and the inchoative construction

The predicates found in the inchoative construction can best be described as externally caused change-of-state (COS) verbs (Levin and Rappaport Hovav 1995). Levin (1993: 28–29) has identified the following main categories:

(i) Break Verbs: break, *romperse, ...*
(ii) Bend Verbs: bend, *doblarse, ...*
(iii) Roll Verbs: move, *moverse, ...*
(iv) Other Alternating Verbs of Change of State: open, *abrirse, ...*
(v) Amuse Type Psych Verbs: sadden, *entristecerse, ...*

3.2.1 Features of the inchoative construction

Verbs regularly taking the inchoative construction disallow the absolute construction, or indefinite object deletion (IOD) (Næss 2007). The inchoative construction designates events under specific time reference, and is thus compatible with the progressive. The theme participant (Subject/Medium) is construed as co-participating actively in the "ergative" process (Davidse 1992).

(10) (a) The glass broke.
(b) *Mary broke.
(c) The glass is breaking now.
(d) What the glass did was break.

3.2.2 Non-derivational analysis

It has been claimed that the inchoative derives from the transitive or lexical causative (Comrie 1981). In cross-linguistic terms, Haspelmath (1993) distinguishes three main types of derivation in the causative/inchoative verb pairs: causative derivation, where the inchoative pair is basic and the causative verb is derived (*rodar, hacer rodar*); anticausative derivation, in which the causative verb is basic and the inchoative is derived (*abrir, abrirse*); and non-directed alternation, one of which variants is the so-called labile alternation, with the same verb form in both causative and inchoative (*boil, boil; hervir, hervir*). With respect to the direction of derivation, Haspelmath (1993) notes that verbs designating events less likely to occur spontaneously (*close*) are lexicalized as basic causative verbs, and thus undergo the anticausative derivation to form the inchoative construction, while those events that are more likely to occur spontaneously are lexicalized as non-causative change-of-state verbs (*roll*) and will take part in the causative derivation.

Non-derivational arguments are put forward by Næss (2007: 145), who includes causative/inchoative verb pairs in a larger category of "ambitransitives" or verbs with both transitive and intransitive uses. Within this category we find two main types, S/O ambitransitives or inchoative-causative verb pairs, where "the single (S) argument of the intransitively used verb corresponds to the O of the transitive", and S/A ambitransitives, where the single (S) argument corresponds to the A of the transitive verb, which undergo indefinite object deletion. Næss (2007: 145) makes the point that whereas indefinite object deletion (IOD) in S/A pairs is primarily a syntactic phenomenon, "S/O ambitransitives are probably only characterisable as genuine verb pairs, that is, as two distinct lexical items with related meanings". These pairs have specific semantic properties: the transitive variant includes the semantic component of "causation of the event by an external agent", which is not present in the intransitive, and the intransitive variant "must denote an event which can be construed as occurring spontaneously", though it is "not necessarily incompatible with the interpretation that the event is externally caused". These semantic properties of the intransitive variant are consistent with Langacker's (1991) analysis of the relation between these verb "pairs" in terms of profiling, which posits both a non-derivational account and explains ambitransitivity without the need to characterize these verbs as two distinct lexical items.

3.2.3 Cause component

The inchoative construction has often been assumed to involve the deletion of the causing subevent (Grimshaw 1982, *inter alia*). Grimshaw's (1982: 103ff) inchoativization rule posits that the CAUSE operator and causer argument are deleted to derive the change-of-state inchoative predicate. Koontz-Garboden (2009), however, observes that since English does not display morphological derivation in the causative/inchoative alternation, any account of anticausativization should focus first and foremost on languages which formally manifest this phenomenon, such as Spanish. He argues that anticausatization should be treated as a reflexivization operation. This analysis would be congruent with the motivation for the extension of the reflexive marker to code anticausativization, which is so frequent cross-linguistically.

Under Koontz-Garboden's (2009: 86) reflexivization analysis, "the CAUSE operator is not removed. Rather the relation denoted by the causative verb is simply reflexivized so that the participants in both the causing and the caused eventualities are specified to be identical". However, it will be argued that rather than reflexivization, the MM *se* schematically denotes non-distinctness of Cause and Affected roles (Langacker and Munro 1975), so that the cause participant initiating the event is underspecified, but nonetheless evoked.

Another argument for the presence of a cause component in the inchoative construction is provided by the facts of negation. As Koontz-Garboden (2009) notes, there are some expressions where negation has scope over the BECOME operator, and others where the scope is over the CAUSE operator, which would entail the existence of the cause component in addition to the change-of-state component. In (11a), the change-of-state is negated, whereas (11b) and (11c) deny that the theme participant was also the initiator of the inchoative event, so that the initiation of the event is attributed to an external cause.

(11) (a) The vase fell, but did not break.
(b) The vase did not break, you broke it.
(c) The vase did not break by itself.

Since the inchoative evokes external causation, typically construed schematically, degree of spontaneity and control of the theme participant may be further specified by the presence of an anaphoric adverbial modifier "by itself" (= without outside help), which restricts the initiating cause to the antecedent subject NP, the theme, and cancels the evocation of some external cause.

(12) The door opened by itself.

This feature contrasts with the case of verbs describing "internally caused eventualities" (Levin and Rappaport Hovav 1995: 94), both unergatives, involving voluntary control of an agent (*laugh*), and unaccusatives, as in the case of existential changes (*appear, disappear*), and other intrinsically spontaneous events described above. In these cases, as Levin and Rappaport Hovav (1995) note, there is typically some property inherent to the argument of the verb which is responsible for the event, such as the emotional reaction of the agent, or change of state which is inherent to the natural course of development of the theme entity. These meanings disallow the use of the anaphoric adverbial modifier, since the notion of "without outside help" designated by the modifier would be redundant, as the event already evokes causal autonomy. Furthermore, since no external cause is evoked, the marked restriction of the causing element to the single participant in the event is incongruent. Spanish, however, allows for the modifier *"por sí mismo/a"*, *"por sí solo/a"* or *"él/ella solo/a"*, in cases where there is a force-dynamic interpretation, in order to invoke causal autonomy.

(13) (a) *Jane laughed by herself.
(b) *The angels appeared by themselves.
(c) Al final, se cayó él solo.
at end MM fall.PST he alone.
"In the end, he fell all by himself".

The type of analyses which posit the deletion of the cause component do not adequately explain the behaviour of the *break*-class and the *cut*-class of verbs with regard to anticausativization. Verbs of the *break*-class regularly display few restrictions on the type of subjects they may choose in the causative construction (agents, instruments, natural forces or even events), whereas the *cut*-class tend to be restricted to human volitional agents.

(14) (a) John/The hammer/The wind/The explosion broke the vase.
(b) The baker/?The knife/*The lightning/*The explosion cut the bread.

This wider scope of possible causes in the *break*-class favours the possibility of evoking an underspecified external cause in the inchoative. Koontz Garboden (2009: 86) argues that "since the participant in the causing subevent need not be an agent, under reflexivization there is no entailment that the undergoer of the COS event (also the EFFECTOR[2] participant in the causing subevent) have agent entailments". In fact, as a consequence of reflexivization, it follows that "only COS verbs with underspecified causes undergo anticausativization" (Koontz-Garboden 2009: 124). Since the initiating and endpoint facets of the event are non-distinct, and since the theme participant in inchoatives is prototypically inanimate, and an external cause is only evoked schematically, it follows that the inchoative construction does not readily accept verbs with agent entailments. This requirement would explain the restriction found in relation to the *cut*-class of verbs (*build, clean, cut, paint, wash,* etc.) (Levin 1993), which are not compatible with the inchoative construction even though they also involve a resultant change-of-state. This restriction on agent entailments similarly applies to the presence of agent-oriented adverbials (*deliberately, willingly, carefully,* etc.), or dynamic adverbs (*vigorously, dynamically,* etc.) in inchoatives. In either case, the interpretation hinders the construal of the event as taking place spontaneously.

(15) (a) *The bread cut.
(b) *The door opened deliberately.

The "*get*-passive" sometimes alternates with the inchoative in the expression of spontaneous events,[3] or makes available an inchoative reading with agentive verbs which do not admit the inchoative construction.

(16) (a) The clothes got washed./*The clothes washed.
(b) The book got read./*The book read.

3.2.4 Theme participant

Variation in the acceptability of the inchoative construction also occurs due to the nature of the theme participant and the different senses of verbs. The inchoative is possible with themes designating elements capable of instigating the event, such as natural forces, or objects capable of undergoing a change of state autonomously through natural causes, without the intervention of a human agent. When the thematic element is an abstract entity, it is not compatible with the construal of the event as autonomous, since it requires the initiation of some sentient agent.

(17) (a) The paint/*The orange peeled.
(b) The vase/The storm/*Our agreement/*The world record broke.

Though the theme participant in the inchoative is prototypically inanimate, there are cases of animate undergoers (*drown, ahogarse*). Koontz-Garboden (2009: 101) observes that these are special cases of reflexivization, where the single argument, the THEME undergoer and underspecified EFFECTOR, "can take an agentive interpretation, a possible interpretation of an EFFECTOR argument". In the context of purpose clauses, which are controlled by an agent, the theme element is interpreted agentively, as in a typical "reflexive" reading. It must be pointed out, however, that the reflexive interpretation is not necessarily valid for all contexts with purpose clauses. In (18) (from Koontz-Garboden 2009: 101), the subject presumably undergoes the change of state (*drowning*) non-volitionally, due to an underspecified cause (*the force of the sea*), but there is a non-specified prior volitional event, that of jumping into the water in order to save his friend, which controls the purpose clause. Thus the THEME undergoer does not necessarily take an agentive interpretation in the context of purpose clauses.

(18) [...] cuando Phil se ahogó para salvarle
[...] when Phil MM drown.PST in order to save.3SG.DAT

la vida a Jim [...]
the life to Jim [...]

"[...] when Phil drowned to save Jim's life [...]"

In addition, the possibility of explicitly referring to some external force in the adjunct points to a non-agentive component in the causing subevent in the inchoative, and thus a non-reflexive interpretation. However, the alternative interpretation of the MM, that of non-distinctness of Cause and Affected roles, does allow for the specification of the indirect cause in adjuncts. Agentivity and causation need to be distinguished as separate notions (DeLancey 1984).

(19) Los supervivientes se ahogaron por la fuerza de las olas.
the survivors MM drown.PST by the force of the waves
"The survivors drowned because of the strength of the waves".

3.3 Facilitative events and the middle construction

Facilitative events are characterized by the presence of a theme participant which by virtue of its inherent properties facilitates (or hinders) the occurrence of the "potential" event, and by an implied potential or virtual agent whose efforts are evoked. The middle construction designating this situation type takes the form of an intransitive clause; it is found with physical and psychological change of state verbs taking the inchoative construction (see §3.2), as well as with verbs involving agent-oriented meaning components (cut, *cortarse*; wash, *lavarse*; build, *construirse*; cook, *cocinarse* tie, *atarse* ...). The middle is also found with basic transitive verbs expressing actions that do not imply a change-of-state (read, *leerse*; sell, *venderse*) (see Levin 1993).

(20) (a) Wholemeal bread cuts easily.
(b) Lamb chops fry well.
(c) Cotton garments wash well.

3.3.1 Features of the middle construction

The middle construction crucially involves a judgement about the feasibility of carrying out the designated event, and thus prototypically requires the presence of some modifier specifying the ease or difficulty of carrying out the event. The middle construction is typically non-eventive (Keyser and Roeper 1984), and lacks a specific time reference (Levin 1993), and is thus incompatible with the progressive. Davidse (1992) has pointed out that the theme participant (Subject/Goal) does not actively co-participate in the "transitive" process. (See García de la Maza, this volume, for a detailed description of the middle).

(21) (a) Wholemeal bread cuts easily.
(b) *Wholemeal bread cuts.
(c) *That wholemeal bread is cutting now.
(d) *What the wholemeal did was cut.

Examples of middles without modifiers are possible in the presence of a modal element; in fact, the meaning of the construction has often been associated with ability or possibility modals (Fagan 1992). Generalized universal statements about the potential event, evoking modal nuances as in (22b), are also possible without modifiers. Yoshimura (1998) notes the effects of "informativity", where the unexpected features of the theme are foregrounded, allowing for the absence of a modifier. Negation is one such context, where typically the most expected, conventional information is cancelled, thus contributing to informativity by foregrounding the unpredictable quality and less expected aspects of the theme, as in (22c). We also find contexts which contribute to informativity by presenting situations which are counterintuitive or counterexperiential, such (22d).

(22) (a) Don't throw this food away. It'll freeze! (i.e. preserve it in the deep freeze) (from J. Taylor, p.c.) (Yoshimura 1998)
(b) Glass recycles. (Fagan 1992)
(c) This dried mud won't scrape off.
(d) I thought we were out of gas, but the car drives! (Fellbaum 1986)

Though the middle construction prototypically instantiates a potential event, examples of "eventive" middles, taking the progressive and participating in the "virtual reflexive alternation" (Levin 1993), are also found. Appropriate contextualization also licenses examples which are not wholly "de-actualized".

(23) (a) Those books are selling very well at the moment.
(b) Those books are selling themselves, as it were.
(c) Two-bedroom apartments, now building in XY Roads, for sale. (publicity notice of a real estate agent, 1997) (Yoshimura 1998)
(d) Your plane is now boarding at Gate 6. (Yoshimura 1998)

3.3.2 Blends

Davidse (1992: 114) has observed the existence of cases, which she terms "blends", which share properties of the middle and the inchoative constructions. The blend allows for a potential externally caused interpretation, as in typical middles, but also for self-instigated action, as in inchoatives.

(24) In the event of an accident the glass will break neatly.
> "In the event of an accident the glass can be broken neatly".
> "In the event of an accident the glass will break (itself) neatly".

Middles with the *break*-class of verbs are special, in that the theme participant can be conceived of as actively co-participating in the process. This blend of features also motivates ambiguity in the interpretation of the adverbial *easily*, which may refer to the efforts of some "potential" external agent or to the quality of the theme and its "potential" initiation of the event.

(25) (a) What that door did was open easily.
(b) This door opens easily.

3.3.3 Cause component

The middle construction typically evokes the efforts of a potential unspecified agent. This feature makes the middle compatible with control of purpose clauses as in (26a). Ackema and Schoorlemmer (1994: 76) point out that the crucial factor is the degree to which the potential sentient agent may be assigned the attendant properties of intentionality and responsibility. Cognitive verbs, verbs of psychological state, and verbs of perception, as in (26b) and (26c), which involve an experiencer instead of an agent, do not readily take the middle construction.

(26) (a) Oven door lifts off to make cleaning easier. (attested, Advertisement notice, 1995), (Yoshimura 1998).
(b) *This poem understands well.
(c) *Spinach dislikes easily.

3.3.4 Theme participant

The theme designates an entity or artefact which by virtue of certain properties facilitates or hinders the potential event. But the theme participant in most of the verbs taking the middle construction (except the *break*-class) can never be attributed initiation of the potential event, since an external agent-cause is always evoked. Thus the use of the modifier "by itself", which restricts the cause to the theme participant, is not readily allowed.

(27) (a) *This cotton shirt washes all by itself.
(b) This door closes all by itself.

3.4 Non-prototypical instances of the middle construction revisited

Non-prototypical instances of the middle construction, such as the existence of middles with instrument, means or locative entities as subject, and the occurrence of the middle construction with basic intransitives, where the subject denotes a location or setting, have been pointed out in the literature (van Oosten 1986; Yoshimura 1998).

(28) (a) Aluminum bakes higher, browns more evenly. (van Oosten 1986)
(b) Linoleum wipes off easily. (Hatcher 1943)
(c) Lakes Wanaka and Hawea still continue to fish well despite the recent spells of heavy rain and rising lake levels. (attested, *Otago Daily Times*, 2/12/1994) (Yoshimura 1998)

All these cases are licensed in events with highly predictable object participants. The potential theme (O) is by-passed as the most eligible participant in the nucleus of the event, and the profiled thematic relation includes the next participant in the action chain, the dependent means or instrument element, which is thus assigned starting-point status and chosen as subject. Similarly, the profile may centre on "the locational 'container-content' relation that the setting bears to a participant therein" (Langacker 2000: 42), as in *setting-subject constructions*, and thus the locative element is foregrounded. In the absence of a newsworthy object as nucleus in the thematic relation, the locative is assigned participant status and chosen as the single element in the profiled thematic relation, and thus as subject.

The middle construction is also found with unergative intransitive verbs (*dance, run*, etc.), and a means or circumstance, or a locative element as subject (van Oosten 1986).

(29) (a) This music dances better than the other one. (van Oosten 1986)
(b) That green plays badly. (Yoshimura 1998)
(c) *Pubs enter into only too easily.
(d) *This stage disappears easily.

As Langacker (1991: 387 n2) notes, "an intransitive clause may also have the structure (D(A)), where the same participant figures in both event components (i.e. as both an energy source and the theme, as in *He jumped*); it is then the thematic role that motivates absolutive case and other manifestations of ergativity". This is the case of initially unergative intransitives, as is (29a–b), whose structure of the conceived event involves the same participant undergoing the thematic process and supplying the energy input. Since the middle typically profiles the nucleus of the event and leaves the agent or energy source unprofiled, the theme-cum-energy source participant is by-passed as the participant in the profiled thematic relation in favour of the other available element for starting point status, the means/accompaniment or the locative. This construal is licensed since these non-prototypical instances bear resemblance relations to the middle prototype, as the themes in (29a–b) display certain properties which facilitate or hinder the potential action of the implied agent. The locative in example (29c), which also involves an unergative verb, however, lacks these facilitative properties specific to the potential action referred to by the predicate.

Non-alternating unaccusatives, (29d), disallow this construal, since they lack an energy source-cum-theme participant. There is no separate conceptual event component involving energy input, and the locative element cannot assume thematic status, since unaccusatives may be viewed as "single-participant thematic processes whose construal is absolute" (Langacker 1991: 390 n5), and as such only the nuclear participant may be assigned starting point status.

4 The inchoative and the middle revisited

Thematic-subject constructions, the inchoative and the middle, have been characterized in terms of a set of parameters: (a) the degree of distinctness of participants in the event, the distinction between a salient cause and an affected element (Kemmer 1993, 1994; Næss 2007); (b) the degree to which the external source of energy is implicit or schematically evoked (Langacker 1991); and (c) the degree to which the thematic participant initiates or facilitates the event (Kemmer 1993, 1994; Langacker 1991).

The inchoative prototype may be characterized as a construction which profiles a single-participant thematic relationship, but which typically evokes an external cause, often abstract and schematic. The theme participant is an entity that undergoes the change of state, and is thus affected, but which is also construed as instigating the event, so that there is a low degree of distinctness between causal and affected roles. The construction designates a spontaneous change-of-state event, which is construed as actual, taking place at a specific time.

The middle prototype is a construction also profiling a single-participant thematic relationship, one in which the agent is non-salient and unspecified, but where the efforts of a potential agent are clearly evoked. The theme designates an entity exhibiting certain inherent properties which facilitate or hinder the occurrence of the potential event, thus endowed with the feature of enabling cause, but which cannot be construed as initiating the event, so that there is certain distinctness between "potential" agent and affected roles. The event is construed as potential and de-actualized.

The occurrence of blends and other non-prototypical phenomena points to the existence of an intermediate domain between the two constructions, a fuzzy area where these instances occur. This middle area is characterized by a set of continua corresponding to the parameters described above in the characterization of the prototypes. The features of non-prototypical expressions may be explained as a result of blending, of conceptual mappings between the two input spaces and of selective projection from the two basic prototypes, creating emergent non-prototypical instances (Fauconnier 1997).

Theme as "potentially" affected	**Theme as affected**
Theme as facilitator	**Theme as initiator**
External "potential" agent	**Schematic "external" cause**
Potential event	**Actual event**
MIDDLE <———— BLENDS —————>	**INCHOATIVE**

Thematic-subject constructions may also be placed in relation to other situation types of reduced transitivity, such as passives and intransitives coding intrinsically spontaneous events (non-alternating unaccusatives). All these constructions choose an affected theme as subject. The passive profiles the whole action chain, involving an initiating agent and an affected theme, though the agent is typically left unspecified. With intrinsically spontaneous events, we find a single-participant thematic process whose construal is absolute.

The feature source of energy input, external vs. internal (cf. Levin and Rappaport Hovav 1995), refers to the degree to which the initiation of the event is construed as externally or internally generated. In the passive, the event is construed as involving an external agent-like cause. In the case of intrinsically spontaneous events, the event is conceptualized as autonomous and inherently generated.

Regarding the feature of degree of control or autonomy of the theme participant, the agentless passive designates events where the theme participant is a purely affected entity, and has no control on the initiation of the event. Intrinsically spontaneous events involve an absolute construal, since the change-of-state of the theme participant is due to its inherent properties and the physiological or physico-chemical processes they are subject to.

Other parameters along which these constructions differ are the roles of the participants and the feature of potentiality or de-actualization characteristic of prototypical middles, in contrast with spontaneous events, which are characterized by their actuality. The main characterizing features

Table 6.2. Characterizing properties of passive, thematic-subject, and intransitive (non-alternating unaccusative) constructions

Features	*Passive*	*Middle*	*Inchoative*	*Unaccusative*
A	High	Medium	Low	None
B	External	External	External (Internal)	Internal
C	(Implicit) Agent	Potential Agent	Schematic Cause	Inherent Cause
D	None	Medium	Medium-High	High
E	Affected	Facilitator	Affected (Effector)	Effector-Affected
F	Actual	Potential	Actual	Actual

of these constructions are summarized in Table 6.2. The features are the following:

A: Degree of distinctness of participants.
B: Source of Energy input
C: Nature of external or internal energy source (Agent or Cause).
D: Degree of control/autonomy of theme participant.
E: Role of theme participant
F: Actual or Potential event

In the network, degree of distinctness and role of participants differs for each construction. There are also distinct differences in the degree of salience, and in the nature, of the agent or cause, and in the conception of the event as actual or potential. The feature source of energy input sets apart intrinsically spontaneous situation types, coded by unaccusative intransitives, from the other constructions. The inchoative is special in both evoking an external underspecified cause, and in designating a theme which has a mixed role of affected-cum-effector, where the initiating feature is quite salient.

5 Conclusion

This paper has re-examined the characterizing properties of thematic-subject constructions (inchoatives and middles) from a cognitive linguistic perspective. The paper has explored some of the central issues discussed in the literature, and argued in favour of a non-derivational analysis of these constructions and the presence of a cause component in the inchoative. Rather than viewing the inchoative and middle as wholly independent constructions, I have posited a middle ground between the two, which accommodates instances of so-called blends and other non-prototypical phenomena, on the basis of a set of continua involving the most relevant features of these constructions. Non-prototypical instances of the middle construction, such as the occurrence of thematic-subjects with means or locative, and middles of inherently intransitive predicates, have been explained on the basis of A/D organization, profiling and resemblance relations to the prototype. The crucial feature licensing these non-prototypical middles appears to be the relevance and informativity of the expression and the properties of the theme element, which facilitate or hinder the potential event. This paper has also presented an account of the network which subsumes thematic-subject constructions and other constructions of reduced transitivity, such as passive and unaccusative intransitives.

Notes

1. Following Langacker (1991: 287), I will be using the term *theme* to refer schematically to the single participant involved in a thematic relationship. The theme may represent a variety of role archetypes, such as the patient (change of state) or the mover (motion) in thematic-subject constructions, and any other role associated with the autonomous core of an event conception.
2. Van Valin and LaPolla (1997: 85) define the participant role of *effector* as "the doer of an action, which may or may not be wilful or purposeful". Koontz-Garboden (2009: 85) uses the label EFFECTOR for the role of the underspecified cause element in the causing subevent. In this paper, I have applied the term *effector* to the role of the theme participant in spontaneous events; the theme in non-intrinsically spontaneous events is primarily construed as initiator and affected at the same time, whereas the role of theme in intrinsically spontaneous events may be a patient or a non-voluntary effector.
3. The aspectual features of change-of-state and the fact that primary responsibility for the event is not wholly attributed to an external (implicit) agent makes the *get*-passive construction an appropriate substitute for the inchoative construction in cases where some human volitional agent is evoked (Marín-Arrese 1993, 2003).

References

Ackema, P. and Schoorlemmer, M. (1994) The middle construction and the syntax-semantics interface. *Lingua* 93(1): 59–90.

Comrie, B. (1981) *Language Universals and Linguistic Typology.* Oxford: Blackwell.

Davidse, K. (1992) Transitivity/ergativity: The Janus-headed grammar of action and events. In M. Davis, J. Martin and L. Ravelli (eds) *Advances in Systemic Linguistics: Recent theory and practice* 105–135. London: Pinter.

Davidse, K. (1998) On transitivity and ergativity in English, or on the need for dialogue between schools. In J. van der Auwera, F. Durieux and L. Lejeune (eds) *English as a Human Language. To honour Louis Goossens* 95–108. München: LINCOM Europa.

DeLancey, S. (1984) Notes on agentivity and causation. *Studies in Language* 8(2): 181–213.

Fagan, S. (1992) *The Syntax and Semantics of Middle Constructions.* Cambridge: Cambridge University Press.

Fauconnier, G. (1997) *Mappings in Thought and Language.* Cambridge: Cambridge University Press.

Fellbaum, C. (1986) *On the Middle Construction in English.* Bloomington, IN: Indiana Linguistics Club.

Fillmore, C. (1967) The grammar of *hitting* and *breaking.* In R. Jacobs and P. Rosenbaum (eds) *Readings in English Transformational Grammar* 120–133. Waltham, MA: Ginn.

García de la Maza, C. (2008) Intransitivity, ergatives and middles. *Estudios Ingleses de la Universidad Complutense* 16: 31–50.

García de la Maza, C. (this volume) The semantics of English middles and pseudo-middles.

Gómez Torrego, L. (1992). *Valores gramaticales de "se".* Madrid: Arco Libros.

Grimshaw, J. (1982) On the lexical representation of Romance reflexive clitics. In J. Bresnan (ed.) *The Mental Representation of Grammatical Relations* 87–148. Cambridge: The MIT Press.

Haspelmath, M. (1993) More on the typology of inchoative/causative verb alternations. In B. Comrie and M. Polinsky (eds) *Causatives and Transitivity* 87–120. Amsterdam: Benjamins.

Hatcher, G. (1943) Mr. Howard amuses easy. *Modern Language Notes* 58: 8–17.

Kemmer, S. (1993) *The Middle Voice.* Amsterdam: Benjamins.

Kemmer, S. (1994) Middle voice, transitivity and the elaboration of events. In B. Fox and P. Hopper (eds) *Voice: Form and function* 179–230. Amsterdam: Benjamins.

Keyser, S. J. and Roeper, T. (1984) On the middle and ergative constructions in English. *Linguistic Inquiry* 15: 381–416.

Koontz-Garboden, A. (2009) Anticausativization. *Natural Language and Linguistic Theory 27*: 77–138.

Langacker, R. W. (1991) *Foundations of Cognitive Grammar, Vol. II: Descriptive application.* Stanford, CA: Stanford University Press.

Langacker, R. W. (2000) *Grammar and Conceptualization.* Berlin: Mouton de Gruyter.

Langacker, R. W. and Munro, P. (1975) Passives and their meaning. *Language* 51(4): 789–830.

Levin, B. (1993) *English Verb Classes and Alternations: A preliminary investigation.* Chicago, IL: University of Chicago Press.

Levin, B. and Rappaport Hovav, M. (1995) *Unaccusativity: At the syntax-lexical semantics interface.* Cambridge, MA: The MIT Press.

Maldonado, R. (1988) Energetic reflexives in Spanish. In S. Axmaker, A. Jaisser and H. Singmaster (eds) *Proceedings of the Fourteenth Annual Meeting of the Berkeley Linguistics Society* 153–165. Berkeley, CA: Berkeley Linguistics Society.

Maldonado, R. (1999) *A media voz: Problemas conceptuales del clítico* se. Mexico: Universidad Nacional de México.

Marín-Arrese, J. (1993) *La pasiva en inglés: Un estudio funcional-tipológico.* Madrid: Editorial de la Universidad Complutense de Madrid.

Marín-Arrese, J. (2003) The middle domain in English and Spanish: Middle and related situation types. In C. Molina, M. Blanco, J. Marín-Arrese, A. L. Rodríguez and M. Romano (eds) *Cognitive Linguistics in Spain at the Turn of the Century, Vol. I: Grammar and semantics* 229–252. Madrid: AELCO and Universidad Autónoma de Madrid.

Næss, A. (2007) *Prototypical Transitivity.* Amsterdam: Benjamins.

Oosten, J. van (1986) *The Nature of Subjects, Topics and Agents: A cognitive explanation.* Bloomington, IN: Indiana University Linguistics Club.

Perlmutter, D. M. (1978) Impersonal passives and the unaccusative hypothesis. In J. J. Jaeger, A. C. Woodbury, F. Ackerman, C. Chiarello, O. D. Gensler, J. Kingston, E. C. Sweetser, H. Thompson and K. W, Whitler (eds) *Proceedings of the Fourth Annual Meeting of the Berkeley Linguistics Society* 157–189. Berkeley, CA: Berkeley Linguistics Society.

Van Valin, R. D. and R. J. LaPolla (1997) *Syntax: Structure, meaning and function.* Cambridge: Cambridge University Press.

Yoshimura, K. (1998) *The Middle Construction in English: A cognitive linguistic analysis.* Ph.D. thesis. University of Otago. Dunedin, New Zealand.

7 The semantics of English middles and pseudo-middles

Casilda García de la Maza[a]

1 Introduction

On the surface, ergatives (*The cup broke*), middles (*This book reads easily*) and passives (*The man has been shot*) are all intransitive one-argument structures. Structurally, however, they hide important differences which have been well documented in the literature. These revolve, on one hand, around the original Agent argument, which is deleted in the case of ergatives, not present though implied in middles, and optionally realized in passives, and, on the other, around the stativity of middles and the eventiveness of ergatives and passives (Keyser and Roeper 1984; Roberts 1987; Fagan 1988, *inter alia*). Comparatively little attention has been devoted to the semantic and pragmatic changes that the transitivity alternations impose on the resulting structures. Whilst in the case of ergatives and passives these changes do not go beyond what we would expect from the grammatical rearrangement of their arguments, they are much more idiosyncratic in middles and yield a highly marked constructional meaning which we refer to as "the middle interpretation". As Jackendoff (1992: 177) puts it, the middle construction is an example of a construction that violates the argument structure of the verb "while imposing characteristic and idiosyncratic changes of meaning". This paper explores the nature and the makeup of this semantic and pragmatic peculiarity and analyses how some even more idiosyncratic English constructions can be made to fall under the middle paradigm.

Consider the middle alternation in (1):

(1) (a) My grandma reads love stories.
(b) Love stories read easily.

a Casilda García de la Maza is Lecturer in English Language and Linguistics at the University of the Basque Country, Spain. E-mail: casilda.garcia@ehu.es

These sentences clearly do not describe the same state of affairs. Sentence (1a) is reporting an event which is performed by an Agent whereas (1b) is not referring to any event. Rather, it is ascribing some property to love stories that makes them easy to read. It is also implying that it is easy for an Agent, which is semantically present, but not superficially expressed, to read love stories. The presence of the adverbial element is crucial to obtain this interpretation. The meaning of middles thus revolves around these two notions: on the one hand, the properties of the subject and on the other, the role of the implied Agent argument, as explored in the following sections.

2 The middle interpretation

2.1 The property reading

The semantic idiosyncrasy of middles has not passed unnoticed in the literature. Dixon (1991: 327) notes that the construction "is only used when the nature of the referent of a non-subject NP is the major factor in the success of some instance of an activity". In a similar vein, Erades (1975: 36) claims that "the construction in question is only found when the subject is represented as having certain inherent qualities which promote, hamper or prevent the realization of the idea expressed by the predicate". Sentence (1b) indeed means that there is some characteristic of love stories (the light-heartedness of the plot, or the straightforwardness of the style) that can be held responsible for the fact that they are easy to read. We refer to this feature as the "property reading" of the middle subject, and take it to be a crucial and defining feature of the English middle construction.

Van Oosten (1977: 461) also emphasizes the semantic relevance of the subject of middles. She claims that, in patient-subject constructions, as she calls middles, "the subject, or a property of it, is understood to be responsible for the action of the verb". She uses this argument to reject the label "middle", which seems to refer to a construction somewhere between the active and the passive, when in fact, as she claims, middles are semantically active in that their subject is like an active subject "since it asserts responsibility for the action of the verb". She goes on to add that "the patient-subject construction [...] is used when we want to say that the patient of the action is to some extent acting as agent". Lakoff (1977: 249) endorses her claims by showing that in prototypical active Agent-Patient sentences, primary responsibility is the central semantic notion to be paired with the grammatical notion of subjecthood, other properties such as control or volition being less important. His examples include sentences like *John hit Mary accidentally*, where the subject is responsible, although not volitional or in control of the action.

There are indeed ways in which the subject of a middle sentence can be seen as an Agent, rather than as a Patient, as will become apparent throughout this paper. However, if we turn to standard notions of agentivity according to which the Agent is the volitional "doer", performer or instigator of an action (Gruber 1967: 943; Fillmore 1968: 24; Jackendoff 1972: 32; Cruse 1973), as is the NP *John* in *John kicked the ball*, then the subject of a middle sentence will be seen to exhibit, if anything, *anti*-Agent-like features. Note that, as the *kick* example shows, agentivity often goes hand in hand with other semantic features like kinesis or action, punctuality, and affectedness of the object, which are some of the components that Hopper and Thompson (1980: 252) list as making up a prototypical transitive clause. Transitivity is here used in the Latin sense of *transire* "to pass" or of "expressing an action which passes over to an object" (OED s.v. *transitive* a. (n.) 2),[1] and is thus seen more as a semantic notion than a purely structural one. In middles, there is no action to be carried out. As our discussion unfolds, it will become apparent that middles are essentially *in*transitive sentences, not only structurally, but also semantically. Middles will reveal themselves as stative, unagentive and uneventive constructions. We could express essentially the same insight by drawing on Halliday's (1967: 38ff) notion of Transitivity, which he defines according to the type of process expressed in the clause. Middles will be seen to be *attributive* clauses, involving primarily a process of *ascription* of an *attribute* to an *attribuant* (the participant to whom the property is ascribed). Halliday's (1967: 47) example of an attributive clause is *She looked happy*, where an attribute (happiness) is being ascribed to an attribuant (*she*). The subject of a middle sentence, like *This book reads easily*, could equally be seen as having the role of an *attribuant* to which the property of being easy to read is being ascribed.

Rosta's (1995) discussion of the semantics of middles goes along the same lines. But he goes a step further and formalizes the property reading of the middle subject by referring to the notion of "the archagonist". The term "archagonist" draws on Talmy's (1985a: 293) application of the theory of force dynamics to the organization of meaning. Force dynamics deals with how "entities interact with respect to force, including the exertion of force, resistance to such a force, the overcoming of such a resistance ...". Talmy uses the term *Agonist* to refer to the force-exerting entity, and *Antagonist* to refer to the force element that opposes it. For example, the sentence *The ball kept rolling because of the wind blowing on it* (Talmy 1985a: 298) involves "an Agonist with an intrinsic tendency towards rest that is being opposed from outside by a stronger Antagonist, which thus overcomes its resistance and forces it to move". In other words, the ball "tends towards rest but is kept in motion by the wind's greater power". The notion of "archagonist" is not part of Talmy's theory, but rather Rosta's own coinage. He does not really explain the motivation for choosing it or how it relates to Talmy's force-exerting entities. He simply uses it to refer to the subject of a middle, whose referent is the "primarily responsible participant" in a middle sentence (Rosta 1995: 128), as discussed above. Explaining the semantics of middles in the context of a theory of force dynamics nevertheless seems appropriate (see also Davidse and Heyvaert 2007). Middles could be perceived as involving a clash of forces. Example (2) (from Van Oosten 1977: 142) illustrates this:

(2) This apple sauce will digest rapidly.

The verb *digest* involves a complicated process in whose successful occurrence whatever is being digested plays a significant role. It is well known that not all kinds of food digest equally well. There seems to be a basic tendency for human beings to have difficulty in digesting food. The apple sauce opposes that tendency and, despite the hindrance, it has such properties that enable it to successfully overcome it. In example (3), where the verb *translate* exhibits a higher degree of agency than the verb *digest*, the role of the implied Agent is seen more clearly.

(3) This book translates easily.

The sentence implies that the process of translating a book is an arduous task and that it normally requires an effort on the part of the translator. But the properties of this particular book are such that, contrary to expectations, it lends itself to an easy translation, or, in other words, it eases the effort required by the implied Agent. If we try to make these intuitions fit into a pattern of clash of forces, the subject would be an Antagonist, the element that opposes (or neutralizes) the force, or the effort, that the implied Agent would have needed to accomplish in order to carry out a successful translation.

2.2 Pragmatic relevance

Fellbaum (1985: 23) and Rosta (1995: 132) point out that in order for middles to be acceptable, they have to provide "newsworthy information".

This idea goes hand in hand with the property reading. Consider the following examples:

(4) ?Cars wash well.

(5) This jumper washes well.

The difference in acceptability between (4) and (5) lies in the different relationship that holds between the properties of the subject and the action denoted by the verb. Under normal circumstances and assuming no context, it is an inherent property of cars that they can be washed, and there is no pragmatic relevance in stating it. The readiness with which a jumper lends itself to being washed, on the other hand, cannot be taken for granted. One could imagine many things that would prevent a jumper from being easily washed, such as its size, fabric or colour. Stating that it can be easily washed conveys newsworthy information, and the corresponding middle is acceptable. Notice that a definite subject (*This car*), instead of the bare plural (*Cars*), would turn Example (4) into a successful middle. It would indeed be more relevant to state that this car in particular can be easily washed (because of some characteristic that this car has but which others lack), than to state that cars in general can be easily washed. In fact, it is often the case with middles that examples with definite subjects are more acceptable than those with indefinite or bare plural NPs as their subjects, as (6a) and (6b) show:

(6) (a) ?A book sells well.
(b) This book sells well.

It is, however, true that middles with bare plural subjects are also common, as (7) exemplifies:

(7) Chickens kill easily.

In this case, it is the specificity of the meaning of the subject, which implies an element of comparison (chickens as opposed to other animals), that accounts for the pragmatic relevance of the middle. A more generic NP would have resulted in a more dubious middle, as shown in (8):

(8) ?Animals kill easily.

But then again, Example (8) would make sense in an imaginary context in which what is being discussed is how to eradicate an unknown and highly contagious disease that strikes humans as well as animals. Culling the affected individuals seems to be the quickest and most efficient way of controlling the epidemic. This is of course a feasible option in the case of animals, hence the relevance of (8), but not so in the case of humans.

2.3 Modification

This section discusses the different types of modification that middles usually appear with, and their contribution to the semantics and pragmatics of the construction. In the light of our discussion so far, the presence of modification in middles can be seen as a means of providing a suitable context and thus helping to convey the middle interpretation, which will in turn make middles more acceptable. We saw above that this was the case with definite subjects. This section explores other linguistic devices that serve the same purpose.

The introduction of an explicit element of comparison is one of them. Consider the sentences in (9):

(9) (a) *This book reads.
(b) ?This book reads but that one doesn't.
(c) This book reads better than that one.

Example (9a) is unacceptable. As the sentence stands, it is difficult to imagine what properties of the book could make it responsible for the fact that it can be read. It is therefore odd for *This book* to appear in the subject position of a construction whose function is to bring to the foreground some property of the subject that can be held responsible for the successful occurrence of the action denoted by the verb. But the situation improves as soon as an element of contrast or comparison is introduced, as in (9b) and (9c). One could think of *this book* as having some particular property, such as simplicity of style, which might make it responsible for the fact that it can be read better than another book. In other words, it is more relevant to state that a particular book, as opposed to another one, can be read, than simply to say that a book can be read. In this sense, (9a) provides less newsworthy information than (9b) and (9c).

Modal auxiliaries, contrastive stress, negation or emphatic *do* are other common types of modification to appear with middles, as Roberts (1987: 195) and Rosta (1995: 132) note. Consider the following examples:

(10) The car will steer, after all. (Rosta 1995: 132)

(11) This book won't translate.

Sentence (10) contains a modal auxiliary, *will*, and the concessive adverbial *after all*, which signals counter-expectation (Traugott 2004: 554). As Rosta (1995: 132) explains, (10) might be said in a context in which the car was not expected to steer, and so displays the clash of forces alluded to in previous paragraphs. Sentence (11), on the other hand, exemplifies a very common and perfectly acceptable kind of middle. Here the expectation is that the book can be translated and the fact that it cannot constitutes newsworthy information. In addition, the sentence is interpreted as if the subject referent may be held responsible for the non-occurrence of the translation, as noted by Rosta (1995: 133). The properties of the book, in this case, are not enough to override the force exerted by the translator. To put it in other words, it is the translator's will to translate the book, but it is the book's fault that it does not lend itself to translation.

Example (12) shows how middles can also occur without any of the elements mentioned above:

(12) Glass recycles. (Fagan 1992: 57)

Here it is the lexical content of the verbs themselves, in combination with their subjects, that makes it possible to create contextual effects. There would not be much relevance in stating, for example, *Rubbish recycles*, since, after all, it is well-known that recycling consists precisely in turning rubbish into reusable material. On the other hand, stating that glass (as opposed to plastic or cardboard, for example) recycles, conveys relevant information, since not all types of materials can be recycled.

But the most common of all possible ways of providing an appropriate context and thus increasing the acceptability of a middle sentence is, without doubt, adverbial modification. In addition, adverbial modification in middles is crucial since it contributes to bringing out the implied Agent argument that characterizes the English middle construction. This is the topic of the next section.

2.4 Adverbial modification

The adverbs that appear in middles are usually of the type referred to as "facility adverbs" (Vendler 1984: 305) or "middle adverbs" (Fellbaum 1989: 126), typically *easily, with difficulty, smoothly, well,* or the like. They point to the "facility" or "ease" with which the action denoted by the verb is accomplished, which is precisely why they fit so well the semantics of middles, as will be explained below.

Facility adverbs differ, amongst other types of adverbs, from Vendler's (1984: 301) group of manner adverbs, like *carefully, skilfully,* etc., which cannot appear in middles:

(13) This book reads easily.

(14) *This book reads carefully.

Manner adverbs are characterized by Vendler (1984: 301) as "positing a trait in the Agent", a feature that facility adverbs lack. Fagan (1992: 155) uses the facts about adverb selection in middles as evidence to show that middles are essentially patient-focused constructions. Manner adverbs, she claims, are not acceptable in middles because they create a "clash of focus". Manner adverbs posit a trait on the Agent, but the focus in a middle is on properties of the Patient, and not the Agent. We might want to make what is essentially the same point, but slightly more in line with our argument about the stativity and unagentivity of middles: The adverb *carefully* in (14) has no Agent to which it can ascribe the property of carefulness, given that the Agent in a middle sentence, although semantically present, is not structurally realized. And we have already noticed that the subject of a middle does not qualify as the Agent of an event. Adverbs like *carefully* or *deliberately*, on the other hand, are incompatible with statives (Dowty 1979: 55–59). Note also that in this respect middles contrast with passive sentences, which do admit modification by adverbs like *carefully*: *The book was read carefully.* Unlike middles, passives are eventive, and they do have an Agent argument that remains grammatically present, and which can be structurally realized in a *by*-phrase: *The book was read carefully by the students.*

Drawing the argument even closer to the semantic ground, the fact that facility adverbs are so frequent in middles should come as little surprise in view of the discussion above on the properties of the middle subject. On the one hand, their presence favours a property reading interpretation, including the idea of newsworthiness. The argument is already a familiar one: while there is nothing special about stating that a book reads, there is some relevance in stating that it reads easily, since it is possible to ascribe the easiness with which the book reads to some of its properties. On the other hand, whereas facility adverbs do not posit a trait in the Agent, they describe the act "with respect to an actual or potential Agent, as performed or performable" (Vendler 1984: 304). They thus bring in the implied Agent argument that is present in middles, the interpretation "it is easy for someone to V". Add to that the crucial fact that their meaning usually revolves around the notions of "easiness" or "difficultness", which helps to instantiate the clash of forces mentioned above.

2.5 Non-eventiveness

As has become apparent from our discussion so far, middles do not refer to events, but are rather descriptive statements which attribute some property to the subject. This is noted by Keyser and Roeper (1984: 381), who claim that middles are generic statements and that, as such, they state propositions that are generally true and do not describe particular events in time. Levin (1993: 26) offers the same insight when she asserts that middles "lack specific time reference". Thus, unlike their transitive counterparts, which are eventive and describe happenings or occurrences, middles describe circumstances or states in which something obtains or holds true (Roberts 1987: 195ff).

However, the following example seems to suggest that eventive middles do exist:

(15) I thought that this book was going to be really difficult to translate, but it wasn't. It translated really easily.

In (15) it is clear that there exists a specific event in the past in which the book was translated. The past tense of the verb is crucial to obtain the eventive reading.[2] And yet, any eventive interpretation that this sentence may have is overridden by the property reading and the lack of agentivity that characterizes middles. While a translation event is indeed implied, the primary function of sentence (15) is not to report that the translation took place, but rather to imply that there were properties of the book that rendered the translation easy, in line with the semantics of the English middle construction. The focus of the sentence is on the subject, rather than on the event denoted by the verb. Thus, though middles can refer to events, they can still be said to be essentially uneventive constructions, in the sense that they do not primarily assert events.

2.6 Modality

Middles typically involve a notion of ability or modality, as shown by the following (attested) example, which appears attached to a laptop case:

(16) Back-pac straps tuck neatly away and the optional waist-pac can be removed to turn e-pac into a briefcase.

The first coordinated sentence is a middle, and could be paraphrased using a modal verb, as shown in (17). This is the construction that appears in the coordinate clause, confirming the parallelism between middles and paraphrases with modals. Otherwise coordination would not be as readily available, as shown by the oddity of (18), where no modality component is present in the second coordinated clause.

(17) Back-pac straps can be easily tucked away.
(18) ?Back-pac straps tuck easily away and the optional waist-pac is made of lycra.

But again, whereas middles typically involve a modality component, not all of them do. Consider example (19) (from Van Oosten 1977: 470) where no modality component is present, and which does not admit a paraphrase with a modal verb, as shown by (20):

(19) A: You didn't leave enough of a margin at the bottom of this page.
B: No, it just photocopied too low.

(20) ??It could be photocopied too low.

In Example (19), the absence of modality goes hand in hand with the absence of an implied Agent, the punctual or watered-down "eventive" interpretation discussed above (for which the past tense is crucial), and the lack of a "middle adverb". Its status as a middle is thus marginal, only warranted in view of two features. One of them is structural, namely, the fact that *photocopy* is a pure transitive verb, and ambiguity with an ergative interpretation is not available. Pages do not photocopy "all by themselves". Someone must do the photocopying. The other one is semantic: the sentence can indeed receive the middle interpretation that we have been characterizing. As noted by Rosta (1995: 128), by making use of the middle pattern, the original Agent shirks off the responsibility for the ill-photocopying, which is shifted to the piece of paper itself. From this perspective, the adverb could indeed be perceived as bringing about a clash of forces and as imputing antagonism to the subject. The fact that the photocopying was too low can be interpreted as going against the speaker's wishes. In other words, it would have been the speaker's wish that the photocopying had turned out successfully, but the sheet's fault that it did not.

2.7 Bringing it all together

Summing up so far, middles can be said to have a clear constructional meaning, which we refer to as the "middle interpretation", and which can be seen compositionally as a function of the meaning of the subject in combination with the verb and the adverb. It clusters, on the one hand, around the property reading and the idea of newsworthiness, which work together, and on the other, around the ever-present implied Agent argument, a force-exerting entity and a kind of beneficiary, which most frequently manifests itself in adverbial modification and which goes hand in hand with the presence of a modality component and uneventiveness.

That is how we would characterize a *paradigmatic* or *prototypical* middle sentence in English. We have already seen that deviations from the prototype do exist. Sentence (15) above did not exhibit the same degree of non-eventiveness as a prototypical middle, although it showed all the other features of the middle interpretation. Example (19) was even less prototypical, since it was more clearly eventive and it lacked a modality component and the interpretation contributed by the implied Agent argument and the middle adverb. The possibility of construing the middle interpretation, however, did exist, and the sentence could still be considered a middle. The important theoretical conclusion to draw from this is that the English middle construction does constitute a construction in the sense of a form-meaning association that exists independently of the lexical items that appear in it. The availability of a "middle" constructional meaning allows for the existence of middles which do not fully conform to our prototype, but which can nevertheless inherit the middle interpretation through the constructional pattern in which they appear.

This is the idea behind Davidse and Heyvaert's (2003: 63) inventory of middle types. By typifying the middle construction exclusively in terms of "the constructional link that exists between a non-agentive subject and an active VP", which contributes the semantic component shared by all middles, they are able to subsume under the middle category a wide range of data. These include, amongst others, the "Location/Subject + intransitive VP" type, exemplified in (21) (their example, p. 65, from the COBUILD corpus), the "Means/Subject + intransitive VP", found in (22) (their example, originally Van Oosten's 1986), and a "Means/Subject + transitive VP" type, shown in (23) (their example, taken from Levin 1993: 173):

(21) The top loch is fishing well.

(22) This music dances better than the other one.

(23) This wood carves beautiful toys.

These examples are considered by them as part of the middle paradigm, on an equal footing with more prototypical examples like *This book reads well.* It has to be acknowledged, however, that they are very marginal and idiosyncratic, and that they deviate significantly, especially structurally (their subject does not correspond to the original object), from our middle prototype. (See also Marín-Arrese, this volume, for an account of the middle prototype and deviations from it.)

3 Lexicalization

We argue that some middles are undergoing a lexicalization process, which constitutes further evidence of their meaning specialization. This is an aspect to which hardly any attention has been devoted in the literature.

It is indeed the case that the most frequent or best-established middles, those formed with the verbs *sell* or *read*, seem to be increasingly lexicalized, their link to their original transitive counterparts becoming gradually less clear.[3] We saw in the previous section that the middle use of the verb *read* has gained a bit of extra semantics and has come to mean something like "having the property of being easy to read by virtue of its style". Something similar happens to middles formed with the verb *sell*, like the one in (24), which do not refer directly to the act of selling in terms of a seller talking a potential customer into buying something and to the subsequent monetary transaction. Rather, they have a very specific and lexicalized meaning, that of "being very successful or in high demand", which has given rise to idiomatic expressions like that shown in (25):

(24) Flats in this part of the city sell very easily.

(25) Isabel Allende's novels sell like hot cakes.

The high degree of lexicalization attained by middles formed from verbs like *sell* or *read*, prototypes of a core middle, is confirmed by the fact that the middle use of these verbs serves as input to word-formation processes, as exemplified in (26)–(28):

(26) This model outsells all the others in our range. (OALD s.v. *outsell*)[4]

(27) They remind me of children's easy-readers. (BBC Radio 4, June 2003)

(28) One of her plays, *My Funeral Tea*, is a best-seller in the United States and is also known in Australia. (BNC, K4P 577)[5]

In sentence (26) the middle subject (*This model*) has assumed a full subject status, and the sentence has been reanalysed as an active sentence, to the point that a new direct object (*all the others in our range*) can be introduced. It constitutes an example of *out*-prefixation applied to a middle verb. Incidentally, another example of the reanalysis of middle *sell* as a fully-fledged active verb can be found in (29), where a direct object has also been introduced:

(29) "This book is buried, it will sell more copies if I put it there" (Ted Heslin, head of classification at Waterstone's bookshop, *The Times Magazine* 15 May 2004, p. 11)

The *-er* nominalizations that we find in (27) and (28), *easy-readers* and *best-seller*, also deserve some comment. The noun *easy-reader* receives a direct object interpretation. Equally, a best-seller refers to a book that sells very well, and not to a particularly successful salesman. These examples are derived from the middle use of the verbs *read* or *sell*, whose subjects also correspond to the original object of the verb. Like the middles from which they are derived, they are dependent on modification for a successful interpretation. Being nominals, modification comes in the form of adjectival premodification (*easy, best*), and yields highly lexicalized expressions. An *easy-reader* does not simply refer to a book that is easy to read. The noun *reader* has acquired a very specific meaning and has come to denote a book intended to give students practice in reading. The object interpretation, based on the middle verb, has become lexicalized. The same happens to *best-seller,* whose meaning is very specific: "one of the books having the largest sale of the year or the season" (OED s.v. *best* a. and adv. B.3b). Indeed, 88% of the occurrences of *best-seller* obtained from an online search in the BNC referred to books, the remaining 12% having to do with cars, games or other. Furthermore, these nominals based on middle verbs have become lexicalized to the point that they can serve as inputs to new formations. From *best-seller*, the OED (s.v. *best* a. and adv. B.3b) cites *best-selling, best-sellerdom* or *sellership* ("the state of achieving of being a best-seller"), and *best-sellerism* ("concentration on best-sellers"). The verb *best-sell* also exists. It could be seen as a back formation derived from *best-seller,* as the OED proposes (s.v. *best* a. and adv. B.3b), or rather, if, as we are assuming, these forms are derived from the middle use of *sell,* we could posit it is an incorporation of the adverbial element onto the middle verb itself:

(30) And, in the words of the elderly, this is a thoroughly "nice" book. I think it may best-sell. (1937 *Observer*, 8 August 6/5) [OED s.v. *best* a. and adv. B.3b]

More generally, from the point of view of the semantics of the English middle construction, the fact that *-er* suffixation can produce nominals related to middles is also significant. *-Er* nominals usually have an agentive interpretation (*writer, murderer*), although they can also have an instrumental role (*peeler, opener*) (Rappaport Hovav and Levin 1992). They all have an external argument reading: the writer is the person who writes, and not the object of his writing. Similarly, a peeler is something that peels, and an opener something that opens something else, and not the other way round. However, we have seen that *-er* nominals based on middle verbs have an internal argument interpretation (Patient or Theme), as Rappaport Hovav and Levin (1992: 146) point out. But there is more. They could be viewed as a sign of the extent to which the subject of a middle assumes subjecthood properties or, rather, exhibits the middle interpretation that we have been outlining. In order to do that, we will show that the *-er* suffix that we find in nominalizations derived from middles is not quite the same as the one we find in *writer* or *peeler*.

The *-er* nominals derived from middle verbs are parallel to the *-er* forms that we find in the following examples:

(31) He's such a looker! (*Sex and the City*, Channel 4 TV, September 2003)

(32) You can have a four-poster if you like. (BNC, AJY 2043)

Whilst they are not derived from middle verbs, these *-er* forms are not agentive or instrumental, as the examples above (*writer*, etc.) are. A looker here is not the person who looks at something, but the person who looks good, or who has the property of looking good, and a four-poster refers to a bedstead that *has* four posts. In other words, these forms pick out the subject of an essentially stative and descriptive statement and attribute some property to it. We will refer to it as the "property *-er*" and thus dissociate it from the more agentive or eventive *-er*. In fact, this semantic distinction correlates with Dowty's (1979: 55–59) distinction between stative and non-stative predicates: the "property *-er*" is essentially stative, and attaches to non-agentive subjects; the other one, which we might term "eventive *-er*", corresponds to predicates denoting eventualities, with a more agentive meaning.

The parallelism with middles is now quite straightforward. It is the property *-er* that we find in nominals derived from middles. When a noun is created by adding the suffix *-er* to a middle verb, the nominal picks out the subject of a middle verb and predicates a property of it, in line with the interpretation of middles we have argued for. Thus, a best-seller is a book that sells well. Rappaport Hovav and Levin (1992: 149) mention a few other examples like *broiler*, or *roaster*. A broiler is "a chicken for broiling, normally reared in close confinement in a broiler house" (OED s.v. *broiler* 2). A roaster is not someone who roasts food, and not simply a roasted pig either, but rather, in line with the property reading associated with the middle semantics, "a pig, or other article of food, fit for roasting" (OED s.v. *roaster* 3).

We will conclude this section by coming back to our original idea of lexicalization. The verb *wash* in (33) provides an example of how the middle use of a verb can not only become lexicalized, but also acquire an idiomatic meaning unrelated even to the standard middle meaning.

(33) The idea that water from the tap is as good as from the bottle doesn't wash, says Dr John Briffa. (*The Observer Magazine*, p. 74, 27 July 2003).

4 Marginal cases

This section concentrates on three types of problematic middle-like expressions. We will deal with the first two rather swiftly, but dwell a bit more on the third, which will deepen our insight into some of the issues that have arisen so far.

Consider first the following data:

(34) She takes a good photograph, though. (BNC, KBC 3850)

(35) Indeed a Rank executive told her she was an ugly girl with no talent who photographed terribly. (*The Week*, p. 40, 21 September 2002)

Example (34) consists of the sequence NP-V-NP, which, despite the oddness of the indefinite post-verbal NP, could well be interpreted as an active sentence, the NP *she* in subject position being an Agent and the NP *a good photograph* being a Patient or Theme. But that is not what the sentence means. Its meaning is the same as that conveyed by (35), which is indeed a middle, and where *she* refers to the person that appears on the photograph. Both are stative statements predicating a particular property of the subject, in this case the property of being photogenic. In these examples, *photograph* and *take a photograph* represent two distinct lexicalizations of the same meaning components. The term "lexicalization" is not being used here in the sense used in the previous section, but in Talmy's (1985b) sense. It refers to the association of meaning elements with surface forms. Thus, the verb *photograph* lexicalizes or "conflates" (Talmy's term) or, less technically, "compresses" in a single morpheme what can also be expressed by three separate morphemes. The modal component is realized as the adjective *good* when it modifies the noun, and as an adverb *well* when it modifies the verb. In both (34) and (35) the subject *she* corresponds to the object of the active sentence, a direct object in *photograph her* and an *of*-complement in *take a photograph of her*. Both sentences are semantically equivalent and (35) can be taken as a pseudo-middle.

The second type of middle-like construction, exemplified in (36), poses a more difficult problem. It illustrates what Lakoff (1977: 251) called "reflexive-patient-subject constructions", also known as "reflexive middles" in the literature:

(36) The subsequent article almost writes itself. (BNC, A6A338)

Fiengo (1980: 52) treats such structures as variants of the English middle construction. He argues that the meaning of the reflexive element is equivalent to an expression like "without aid", which suggests that it is functionally an adverb and that it occupies the adverb slot of the English middle construction. He bases this claim on the complementary distribution that the reflexive exhibits with respect to the adverbs normally found in middles, as (37) and (38) show (Fiengo's (1980: 52) examples):

(37) *Foreign cars sell themselves easily.

(38) *Foreign cars sell easily themselves.

Fellbaum (1989: 128), on the other hand, claims that examples like that in (36) are not middles at all, but plain reflexive sentences, in which the subject, which is a Theme, is interpreted metaphorically as an Agent. There is some appeal in both views. Dissociating examples like (36) from middles seems a reasonable proposal, given that both constructions are subject to different restrictions, reflexive middles being available with a narrower set of verbs than plain middles, as noted by Lakoff (1977: 252). Consider the following contrasts:

(39) This bread cuts easily./??This bread cuts itself.

(40) This book reads easily./??This book reads itself.

On the other hand, considering examples like (36) as pseudo-middles seems to be warranted on semantic grounds. Whereas, unlike in plain middles, the force exerted by the implied Agent is reduced to nothing, the responsibility or agent-like properties of the subject are compensatorily augmented, to the point that the subject bears exclusive responsibility for the action denoted by the verb. It could thus be said to epitomize the property reading characteristic of middles. And it is not exempt from a certain degree of lexicalization either. Example (36) means that there is something about the article that makes it *extremely* easy to write. I would consider it as an "emphatic" middle.

The third type of marginal middle-like structure we will consider is exemplified by the following sentences:

(41) Futon Company new sofa seats 3, sleeps 2, and costs just £199. (Advertisement in *The Independent Magazine*, Autumn 2001)

(42) This foldaway table seats four, folds into a carrying case and weighs just 21 lb. £69. (plus £10 p&p), from Huzar co. (BNC, FBL 3307)

(43) In other words it sleeps six erm and the landlady's willing to have one person sleeping on the floor officially. (BNC, JP7 345)

(44) The broader objectives were to provide a vehicle that was fun to drive, docile in traffic, quiet and refined and a comfortable four-seater. (BNC, A6X 351)

(45) The London-to-Edinburgh sleeper. (OALD s.v. *sleeper* 2(a))

Despite appearances, the structures in which the verbs *seat* and *sleep* appear in (41)–(43) bear little resemblance to middles. An object is present in both cases, and this time, unlike in the *photograph* example above, lexicalization facts (in Talmy's sense) cannot be invoked. The presence of an object in the case of *sleep* is most bizarre. It is semantically an Agent, and would appear in subject position in the canonical, intransitive usage of *sleep*, as in *I sleep on the sofa*. *Seat*, on the other hand, is a transitive, causative verb, as in *I seated the baby on my lap* although this is not the meaning that we find in the examples above. Furthermore, the subject in both (41) and (42) corresponds to what would normally be a locative adjunct. Notice too that these sentences lack an implied Agent argument, which was one of the distinctive features of the English middle construction. Structurally, therefore, these examples are very distant from our prototypical middle, and any resemblance we might see in them is simply due to their superficial makeup or stress pattern. They consist, like middles, of an NP followed by a verb, typically, like in middles, in simple present tense, and a post-verbal element, which is reminiscent of the adverbial modification found in middles. They are very fixed expressions. Their use seems to be limited to these two verbs and the post-verbal element most often consists of a single numeral. They might be better treated by positing separate verbs *seat* and *sleep*, with their own lexical entries and semantic and configurational properties.

A closer look at their semantics, however, reveals that, like middles, they are essentially stative structures predicating a property of the subject, namely, the property to fit a certain number of people. As in middles, a modality component is present here too. A sofa that seats four is a sofa that has the capacity of fitting four people or that can fit four people. Similarly, a flat that sleeps six is a flat that has the ability of fitting six people. The fact that *-er* nominalizations derived from these verb forms are available, as shown in (44) and (45) (*four-seater*, *sleeper*), provides additional motivation for the identification of our "property *-er*". Their semantic parallelism with middles, in turn, further highlights the property reading of the construction.

Consider now these data:

(46) In other words, the rear seats should only sit two children or two small adults uncomfortably, otherwise your four-sitter will not be shown on this Page. (*My Sports Car Pictures* webpage)

(47) Luxury Limousine. Sits 10 people comfortably. Ideal for groups or large families who want to have it all. (*Royal Dynasty Tour* webpage)

It is quite common for verbs to be able to be used both transitively and intransitively (e.g. *I broke the glass* vs. *The glass broke*), but it is only in a few verbs in English that this alternation shows up morphologically in an ablaut change in the root vowel of the verb. The pair *sit-seat* is one of them, together with others like *rise-raise or fall-fell.* In (46) and (47), unlike in the set of data above, the intransitive variant (*sit*) is used instead of the transitive one (*seat*). It could be argued that the source of these examples, the web, is less reliable than the corpus or magazine from which the data in (41), (42) and (43) have been obtained, and so we could dismiss them as instances of sloppy spelling. On the other hand, the OED does contain an entry for *sit* as a transitive verb, with the meaning of "to cause (a person) to sit". The most recent quotation with this usage, however, dates from 1895, and the entry itself is number 34 out of the 39 entries given for the verb *sit.*[6] The third possible explanation is more plausible and much more interesting from a grammatical point of view, namely, that these examples reflect a genuine use of the intransitive *sit.* Hesitation in the use of one form or the other would, at the very least, point to the perceived intransitive status of these structures, despite the presence of a post-verbal NP. Once more, this highlights the relationship between intransitivity, stativity and the predication of properties, as opposed to the agentivity and transitivity associated with the expression of eventualities. And again, the parallelism in this respect carries over to middles, which are also intransitive, not only structurally, but also semantically, in the sense of being stative statements predicating a property of the subject.

5 Conclusion

The property reading of the middle subject and the presence of a semantically present but unexpressed Agent argument are the two crucial ingredients around which the meaning of middles is construed. The notion of facility or easiness, from which the implied Agent benefits, modality and uneventiveness are also key features of what we have defined as a prototypical middle. Middles have been presented as semantically intransitive constructions. We have highlighted the lexicalization process that some middles are undergoing, which has come to confirm the very marked and idiosyncratic meaning of the construction. Some facts arising from it, and from our discussion of some marginal middle-like examples, have further supported our view of middles as essentially stative, unagentive and attributive sentences, pointing to their semantic intransitivity.

Notes

1. *Oxford English Dictionary*. Available online at http://dictionary.oed.com/entrance.dtl. Last accessed January 2006.
2. It is true, however, that a generic reading in the past is also possible.
3. See García de la Maza (2004) for quantitative data showing how middles formed from the verbs *sell, read, wash* and *cut* can be considered to form the group of "core" or "best-established" middles in English.
4. *Oxford Advanced Learner's Dictionary* (1995) (Fifth edition.) Ed. J. Crowther. Oxford: Oxford University Press.
5. Examples marked BNC are taken from the British National Corpus. Available online at http://sara.natcorp.ox.ac.uk/lookup.html. Accessed January 2004–January 2006.
6. A reviewer points out that this usage is common in present-day English, particularly in colloquial examples like *Sit yourself down*. This transitive use, however, is very different from the "middle" one investigated here.

References

Cruse, D. A. (1973) Some thoughts on agentivity. *Journal of Linguistics* 9: 11–23.

Davidse, K. and Heyvaert, L. (2003) On the so-called "middle" construction in English and Dutch. In S. Granger, J. Lerot and S. Petch-Tyson (eds) *Empirical Approaches to Contrastive Linguistics and Translation Studies* 57–73 Amsterdam: Rodopi.

Davidse, K. and Heyvaert, L. (2007) On the midde voice: An interpersonal analysis of the English middle. *Linguistics* 45(1): 37–82.

Dixon, R. M. W. (1991) *A New Approach to English Grammar, on Semantic Principles.* Oxford: Clarendon Press.

Dowty, D. R. (1979) *Word Meaning and Montague Grammar*. Dordrecht: Reidel.

Erades, P. A. (1975) *Points of Modern English Syntax: Contributions to English studies by P. A. Erades.* Amsterdam: Swets and Zeitlinger.

Fagan, S. (1988) The English middle. *Linguistic Inquiry* 19(2): 181–203.

Fagan, S. (1992) *The Syntax and Semantics of Middle Constructions.* Cambridge: Cambridge University Press.

Fellbaum, C. (1985) Adverbs in agentless actives and passives. In W. H. Eilfort, P. D. Kroeber and K. L. Peterson (eds) *Papers from the Twenty-first Regional Meeting of the Chicago Linguistics Society, Part 2: Papers from the parasession on causatives and agentivity* 21–31 Chicago, IL: Chicago Linguistics Society.

Fellbaum, C. (1989) On the reflexive middle in English. In C. Wilshire, R. Graczyk and B. Music (eds) *Papers from the Twenty-fifth Regional Meeting of the Chicago Linguistics Society* 123–132. Chicago, IL: Chicago Linguistics Society.

Fiengo, R. (1980) *Surface Structure: The interface of autonomous components.* Cambridge, MA: Harvard University Press.

Fillmore, C. (1968) The case for case. In E. Bach and R. T. Harms (eds) *Universals in Linguistic Theory* 1–90. New York: Holt, Rinehart and Winston.

García de la Maza, C. (2004) *The Grammar, Semantics and Productivity of the English Middle Construction.* Ph.D. dissertation. Dept. of Linguistics, University of Cambridge.

Gruber, J. (1967) Look and see. *Language* 43(4): 937–947.

Halliday, M. (1967) Notes on transitivity and theme in English. Part I. *Journal of Linguistics* 3(1): 37–81.

Hopper, P. and Thompson, S. (1980) Transitivity in grammar and discourse. *Language* 56: 251–299.

Jackendoff, R. (1972) *Semantic Interpretation in Generative Grammar.* Cambridge, MA: The MIT Press.

Jackendoff, R. (1992) Babe Ruth homered his way into the hearts of America. In T. Stowell and E. Wehrli (eds) *Syntax and the Lexicon* 155–178. San Diego, CA: Academic Press.

Keyser, S. and Roeper, T. (1984) On the middle and ergative constructions in English. *Linguistic Inquiry* 15: 381–416.

Lakoff, G. (1977) Linguistic Gestalts. In W. Beach, S. Fox and S. Philosoph (eds) *Papers from the 13th Regional Meeting of the Chicago Linguistics Society* 225–235. Chicago, IL: Chicago Linguistics Society.

Levin, B. (1993) *English Verb Classes and Alternations: A preliminary investigation.* Chicago, IL: University of Chicago Press.

Marín-Arrese, J. I. (this volume) Spontaneous and facilitative events revisited.

Rappaport Hovav, M. and Levin, B. (1992) *-Er* nominals: Implications for the theory of argument structure. In T. Stowell and E. Wehrli (eds) *Syntax and the Lexicon* 127–153. San Diego, CA: Academic Press.

Roberts, I. (1987) *The Representation of Implicit and Dethematized Subjects.* Dordrecht: Foris.

Rosta, A. (1995) The semantics of English mediopassives. In B. Aarts and C. Meyer (eds) *The Verb in Contemporary English* 123–144. Cambridge: Cambridge University Press.

Talmy, L. (1985a) Force dynamics in language and thought. In W. H. Eilfort, P. D. Kroeber and K. L. Peterson (eds) *Papers from the Twenty-first Regional Meeting of the Chicago Linguistics Society, Part 2: Papers from the parasession on causatives and agentivity* 293–337. Chicago, IL: Chicago Linguistics Society.

Talmy, L. (1985b) Lexicalization patterns: Semantic structure in lexical forms. In T. Shopen (ed.) *Language Typology and Syntactic Description* 57–149. Cambridge: Cambridge University Press.

Traugott, E. (2004) Historical pragmatics. In L. Horn and G. Ward (eds) *The Handbook of Pragmatics* 538–561. Oxford: Blackwell.

Van Oosten, J. (1977) Subjects and agenthood in English. In W. Beach, S. Fox and S. Philosoph (eds) *Papers from the Thirteenth Regional Meeting of the Chicago Linguistics Society* 459–471. Chicago, IL: Chicago Linguistics Society.

Van Oosten, J. (1986) *The Nature of Subjects, Topics and Agents: A cognitive explanation*. Bloomington, IN: Indiana University Linguistics Club.

Vendler, Z. (1984) Adverbs of action. In D. Testen, V. Mishra and J. Drogo (eds) *Papers from the Parasession on Lexical Semantics* 297–305. Chicago, IL: Chicago Linguistics Society.

8 An antipassive interpretation of the English "conative alternation": Semantic and discourse-pragmatic dimensions*

Pilar Guerrero Medina[a]

1 Introduction

Authors like Hopper and Thompson (1980), Cooreman (1994), Givón (2001b) and Polinsky (2008) show the correlations between the antipassive and "de-transitivized" constructions in nominative languages such as English, where the non-topical patient is demoted from a direct object into an oblique case. According to Cooreman:

> The domain of functions identified for the antipassive construction is by no means restricted to antipassives only. These same functions can be also expressed in many languages, ergative and accusative alike, that do not have an antipassive, sometimes by means of de-transitivized constructions, e.g. through deviations in the basic transitive case frames. (1994: 65)

Givón presents the examples in (1) to illustrate the connection between the conative and the antipassive in a nominative language like English, where "an object may be demoted into an oblique case to render a sense of low affectedness" (2001b: 171). The English expressions in (1b) and (1d) are characterized by the author as "antipassive intransitive" constructions as compared with their transitive counterparts in (1a) and (1c):[1]

(1) (a) He *shot* the deer.
    (b) He *shot* at the deer.

a Pilar Guerrero Medina is Lecturer in English Grammar at the University of Córdoba, Spain. E-mail: ff1gumep@uco.es

(c) She *kicked* the mule.
(d) She *kicked at* the mule.

In derivational accounts of argument structure, argument patterns such as the ones in (1a–b) and (1c–d) are presented as examples of the so-called "conative alternation", a type of transitivity alternation whereby the semantically affected transitive object becomes an oblique complement.[2] The conative variant has been associated with "attempted" action (Pinker 1989: 104; Levin 1993: 42; Tenny 1994: 45), "endeavour" (Huddleston 2002: 298), "non-achievement" (Dixon 2005: 298) or "lack of Completion" (Schlesinger 1985: 64).

In what follows I will attempt to analyse the semantic and discourse-pragmatic dimensions of the English conative, exploring the connections between the conative construction itself and what is considered to be an "antipassive" in the functional-typological literature.[3]

This article is organized as follows. In §2 I will address the question of the interaction between verb meaning and diathesis alternations, giving a brief overview of Levin's (1993), Tenny's (1994), Dowty's (2001) and Goldberg's (1995) analyses of the English conative alternation. The dual-transitivity verbs on which I have based my analysis will be presented in §3. In §4 I will explore the connections between the conative construction and the antipassive, drawing on data from the World Edition of the British National Corpus (henceforth BNC).[4] The main conclusions of this study will be summarized in §5.

2 The conative alternation in the linguistic literature: The lexically-based vs the construction-based approach

Levin (1993: 1) argues that "the behaviour of a verb, particularly with respect to the expression and interpretation of its arguments, is to a large extent determined by its meaning", and moreover that "verbs that fall into classes according to shared behaviour would be expected to show shared meaning components" (1993: 5).

In Levin's lexically-based approach to argument alternations, the conative alternation is restricted to verbs "whose meanings include notions of both contact and motion" (1993: 42) (cf. also Pinker 1989: 107). This would explain why *cut* and *hit* (whose meanings involve both components) are compatible with the conative alternation, while *break* (which lacks both components) and *touch* (which is a "pure verb of contact") are not.

In (2) I reproduce Levin's (1993: 41–42) list of the semantic verb classes which do and do not allow the conative alternation, including just some of the examples mentioned by the author. Classes of verbs that do not undergo the alternation are preceded by an asterisk.

(2) VERBS OF CONTACT BY IMPACT:
 (a) HIT VERBS: bang, bash, batter, beat, bump, hit, kick ...
 (b) SWAT VERBS: bite, claw, shoot (gun) ...
 (c) *SPANK VERBS: belt, birch, bludgeon, bonk ...
 POKE VERBS (some): dig, jab, poke, stick
 VERBS OF CUTTING:
 (a) CUT VERBS: chip, clip, cut, hack ...
 (b) *CARVE VERBS: bore, bruise, carve, chip ...
 SPRAY/LOAD VERBS (some): dab, rub, splash, spray ...
 *ALTERNATING VERBS OF CHANGE OF STATE including:
 (a) *BREAK VERBS: break, chip, crack, crash, crush, rip, tear ...
 (b) *BEND VERBS: bend, crease, crinkle, crumple ...
 *TOUCH VERBS: caress, graze, kiss, lick, touch ...
 PUSH/PULL VERBS: heave, jerk, press ...
 *DESTROY VERBS: annihilate, blitz, decimate, demolish, destroy ...
 VERBS OF INGESTING:
 (a) EAT VERBS: drink, eat
 (b) CHEW VERBS: chew, crunch, gnaw, lick, munch, nibble, sip ...
 (c) *GOBBLE VERBS: bolt, gobble, gulp, guzzle ...
 (d) *DEVOUR VERBS: consume, devour, imbibe, ingest ...
 *VERBS OF SENDING AND CARRYING:
 (a) *SEND VERBS: airmail, convey, deliver, dispatch, express ...
 (b) *SLIDE VERBS: bounce, float, move, roll, slide ...

It should be observed, however, that some of the asterisked verbs in Levin's list actually allow the conative alternation, as exemplified in (3a–b):

(3) (a) African hunting dogs attack their prey in a pack [...] They simply *tear at* the flesh of the victim until the animal is weak from loss of blood [...] (BNC, BLX 1773)
 (b) The spurs *ripped at* the Muslim's bird and drew blood on its back, just above the wing. (BNC, H89 231)

The fact that the two BREAK verbs *tear* and *rip* can be associated with the conative pattern indicates that a verb's eligibility for participation in the conative alternation is not exclusively dependent on its class membership, as claimed by authors such as Levin (1993: 7–8) and Guerssel *et al.* (1985: 50).[5]

Tenny (1994) and Dowty (2001) offer a more satisfactory explanation of the English conative, as they also account for the aspectual ingredients of the verbs involved in this alternation. Tenny (1994: 122) observes that the [+motion, +contact] constraint is not sufficient to explain why a verb like *break* does not undergo the alternation. Examining the aspectual role of verbs of motion and contact, the author concludes that there is also an aspectual condition on the alternation:

> Motion-towards and contact are two non-aspectual ingredients of the meaning of verbs that can undergo the conative alternation in modern English. The constraint that these verbs may not unambiguously specify a measuring argument is an aspectual condition on the alternation. These aspectual and non-aspectual elements of meaning combine to isolate a class of verbs that undergo the conative alternation in English. (Tenny, 1994: 123)

According to Tenny (1994: 47), when the conative construction applies to a verb which is ambiguous with respect to measuring arguments, it removes its measuring properties. It is only when the event participant is represented as a direct argument that it can be converted into a "measuring argument" by the addition of a resultative predicate, as in (4a), or a verb particle, as shown in (4c):

(4) (a) *hit* the fence to pieces
(b) **hit at* the fence to pieces
(c) *chew* the cheese *up*
(d) **chew at* the cheese *up*
Examples taken from Tenny (1994: 46).

Verbs of change of state (such as *break, crack, splinter,* etc.) which obligatorily require a "measuring argument", as they "enforce a delimiting change of state or impart an endstate entailment on the interpretation" (Tenny 1994: 46), cannot enter into the conative alternation. The change-of-state verbs *rip* and *tear,* which do not *unambiguously* require a measuring argument (see also §4.1.2), would therefore be allowed in the conative construction.

Along these lines, Dowty (2001) proposes an analysis where the semantic change that arises through a particular alternation "filters" the verbs can enter into it.[6] In the particular case of the English conative, the construction entails that the action is incomplete in one of two different ways:[7]

> With verbs that entail physical change in the patient, the derived construction means that some but not all of the patient is affected, and is consistent with the possibility that very little is affected, cf. *eat at the cake.*

> The remaining verbs in this construction entail motion and contact but not necessarily any physical change in the Patient at all, but they do involve a distinguishable manner or shape of movement by the agent even if contact fails to be achieved (*hit, swat, slap at the fly,* etc.). With these verbs, the action is understood not to involve contact but only to involve this characteristic movement. (Dowty, 2001: 184–185)

Contrary to lexically-based derivational approaches to argument structure, Goldberg (1995: 8) claims that the syntactic configuration of the conative construction cannot be uniquely predicted from the lexical semantics of the main verb. In Goldberg's constructionist approach, "the semantics of the verb classes and the semantics of the constructions are integrated to yield the semantics of particular expressions" (1995: 60). In order to delimit the verb classes that can be associated with the conative construction it is thus necessary to examine the types of relation that the verb's semantics bears to the semantics of the construction. As shown in (5), where I have adapted the notation of Goldberg (1995: 64), the event type designated by the verb can be related to the event type designated by the construction in two ways: [+motion, +contact] verbs like *shoot, hit, kick* or *cut* are related to the construction by the "intended-result relation", while verbs of "attention" like *look* and *aim* (which are not [+motion, +contact] verbs) may "fuse" with the conative construction, being thus regarded as "instances" of DIRECT-ACTION-AT:

(5) Syntax: Subj V Obl ("at")
Semantics: DIRECT-ACTION-AT <**agent** theme>[8]
INTENDED RELATION:
[verbal subevent: +motion, +contact] e.g. *shoot, hit, kick, cut*
INSTANCE: e.g. *look, aim, shout, growl*

This representation would allow us to assimilate expressions such as *Ethel struck at Fred* or *Ethel shot at Fred,* where "striking him" or "shooting him" is the intended result of the directed action, to other related expressions such as *Fred looked at Ethel* or *Ethel aimed at Fred,* where "the verb's semantics is an instance of the semantics of the construction" (Goldberg 1995: 64). Similarly, as Ikegami (1985: 282) points out, verbs of "shouting", "growling" and "scoffing", involving some notion of "directed action", could also be used as instances of the construction (e.g. *shout at a person, growl at a person, sneer at a person*).

Goldberg's (1995: 63) constraint that the verb that is related to the conative construction by the intended-result relation must be [+motion, +contact] serves to rule out verbs such as **move* (no contact) and **touch* (no motion), as predicted by Levin, but it does not clearly explain why the

BREAK verbs *tear* and *rip*, which may be said to involve some notions of motion and contact but which do not exemplify the "intended result relation", are actually allowed in the conative construction.

I believe that a constructionist account of the English conative is in principle superior to a lexically-based one: argument structure patterns such us those presented in (1) above cannot be *only* considered in terms of alternations (cf. Goldberg 2006: 34).[9] However, in my view, the Goldbergian approach still provides an incomplete picture of the problem. The conative linguistic pattern can be understood to form a construction, i.e. "a conventionalized pairing of form and function" (Goldberg 2006: 3), but Goldberg's representation in (5), where the meaning of the construction ("X DIRECTS ACTION AT Y") would remain constant independently of the relation existing between the meaning of the verb and the meaning of the construction, still needs to be further refined in order to fully reflect the semantic and discourse-pragmatic properties of the English conative.

3 The corpus

In this article I will restrict my analysis to one subtype of dual-transitivity verbs involving a contrast between transitive and prepositional uses in English, as illustrated by the examples in (1) above. My discussion will be based on data extracted from the BNC with verbs from four of the semantic classes presented in (2): three verbs of CONTACT BY IMPACT of the HIT and SWAT subtypes (i.e. *hit (at), kick (at), shoot (at)*), two verbs of BREAKING (i.e. *tear (at), rip (at)*), which appear as asterisked verbs in Levin's list, two verbs of CUTTING (i.e. *cut (at), hack (at)*) and two verbs of INGESTING of the CHEW subtype (i.e. *sip (at/on), nibble (at/on)*).

The definitions in (6) correspond to the transitive uses of these verbs, as found in the *Compact Oxford Dictionary*:[10]

(6) (a) CONTACT BY IMPACT
Hit: "(of a moving object or body) come into contact with (someone or something stationary) quickly and forcefully".
Kick: "strike or propel forcibly with the foot".
Shoot: "kill or wound (a person or animal) with a bullet or arrow".
(b) BREAKING
Tear: "to pull or rip apart or into pieces".
Rip: "tear or pull forcibly away from something or someone".
(c) CUTTING
Cut: "make an opening, incision, or wound in (something) with a sharp implement".
Hack: "cut with rough or heavy blows".

(d) INGESTING
Sip: "drink (something) by taking small mouthfuls".
Nibble: "take small bits of".

I have selected a manageable but representative sample of verbs allowing the conative construction. The three first classes (CONTACT BY IMPACT, BREAKING and CUTTING) include verbs that Dixon (2005: 110) classifies as AFFECT verbs. However, not all the AFFECT verbs selected for this analysis are actually prototypically transitive verbs. Using Tsunoda's (1985: 387) terminology, I will thus distinguish between inherently "resultative" AFFECT verbs, i.e. "those verbs which describe an action that not only impinges on the patient but necessarily creates a change in it" (such as *tear, rip, cut* and *hack*) and inherently "non-resultative" (and therefore less prototypical) AFFECT verbs (such as *shoot, hit* and *kick*), which do not necessarily involve any physical change in the patient.[11]

As shown in (2), the semantic class of verbs of INGESTING (which could also be characterized as "resultative" verbs, inflicting some change in the patient) is subdivided by Levin in four subclasses: EAT, CHEW, GOBBLE and DEVOUR verbs. Only the EAT and CHEW subsets allow the conative alternation. For this study I have chosen two verbs of the CHEW type (i.e. *sip* and *nibble*), whose meaning "involves a specification of the manner of ingesting" (Levin 1993: 214) and which are used in the conative construction more frequently than verbs of the EAT type. GOBBLE and DEVOUR verbs, which cannot occur without a holistic object, as exemplified in (7), would be filtered out by the "incompleted entailment" of the construction, to use Dowty's (2001) terminology:

(7) (a) I must confess I *gobbled* the meat *down* and I didn't notice the bone until it was too late. (BNC, HJC 1139)
(b) [...] he dropped his food and had to watch helplessly while they *devoured* every last scrap of it. (BNC, ACW 547)

4 Functional correlates of the English conative: Semantic and discourse-pragmatic dimensions

Cooreman (1994: 51) identifies one general function of the antipassive, under which all the other different subfunctions can be subsumed:

(8) The antipassive which is used for semantic/pragmatic reasons is best described as indicating a certain degree of difficulty with which an effect stemming from an activity by A on an identifiable O can be recognized.

The different subfunctions of the antipassive construction (presented in (9) below) will be determined by the particular way in which this difficulty may arise in a particular language. In what follows I will focus on the semantic and discourse-pragmatic functions of the English conative, analysing to what extent the conative construction fulfils similar functions to the antipassive. In §4.1 I will explore the semantic correlates of the conative construction; its discourse-pragmatic dimensions will be analysed in §4.2.

4.1 Semantic dimensions

Hopper and Thompson (1980: 252) identify ten semantic and grammatical components of Transitivity, each of which "involves a different facet of the effectiveness or intensity with which the action is transferred from one participant to another". "Low Transitivity" parameters in Hopper and Thompson's list (such as atelic aspect, non-punctuality, non-volitionality, negation, irrealis modality, low affectedness and low individuation of the Object) are reflected in the functions that Cooreman (1994: 52–64) regards as crucial parameters for the antipassive in ergative languages, which I reproduce in (9):[12]

(9) (a) Property of the O(bject): identifiability
(b) Property of the predicate: aspectual changes
(c) Property of the O(bject): affectedness
(d) Lack of volitionality on the part of A(gent)[13]

In the remainder of this section I will attempt to account for the correlations between the subfunctions of the antipassive in (9) and the specific functions of the English conative construction.

4.1.1 Property of the O: Identifiability

Cooreman (1994: 52–53) establishes a correlation between the property of O identifiability and the use of the antipassive in ergative languages. As illustrated in (10), the antipassive construction is obligatory in Mam, a Mayan language, when the O is unidentified:[14]

(10) (a)

ma	Ø-	-w	-aq'na	-7n	-a.
ASP	ABS.3SG	-ERG.1SG	-work	-DS	-1SG

"I worked it". (something)

(b) ma chin aq'na -n -a.
ASP ABS.1SG work -ANTIP -1SG
"I worked". (no implication of what was worked)
Examples taken from England (1988: 533), in Cooreman (1994: 53).

According to Cooreman (1994: 81), the functional domain of the antipassive, comprising its individual functions, can be described in general as "involving some level of difficulty with which the O participant of a proposition is or can be clearly and uniquely identified". Cooreman's scalar notion of "identifiability" corresponds in part to the notion of "individuation", defined by Timberlake (1975: 124) as "the degree to which the participant is characterized as a distinct entity or individual in the narrated event". The following binary hierarchies of O individuation are given by Hopper and Thompson (1980: 253): *proper/common*; *concrete/abstract*; *count/mass*; *animate/inanimate*; *singular/plural*, *definite/indefinite* and *referential/non-referential.*

In the sample of data on which this paper is based, highly individuated entities (i.e. [+concrete], [+count], [+singular]) were frequently presented as the oblique counterparts of the direct object in the conative construction:[15] 81.42% of the analysed examples with verbs of INGESTING (114 out of 140) had highly individuated objects, while in examples with AFFECT verbs the proportion was only 56.98% (102 out of 179).[16]

According to Hopper and Thompson (1980: 253), a highly individuated object is more likely to be regarded as totally affected than a non-individuated object. However, I have found that there is no one-to-one correspondence between O individuation and O affectedness in the English conative construction, as highly individuated objects may be presented as non-affected or partially affected entities (see the examples in §4.1.3 below).

4.1.2 Property of the predicate: Aspectual changes

Cooreman (1994: 57) reports that the antipassive is "likely to describe an activity without a perceptible onset or conclusion". The author's Chamorro example in (11) illustrates the use of the antipassive to describe an iterative event:

(11) Mang-galuti gue' ni ga'lago.
ANTIP-hit ABS.3SG OBL dog
"He pounded on/repeatedly hit the dog".

As Polinsky (2008: 5) observes, comparable effects can be found in the English conative, which, like the antipassive, frequently carries an iterative meaning:[17]

(12) At a meal have a glass of water as well as wine and keep *sipping at* the water so that it is not your wine glass which is being constantly refilled. (BNC, BNA 1202)

Tenny (1994: 47) claims that "the conative construction removes the measuring properties of the verb's internal argument, if it has any". However, as illustrated by Dixon's example in (13), the conative construction does not necessarily remove the measuring properties of the verb altogether when it applies to a resultative verb describing a gradual change of state:

(13) He kept *tearing at* the wrapping paper until it was all removed.

The NP that measures out the event in (13), *the wrapping paper*, acts here like an Incremental Theme (Dowty 1991: 568): the action was done several times, "bit by bit until a result was achieved" (Dixon 2005: 119).

With non-measuring verbs of contact which do not describe a gradual change, the plural object frequently triggers a non-delimited repetitive reading in the conative construction:

(14) (a) *Kicking at* pine cones on the path, Mungo was halfway to the top of the slope when a slight figure appeared round the corner of the station entrance. (BNC, ACV 92)
(b) Up in the chestnut branches girls and boys were clambering about, *hitting at* the spiked green conkers and knocking them down on to the heads below. (BNC, A0N 627)
(c) Gourmets lured them to piles of turnips, then *shot at* them with duck-guns. (BNC, F9H 1749)

An adjunct of frequency may force the bounded iterative reading when the verb combines with a singular object, as is the case with *shoot* in (15):

(15) The Australian case of McKay [...] involved a chicken farmer who, when he found an intruder stealing chickens, *shot at* him five times, killing him. (BNC, ACJ 273)

The aspectual nature of the verbs that can be associated with the conative pattern is thus decisive in two main respects: on the one hand, only verbs which do not involve "a strong enough entailment of completion of action" (Dowty 2001: 185) are compatible with the construction; on the other, the way in which the conative construction cancels the entailment of completion of its transitive counterpart is strongly dependent on the measuring properties, if any, of the verbal predicate.

4.1.3 Property of the O: Affectedness

As stated in §1, the demotion of the patient into an oblique case to cancel the affectedness entailment of the transitive verb is commonly regarded as the main function of the English conative alternation in the linguistic literature. According to Dixon (2005: 297–298), the insertion of a preposition between a transitive verb and its object NP is a reflection of the conceptual deviance from "an 'ideal' transitive event" in English. Along these lines, Halliday and Matthiessen (2006/1999: 173) distinguish between "entity as participant" (in *shoot the pianist*) and "entity as circumstance" (in *shoot at the pianist*) and point out that "the pianist is more likely to escape unscathed as a circumstance than as a participant".

This deviation from an "ideal" transitive event is also illustrated by the examples in (16), where the insertion of *at* creates a semantic distance between the CONTACT BY IMPACT verb and the (highly individuated) Object:

(16) (a) I drove and would you believe, my ball *hit* the marker and bounced back. And Willie admonished me. "I told ye to *hit at* it, I didna' tell ye to *hit* it, he muttered." (BNC, CBC 11404)

(b) In front and to each side, people were *shooting at* him, but they all missed. (BNC, G0L 3632)

(c) For example, the question may state that the defendant *shot at* a burglar when a bystander was standing dangerously close, and hit the bystander. (BNC, FRA 636)

As stated by Dowty (2001: 184–185), the entailment of incompletion may manifest itself in two different ways (see §2). With verbs of contact, the conative construction may be used to indicate that contact is not achieved, as in (16). There are other cases, however, where the conative seems to impose "a sense of partial Affectedness of the O" (Hopper and Thompson 1980: 268).[18] The sentence pairs in (17) exemplify this "holistic/partitive" effect, which I have found to be frequent with resultative verbs like *nibble* and *tear* in their transitive and conative uses.

(17) (a) [...] when he could not immediately think of an answer he *nibbled* the canapé and viewed the questioner with cold button eyes. (BNC, CDN 1047)

(b) Moodie, more like a mouse than ever, *nibbled at* a bit of cheese. (BNC, HU0 156)

(c) Oliver *tore* the meat to pieces with his teeth as if he were a wild animal. (BNC, FRK 159)

(d) [...] and [she] did the only thing possible – *tore at* the bread with her teeth, one bite, two ... three – stuffing her mouth till the bread protruded and she could hardly chew. (BNC, C85 486)

But the conative construction with non-resultative verbs of CONTACT BY IMPACT such as *kick, hit* or *shoot* does not necessarily correlate with a marked decrease in O affectedness, as exemplified in (18):

(18) (a) Philip *kicked at* the pile of sticks he'd gathered for his trap, scattering them. (BNC, ABX 413)

(b) Up in the chestnut branches girls and boys were clambering about, *hitting at* the spiked green conkers and knocking them down on to the heads below. (BNC, A0N 627)

(c) (...) Mr J. Vicars, nearly thirty years ago, *shot at*, and wounded both the eagles at the same time; one being descried immediately behind the other. The eagles were afterwards found dead. (BNC, B3H 1073)

The oblique objects in (18) are presented as affected entities. The achievement of the particular result denoted by the verb in each case is signalled either by a non-finite clause, as in (18a–b), or by an independent finite clause, as in (18c). It should be noted that, with these verbs, the conative construction may also be understood to indicate that "the emphasis is not on the effect of the activity on some specific object [...] but rather on the subject's engaging in the activity" (Dixon 2005: 299).

The meaning difference between the transitive and prepositional uses of the same verb in terms of "endeavour" vs "success" is not always evident with resultative verbs of BREAKING and INGESTING either, as shown by the sentence pairs in (19):

(19) (a) [...] he *tore* the books as his father weakened. (BNC, A0P 418)

(b) The mongrel *tore* savagely *at* the newspapers [...] (BNC, EA5 621)

(c) Jay sprawled on the floor, *sipped* wine, stopped herself grabbing Lucy's grabbable ankles, held herself back. (BNC, A0L 1533)

(d) Our Gallic neighbours *sipped* disdainfully *at* orange juice. (BNC, CJV 1355)

The examples with *tear* in (19a–b) above contain clearly affected Objects, irrespectively of whether they are presented as direct or oblique arguments. In (19c–d), on the other hand, the mass noun triggers an unbounded and "unaffectedness" interpretation in both the transitive and prepositional variants of *sip*.

It should also be observed that the conative construction (with both resultative and nonresultative verbs) is frequently used in contexts where there is a certain degree of ambiguity as to whether the object was actually affected or not, as shown in (20):

(20) (a) For a moment she almost hated him. She *kicked at* the hay in a burst of frustration. (BNC, C85 2351)

(b) A figure popped out of a doorway to Alexei's left, and he *cut at* it with his sword and ran on. (BNC, G17 1991)

(c) Soldiers also *shot at* mourners burying the dead at two cemeteries in Bamako. (BNC, A03 86)

There are even cases where the action denoted by the verb rather affects the instigator of the action, and not the object, as exemplified in (21):

(21) (a) A rock lay in his way and in revenge he *kicked at* it, catching the lower eye of one of his boots against its sharp side [...] (BNC, BN1 2064)

(b) I *kicked at* his leg but almost overbalanced. (BNC, HR7 1578)

(c) There was frost on his hair, on the fur of his hood, but soon, as he *hacked at* the tree, his skin began to glow and a fine, warm moisture gleamed on his face. (BNC, HTM 2495)

As is the case with the antipasssive, "which *sometimes* correlates with a low degree of affectedness of the O" (Cooreman 1994: 58; my emphasis, PGM), I have found that the conative construction does not necessarily correlate with a marked decrease of O affectedness in the examples selected for analysis in this paper. According to Ikegami (1985: 280), one possible way of accounting for the restriction on the choice of the prepositional pattern "v_i + *at*" would be "to say that the verb implies a goal-achieving intention". It should be emphasized, however, that it is the undertaking of the action rather than the achievement of a definite result which is frequently taken as the goal.

4.1.4 Lack of volitionality on the part of A

Hopper and Thompson (1980: 269) observe that in ergative languages "the degree of planned involvement" of the Agent is an important factor in the selection of an ergative (i.e. more transitive) construction. However, Cooreman (1994: 62) shows some reservations as to the nature of the correlation between the lack of volitionality on the part of the Agent and the use of the antipassive. According to the author (1994: 71), the antipassive coding for a relative decrease in the involvement of A is due to a "cross-over" from the functional domain of the passive.

Tsunoda (1985: 393) regards the volitionality and agency features in Hopper and Thompson's list as irrelevant notions, as far as the manifestation of the transitive case frame NOM-ACC is concerned. As shown in (21), it is the affectedness of the patient that is taken to be the crucial parameter for Transitivity.

(22) (a) I *hit* him. NOM-ACC; patient affected; either volitional or non-volitional; either agentive or non-agentive.

(b) I *hit at* him. NOM-*at*; patient not affected; volitional; agentive.

I agree with Tsunoda that the conative construction frequently correlates with a high degree of volitionality of the Agent. However, there also seems to be a certain degree of correlation between the degree of involvement of the Agent and the aspectual delimitedness of the predication.

Collocations of verbs of INGESTING with agent-oriented adverbs such as *appreciatively, thoughtfully, cautiously* or *carefully* reveal that the conative construction with these verbs, which commonly co-occur with highly individuated objects (see §4.1.1), is also frequently associated with the deliberate involvement of the Agent:

(23) (a) Mrs Stych, however, *nibbled* appreciatively *at* one of the chocolate morsels. (BNC, CDN 1860)
(b) Melissa *nibbled* thoughtfully *at* a cookie. (BNC, HNJ 2571)
(b) A crewman served him with a cup of mediocre wine, and he *sipped at* it cautiously. (BNC, FSE 174)
(c) She carefully *nibbled at* the pizza. Jack was on his fifth piece and Zack was eating his seventh.
http://www.quizilla.com/stories/6344109/alex-gaskarth-this-four-leaf-clover-is-all-but-useless-now-10-21k-
Accessed on 13 March 2009.

Non-resultative verbs of CONTACT BY IMPACT such as *shoot, kick* and *hit* can be used to express situations involving a lower degree of deliberate intervention of the Agent:

(24) (a) They wandered on, aimlessly *kicking at* the pine cones. (BNC, B3J 2291)
(b) Without warning the shower curtain was ripped off and all she could do was scream and *hit* aimlessly *at* the air. http://forum.lu.scio.us/showthread.php?t=2360&page=2 -72k -
Accessed on 13 March 2009.
(c) They aimlessly *shot at* innocent people. It's not like they sought them out and chose who to kill.
http://www.youtube.com/user/koljastar - 98k -
Accessed on 13 March 2009.

In the examples above, the co-occurrence of *aimlessly* with non-individuated (and non-delimiting) objects (*the pine cones, the air* and *innocent people*) clearly indicates that the action was not geared towards achieving a definite result. There is not an "intended endpoint" (Depraetere 1995: 2–3), and therefore, in these cases, the action is presented (and perceived) as unbounded. As stated in §4.1.3, the conative construction may be understood to focus on the activity itself, and not necessarily on the result of the action.

A verb like *shoot*, however, also co-occurs freely with an agent-oriented adverb like *carefully* in bounded linguistic expressions, as exemplified in (25):[19]

(25) He carefully *shot at* the engine, which was luckily vulnerable. It exploded and Jack grinned. http://runescape.salmoneus.net/forums/index.php?act=Print&client=printer&f=102&t=177507 - 114k
Accessed on 13 March 2009.

Finally, I have also found that in 37.03% (20 out of 54) of the examples with the two BREAK verbs *tear* and *rip*, the conative variant has been used to express non-volitional situations with inanimate instigators and highly affected objects, as exemplified in (26).

(26) (a) The front of the hurricane *tore at* the lower flanks of the mountains, rending great trees from the rain forest and tossing them aside as if they were little more than sticks. (BNC, AMU 1905)
(b) [...] her eyes following the vigorous heave and surge of the mole-brown water as it tore down past them and *ripped at* the curve of the bank, lipping half across the trodden right of way. (BNC, H8L 421)

It should be noted, however, that inanimate subjects are not uncommon when these verbs are used transitively, as in (27):[20]

(27) (a) Then came the terrifying crash as the coral *tore* the ship's bottom out. (BNC, AMU 1568)
(b) Each burst *ripped* the air like split canvas. (BNC, HRA 4382)

To recap the argument so far, in this section I have tried to show that the English conative parallels some of the features of the antipassive construction in ergative languages. The semantic properties of the English conative can be described in terms of Cooreman's (1994) general function of the antipassive, which can in turn be decomposed into scalar subfunctions determining the "degree of difficulty" with which a particular action is transferred from the Agent to the (oblique) Object. The necessary level of difficulty for the conative construction to be used in English is to a great extent dependent on the aspectual nature of the verb, which determines the way in which the entailment of incompletion of the construction is manifested. The degree of involvement of the Agent, which frequently correlates with the degree of individuation of the Object, two factors which are not exclusively dependent on the semantic properties of the verbal predicate, have also proved to be relevant (though not decisive) features to determine the level of difficulty with which the effect of the action on the Object can be recognized.

4.2 Discourse-pragmatic dimensions

A discourse-pragmatic approach to the functional domain of the conative alternation should take into account the dimension of *topicality*, which Givón (2001a: 198) defines as "a cognitive dimension, having to do with the focus of attention on one or two important event-or-state participants during the processing of multi-participant clauses".

Givón (1994: 9–11, 2001b: 123) proposes two text-based methods in order to assess the topicality of the participants in discourse, i.e. *anaphoric distance* (AD) and *cataphoric persistence* (CP). The AD method measures the number of clauses between the referent's present appearance and its previous occurrence in the preceding discourse; the CP method, on the other hand, measures the number of times the referent occurs in the subsequent discourse.[21]

I have applied Givón's text-based methods of *anaphoric distance* and *cataphoric persistence* to assess the object topicality in the sample of contextualized BNC examples illustrating the conative uses of the AFFECT verbs presented in (6). These methods are based on the assumption that more topical arguments "tend to be more *anaphorically accessible* ('continuous') and more *cataphorically persistent* ('recurrent')" (Givón 1994: 10).

The following AD values have been assigned: low AD (1–2), when the referent occurs within the preceding two clauses from its present use, vs. high AD (>2), when the referent is not found in the immediately preceding two clauses. As for CP values, low CP (0) has been assigned when the argument does not recur in the next two or three clauses following its use vs. high CD (1/>1), when the argument recurs once or more following its use in the construction. The average CP and AD measures for the analysed conative structures are presented in Table 8.1.

The results of my analysis corroborate Cooreman's (1994) and Givón's (2001b) claims regarding the topicality of the object in the antipassive

Table 8.1. AD and CP of oblique objects in the conative construction with AFFECT verbs

AFFECT verbs	*Low AD*	*High CD*
CONTACT BY IMPACT	45.23%	33.33%
BREAKING	31.14%	29.50%
CUTTING	35.29%	14.30%
Total (%)	38.54%	28.49%

construction. In Givón's words, "the object in an antipassive clause may be semantically referring or even definite and thus anaphoric, but still non-topical and unlikely to persist in the subsequent (cataphoric) discourse" (2001b: 168).

As shown in Table 8.1, the *backgrounding* of the Object's referential identity can also be regarded as a "core" function of the English conative (Cooreman 1994: 67). I have found that 38.54% of the oblique objects with AFFECT verbs (69 out of 179) were anaphorically accessible; however, only in 28.49% of the cases (51 out of 179) did the object referent persist in the subsequent discourse.

Not surprisingly, examples of cataphorically persistent objects with AFFECT verbs corresponded mainly to human participants, including first person and second person natural topics ranking high in the animacy hierarchy (Silverstein 1976):[22]

(28) (a) I was looking at a muzzle *shooting at* me and I was quite content. I knew what was happening. (BNC, CBE 2559)

(b) He swung left to right, back again, careered across the road, in and out of the trees. In front and to each side, people were *shooting at* him, but they all missed. He unswung the machine-gun and sprayed the bullets into the trees [...]. (BNC, G0L 3632)

(c) The Prince was *hitting at* the running men with the flat of his sabre, but they feared an emperor far more than they feared a prince and so they kept on running. (BNC, CMP 2756)

5 Final remarks

In this article I have explored the connections between the English conative construction and the antipassive, with the aim of throwing more light on the semantic and discourse-pragmatic functions of the English conative construction itself. The main conclusions of this study are summarized below:

1. The conative construction often entails a modification of the *Aktionsart* properties of the predication.[23] As shown in §4.1.2, the aspectual nature of the verbs that can be integrated with it has proved to be relevant in determining the semantic properties of the conative construction, which (like the antipassive) is frequently associated with non-delimited readings.
2. The interaction between lexical and constructional meaning should be here addressed from a double perspective: on the one hand, a

semasiological approach seems to be in order, since the English conative is sensitive to aspectual and non-aspectual components of verb meaning. But a lexically-based approach is not entirely satisfactory to account for the interaction between verb meaning and argument structure in the conative construction, as there are semantic (and discourse-pragmatic) constraints that should be associated directly with the conative construction itself. However, as stated in §2, Goldberg's (1995) rough representation of the semantics of the English conative as "X DIRECTS ACTION AT Y" still needs to be further refined to give a full account of the conative construction. The semantic and discourse-pragmatic dimensions of the construction would be better captured under Cooreman's (1994: 65) general function of the antipassive, presented in (8).

3. Finally, it has also been my contention that the English conative is also sensitive to the pragmatics of topicality. The conative variant allows the speaker to focus on the activity itself, and not necessarily on the result of the action the verb denotes, which is frequently transferred to an object which does not tend not occur again soon in the discourse, thus showing a low degree of cataphoric persistence.

   As in the case of the antipassive, the notion of *referential backgrounding* (Cooreman 1994) can be understood to be a "core" function of the conative construction. The correlation of the construction with the notion of *propositional backgrounding* (cf. Hopper and Thompson 1980: 200ff, Cooreman 1994: 69) remains an issue for future research.

Notes

* The research reported here has been conducted within the framework of the projects FFI 2008-04448/FILO and FFI 2008-04585/FILO, funded by the Spanish Ministry of Education and Innovation. I am grateful to Christopher Butler and to two anonymous referees for their useful comments and suggestions on earlier versions of this paper.

1. Cooreman (1994: 82 n1) is, however, reluctant to use the term "antipassive" to refer to de-transitivization processes in nominative/accusative languages like English. Her structural definition of the antipassive is restricted to ergative languages, where the agent is typically coded as an absolutive NP, and the object (if present) is marked otherwise.

2. In the intransitive variant the object is rendered by a prepositional phrase most frequently headed by the preposition *at* (or sometimes *into* or *on* with verbs of INGESTING like *bite, sip* and *nibble*, or the PUSH/PULL verbs). See Levin's (1993) taxonomy in (2).
3. The term "antipassive" was introduced by Silverstein (1972: 395) in the linguistic literature to refer to a construction which is the inverse equivalent of the passive in ergative languages.
4. See http://www.natcorp.ox.ac.uk/. BNC examples will be identified by means of a three-letter code and the sentence number within the text where the hit was found.
5. Cf. also Rodríguez Arrizabalaga (2003: 115).
6. In Dowty's lexically-based approach to argument alternations, the "alternation" is analysed "as the application of a lexical rule to a verb, changing the subcategorization it has in X to the new categorization it has in Y" (2001: 173).
7. The verbs investigated in this study are representative of the two subsets mentioned by Dowty (see §2). Verbs of BREAKING, CUTTING and INGESTING would be included in the group of "physical change" verbs. The "remaining verbs" correspond to the CONTACT BY IMPACT subset.
8. The "agent" (a profiled argument role, expressed by a direct grammatical relation) is indicated by boldface. The "theme" argument is defined as an "argument which undergoes a change of state or location" (Goldberg 1995: 112).
9. I do not, however, fully support Goldberg's (2006: 25) claim that "each argument structure pattern is best analyzed on its own terms, without relying on explicit or explicit reference to a possible alternative paraphrase" and that "the robust generalizations are surface generalizations" (p. 33). In contrast to Goldberg's approach, I agree with Davidse (this volume) that verb-specific alternations are "semantically relevant *both* to verb meaning and to the semantics of constructions" (p. 12).
10. Available online at http://www.askoxford.com/dictionaries/. Last accessed on 21 November 2009.
11. These verbs may include a resultative predicate to describe the precise effect of the action denoted by the verb on the object, as in *kick someone unconscious* or *shoot someone dead* (Dixon 2005: 113). See also Tenny's (1994) example in (4a).
12. The functional correlates of the antipassive are presented in order of frequency of occurrence in the 19 ergative languages on which Cooreman (1994) bases her study.
13. Two characteristics are subsumed by Cooreman (1994: 52–64) under "Other marginal or infrequent functional correlates of the antipassive": *Lack of volitionality on the part of A* and *Counterfactualness*. The latter will not be regarded as a relevant feature in the present study, where all of the analysed examples will be affirmative and in the "realis" mode.

14. The meanings of the abbreviations in (10) and (11) are as follows: ANTIP: antipassive; ASP: aspectual marker; ABS: absolutive; ERG: ergative; DS: directional suffix; OBL: oblique.
15. As definiteness and referentiality are predictable properties of discourse topicality these two features will be computed in §4.2, where I will assess the Object topicality in the corpus examples with AFFECT verbs. The definiteness vs indefiniteness relation obviously correlates with the accessibility of referents in the preceding discourse, and therefore with givenness (cf. Chafe 1976: 42). "Anaphorically accessible" objects (Givón 2001a: 198) tend to be [+definite] and [+referential] objects with a specific referent playing some role in the discourse.
16. The proportion of highly individuated objects to each of the verb classes was as follows: 60.71% (51/84) to CONTACT BY IMPACT verbs; 50.81% (31/61) to BREAKING verbs and 58.82% (20/34) to verbs of CUTTING. Examples illustrating metaphorical uses of these verbs were discarded from the present study, e.g. *Every racking pain tore at him* (BNC, CDY 1855) or *He hacked at Mr Lawson's trade deficit* (BNC, A4U 196).
17. The addition of the verb particle *away* may reinforce the iterative reading, e.g. (...) *almost all the other tables seemed to be occupied by ladies of Habsburg vintage who sipped away at their camparis or white wine or, in two cases, glasses of beer* (BNC, AE8 1371).
18. As Pinker (1989: 108) points out, "If *John cuts at the bread*, it's not that the knife never arrives at the bread; rather, the bread was not properly cut".
19. I have found ca. 9000 occurrences where *carefully* collocates with *shot at* on Google; only 73 solutions have been found for the entry *shot aimlessly at*. Collocations of *nibble* and *sip* with the adverb *aimlessly* are however very rare on Google. I have only retrieved 3 occurrences of *nibbled aimlessly at* and 1 of *sipped aimlessly at*.
20. Inanimate subjects were presented as the instigators of the action in 10.53% (67 out of 636) of the examples in the corpus where *rip* and *tear* were used as transitive verbs.
21. Givón (2001b: 123) counts how many times a particular referent recurs in the next 10 clauses following its appearance in a particular construction. The author assigns different AD and CD values: low AD (1-3) vs high AD (>3); high CP (>2) vs low CP (0-2).
22. The notion of "Natural topicality" refers to "the preference to assign topicality to NPs higher in the animacy hierarchy" (Croft 1991: 151).
23. Following Dik (1997: 106–107), the term *Aktionsart* (or "Mode of Action") is here used to refer to those aspectuality distinctions concerning "the internal semantics of the predication".

References

Chafe, W. L. (1976) Givenness, contrastiveness, definiteness, subjects, topics, and point of view. In Ch. N. Li (ed.) *Subject and Topic* 25–55. New York: Academic Press.

Cooreman, A. (1994) A functional typology of antipassives. In B. Fox and P. J. Hopper (ed.) *Voice: Form and function* 49–88. Amsterdam: Benjamins.

Croft, W. (1991) *Syntactic Categories and Grammatical Relations*. Chicago, IL: University of Chicago Press.

Davidse, K. (this volume) Alternations as a heuristic to verb meaning and the semantics of constructions.

Depraetere, I. (1995) On the necessity of distinguishing between (un)boundedness and (a)telicity. *Linguistics and Philosophy* 18(1): 1–19.

Dik, S. C. (1997) *The Theory of Functional Grammar, Part I: The structure of the clause*. Berlin: Mouton de Gruyter.

Dixon, R. M. W. (2005) *A Semantic Approach to English Grammar*. Oxford: Oxford University Press.

Dowty, D. R. (1991) Thematic proto-roles and argument selection. *Language* 67(3): 549–619.

Dowty, D. R. (2001) The semantic asymmetry of "argument alternations" (and why it matters). In G. van der Meer and A. G. B. ter Meulen (eds) *Making Sense: From lexeme to discourse* 171–186. Groningen: Centre for Language and Cognition. [Groninger Arbeiten zur germanistischen Linguistik 44].

England, N. M. (1988) Mam voice. In M. Shibatani (ed.) *Passive and Voice* 525–545. Amsterdam: Benjamins.

Givón, T. (1994) The pragmatics of de-transitive voice: Functional and typological aspects of inversion. In T. Givón (ed.) *Voice and Inversion* 3–44. Amsterdam: Benjamins.

Givón, T. (2001a) *Syntax: An introduction. Volume I*. Amsterdam: Benjamins.

Givón, T. (2001b) *Syntax: An introduction. Volume II*. Amsterdam: Benjamins.

Goldberg, A. E. (1995) *Constructions: A construction grammar approach to argument structure*. Chicago, IL: University of Chicago Press.

Goldberg, A. E. (2006) *Constructions at Work: The nature of generalization in language*. Oxford: Oxford University Press.

Guerssel, M., Hale, K., Laughren, M., Levin, B. and Eagle, J. W. (1985) A cross-linguistic study of transitivity alternations. *Papers from the Twenty-first Regional Meeting of the Chicago Linguistics Society, Part 2: Papers from the parasession on causatives and agentivity* 48–63. Chicago, IL: Chicago Linguistics Society.

Halliday, M. A. K. and Matthiessen, C. M. I. M. (2006/1999) *Construing Experience through Meaning: A language-based approach to cognition*. London: Continuum. (Originally published by Cassell, 1999.)

Hopper, P. J. and Thompson, S. A. (1980) Transitivity in grammar and discourse. *Language* 56(2): 251–299.

Huddleston, R. (2002) The clause: Complements. In R. Huddleston and G. K. Pullum (eds) *The Cambridge Grammar of the English Language* 213–321. Cambridge: Cambridge University Press.

Ikegami, Y. (1985) "Activity" – "accomplishment" – "achievement" – A language that can't say "I burnt it, but it didn't burn" and one that can. In A. Makkai and A. K. Melby (eds) *Linguistics and Philosophy: Essays in honor of Rulon S. Wells* 265–304. Amsterdam: Benjamins.

Levin, B. (1993) *English Verb Classes and Alternations: A preliminary investigation.* Chicago, IL: University of Chicago Press.

Pinker, S. (1989) *Learnability and Cognition: The acquisition of argument structure.* Cambridge, MA: The MIT Press.

Polinsky, M. (2008) Antipassive constructions. In M. Haspelmath, M. S. Dryer, D. Gil and B. Comrie (eds) *The World Atlas of Language Structures Online* 1–8 (Chapter 108). Munich: Max Planck Digital Library. Retrieved on 6 February 2009 from http://wals.info/feature/108

Rodríguez Arrizabalaga, B. (2003) Sobre verbos de cambio ingleses y españoles: las clases de "breaking" y "cutting" frente a las de "romper" y "cortar". In M. Martínez Vázquez (ed.) *Gramática de Construcciones: Contrastes entre el inglés y el español* 91–140. Huelva: University of Huelva.

Schlesinger, I. M. (1985) On the semantics of the object. In B. Aarts and Ch. F. Meyer (eds) *The Verb in Contemporary English* 54–74. Cambridge: Cambridge University Press.

Silverstein, M. (1972) Chinook Jargon: Language contact and the problem of multi-level generative systems, I. *Language* 48(2): 378–406.

Silverstein, M. (1976) Hierarchy of features and ergativity. In R. M. W. Dixon (ed.) *Grammatical Categories in Australian Languages* 112–171. Canberra: Australian Institute of Aboriginal Studies.

Tenny, C. L. (1994) *Aspectual Roles and the Syntax-semantics Interface.* Dordrecht: Kluwer.

Timberlake, A. (1975) Hierarchies in the genitive of negation. *The Slavic and Eastern European Journal* 19(2): 132–138. Retrieved on February 2009 from http://www.jstor.org/stable/306765

Tsunoda, T. (1985) Remarks on transitivity. *Journal of Linguistics* 21(2): 385–396.

II.2 Alternations involving a change in the morphosyntactic expression and/or placement of arguments

9 A frame-semantic approach to syntactic alternations: The case of *build* verbs*

Hans C. Boas[a]

1 Introduction

Levin (1993: 1) proposes that "the behavior of a verb, particularly with respect to the expression and interpretation of its arguments, is to a large degree determined by its meaning". To demonstrate this relationship between form and meaning Levin identifies a number of syntactic alternations. The idea is that verbs that are closely related in meaning show similar alternating behavior.

While this methodology has been applied successfully to a broad number of English verb classes and alternations, more recent work by Nemoto (1998), Baker and Ruppenhofer (2002), Goldberg (2002), Boas (2003a, 2008b), Iwata (2008), and Neale (this volume) has shown that Levin's verb classes are not as homogeneous as previously thought. This paper contributes to this ongoing discussion by offering a frame-semantic analysis of the various syntactic alternations claimed by Levin to occur with her so-called *build* verbs.

The remainder of the paper is structured as follows. §2 reviews Levin's (1993: 173–174) analysis of *build* verbs such as *arrange, assemble, bake,* and *build,* which are claimed to exhibit a number of specific alternations. §3 tests Levin's claims and shows that not all of her *build* verbs exhibit identical alternating behavior. Following Boas (2003a, 2008a) I claim that the differences in syntactic behavior are best explained in terms of the different polysemy networks of senses associated with each verb. §4 offers an alternative approach to syntactic alternations with *build* verbs. Adopting key ideas from Fillmore's (1982) Frame Semantics and its practical

a Hans C. Boas is Associate Professor of Germanic Linguistics at the University of Texas at Austin. E-mail: hcb@mail.utexas.edu implementation in FrameNet (Fillmore *et al.* 2003), I claim that syntactic behavior is not always the most effective method for determining membership in a semantic class of verbs. §5 summarizes my findings and provides an outlook on further research.

2 Levin's (1993) analysis of *build* verbs

Levin's (1993) seminal work is based on the idea that the syntactic behavior of a verb can be predicted from its meaning (see also Fillmore 1967; Hale and Keyser 1987, among others, on this idea). In this view, "verbs that fall into classes according to shared behavior would be expected to show shared meaning components" (Levin 1993: 5). Levin's verb classification is based on a total of 79 syntactic alternations, leading her to posit 193 distinct verb classes that cover 3024 verbs (or 4186 senses), such as verbs of putting, verbs of communication, etc. One of her verb classes is the so-called *build* verbs, a sub-type of verbs of creation and transformation, which includes the following members:

(1) *Build* verbs: arrange, assemble, bake, blow (bubbles, glass), build, carve, cast, chisel, churn, compile, cook, crochet, cut, develop, embroider, fashion, fold, forge (metal), grind, grow, hack, hammer, hatch, knit, make, mold, pound, roll, sculpt, sew, shape, spin (wool), stitch, weave, whittle. (Levin, 1993: 173)

According to Levin (1993: 174), these verbs form a specific class because they are closely related in meaning, i.e., they "describe the creation of a product through the transformation of raw materials". As such, they also exhibit similar syntactic behavior with respect to a number of syntactic alternations. More specifically, *build* verbs occur in the material/product alternation, as in (2), the unspecified object alternation, as in (3), and the benefactive alternation, as in (4):

(2) (a) Martha carved a toy out of the piece of wood.
(b) Martha carved the piece of wood into a toy.

(3) (a) Martha carves toys.
(b) Martha carves.

(4) (a) Martha carved a toy (out of a piece of wood) for the baby.
Martha carved the baby a toy (out of a piece of wood).
(b) Martha carved a piece of wood (into a toy) for the baby.
*Martha carved the baby a piece of wood (into a toy).
Examples taken from Levin (1993: 173).

With respect to the benefactive alternation in (4), Levin (1993: 174) points out that *build* verbs may exhibit particular properties of other verb classes: "If the creation is done on someone's behalf, then these verbs are like verbs of obtaining and, like the *get* verbs, are found in the benefactive alternation." In other words, *build* verbs may take on syntactic properties of *get* verbs, if the context allows for the appropriate interpretation. While all *build* verbs are capable of participating in the alternations in (2)–(4), according to Levin, they share another property, namely that they disallow other types of alternations, such as the total transformation alternation (transitive) as in (5), among others.

(5) (a) Martha carved the piece of wood into a toy.
(b) *Martha carved the piece of wood from a branch into a toy.
Examples taken from Levin (1993: 173)

Interestingly, *build* verbs do not always exhibit clear-cut syntactic behavior. For example, Levin (1993: 173) observes that only some verbs but not others participate in the raw material subject alternation as in (6) and the sum of money subject alternation as in (7).

(6) (a) Martha carved beautiful toys out of this wood.
(b) This wood carves beautiful toys.
Examples taken from Levin (1993: 173)

(7) (a) The contractor will build (you) a house for $100,000.
(b) $100,000 will build (you) a house.
Examples taken from Levin (1993: 174)

The irregular behavior of *build* verbs with respect to the alternations in (6) and (7) suggests that there are some inconsistencies when systematically predicting a verb's syntactic behavior based on its meaning. Another problem is that not all *build* verbs may occur – like *carve* – in the material/product alternation as in (2) (e.g. *Joe builds houses out of bricks/*Joe builds bricks into houses*) or in the unspecified object alternation in (4) (e.g. *Joe builds houses/*Joe builds; Miriam assembles toys/*Miriam assembles*; etc.) In other words, despite the fact that all the verbs in (1) are classified by Levin (1993) as *build* verbs, this verb class membership does not seem to be predictive of a verb's syntactic behavior as claimed by Levin.

3 Problems with syntactic alternations as classificatory criteria

I propose that the irregular syntactic behavior of verbs in the *build* class is caused by the fact that there is not always a one-to-one mapping between semantics and syntax across the board. In other words, a number of verbs describing "the creation of a product through the transformation of raw materials" (Levin 1993: 174) participate in the syntactic alternations, but a fair number of verbs do not despite their semantic similarities.

3.1 Exclusion of semantically related verbs based on syntactic criteria

Consider Levin's characterization of *build* verbs as describing "the creation of a product through the transformation of raw materials" (Levin 1993: 174). Given this definition, we would expect *construct,* which involves the creation of a product through the transformation of raw materials, to be a member of the *build* class. However, it does not exhibit the same syntactic alternation characteristics of other *build* verbs, and is therefore not included in Levin's *build* class.

(8) (a) Lena constructed a building out of the bricks.
(b) *Lena constructed the bricks into a building.

(9) (a) Lena constructs buildings.
(b) *Lena constructs.

The examples show that *construct* does not occur in the material/product alternation as in (8) and the unspecified object alternation as in (9). This raises the following question: If only some *build* verbs occur in these two alterations, and others do not, what is the practical value of syntactic alternations for determining class membership? In other words, how many syntactic alternations should a verb participate in (or not) in order to be classified as belonging to a particular verb class?

A comparison with the alternating behavior of other verbs that fit the semantic characterization of *build* verbs such as *erect* presents similar problems. This verb does not exhibit the characteristic syntactic behavior of *build* verbs, and is not classified by Levin (1993) as a *build* verb, yet it is clearly capable of expressing the semantics of *build* verbs ("the creation of a product through the transformation of raw materials") by other syntactic means as in *They erected the skyscraper* where the materials used to create the end product are implicitly understood and do not need to be mentioned.

Next, consider the definition of *weld,* which also fits the semantic characteristics of the *build* class: *To soften by heat and join together (pieces of metal, esp. iron, or iron and steel) in a solid mass, by hammering or by pressure; to forge (an article) by this method* (OED).

(10) (a) Samuel welded a sword out of the iron.
(b) Samuel welded the iron into a sword.

(11) (a) Samuel welds swords.
(b) Samuel welds (again).

(12) (a) Samuel welded a sword (out of iron) for his friend.
(b) Samuel welded his friend a sword (out of iron).

The examples in (10)–(12) show that *weld* occurs in three of Levin's syntactic alternations used to characterize the *build* verb class. At the same time, *weld* does not appear in the total transformation alternation (transitive), the causative alternations, the raw material subject alternation, and the sum of money subject alternation. Given these syntactic characteristics, one would expect *weld* to also be classified as a *build* verb, but it is not. Instead, Levin (1993: 161–162) classifies *weld* as a *shake* verb, which specifies "the manner in which things are combined, rather than the result of the combining".

The data demonstrate that although alternating syntactic behavior may be taken as an indication of verb class membership, it does not always work, thereby excluding other relevant verbs from the same semantic class. While some *build* verbs such as *carve* neatly fulfill all of Levin's syntactic criteria, others do not. Furthermore, verbs with meanings that would warrant a semantic classification as *build* verbs such as *construct* or *weld* are not included in this semantic class because they either do not fulfill the syntactic criteria set out by Levin, or they are grouped into a different semantic class based on other syntactic alternations. In sum, the fact that the putative members of Levin's *build* class do not behave uniformly challenges the very notion of a verb class based on syntactic criteria alone.

3.2 Syntactic criteria are often unreliable

In my view, this problem is largely due to the fact that Levin's verb classes are not defined independently of syntactic criteria. To this end, Baker and Ruppenhofer (2002) argue that Levin's syntactic classification system does not always provide clear-cut results. Drawing on earlier insights by Dang *et al.* (1998) they discuss cases in which verbs that occur in the same set of alternations are classified as belonging to different semantic classes, which is inconsistent with Levin's approach. This leads them to argue that Levin's classes are at least partially semantically motivated and that "a classification rigorously and solely based on alternations would give much finer distinctions, including splitting of many semantically coherent classes" (Baker and Ruppenhofer 2002: 37). Similarly, Schnorbusch (2004: 36) points out that Levin's classification does not provide any inventory of meaning components that would allow for a systematic comparison and classification based on semantic criteria. This observation leads him to claim that Levin's classification is at least partially circular because semantic properties are not defined or motivated independently of syntactic properties. Thus, Schnorbusch points out, syntactic alternations are always taken as an indicator of semantic differences despite no systematic discussion of these semantic differences.

All of these issues point to a common problem with Levin's classification system, namely the heavy reliance on syntactic alternations to define semantic classes without recognizing that these alternations do not work across the board. To illustrate this point, consider *arrange*, which is a member of Levin's *build* class, and *erect*, which is not. The former alternates in the material/product alternation (transitive), but the latter does not, hence its exclusion from that class:

(13) (a) They arranged piles out of the rocks.
(b) They arranged the rocks into piles.

(14) (a) They erected skyscrapers out of steel and concrete.
(b) *They erected steel and concrete into skyscrapers.

This contrast illustrates that although both verbs are very close in meaning (they describe the creation of an entity out of smaller parts), they are not grouped in the same semantic class because of different alternating behavior. Given their closely related meanings it does not make sense to classify them differently according to syntactic criteria.

Another issue with Levin's (1993) syntactic classification concerns the availability of independently motivated criteria for deciding what types of syntactic patterns should be regarded as valid classificatory diagnostics. Recall from §2 that not all of Levin's *build* verbs behave uniformly in the raw material subject alternation and the sum of money subject alternation. If verbs from the same class differ with respect to their ability to occur in these two alternations, what empirical status do these two alternations have? In other words, what are the criteria used to identify a specific alternation as a valid classificatory instrument to determine verb class membership? If we were to apply a similar line of thinking to the classification of *erect*, we might be led to classify it as a *build* verb as well despite its inability to occur in the material/product alternation (transitive) (see (14)) because it occurs in the benefactive alternation. To put it differently, what number and what types of syntactic alternations does a verb have to participate in order to be classified as belonging to a specific class? What criteria are used to characterize the number and types of alternations and how can these be falsified, if at all?

Closely related to this issue is the theoretical status of other syntactic patterns that do not necessarily participate in any alternations. Consider, for example, Levin's (1993: 95–106) "other constructions" such as the cognate object construction, reaction object construction, and resultative construction, among many others. Sometimes these other constructions are discussed among the syntactic properties of Levin's verb classes (even when they do not occur in those constructions), sometimes they are not. More specifically, these other constructions are not included in Levin's discussion of *build* verbs. This omission raises the question of whether there are any objective criteria that would indicate when an alternation or other syntactic construction should be considered in the discussion of a verb class and when not.

Next, consider the many syntactic patterns that are not covered by Levin's alternations and other syntactic constructions. What is their theoretical status? Why are they not investigated in more detail to arrive at a more complete picture about the syntactic distributions of the members of a verb class? To answer these questions, consider the following syntactic frames that occur with *build*, arguably the most prototypical member of Levin's *build* class, and other verbs from the same syntactic class.

(15) (a) We built a house.
(b) *We arranged a hut.

(16) (a) We are building our way out of the housing crisis.
(b) *We are rolling our way out of the dough crisis.

(17) (a) We need to build windows into the house.
(b) *We need to assemble the screw into the furniture.

(18) (a) They built the house on a bad foundation.
(b) They carved a toy on a couch.

The examples in (15)–(18) represent a small number of syntactic patterns that may occur with *build*, but not with other verbs of the *build* class. They show that despite their common semantic classification these verbs differ substantially with respect to their syntactic distribution, reminiscent of the syntactic variation pointed out by Salkoff (1983) for verbs occurring in the locative alternation. These differences clearly show that Levin's semantic classification of verbs based on syntactic alternations is insufficient when it comes to accounting for a more complete syntactic distribution of verbs in the *build* class. In the following section I address some of the reasons why Levin's classification exhibits these issues and propose a frame-semantic alternative that seeks to overcome these problems.

4 Towards a frame-semantic classification of *build* verbs

4.1 Frame Semantics and FrameNet

Frame Semantics (Fillmore 1982) is based on the idea that "a word's meaning can be understood only with reference to a structured background of experience, beliefs, or practices, constituting a kind of conceptual prerequisite for understanding the meaning" (Fillmore and Atkins 1992: 76–77). In this view, meanings of words are understood in terms of semantic background frames that motivate the concept encoded by a word. Since the late 1990s, Frame Semantics has been applied to the construction of a corpus-based lexical database of English, FrameNet, which is built around the concept of semantic frames that can be evoked by words (Fillmore *et al.* 2003).[1] FrameNet differs from other lexical databases in that it is not structured around sense relations like WordNet (Fellbaum 1998). Instead, semantic frames are taken as structuring devices to model the types of knowledge necessary for interpreting utterances in the language (see Petruck 1996; Boas 2005).

FrameNet describes lexical units (LUs) in terms of the semantic frames they evoke, and presents for each LU a lexical entry that lists different types of interconnected information (see Ruppenhofer *et al.* 2006 for details).[2] Consider the verb *load*, which has multiple senses, and is thus represented in terms of multiple LUs in FrameNet. One such LU evokes the `Filling` frame, which is also evoked by other LUs such as *fill*, *glaze*, *smear*, *spatter*, *spray*, and *tile*, among many others. The lexical entry of the LU *load* in the `Filling` frame consists of three parts: the frame description, an exhaustive inventory of how frame elements are realized syntactically, and annotated example sentences from the British National Corpus. Each frame description consists of frame elements (FEs) that are essential for a full understanding of the associated situation type.

For example, the frame description of the `Filling` frame is defined as "words relating to filling CONTAINERS and covering AREAS with some thing, things or substance, the THEME. The AREA or CONTAINER can appear as the direct object with all these verbs, and is designated GOAL because it is the goal of motion of the THEME. Corresponding to its nuclear argument status, it is also affected in some crucial way, unlike goals in other frames. The AGENT is the actor who instigates the filling." The frame description also contains detailed definitions of all FEs as well as a list of all LUs that evoke the frame (see Ruppenhofer *et al.* 2006). The second part of a lexical entry, the Lexical Entry Report, provides a definition for that LU (*load*: fill a container-like entity with something, often in abundance), a list of FEs and their syntactic realizations, and the valence patterns (see Figure 9.1), illustrating how frame element configurations (FECs) are realized syntactically by that LU.

The third part of a lexical entry contains the Annotation report, which provides annotated corpus sentences from the BNC exemplifying how the FEs are realized in context. Compare, for example, the following sentences illustrating how the FEs of the `Filling` frame are realized syntactically.

(19) (a) [Two girls]$_{AGENT}$ are loading^{tgt} [the donkeys]$_{GOAL}$ [with water containers and sacks]$_{THEME}$.

(b) Did you know that [Cecil Beaton]$_{AGENT}$ couldn't even load^{tgt} [his own camera]$_{GOAL}$? <INI>

(c) We'd have [our packs]$_{GOAL}$ loaded^{tgt} [with various weights]$_{THEME}$ ...

Number Annotated	**Patterns**		
15 TOTAL	Agent	Goal	Theme
(3)	CNI –	NP Ext	PP [with] Dep
(1)	CNI –	NP Obj	PP [with] Dep
(1)	NP Ext	DNI –	INI –
(1)	NP Ext	DNI –	PP [with] Dep
(2)	NP Ext	NP Obj	INI –
(7)	NP Ext	NP Obj	PP [with] Dep

Figure 9.1. Valence Information for *load* in `Filling` frame[3]

In contrast to Levin (1993), who classifies verbs according to their ability to appear in syntactic alternations, Frame Semantics assumes that semantic criteria are primarily for identifying whether a given LU belongs to a semantic class. In this alternative view, semantic frames are structuring devices that help linguists to identify verb classes based on their ability to describe similar types of scenes or situations. While identifying frames and contrasting them with other frames may sometimes raise a number of problems (see Petruck *et al.* 2004; Ruppenhofer *et al.* 2006), frame-semantic definitions are nevertheless advantageous because they are intuitive and can be checked against corpus evidence. Another benefit of Frame Semantics is that syntactic criteria are regarded as secondary for the identification of verb classes, thereby steering clear of the problems associated with Levin's syntactic approach. This does not imply that syntactic information is irrelevant. As Figure 9.1 and the examples in (19) show, FrameNet provides syntactic information by presenting information about how frame element configurations are realized syntactically. Note, however, that the type of syntactic information presented by FrameNet is only secondary as it relies on the presence and combinations of FEs, which are defined semantically. Thus, if certain aspects of the semantics of a frame are not perspectivized by a particular LU, they do not occur syntactically either. This methodology also implies that no special preference is given to particular syntactic alternations, grammatical constructions, or other syntactic patterns, thereby avoiding the issue of having to arrive at independent criteria that would allow us to empirically identify (or falsify) those syntactic patterns that are relevant for the definition of a particular verb class (see also Baker and Ruppenhofer 2002).

Such a frame-semantic classification not only makes it possible to avoid the problems associated with Levin's (1993) syntactic approach discussed above. In addition, frame-semantic criteria allow for a more systematic cross-linguistic application and comparison without having to rely on syntactic differences and idiosyncrasies between languages. For example, several studies have investigated how semantic frames developed on the basis of English data such as `Commitment` (Subirats 2009), `Communication` (Subirats and Petruck 2003; Boas 2005b), `Revenge` (Petruck *et al.* 2004; Petruck 2009), `Risk` (Fillmore and Atkins 1992; Ohara 2009), and `Self_motion` (Fillmore and Atkins 2000; Boas 2001; Iwata 2002) can be applied to the analysis of other languages such as Spanish, German, Japanese, French, and Hebrew. The consensus emerging from these studies is that frame-semantic information allows us to characterize semantically coherent classes, both within a single language and cross-linguistically (see Boas 2009 for details). At the same time, however, these studies also point out that the range of syntactic frames occurring with a given LU is to a certain degree idiosyncratic, and cannot always be automatically deduced from semantic information.

4.2 Syntactic alternations in FrameNet

At this point one might wonder about the status of syntactic alternations in FrameNet. In other words: how are they captured and analyzed? Because FN does not regard syntactic information as primary for the identification of verb classes (LUs are classified based on the frames they evoke), it does not provide an inventory of alternations *per se*. However, since FN lexical entries provide exhaustive valence information for each LU, the types of syntactic alternations discussed by Levin are included in FN, but not overtly. Consider, for example, our discussion of *load* in the previous section, where I pointed out that it evokes the `Filling` frame (cf. *Michael loaded the table with books*). In fact, FN contains a second LU for *load,* which evokes a different frame, namely the `Placing` frame (cf. *Michael loaded the books on the table*).

This frame describes situations in which an AGENT places a THEME at a LOCATION (the GOAL), which is profiled. The THEME is under the control of the AGENT at the time of its arrival at the GOAL. The `Placing` frame is also evoked by a number of different LUs, such as *archive, brush, hang, heap,* and *smear*. As such, the lexical entry for the LU *load* in the `Placing` frame points to the frame description (including its FEs), includes a definition of this particular sense of *load,* lists the valence information (which are different from those in Figure 9.1 above), and provides annotated corpus sentences similar to the ones in (19) above.

The comparison of the two LUs of *load* shows that they evoke two different frames, and that their two lexical entries contain the relevant syntactic information about how the semantics of the two frames are realized. However, FrameNet does not provide any explicit link between the different syntactic patterns of the two lexical entries so that the alternating behavior of *load* (cf. *Michael loaded the books onto the table* vs. *Michael loaded the books on the table*) would become immediately apparent. Given our observations regarding the primacy of semantic information over syntactic information in FrameNet, this does not come as a surprise. But how is it possible to account for syntactic alternations?

When verbs exhibit alternating behavior of the type cataloged by Levin (1993), they evoke different semantic frames in FrameNet. With *load,* this means that both the `Placing` frame and the `Loading` frame are evoked by two separate LUs of *load*. Frames differ in their level of granularity and how they are related to each other. Figure 9.2 illustrates a small part of the complex ontology of frames from the domain of `Transitive_action`. Figure 9.2 is a partial representation of the relations between frames in FrameNet, with "parent" frames pointing to "child" frames. Various frame-to-frame relations capture semantic relationships between frames, including: 1. Inheritance (a child frame is a more specific elaboration of a parent frame); 2. Subframe (used to characterize the different sequential parts of a complex event); 3. Perspective_on (expressing different points of view of an event); 3. Using (when a part of the scene evoked by the Child frame refers to the Parent frame); and others (for more details, see Petruck *et al.* 2004; Ruppenhofer *et al.* 2006). For example, both the `Placing` and `Filling` frames inherit from the `Transitive_action` frame, which is at a more abstract level in the ontology of frames. In addition, the `Filling` frame also uses the `Placing` frame, because reaching the endpoint of a filling event requires a number of placing events that temporally precede this endpoint.

Since the frame-to-frame relations depicted in Figure 9.2 are all at the semantic level, they do not directly represent the syntactic behavior of verbs. However, if one looks at the frame descriptions of the `Placing` and `Filling` frames, one sees that the latter has a use-relation with the former, and is therefore semantically related to it. Thus, if both frames are

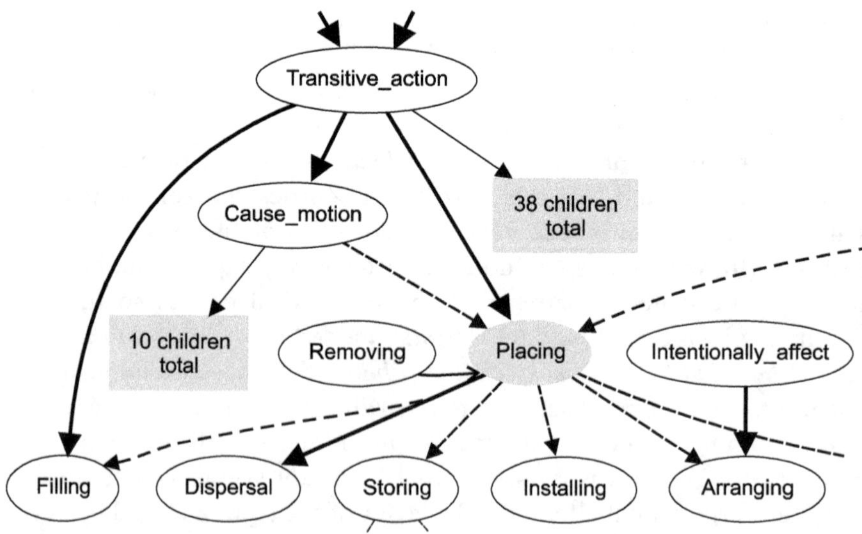

Figure 9.2. Frame-to-frame relation between `Placing` and `Filling` frames in FrameNet

evoked by two LUs with the same name, such as *load*, then we know that the two LUs are related to each other because the frames they evoke are related to each other. This means that if we look at the syntactic frames of the two LUs of *load* (one evoking the `Placing` frame, the other the `Filling` frame) we are able to learn more about their syntactic behavior, including the types of alternations cataloged by Levin (1993).

Capturing syntactic alternations by relating those semantic frames to each other that are evoked by two related LUs means that if one wants to learn about alternating verb behavior, one must first know whether semantic frames are related to each other (see Figure 9.2). If a semantic frame is not related to another semantic frame, then one would not expect any semantic relatedness between the LUs evoking the two frames either. The next step involves a comparison between the lists of LUs that evoke the two different frames. For example, in comparing an alphabetically organized sample of

Table 9.1. Sample of alphabetically ordered LUs evoking the `Placing` and `Filling` frames

Placing frame	*Filling frame*
hang	*hang*
heap	*heap*
immerse	
implant	
inject	*inject*
insert	
jam	*jam*
lay	
lean	
load	*load*
lodge	
pack	*pack*
	paint
	panel
park	
perch	
	pave
pile	*pile*
	plant
	plaster
	pump
	scatter
	seed

LUs evoking the `Placing` frame with an alphabetically organized sample of LUs evoking the `Filling` frame, we see that some LUs are found in both lists. Compare the two lists in Table 9.1.

The samples of alphabetically ordered verbal LUs from the two frames illustrate how some verbs have two LUs that evoke different semantic frames. Those that are found in both lists such as *hang, heap, load,* and *pack* are semantically related (they are polysemous and hence alternate syntactically) because their semantic frames are related to each other (cf. Figure 9.2). The alternating behavior of these verbs can then be compared by looking at the FN entries of the two LUs side by side. LUs which do not have counterparts in the respective other frame such as *immerse, implant,* and *park* in the `Placing` frame or *paint, panel,* and *pave* in the `Filling` frame in Table 9.1 do not alternate because there is no corresponding LU whose lexical entry could provide the corresponding syntactic frame to "provide" the alternating behavior.

There are a number of advantages to capturing syntactic alternations with Frame Semantics. First, the splitting approach to polysemy allows for a more finely-grained analysis of verb meanings. This implies that the different meanings associated with the individual members of pairs of syntactic frames that make up syntactic alternations can be captured more straightforwardly. Second, syntactic alternations are not given any special status for identifying semantic verb classes. Instead, syntactic alternations are an epiphenomenon caused by a significant type frequency of semantically related verbs, and there is no need to pay special attention to the role of syntactic alternations. This means that the syntactic frames of the alternations are treated like any other syntactic frames and can be compared and contrasted using the same set of criteria. Third, the frame-semantic approach to syntactic alternations provides a set of semantic criteria that can be verified (and falsified) on independent grounds. More specifically, the definitions of semantic frames are structured in such a way that it is relatively easy to determine whether a given LU evokes a frame or not, given the frame's description and coverage. Fourth, and perhaps most importantly, this alternative methodology allows for a finer-grained analysis of semantic verb classes that avoids the problems noted with Levin's (1993) approach: 1. not all members of a semantic verb class exhibit the same alternating behavior; 2. verbs that should be included in a semantic class are not included because they do not alternate; 3. verbs that show similar alternating behavior are not included in the verb class because their semantics are not similar enough; and 4. syntactic patterns that are not part of alternations are less important (see also Baker and Ruppenhofer 2002).

4.3 The role of frame-semantic criteria for identifying subclasses in Levin's *build* class

Returning to our discussion of *build* verbs, it should now be clear that the inconsistent syntactic distribution of Levin's *build* verbs is due to their different polysemy patterns. In other words, some verbs exhibit similar polysemy patterns where their respective LUs evoke the same semantic frames. At the same time, however, other verbs do not exhibit the same types of polysemy patterns, and their respective LUs may differ in number and types of semantic frames they evoke. To illustrate, consider *carve*, which occurs in the material/product alternation, the unspecified object alternation, and the benefactive alternation (see (3)–(5) above). Recall Levin's claim that other verbs should also be considered as belonging to the *build* verb class, because they share the syntactic behavior of *carve* and are semantically similar.

In contrast to Levin (1993), an alternative frame-semantic approach analyzes the alternating behavior of *build* verbs by first determining the different types of LUs associated with each verb, and the types of semantic frames these LUs evoke. Then it is necessary to find out which valence patterns (syntactic frames) represent the overt realization of the semantics of a LU evoking a specific semantic frame. To illustrate, let us see which semantic frames are evoked by the two syntactic frames of the material/product alternation. First, consider the `Building` frame in FrameNet, which describes assembly or construction actions, where an AGENT joins COMPONENTS together to form a CREATED_ENTITY, which is profiled, and hence the object of the verb. Verbal LUs evoking the `Building` frame include *assemble, build, construct, erect, fashion, fit together, glue, make, piece together, put together, raise,* and *weld,* but not *carve.*[4] This raises the following question: why do some verbs categorized as *build* verbs by Levin (1993) evoke the `Building` frame, but not others? To answer this question, let us take a closer look at the semantic definition of Levin's *build* class, which states that its members "describe the creation of a product through the transformation of raw materials" (1993: 174). Comparing this definition with the definition of the `Building` frame reveals a number of important differences.

First, Levin's characterization of the activities described by her 35 *build* verbs is rather coarse-grained, labeling them as "creation." In contrast, the `Building` frame specifies the activities denoted by its 12 verbal LUs as "assembly or construction actions". As such, the `Building` frame does not only specify in greater semantic detail the types of activities considered as building actions. It also offers a more fine-grained semantic distinction between Levin's *build* verbs, thereby identifying a specific sub-class. Thus, while some of Levin's *build* verbs such as *assemble, build,* and *construct* clearly fall within the definition of the `Building` frame, others do not because they do not fit the definition of building activities. In other words, *carve* does not evoke the `Building` frame because it does not typically denote assembly or construction actions. Instead, *carve* describes an activity by which an object is transformed into a different object by altering its original shape (typically by using an instrument to take off parts so it takes on a different shape). In short, *carve* does not evoke the `Building` frame because of a crucial difference in the type of creation activity. Note also that one of Levin's syntactic criteria for defining membership in the *build* class – ability to participate in the material/product alternation – becomes superfluous: Some of Levin's *build* verbs such as *carve* occur in the material/ product alternation, but do not evoke the `Building` frame. In contrast, verbs that are typically considered as prototypical *build* verbs, such as *build* itself, do not exhibit this alternating behavior despite belonging both to Levin's *build* class and evoking the `Building` frame (e.g. *Joe builds houses out of bricks/*Joe builds bricks into houses*). This unsystematic alternating behavior demonstrates once again the problematic nature of relying on syntactic criteria for identifying semantic classes of verbs.

The second difference concerns the nature of the entity that results from the activity. Levin (1993) characterizes entities resulting from the activities of her 35 *build* verbs as "product". In contrast, the `Building` frame offers more specific semantic information by defining the product as resulting from an AGENT joining COMPONENTS together to form a CREATED_ENTITY. As in the previous paragraph, this difference in semantic granularity has direct consequences for the range of Levin's *build* verbs that can also evoke the `Building` frame. For example, some of Levin's *build* verbs such as *assemble, build,* and *fashion* also fit the definition of the `Building` frame because the CREATED_ENTITY is the result of the AGENT joining components together. Other verbs such as *cut, grind,* and *hammer* do not involve the joining of COMPONENTS to form a CREATED_ENTITY and do therefore not evoke the `Building` frame. Note also that these verbs do not appear in the same alternations as *carve* (Levin's example verb for illustrating the alternating behavior of *build* verbs): they do not participate in the material/product alternation, the unspecified object alternation, or the benefactive alternation.

The third difference lies in the types of raw materials. Levin's 35 *build* verbs differ quite drastically in terms of the types of raw materials being transformed. While some verbs do not provide any specific information with respect to the quality or type of the materials (*arrange, assemble, compile, make,* and *shape*), other verbs are more specific, such as *bake* and *cook* (requiring some edible materials), or *knit, spin, stitch,* and *weave* (requiring some type of clothes or thread). In contrast, the `Building` frame offers a definition of raw materials that is both more specific and more general at the same time. It is more specific because "an AGENT joins COMPONENTS" implies the presence of different parts that can be put together. This definition is more specific than Levin's "raw materials" because it requires the COMPONENTS to be able to be joined together (as opposed to *hack,* which assumes separation; or *blow bubbles/glass,* which assumes creation of a new entity (not joining existing parts together)). As such, this definition of the types of materials is more fine-grained than Levin's raw materials. At the same time, this frame-semantic definition is more general because it involves any type of COMPONENTS that can be joined together by an AGENT to form a CREATED_ENTITY and therefore has the potential of applying to a broader variety of verbs. Given this definition, *glue* and *weld* also evoke the `Building` frame. However, these two verbs are not included in Levin's (1993) *build* class – perhaps because they do not fulfill Levin's syntactic criteria.

Returning to the initial question ("Why do some verbs categorized as *build* verbs by Levin (1993) evoke the `Building` frame, but not others?"), it should be clear by now that the different classifications are due to: 1. granularity of verb sense and verb class definitions; 2. reliance on syntactic criteria for establishing semantic classes; and 3. irregular relationships between a verb's meanings and its syntactic distribution. More specifically, Levin's *build* class encompasses a fairly large group of verbs because its semantic definition is rather broad. The verbs in this class share only a relatively broad range of definitional criteria, such as "creation", "product", "transformation", and "raw materials". This differs from the `Building` frame, which offers a more nuanced set of classificatory criteria that cover only a small sub-set of Levin's 35 *build* verbs. At the same time, however, these fine-grained semantic criteria also cover semantically related verbs such as *glue* or *weld,* which are not included in Levin's *build* class. In contrast to Levin's approach, which heavily relies on syntactic alternation criteria to establish semantic classes of verbs, the frame-semantic approach relies primarily on semantic criteria to determine which verbs (or: LUs) evoke a particular semantic frame and should therefore be classified as belonging to the same class.

To substantiate my proposals, I now present a case study of how frame-semantic criteria can be implemented to arrive at alternative classifications of Levin's *build* verbs without having to rely on syntactic criteria. Consider the verb *grind,* which is also classified by Levin as a *build* verb because it involves the creation of a product through the transformation of raw materials. Although this classification appears to be unproblematic at first sight, there are a number of issues that argue for a re-classification of *grind.*

The first issue concerns the verb's ability to conform to the alternation patterns most characteristic of Levin's *build* class verbs. While *grind* occurs in the benefactive alternation, it is typically not acceptable in the material/product alternation (e.g. **Michael grinds fine powder out of the coriander seeds/Michael grinds the coriander seeds into fine powder*) and the unspecified object alternation (e.g. *Russell grinds pepper/*Russell grinds*). The second issue concerns the broader syntactic distribution of *grind.* Compare the following examples:

(20) (a) She is grinding her cigarette to ash.
(b) *She is assembling the rocks to piles.
(c) She is cutting the wood to pieces.
(d) *She is knitting the wool to sweaters.
(e) *She is sewing the rags to clothes.
(f) She is hammering the metal to pieces.

The examples in (20) show that not all verbs from Levin's *build* class exhibit the same syntactic behavior in resultative constructions. Some allow a resultative PP headed by *to,* while others do not. This observation has led me to argue that each sense of a verb should be represented in terms of a mini-construction, representing the particular syntactic, semantic, and pragmatic restrictions of individual verb senses (Boas 2003a). While there are parallels in the distribution of syntactic frames among semantically related verbs (e.g. (20a) and (20c)), I have also demonstrated that certain types of semantic generalizations are best reached by comparing the distributional properties of particular verb senses with respect to specific grammatical constructions (Boas 2003a, 2008a). In the case of resultatives, the distribution is often highly irregular. In other cases, such as the locative alternation, the distribution is more regular, but still with a fair number of exceptions (for examples, see Boas 2003b; Iwata 2008).

At this point, the following question is fairly obvious: What does it mean to have a semantic class such as the *build* class that is supposedly predictive of syntactic behavior? As seen above, it does not predict the same alternation patterns for all members of a semantic class, and it also does not help predict other syntactic patterns. This suggests that such a semantic class does not provide us with notable predictive powers about alternating behavior.[5] However, I would argue that some of Levin's alternation classes are fairly close to an intersection or overlapping of two frame-semantic classes. In other words, verbs that share a common pair of semantic frames might participate in the same pair of syntactic patterns. On this view, we need two related semantic frames for accounting for a single syntactic alternation. Another problem, which we already discussed at length, concerns membership in a specific class. That is, in the case of *grind*, we know that it is included in Levin's *build* class. But what about other semantically related verbs that also involve the creation of a product through the transformation of raw materials such as *pulverize, shred, grate*, and *flake*, among others? Why are these not included in Levin's *build* class?

In my view, the frame-semantic approach to verb classification offers a more elegant alternative by capturing the relevant semantic distinctions between verbs, thereby arriving at a more coherent verb classification. Instead of classifying *grind* as a *build* verb together with a broad range of 34 other vaguely related verbs, I suggest that we pay more attention to the individual semantics of *grind* and the type of frame it evokes. In other words, while *grind* involves the "creation of a product through the transformation of raw materials" (Levin 1993: 174), it also involves much more idiosyncratic information. To wit, FrameNet contains a particular `Grinding` frame, in which "a GRINDER or a GRINDING_CAUSE causes an UNDERGOER to be broken into smaller pieces. A RESULT or GOAL can be present."[6] Verbal LUs evoking the `Grinding` frame include *crumble, crunch, crush, flake, grate, grind, mill, pulverize*, and *shred*, among others. As with other FN entries, each entry for these LUs contains information about their specific valence patterns, together with an annotated example sentence. The important point here is that the classification of verbs (or: LUs) is based on frame-semantic criteria, and not on syntactic criteria, while at the same time still capturing the syntactic distribution of LUs evoking the `Grinding` frame. To illustrate this point, compare the syntactic distribution of the core FEs of the `Grinding` frame among the verbs evoking it.

Table 9.2 summarizes the valence patterns of the nine verbal LUs evoking the `Grinding` frame in FrameNet. The top row lists the names of FEs (GRINDER and UNDERGOER, and GRINDING_CAUSE and UNDERGOER) together with their varied syntactic realizations in terms of phrase types and grammatical functions. For example, the third column from the left represents one particular type of FE realization where the GRINDER is realized as an external NP, and the UNDERGOER is realized as an object, which is also a NP. Eight of the nine verbs share this valence pattern. In contrast, the sixth column from the left lists which LUs realize the GRINDER as a dependent PP headed by *by* and the UNDERGOER as an external NP. Only one out of the nine verbs exhibits this particular valence pattern.

Table 9.2. Comparison of valence patterns of verbal LUs in the `Grinding` frame

	Grinder, Undergoer (CNI/–), (NP/Ext)	Grinder, Undergoer (CNI/–), (NP/Obj)	Grinder, Undergoer (NP/Ext), (NP/Obj)	Grinder, Undergoer (CNI/–), (CNI/–)	Grinder, Undergoer (DNI/–),(NP/Ext)	Grinding_cause, Undergoer (PP[by]/Dep),(NP, Ext)	Grinding_cause, Undergoer (NP/Ext), (NP/Obj)	Grinding_cause, Undergoer (PP[beneath])/Dep), (NP/Ext)	Grinding_cause, Undergoer (PP[by]/Dep), (NP/Ext)
crumble	X	X	X				X		
crunch			X				X		
crush		X	X	X	X		X	X	X
flake	X	X							
grate		X	X						
grind	X	X	X				X		
mill	X		X						
pulverize	X		X						
shred		X	X			X			X

Comparing the valence patterns of the nine LUs evoking the `Grinding` frame reveals a rather divergent range of valence patterns. Of the nine verbs, there are only two groups of two LUs each of which share the same set of valence patterns. The first group consists of *crumble* and *grind*, the second group consists of *mill* and *pulverize*. The remaining five LUs exhibit idiosyncratic valence patterns that differ from each other as well as from the two pairs that each share a common set of valence patterns. Taken together, the distribution of valence patterns in Table 9.2 demonstrates that finding syntactic generalizations among LUs closely related in meaning is complicated (see also Salkoff 1983; Gross 1994). More specifically, the rather high degree of syntactic variation demonstrates that using syntactic criteria for identifying semantic classes of verbs is highly problematic. Note that the valence information in Table 9.2 does not even capture alternating behaviors of verbs, but only represents the valence patterns of verbal LUs evoking one semantic frame. In sum, our discussion of LUs evoking the `Grinding` frame has shown that a classification of verbs based on frame-semantic criteria offers a more coherent methodology for identifying semantically related verbs than a classification that heavily relies on syntactic information.

4.4 Modeling alternating behavior of *build* verbs

Based on the identification of one semantically coherent class of verbs such as those evoking the `Grinding` frame, the question remains as to how to account for their assumed alternating behavior – after all, *grind* is classified by Levin as a *build* verb. However, when one considers the range of alternations used by Levin to identify verbs belonging to her *build* class, an interesting observation emerges: Verbs evoking the `Grinding` frame do not typically participate in the alternations in which *build* verbs are assumed to participate, such as the material/product alternation and the unspecified object alternation. However, they may occur, like other *build* verbs, in the benefactive alternation (e.g. *Carlos grated some parmesan for Michael/ Carlos grated Michael some parmesan*). Whether this alternating behavior is best modeled in terms of semantic classes of verbs whose members all participate in this alternation is not entirely clear. For example, Goldberg (1995) argues for an alternative constructional account involving the ditransitive construction. On this view, lexical entries of verbs can fuse with independently existing meaningful constructions in order to license different kinds of syntactic frames. Thus, the occurrence of verbs like *grate* in Levin's benefactive alternation is not necessarily due to their membership in a particular semantic class. Instead, verbs such as *grate* exhibit this varied syntactic distribution because their semantics are compatible with different types of grammatical constructions, each licensing distinct syntactic realizations of a verb's Frame Elements.

This short overview shows that a sub-class of Levin's *build* verbs – those evoking the `Grinding` frame – does not exhibit the specific types of alternating behaviors that characterize Levin's (1993) class of *build* verbs. As such, our frame-semantic analysis does not need to account for their alternating behavior as we did for verbs participating in the locative alternation in §4.2 above.[7] There we saw that we needed to posit two separate but related frames, namely `Placing` and `Filling` to account for the alternating behavior of verbs such as *load* and *spray*.

But what about the alternating behavior of other *build* verbs? Because of space limitations I only discuss a few illustrative examples and sketch out a methodology for applying my proposals to the full range of Levin's *build* verbs. Consider the alternating behavior of another group out of 35 of Levin's *build* verbs, namely those evoking the Building frame, as discussed in §4.3. As the following examples illustrate, the picture is rather mixed as some verbs exhibit alternating behavior while others do not.

(21) (a) They assembled the pile out of rocks.
(b) They assembled the rocks into a pile.

(22) (a) They built a new house out of old bricks.
(b) *They built old bricks into a new house.

Both (21a) and (22a) are licensed by LUs evoking the Building frame (which requires that the CREATED_ENTITY be profiled, and hence the object of the verb), i.e. *assemble* and *build*. However, while *assemble* participates in the material/product alternation, *build* does not. To capture this distinct syntactic behavior, I tentatively propose that the syntactic frame in (21b) is licensed by a distinct LU of *assemble* that evokes a semantic frame different from Building.[8] This frame, which I tentatively call Assemble, and which is semantically related to Building, is evoked by LUs such as *assemble, piece, put together, tack,* and *tack together.* This frame differs from Building in that it does not profile the CREATED_ENTITY, but rather the COMPONENTS used in creating it. While some verbs, such as *assemble* and *put together,* have LUs that evoke both the Building and the Assemble frames, others have only one LU that evoke only one of the two frames. This means that alternating verbs such as *assemble* have two distinct LUs evoking different semantic frames, while non-alternating verbs such as *build* or *piece* have only one LU evoking only one of the two frames. Similar to the analysis of the locative alternation in §4.2, the different valence patterns expressing the syntactic alternations are a part of the lexical entries of the respective LUs.

This brief discussion of how to capture the alternating behavior of two sub-classes of Levin's *build* verbs (i.e. those evoking the Grinding, Building, and Assemble frames) offers a roadmap for the further analysis of the remaining *build* verbs without having to depend on unreliable syntactic criteria. To achieve this goal it will first be necessary to identify the different types of semantic frames evoked by the verbs in Levin's *build* class. The discussion above suggests that this step may result in a much broader variety of semantic (sub-)classes that may also cover many more verbs (cf. our discussion of *glue* and *weld* above, which – despite their semantic similarity – are not included in Levin's *build* class). Next, it will need to be determined which LUs evoking a particular frame truly exhibit alternating behavior and which ones do not. As outlined above, this investigation will result in a list of related semantic frames, each of which will be evoked by a LU that is related to the original LU. Verbs that alternate will have two distinct LUs, each evoking semantic frames that are related to each other in some way. Finally, the alternating behavior of *build* verbs will be captured in terms of valence patterns contained in the lexical entries of LUs of the same verb that evoke semantically related frames.

5 Conclusions and outlook

In this paper I proposed an alternative frame-semantic classification of Levin's (1993) *build* verbs. Showing that Levin's syntactic criteria for identifying semantic class membership do not always provide adequate results led me to argue that her definitions of semantic classes is too coarse-grained (see also Neale, this volume). More specifically, while some verbs of her *build* class exhibit alternating behavior with respect to her range of definitional criteria, others do not. Other verbs, which are semantically closely related to Levin's *build* class and should therefore be classified as *build* verbs are not included because they do not exhibit the relevant alternating behavior.

Levin's inconsistent syntactic criteria for defining verb class membership led me to propose an alternative frame-semantic approach toward defining verb classes and identifying their members. Based on previous work by Baker and Ruppenhofer (2002) and Boas (2003b, 2008b), I argued that verb classes defined in terms of frame-semantic criteria offer a number of advantages. First, frame-semantic criteria offer a more coherent methodology for identifying semantically related verbs than a classification that heavily relies on syntactic information. In other words, determining the number of LUs of a verb and the different types of semantic frames they evoke allows us to distinguish clearly between the different senses of verbs.

Second, a frame-semantic classification of verbs also captures the alternating behavior of verbs more systematically. Although this alternative approach does not rely on syntactic criteria for verb classification, it includes the relevant valence information in the lexical entry of each LU. Thus, alternating verbs are associated with (at least) two different LUs that each evokes different but semantically related frames. The alternating behavior of these verbs is accounted for by the different valence patterns of the two LUs associated with the verb. This means that certain non-alternating verbs that are closely related in meaning to alternating verbs are associated with only one LU evoking one of the two frames evoked by one of the two LUs of the alternating verb, but not a second LU. Following this approach captures a verb's alternating behavior (or non-alternating behavior) while at the same time ensuring that semantic classes contain only those LUs that really evoke the same frame.

Third, the frame-semantic approach allows us to establish more finely-grained categories of verb classes which in turn allow for a broader coverage. Recall that Levin's *build* class includes 35 verbs. My analysis in §4 has shown that Levin's class is both too broad and too narrow at the same time. It is too broad because it includes verbs that differ quite drastically in their meanings, e.g. the types of products derived as the result of the activity described by the verb, or the kinds of activities involved. This observation led me to describe and analyze three distinct semantic sub-classes of Levin's *build* verbs, namely those evoking the `Building`, `Grinding` and `Assemble` frames. Applying the same methodology will result in the identification of further distinct semantic frames evoked by the remaining members of Levin's *build* verbs. I proposed above that these differences in meaning may perhaps be causing the varying alternating behaviors of Levin's 35 *build* verbs. Levin's *build* class is too narrow, because it does not include verbs such as *glue* or *weld* that fit the semantic description of her *build* class but are excluded on the grounds that they do not exhibit the alternating behavior characteristic of Levin's other *build* verbs.

I am not abandoning Levin's (1993) basic assumption, namely that certain aspects of a verb's meaning may determine its syntactic behavior. Her groundbreaking research is the first systematic work on the English verb lexicon to arrive at this important insight. However, I think I have convincingly shown that her methodology of using syntactic criteria to arrive at coherent semantic classes predictive of syntactic behavior is problematic. I have argued that since syntactic alternations are an epiphenomenon caused by a significant type frequency of semantically related verbs, there is no need to pay special attention to the role of syntactic alternations. This means that the syntactic frames of the alternations are treated like any other syntactic frames and can be compared and contrasted using the same set of criteria.

The frame-semantic approach outlined in this paper is only a first step toward developing a broad-scale alternative account of Levin's (1993) verb classes. Future research needs to identify the other semantic frames evoked by the remaining members of Levin's *build* class to see whether the types of proposals put forward in this paper can be applied across the board. Next, this methodology should be applied to other verb classes identified by Levin (1993). At the same time some important questions remain: 1. How finely-grained should semantic verb classes be (see e.g. Croft 2003; Boas 2003a, 2008a; Iwata 2008)? 2. Is it possible to arrive at systematic predictions about a verb's syntactic distribution based on its frame-semantic classification (see e.g. Taylor 1996; Boas 2006, 2008b)? 3. If certain aspects of meaning do in fact influence a verb's syntactic behavior, are these meaning components the same cross-linguistically (see e.g. Frense and Bennett 1996 and the papers in Boas 2009)? Clearly, much research remains to be done.

Notes

1. Thanks to Marc Pierce, Seizi Iwata, Jaakko Leino, Francisco Gonzálvez-García, Christopher Butler and the editor of this volume for extensive comments. The usual disclaimers apply. FrameNet: http://framenet.icsi.berkeley.edu
2. A lexical unit is a word in one of its senses (see Cruse 1986). Throughout this paper I often use the terms LU and verb interchangeably because a verb may have separate senses each of which evokes a different semantic frame and hence represents a different LU.
3. Please see Fillmore *et al.* (2003) for how the valence information is structured.
4. Other LUs evoking the `Building` frame include nouns such as *assembly* and *construction*.
5. In this paper I limit my critique of Levin's approach to *build* verbs; further investigations need to determine whether the same issues are found with other verb classes identified by Levin.
6. The non-core FEs of the `Grinding` frame are the following: DURATION, GOAL, INSTRUMENT, LOCUS, MANNER, MEANS, PLACE, PURPOSE, RESULT, and TIME.
7. This assumes a constructional analysis of the benefactive alternation in terms of Goldberg's (1995) ditransitive construction.
8. See Jackendoff (1990) for an alternative analysis involving the determiner restriction.

References

Baker, C. and Ruppenhofer, J. (2002) FrameNet's frames vs. Levin's verb classes. In J. Larson and M. Paster (eds) *Proceedings of the Twenty-eighth Annual Meeting of the Berkeley Linguistics Society* 27–38. UC Berkeley: Berkeley Linguistics Department.

Baker, C., Fillmore, C. J. and J. B. Lowe (1998) The Berkeley FrameNet Project. In A. Polguère and S. Kahane (eds) *Proceedings of the COLING-ACL '98, Vol. 1* 86–90. Montréal, Quebec, Canada.

Boas, H. C. (2001) Frame Semantics as a framework for describing polysemy and syntactic structures of English and German motion verbs in contrastive computational lexicography. In P. Rayson, A. Wilson, T. McEnery, A. Hardie, and S. Khoja (eds) *Proceedings of the Corpus Linguistics 2001 Conference: Technical Papers, Vol. 13* 64–73. Lancaster, UK: University Centre for Computer Corpus Research on Language.

Boas, H. C. (2003a) *A Constructional Approach to Resultatives.* Stanford, CA: CSLI Publications.

Boas, H. C. (2003b) A lexical-constructional account of the locative alternation. In L. Carmichael, C.-H. Huang and V. Samiian (eds) *Proceedings of the 2001 Western Conference in Linguistics, Vol. 13* 27–42. Fresno, CA: CSU Publications.

Boas, H. C. (2005) From theory to practice: Frame Semantics and the design of FrameNet. In S. Langer and D. Schnorbusch (eds) *Semantik im Lexikon* 129–160. Tübingen: Narr.

Boas, H. C. (2006) A frame-semantic approach to identifying syntactically relevant elements of meaning. In P. Steiner, H. C. Boas and S. Schierholz (eds) *Contrastive Studies and Valency: Studies in honor of Hans Ulrich Boas* 119–149. Frankfurt: Peter Lang.

Boas, H. C. (2008a) Determining the structure of lexical entries and grammatical constructions in Construction Grammar. *Annual Review of Cognitive Linguistics* 6: 113–144.

Boas, H. C. (2008b). Towards a frame-constructional approach to verb classification. In E. Sosa Acevedo and F. J. Cortés Rodríguez (eds) *Grammar, Constructions, and Interfaces: Special issue of Revista Canaria de Estudios Ingleses* 57: 17–48.

Boas, H. C. (ed.) (2009) *Multilingual FrameNets in Computational Lexicography: Methods and applications.* Berlin: Mouton de Gruyter.

Croft, W. (2003) Lexical rules vs. constructions: A false dichotomy. In H. Cuyckens, T. Berg, R. Dirven and K.-U. Panther (eds) *Motivation in Language: Studies in honor of Günter Radden* 49–68. Amsterdam: Benjamins.

Dang, T. H., Kipper, K., Palmer, M. and Rosenzweig, J. (1998) Investigating regular sense extensions based on intersective Levin classes. In A. Polguère and S. Kahane (eds) *Proceedings of COLING-ACL '98, Vol. 1* 293–299. Montréal, Quebec, Canada.

Fellbaum, C. (1998) *WordNet.* Cambridge, MA: The MIT Press.

Fillmore, C. J. (1967) The grammar of hitting and breaking. In R. Jacobs and P. Rosenbaum (eds) *Readings in English Transformational Grammar* 120–133. Waltham, MA: Ginn.

Fillmore, C. J. (1982) Frame Semantics. In Linguistic Society of Korea (ed.) *Linguistics in the Morning Calm* 111–138. Seoul: Hanshin.

Fillmore, C. J. and Atkins, B. T. S. (1992) Toward a frame-based lexicon: The semantics of RISK and its neighbors. In A. Lehrer and E. Kittay (eds) *Frames, Fields, and Contrasts: New essays in semantic and lexical organization* 75–102. Hillsdale, NJ: Erlbaum.

Fillmore, C. J. and Atkins, B. T. S. (2000) Describing polysemy: The case of "crawl". In Y. Ravin and C. Laecock (eds) *Polysemy* 91–110. Oxford: Oxford University Press.

Fillmore, C. J., Johnson, C. R. and Petruck, M. R. L. (2003) Background to FrameNet. *International Journal of Lexicography* 16(3): 235–250.

Frense, J. and Bennett, P. (1996) Verb alternations and semantic classes in English and German. *Language Sciences* 18: 305–317.

Goldberg, A. (1995) *Constructions: A construction grammar approach to argument structure.* Chicago, IL: University of Chicago Press.

Goldberg, A. (2002) Surface generalizations: An alternative to alternations. *Cognitive Linguistics* 13(4): 327–356.

Goldberg, A. (2006) *Constructions at Work: The nature of generalization in language.* Oxford: Oxford University Press.

Gross, M. (1994) Constructing Lexicon Grammars. In B. T. S. Atkins and A. Zampolli (eds) *Computational Approaches to the Lexicon* 213–58. Oxford: Oxford University Press.

Hale, K. and S. J. Keyser (1987) A view from the middle. *Lexicon Project Working Papers* 10. Cambridge, MA: MIT Center for Cognitive Science.

Iwata, S. (2002) Does MANNER count or not? Manner-of-motion verbs revisited. *Linguistics* 40: 61–110.

Iwata, S. (2008) *A Lexical-constructional Approach to the Locative Alternation.* Amsterdam: Benjamins.

Jackendoff, R. (1990) *Semantic Structures.* Cambridge, MA: MIT Press.

Levin, B. (1993) *English Verb Classes and Alternations: A preliminary investigation.* Chicago, IL: University of Chicago Press.

Neale, A. (this volume) Alternation and Participant Role: A contribution from a Systemic Functional Grammar.

Nemoto, N. (1998) On the polysemy of ditransitive SAVE: The role of Frame Semantics in Construction Grammar. *English Linguistics* 15: 219–242.

Ohara, K. (2009) Frame-based contrastive lexical semantics in Japanese FrameNet: The case of *risk* and *kakeru*. In H. C. Boas (ed.) *Multilingual FrameNets in Computational Lexicography: Methods and applications* 163–182. Berlin: Mouton de Gruyter.

Petruck, M. R. L. (1996) Frame Semantics. In J. Verschueren, J.-O. Östman, J. Blommaert and C. Bulcaen (eds) *Handbook of Pragmatics* 1–13. Amsterdam: Benjamins.

Petruck, M. R. L. (2009) Typological considerations in constructing a Hebrew FrameNet. In H. C. Boas (ed.) *Multilingual FrameNets in Computational Lexicography: Methods and applications* 183–208. Berlin: Mouton de Gruyter.

Petruck, M. R. L., C. J. Fillmore, C. Baker, M. Ellsworth, and J. Ruppenhofer (2004) Reframing FrameNet data. In G. Williams and S. Vessier (eds) *Proceedings of the Eleventh EURALEX International Congress* 405–416. Lorient, France.

Ruppenhofer, J., M. Ellsworth, M. R. L. Petruck, C. Johnson, and J. Scheffczyk (2006) FrameNet II: Extended theory and practice. Retrieved on 1 February 2010 from http://framenet.icsi.berkeley.edu

Salkoff, M. (1983) Bees are swarming in the garden. *Language* 59(2): 288–346.

Schnorbusch, D. (2004) Semantische Klassen aus syntaktischen Klassen? In S. Langer and D. Schnorbusch (eds) *Semantik im Lexikon* 33–58. Tübingen: Narr.

Subirats, C. (2009) Spanish FrameNet: A frame-semantic analysis of the Spanish lexicon. In H. C. Boas (ed.) *Multilingual FrameNets in Computational Lexicography: Methods and applications* 135–162. Berlin: Mouton de Gruyter.

Subirats, C. and Petruck, M. R .L. (2003) Surprise: Spanish FrameNet! In E. Hajicova, A. Kotesovcova and J. Mirovsky (eds) *Proceedings of CIL 17.* CD-ROM. Prague: Matfyzpress.

Taylor, J. (1996) On running and jogging. *Cognitive Linguistics* 7(1): 21–34.

10 Acquiring particle placement in English: A corpus-based perspective*

Stefan Th. Gries[a]

1 Introduction

1.1 General introduction

One of the most challenging areas for infants acquiring English as their native language are multi-word verbs: There are many different kinds of such verbs – e.g., prepositional verbs, phrasal verbs, phrasal-prepositional verbs, verb-adjective combinations, in Quirk *et al.*'s (1985) terminology – and they come with different kinds of semantic and syntactic patterns. One particularly multi-faceted type are transitive phrasal verbs, which exhibit the constituent order called particle placement (henceforth PrtPlc) exemplified in (1):

(1) (a) He $[_{VP}$ picked $[_{Prt}$ up$]$ $[_{DirObj}$ the book$]]$ V-Prt-DirObj
    (b) He $[_{VP}$ picked $[_{DirObj}$ the book$]$ $[_{Prt}$ up$]]$ V-DirObj-Prt

Not only can the same situation be described by two constituent orders, but the choice of constituent order is also nearly completely unconscious and influenced by many different variables. For instance, in the probably most comprehensive study of PrtPlc, Gries (2003a) has shown that the likelihood of V-Prt-DirObj significantly increases with

- phonological variables: long and/or contrastively stressed direct objects;
- syntactic variables: syntactically complex and indefinite determiners;
- semantic variables: abstract referents of the direct object and non-spatial meanings of verb-particle constructions (henceforth VPCs);

a Stefan Th. Gries is Full Professor of Linguistics at the University of California, Santa Barbara. E-mail: stgries@linguistics.ucsb.edu

- discourse-pragmatic variables: new/uninferrable referents of the direct object.

(Cf. also Bolinger 1971.)

These factors influence PrtPlc strongly and significantly and are interrelated such that they can all be (a) related to how amounts of processing effort drive speakers' constructional choices; and (b) integrated into an interactive activation model of linguistic processing (cf. Gries 2003a, in particular Chapter 4 and pp. 159–161). Prototypically, the direct object of a V-Prt-DirObj construction is harder to process because it involves a new referent, which incurs more processing effort than a given one, with an indefinite determiner marking its newness, maybe with additional modification (increasing its length and complexity, etc.). By contrast, the prototypical direct object of a V-DirObj-Prt construction is an easy-to-process given and short pronominal object.

Some additional factors influencing PrtPlc that were uncovered later are also related to psycholinguistic processing. For example,

- PrtPlc is subject to priming effects: the occurrence of V-Prt-DirObj increases the likelihood of another such construction later in the discourse/text (Gries 2005);
- rhythmic alternation (Couper-Kuhlen 1986; Schlüter 2003) appears to play a role such that V-Prt-DirObj is preferred if it results in a sequences of one stressed and maximally two unstressed syllables (Gries 2007);
- on the basis of Gries's (2003a) data, Schnoebelen (2008) uses information-theoretic entropy-based measures inspired by Moscoso del Prado Martín to quantify the degree of compositionality of phrasal verbs, which in turn is a significant predictor of PrtPlc. (Schnoebelen refers to Moscoso del Prado Martín for how such measures relate to processing.)

A few other studies, however, have found determinants of PrtPlc that are not as easily subsumed under a single processing/activation-related hypothesis. For example, Browman (1986) has argued there is a preference of particles beginning with a vowel and high-frequency phrasal verbs for V-Prt-DirObj.[1] In addition, she points out individual lexically-specific preferences such that *up* and in particular *pick up* have a special preference for V-Prt-DirObj (cf. also Bolinger 1971: 10), and later corpus-based work has shown more comprehensive evidence for verb-specific preferences (cf. Gries and Stefanowitsch's 2004 distinctive collexeme analysis and

Schnoebelen 2008, where verb-specificity is included in a mixed-effects model).

Despite the complexity of the use of these constructions, there is very little work on the acquisition of PrtPlc. In this paper, I will examine data from the CHILDES set of corpora to explore some aspects of this alternation. More specifically, after a brief review of previous studies in §1.2, §2 describes the data selection and coding procedures. §3 discusses the results separately for each child. Finally, §4 concludes. One caveat is in order, however, which has to do with the facts that (a) PrtPlc is determined by at least two dozen highly interrelated factors; and that (b) the construction in (1a) is much rarer than that of (1b), which is why the results of this paper must be considered a starting point rather than a comprehensive analysis.

1.2 Previous studies

As mentioned above, there are only few empirical studies of the acquisition of PrtPlc. One robust finding is that V-DirObj-Prt appears in children's speech earlier and more often than V-Prt-DirObj. This finding may seem surprising because, as Gries (2003a: 141f) has shown, V-Prt-DirObj

- instantiates the cognitively basic scenario of transitive events, in which an agent acts on a patient (cf. Hopper and Thompson 1980);
- has the optimal configuration for parsing because the particle need not be kept in working memory until the direct object's processing has been completed;
- is less marked because the only near-categorical distributional restriction on its use is that it cannot occur with pronominal direct objects (and even that is not completely categorical because with contrastively-stressed pronominal direct objects,V-Prt-DirObj is possible);
- Dehé (2000) and Peters (2001) found that native speakers who are asked to combine words into a VPC more frequently create V-Prt-DirObj.

Nevertheless, studies unequivocally report a strong early preference for V-DirObj-Prt, in what Hyams *et al.* (1993) and Broihier *et al.* (1994) called the "stranded particle stage" (based on data for Eve, Sarah (Brown 1973) from the CHILDES archive and an additional unspecified child; cf. also Sawyer 2001). While these studies' focus on English and other Germanic VPCs from the perspective of Government and Binding Theory limits their relevance to this study, Broihier *et al.* (1994: 8) do also briefly comment on the productivity of the alternation: "the alternation exists with individual particle verbs (e.g., *put on, pick up*), which argues against the view that the order of NP and particle is lexically governed by the choice of particular verbs."

The study closest in spirit to the present one is Diessel and Tomasello (2005), essentially a replication of Gries's (2003a) study of adult data to first language acquisition data. In 450 VPCs in the speech of Eve (Brown 1973) and Peter (Bloom 1973), Diessel and Tomasello observe 421 instances of V-DirObj-Prt (93.5%) but only 29 instances of V-Prt-DirObj (6.5%). They then code all VPCs for six different variables: the length, complexity, NP type, and definiteness of the direct object, the meaning of the particle, and the presence/absence of a directional adverbial. Just like Gries, they start out with a monofactorial analysis before turning to a multifactorial approach with a binary logistic regression.

Their monofactorial results are similar to Gries's (2003a): with some simplification, V-DirObj-Prt prefers short, simple, pronominal, or definite direct objects in constructions with spatial meanings whereas, on the whole, V-Prt-DirObj is associated with the opposite characteristics. The more sophisticated multifactorial approach, however, showed that, in the context of all variables, only NP type and spatial vs. non-spatial meaning are significantly correlated with the constructional choice. In addition, Diessel and Tomasello found that the caretakers' language exhibits the exact same patterning, both in terms of the constructions' frequencies and the question which factors are significantly correlated with PrtPlc.

Diessel and Tomasello (2005) broke interesting ground, and I follow their lead. However, given the little work on PrtPlc so far and the sparsity of their data – recall their mere 29 instances of V-Prt-DirObj – the field still needs additional exploration, but there are some ways in which I will depart from their approach. First, they conflated the data for their children, which is understandable given their objective of statistical modeling and data scarcity, but also rather untypical of acquisition studies because it hides potential differences between children; I will therefore study all children separately. Second, data scarcity also did not allow them to explore lexical effects in the two constructions in more detail, which is what I will attempt. Third, I will consider some phonological variables not previously examined and also informally explore the role of phrasal verb frequency. Finally, with regard to productivity, Diessel and Tomasello argue that, since the two children used many phrasal verbs and also phrasal verbs in both constructions, it does not make sense to assume the children's use is based on imitative rote-learning only:

> While it is possible that children memorize both particle positions in some of these cases, we believe that the variation is so extensive that rote-learning cannot account for all of the data. (2005: 107)

However, in the absence of a clearly-defined operationalization of "extensive", this is somewhat speculative, and a superficial glance at data will in fact suggest the opposite, which is why I will explore this claim in more detail below. In sum, I will

- provide a descriptive overview of how transitive phrasal verbs are used on the basis of a larger corpus of VPCs;
- explore phonological and frequency variables that have so far received little attention in the scarce literature on the acquisition of VPCs;
- describe lexical variation in a larger corpus especially with an eye to degrees of productivity and with regard to children's first uses of V-Prt-DirObj.

2 Methods: Data and coding

This study is based on data from the CHILDES archive (cf. <http://childes.psy.cmu.edu/>), more specifically, on data from the Abe (Kuczaj 1976), Adam (Brown 1973), and Nina (Suppes 1974) corpora from the CHILDES databank. Instead of the raw data files, I used a version from the syntactically-annotated ReVerb database. The ReVerb project was supervised by Michael Israel during his postdoc at the Department of Psychology at the Max Planck Institute for Evolutionary Anthropology and aimed at providing a database of the development of verbal constructions in English-speaking children between (approximately) 1;6 and 5 years of age (cf. Michael Israel's website at <http://terpconnect.umd.edu/~israel/research.html>). In the original version of this database, multi-word verbs are annotated in terms of the verbs and prepositions/particles they involve; for example, the utterance *take your coat off* would be coded as involving the lexical material "$TAKE $P=OFF". While this annotation facilitates the identification of multi-word verbs, it does not reliably distinguish between intransitive prepositional verbs and transitive phrasal verbs. I therefore manually inspected a cleaned-up version of the ReVerb database by determining for each annotated verb that was

- produced by Abe (age range: 2;5.0 to 5;0.11), Adam (age range: 2;3.4 to 5;2.12), or Nina (age range: 1;11.16 to 3;3.8);
- lexically annotated as involving a "$P=";
- syntactically annotated as not being intransitive;

whether it constituted a transitive phrasal verb and, if so, which VPC. Given the messy nature of corpus data in general and language acquisition data in particular, several coding decisions merit brief mention here. The potentially most controversial of these is counting utterances such as (2) as VPCs:

(2) gonna put that umbrella on here (Nina, 2;9.26)

On the one hand, one may disagree and point out that *on here* can be replaced by *here* or *there*, yielding (3), which is not a VPC since it does not allow the alternation in question (cf. (4)).

(3) gonna put that umbrella here/there

(4) *gonna put here/there that umbrella

On the other hand, the children used *put on* as a phrasal verb as in, say, (5). Second, if a direct object becomes long/complex enough, even a "bipartite particle" such as *on here* can, in fact needs to, be preposed, as in the hypothetical example in (6).

(5) I put on a nightgown (Nina, 2;5.24)

(6) I put on here all the books that my parents had brought with them when they were last in Europe.

By analogy, I also included "bipartite particles" such as *back in* and *back on* as exemplified in (7) and six utterances with "tripartite particles" of the type in (8) in the data. (Naturally, the influence of a mere six such examples will be negligible.)

(7) you gonna put it back in? (Adam, 3;4.1)

(8) Mommy I'm gonna put it back in here (Nina, 3;0.10)

On the other hand, mostly I decided to err on the side of caution, especially when considering to count a tricky utterance as an instance of the (rarer) V-Prt-DirObj pattern. For example, utterances such as (9) could be a VPC with a direct object beginning with *this*, but also a case where a direct object has been omitted and *this* is used as a deictic accompanying a gesture, as in the hypothetical example of (10).

(9) put on this (Nina, 3;0.16)

(10) put the doll on this [pointing onto a table]

Similarly, utterances such as (11) look like a VPC but I have considered them an elided version of something like (12).

(11) get out my chair (Adam, 3;11.14)

(12) get out of my chair

After the VPCs were retrieved as mentioned above, they were manually annotated for several variables. Since the number of matches was too large to annotate all, I annotated

- all instances of V-Prt-DirObj; and
- a number of instances of V-DirObj-Prt such that I coded minimally one randomly chosen instance in each recording and maximally as many pseudo-randomly chosen instances as the recording contributed proportionally to all instances of V-DirObj-Prt for each child; the choice was *pseudo*-random because, when the next randomly-chosen utterance contained the same VPC as the previous one, I picked another one.

The variables that were coded are the following:

- Construction: V-Prt-DirObj vs. V-DirObj-Prt;
- Length of the direct object in morphemes: for instance, *you can match up the story with the pictures on here* (2) or *we can open up our presents* (3); a *plurale tantum* such as *clothes* was coded as one morpheme;
- ObjType of the direct object: clause (as in *you find out where my piece goes*), definite lexical NP (as in *let's turn on the record*), indefinite lexical NP (as in *kick off a sock*), lexical NP with possessive pronoun (as in *can I put on my moccasins?*), lexical NP without determiners/premodification (as in *take away parachute*), name (as in *I bate Paul up*), pronominal (as in *(ex)cept how long will it take to pick up it?*);
- Semantics of the particle: end states vs. completives. VPCs were coded as end states if one could say "after the action denoted by the VPC, the [referent of the direct object] is [particle]", as in *turn the light on* (after which the light is on) or *chop down a dead pear tree* (after which the tree is down); this coincides with what other studies categorized as spatial/locative uses. On the other hand, VPCs were coded as completives when the particle "solidified" the action by the verb so one could say "after the action denoted by the VPC, the [referent of the direct object] is completely [verb-ed]", as

in *wake up kitten* (then, the kitten is awake but not necessarily up) or *them guys can beat up this guy* (after which this guy is beaten, but most likely not up); completives also cover (a tiny number of) metaphorical/idiomatic uses;

- the type of initial SEGMENT of the particle: V as for *pick up* and C as for *bring back*;
- CV ALTERNATION: the type of initial segment of the particle (from above) and the type of final segment of the verb.[2]

In the next section, I will discuss the results of the corpus analysis.

3 Findings

3.1 Overview

As a result of the above procedures, I obtained the data summarized in Table 10.1.

Table 10.1. Frequencies of Abe, Adam's, and Nina's VPCs

	Abe	*Adam*	*Nina*	*Totals*
V-Prt-DirObj	72	66	49	187
V-DirObj-Prt	1010	1578	898	3486
Totals	1082	1644	947	3673

The ratio of V-Prt-DirObj of all VPCs is reassuringly close to that reported in Diessel and Tomasello (2005), and while Table 10.1 indicates that the frequencies of the constructions differ significantly across the children (χ^2 = 9.43; df = 2; p<0.01), the size of this effect is very small (Cramer's V=0.05), given the children's rather different age and MLU ranges.

3.2 The effect of LENGTH

The three panels of Figure 10.1 illustrate the correlation between CONSTRUCTION and LENGTH for each child separately with box-and-whisker plots, where the thick horizontal line/the plotted "x" represent the constructions' medians/means respectively, and where the boxes cover the central 50% of the data around the medians.

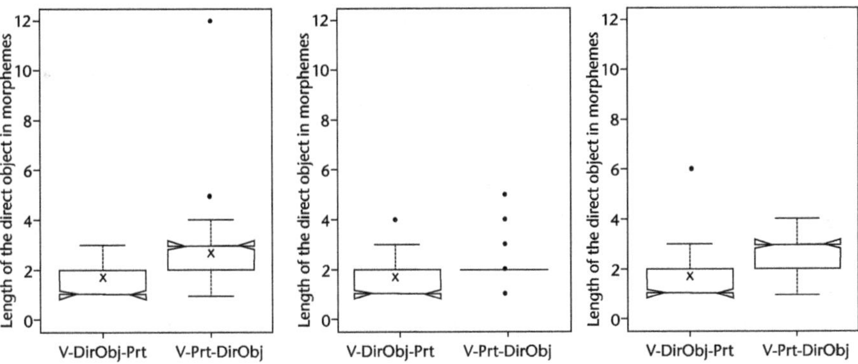

Figure 10.1. CONSTRUCTION × LENGTH (left: Abe; center: Adam; right: Nina)

U-tests show each child exhibits a significant tendency to use V-DirObj-Prt with, on average, shorter direct objects than V-Prt-DirObj (Abe: 1.6 vs. 2.8 morphemes; $W = 2780$; $p<0.001$; Adam: 1.4 vs. 2.1 morphemes; $W = 1666$; $p<0.001$; Nina: 1.8 vs. 2 morphemes; $W = 1468.5$; $p<0.05$; all reported averages are medians). These effects are in the direction expected from, but smaller than found in, adult data, but they are very similar to those observed by Diessel and Tomasello (2005: 100) for acquisition data. They can therefore be explained in terms of the workings of an interactive activation model or in terms of widely-attested processing effects as mentioned above. The fact that the effects observed in acquisition data are weaker than in adult data is of course due to the fact that children's utterances are in general shorter and thus do not contain the long objects necessary for stronger effects.

3.3 The effect of NP TYPE

The three panels of Figure 10.2 illustrate the correlation between CONSTRUCTION and OBJTYPE for each child with a cross-tabulation plot (cf. Gries 2009: 176f.); I have omitted four instances of V-Prt-DirObj. The color of the numbers and the parenthesized sign indicate whether an observed frequency is larger than expected (black and "(+)") or smaller than expected (gray and "(–)"), and the physical size of the number indicates the size of the effect (as a proportion of the Pearson residuals).

All panels deviate significantly from a random distribution (Abe: $\chi^2 = 58$; $df = 5$; $p<0.001$; Cramer's $V = 0.47$; Adam: $\chi^2 = 37.55$; $df = 5$; $p<0.001$; Cramer's $V = 0.49$; Nina: $\chi^2 = 26.54$; $df = 5$; $p<0.001$; Cramer's $V = 0.46$). The children are remarkably similar to each other. For most object types – (in)definite NPs, NPs without premodifiers, and pronouns – they pattern

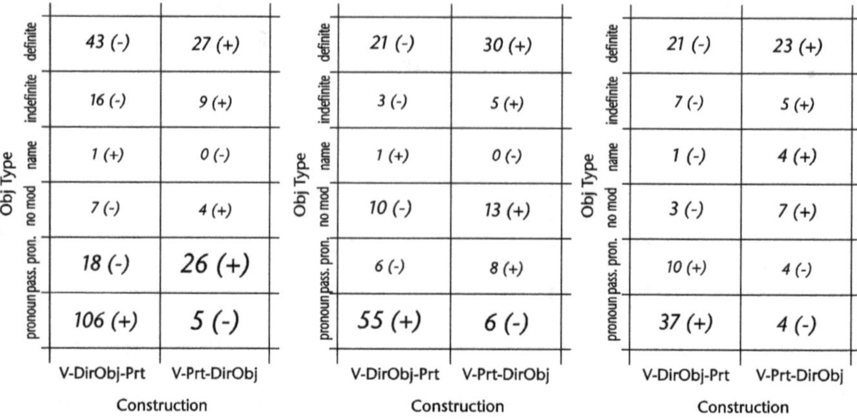

Figure 10.2. CONSTRUCTION × OBJTYPE (left: Abe; center: Adam; right: Nina)

alike. However, they pattern differently for names such that there is a very tiny effect due to Abe's and Adam's preference, and Nina's dispreference, for V-DirObj-Prt. Comparable data from adults also show only a very weak preference (for V-DirObj-Prt; cf. Gries 2003a: 85). More prominent, however, is the larger difference for lexical NPs with possessive pronouns: Adam and Abe prefer V-Prt-DirObj for these (the former strongly) while Nina (slightly) prefers V-DirObj-Prt.

Interestingly, most effects are identical to findings from adult data. However, each child violates the otherwise virtually categorical preference of pronominal objects for V-DirObj-Prt. Abe's five cases involve the particle *up*, three of these involve *pick up* and in 10 of the 15 cases the pronoun is either *yours* or the demonstrative pronouns *this*/*dis* and *that*; the remaining cases are one *everything* and four *it*s. These observations are compatible with, for example, Browman's (1986) mention of the special status of *up* and *pick up* (but cf. below), and the fact that demonstrative pronouns preference for V-Prt-DirObj can be explained by their prominent/contrastive information status in their VP-final position.

Second, while adults prefer definite NPs and indefinite NPs in V-DirObj-Prt and V-Prt-DirObj respectively, the children studied here prefer V-Prt-DirObj with both kinds of determiners, which conforms to Diessel and Tomasello's (2005: 102) findings. The data therefore suggest that Abe's and Adam's main distinction with regard to PrtPlc is between longer lexical NPs (definite, indefinite, no premodification, and premodification with a possessive pronoun), which they strongly prefer with V-Prt-DirObj, and a class consisting of shorter names and pronouns, which they strongly prefer with V-DirObj-Prt. In other words, Abe and

Adam are sensitive to a coarse formal distinction – names/pronouns vs. lexical nouns – and, presumably its discourse-functional/information-structural motivation: referents of names and pronouns are generally more identifiable than referents of lexical nouns. Accordingly, the children's data can be integrated well into Gries's (2003a) above-mentioned accounts in terms of activation or processing cost. However, Abe and Adam are apparently *not* sensitive to the more fine-grained formal distinction – definite vs indefinite within the lexical objects – and its information-structural motivation: referents of definite NPs are generally more given than referents of indefinite NPs. Nina patterns nearly the same way, differing from Abe and Adam only with regard to her weak opposite preferences for names and lexical NPs with possessive pronouns.

3.4 The effect of SEMANTICS

The three panels of Figure 10.3 represent the correlations between CONSTRUCTION and SEMANTICS with cross-tabulation plots. (I have omitted 13 VPCs from these data for reasons discussed below.)

The results indicate that, on the whole, the children's use of VPCs is the one expected from, and explained for, adult data (cf. Gries 2003a: 87f.) and acquisition data (cf. Diessel and Tomasello 2005: 102); the distributions found for Abe and Nina are significant, while the one for Adam is only in the expected direction, but not significant (Abe: $\chi^2 = 6.38$; $df = 1$; $p<0.05$; Cramer's $V = 0.16$; Adam: $\chi^2 = 1.09$; $df = 1$; $p = 0.3$; Cramer's $V = 0.08$; Nina: $\chi^2 = 13.09$; $df = 1$; $p<0.001$; Cramer's $V = 0.32$).

In addition to the above correlation, 13 VPCs were classified in ways other than "end state" and "completive". Six were cases where the child seems to have used the 'wrong' direct object, cf. the examples in (13) and (14).

(13) (a) did Mommy already start picking up the living room? (Abe, 4;7.11)
(b) she left for me to pick up the living room (Abe, 4;7.11)
(c) I picked up the kitchen (Abe, 4;7.11)

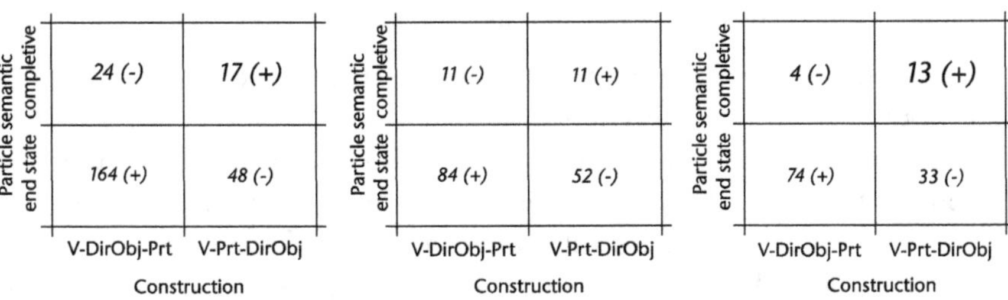

Figure 10.3. CONSTRUCTION × SEMANTICS (left: Abe; center: Adam; right: Nina)

(14) (a) I already ate cucumber I even ate the fridge up (Abe, 4;5.28)
(b) shovel up the street (Adam, 3;8)
(c) you (sup)posed to cut out de lines (Adam, 4;7)

The constructions in (13) all involve *pick up* $\text{DirObj}_{\text{location}}$ used by Abe in the sense of "clean up $\text{DirObj}_{\text{location}}$ by picking up $\text{DirObj}_{\text{things in location}}$", a use that Adam and Nina do not exhibit. This observation is unusual because Abe uses *pick up* like this only in one recording, but correctly in all remaining recordings. In fact, after Abe's uttering (13a), his father responds "yea, she picked up a lot", exemplifying the canonical use, to which Abe, however, responds with (13b). This is directly followed by another exchange in which the father provides the canonical use and Abe then picks up (no pun intended) the canonical use, too: Abe's father says "she picked up most of it", to which Abe responds "oh yea, she left me to pick up this stuff" followed by, one turn later, "I didn't have to pick up too much." But even after two utterances with canonical uses of *pick up*, Abe later reverts to his idiosyncratic use by uttering (13c), to which his mother responds (twice) "did you pick up all your toys" (Abe's answer to this does not involve *pick up*). It seems, therefore, that Abe definitely knows the canonical use of *pick up*, but assumes, if only briefly, the argument structure construction exemplified in (14) is normal, too.

The constructions in (14) are special in various senses. (14a) may be a canonical use if Abe used it to jocularly say "I ate very much", and (14b) could be a creative use of *shovel up* as "dig up" and, thus, a creative but otherwise canonical use just like *dig up the street*. In order to annotate the data conservatively, neither was not counted as a regular completive. Finally, (14c) is supposed to mean "cut out [some paper] *along* the lines".

Another set of VPCs not lumped together with the clear-cut cases is shown in (15).

(15) (a) wash off my hands (Abe, 2;11.18)
(b) wash my hands off (Abe, 3;1.18)
(c) would you wipe off my legs (Abe, 3;6.10)
(d) I wipe it off (Adam, 2;10.16)
(e) you clean it off (Nina, 2;3.28)

Here, the particle does not necessarily modify the referent of the direct object but the referent of another object that is not mentioned. For instance, after performing the action described in (15a), it is not the hands that are off, but, say, the dirt on my hands or legs, as described in <u>*wash*</u> *the dirt* <u>*off my hands*</u> (for (15a)), where the underlined parts indicate the material that made it into the utterance. For this reason, these constructions were not grouped with the cases where the particle denotes the resultant state of the direct object's referent.

The final two special cases shown in (16) were cases where I was not certain enough how to analyze them.

(16) (a) Beat two out Mommy beat two out (Abe, 2;8.8)
(b) I tear off a hole (Adam, 3;3.4)

In (16a), Abe may mean "beat a line with his brush" (judging from what appears to be a clarification from his father), but the meaning is not completely clear. Finally, (16b) is similar to examples in (15) in that the particle seems to refer to an unmentioned object – Abe seems to mean "I tore off something$_1$ of something$_2$, thereby creating a hole in something$_2$" – but it is also different in that the paraphrase that would turn it into a canonical adult utterance is more complex than those required for the cases in (15).

The previous sections were concerned with variables that were, sometimes slightly differently, also studied by Diessel and Tomasello. The following section explores phonological variables that have one rarely been studied in PrtPlc data from adults and not at all in PrtPlc data from children.

3.5 The effects of Segment and CV alternation

Figure 10.4 shows cross-tabulation plots for the relation between Construction and Segment.

Browman found a significant preference of particles beginning with a vowel for V-Prt-DirObj, but all three children exhibit only insignificant tendencies in this direction (Abe: $\chi^2 = 2.63$; $df = 1$; $p = 0.1$; Cramer's $V = 0.05$; Adam: $\chi^2 = 2.73$; $df = 1$; $p = 0.098$; Cramer's $V = 0.04$; Nina: $\chi^2 \approx 0$; $df = 1$; $p = 0.98$; Cramer's $V<0.001$). However, this insignificant result is less disappointing than it seems. First, the expected tendency was observed. Second, as discussed in note 1, the level of resolution – particle-initial segment: vowel vs. consonant – is not particularly high and maybe confounded with other factors. Finally, unlike most determinants of PrtPlc, this one does not appear to be integratable into a psycholinguistically

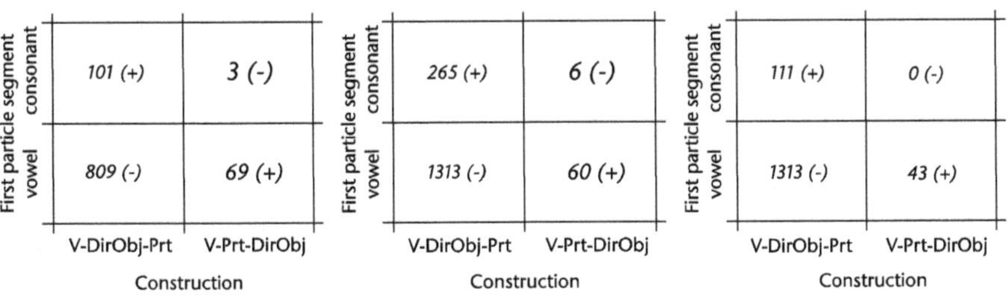

Figure 10.4. Construction × Segment (left: Abe; center: Adam; right: Nina)

motivated account: there seems to be no psycholinguistic motivation for why the particle-initial segment should play a role. However, once a more precise resolution is adopted, the situation changes. If one considers not only the type of particle-initial segment, but also its interaction with the verb-final segment, something that Browman (1986: 319–320) alludes to, but does not study, a different picture emerges; consider Figure 10.5.

If CV ALTERNATION played a role, then in V-Prt-DirObj, where the verb-final segment is immediately followed by the particle-initial segment, the type of the verb-final segment should be different from the particle-initial segment more often than expected by chance. This is the tendency that all three children exhibit, and preference is significant in the case of Abe (Abe: $\chi^2 = 6.5$; $df = 1$; $p = 0.01$; Cramer's $V = 0.08$; Adam: $\chi^2 = 0.23$; $df = 1$; $p = 0.63$; Cramer's $V = 0.01$; Nina: $\chi^2 = 1.11$; $df = 1$; $p = 0.29$; Cramer's $V = 0.03$).

The fact that one child exhibited a significant tendency for CV ALTERNATION is one reason to assume that this variable is a better predictor than SEGMENT. A second one is that CV ALTERNATION is better motivated as a predictor. First, the variable SEGMENT is merely a stipulation or even only a generalization already based on PrtPlc data, whereas CV ALTERNATION is not only a phenomenon observed independently of PrtPlc, it is in fact just one instance of more general and well-known dispreference of very similar structures to appear in very close succession, a tendency that is, so to speak, the opposite of priming and is sometimes referred to as *horror aequi* (cf. Rohdenburg 2003). We know that speakers disprefer successive occurrences of stressed syllables, so-called stress clashes, or successive occurrences of unstressed syllables, so-called stress lapses (cf. Selkirk 1984; Schlüter 2003). In fact, we already know that adult PrtPlc itself is correlated with at least one instantiation of *horror aequi*, namely a preference for rhythmic alternation (cf. Gries 2007). Second, given that CV ALTERNATION is a realization of a more general phenomenon, it comes as no surprise that an explanation for this kind of patterning is available, and the explanation I favor involves exactly the activation-based model of language production that Gries (2003a) uses to unite all known determinants of PrtPlc.

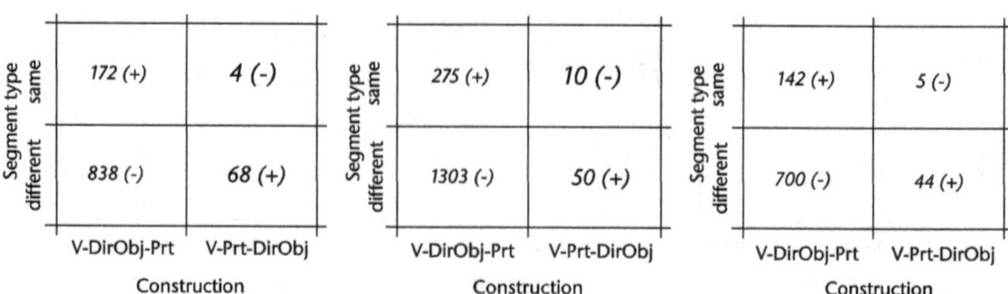

Figure 10.5. CONSTRUCTION × CV ALTERNATION (left: Abe; center: Adam; right: Nina)

From this perspective, CV ALTERNATION and other *horror aequi* effects result from how activation cycles of nodes function in interactive activation models. Such models (of linguistic knowledge) involve nodes (representing linguistic units on different hierarchical levels) and links between them, and nodes send and receive activation from other nodes via these links. When a node receives enough activation, it can be "selected", which means that, for example, the linguistic unit (or action routine) that it represents will be executed. Crucially, once a node, e.g., one representing "consonants", has fired and thereby facilitated the production of a consonant, it undergoes a short period of self-inhibition during which it is unlikely to be chosen for activation again, which is why the node for vowels is more likely to be chosen next, which naturally leads to, or at least favors, the kinds of alternating patterns often found (cf. MacKay 1987, esp. Chapters 1 and 2, for details and various kinds of neurological evidence for this model).

3.6 Lexically-specific results

One question that naturally arises with regard to all sorts of acquisition data is to what degree children's production consists just of verbatim repetitions or, in this case, rote-learned pairs of particular phrasal verbs in particular constituent orderings. Both Broihier *et al.* (1994) and Diessel and Tomasello (2005) argue against rote-learned VPCs, showing that there are phrasal verbs used in both constructions. However, Broihier *et al.* (1994) do not provide a systematic overview let alone frequencies of the phrasal verb types, tokens, and their occurrences in both constructions. Diessel and Tomasello are more systematic: they compare the effects of the variables they study in child language to the effects these variables exhibit in caretaker language, but also provide both phrasal-verb type frequencies (65 and 83 in Peter's and Eve's data from CHILDES) and several examples of phrasal verbs Peter and Eve use in both VPCs. However, the problem of data scarcity – recall their database contained only 421 and 29 (!) instances of V-DirObj-Prt and V-Prt-DirObj respectively – makes it difficult to get a reliable picture of how especially the latter construction is used and calls for more comprehensive description. This section will provide some descriptive overview data and explore the relation between the frequency of phrasal verbs and the constructional choices.

Since the main objective of this section is descriptive, I will begin with some summary tables. Tables 10.2, 10.3, and 10.4 list the frequencies of VPCs (abbreviated as *VPO* and *VOP* for reasons of space) for the most frequent phrasal verbs, verbs, and particles in Abe's, Adam's, and Nina's speech respectively.

Table 10.2. Frequencies of Abe's most frequent phrasal verbs, verbs, and particles; figures larger than expected are in bold

Phrasal verb	*VPO : VOP*	*Verb*	*VPO : VOP*	*Particle*	*VPO : VOP*
put in	0 : **124**	*put*	11 : **307**	*up*	**38** : 201
put on	**9** : 112	*get*	2 : **124**	*on*	**16** : 218
turn on	3 : **44**	*take*	0 : **75**	*in*	0 : **149**
get off	0 : **37**	*turn*	4 : **71**	*off*	4 : **132**
get out	1 : **35**	*cut*	3 : 40	*out*	**9** : 124
pick up	**18** : 16	*pick*	19 : 18	*down*	3 : **70**
take off	0 : **34**	*throw*	0 : **32**	*away*	0 : **51**
eat up	2 : **29**	*eat*	2 : **29**	*back*	0 : **21**
take out	0 : **26**	*knock*	1 : **23**	*over*	**2** : 15
throw away	0 : **26**	*bring*	2 : 16	*around*	0 : **6**
186 more types	39 : 527	91 more types	28 : 276	10 more types	0 : 23

Table 10.3. Frequencies of Adam's most frequent phrasal verbs, verbs, and particles; figures larger than expected are in bold

Phrasal verb	*VPO : VOP*	*Verb*	*VPO : VOP*	*Particle*	*VPO : VOP*
put in	1 : **196**	*put*	12 : **498**	*up*	11 : **335**
put on	**11** : 145	*take*	9 : **227**	*on*	**14** : 235
take off	**7** : 127	*get*	3 : 66	*off*	**13** : 227
take out	1 : **78**	*knock*	0 : **65**	*in*	3 : **222**
eat up	0 : **54**	*turn*	4 : 57	*out*	**15** : 204
knock down	0 : **53**	*eat*	0 : **55**	*down*	6 : **161**
pick up	**2** : 39	*cut*	10 : 44	*back*	0 : **50**
put up	0 : **38**	*push*	1 : **46**	*away*	1 : **37**
get out	**3** : 29	*pick*	2 : 39	*over*	**2** : 26
punch out	0 : **29**	*punch*	0 : **30**	*back in*	0 : **18**
229 more types	41 : 790	103 more types	25 : 451	20 more types	1 : 63

Table 10.4. Frequencies of Nina's most frequent phrasal verbs, verbs, and particles; figures larger than expected are in bold

Phrasal verb	*VPO : VOP*	*Verb*	*VPO : VOP*	*Particle*	*VPO : VOP*
put on	5 : **129**	*put*	7 : **346**	*on*	5 : **238**
put in	0 : **104**	*take*	9 : **168**	*up*	**22** : 144
take off	7 : 94	*want*	0 : **47**	*off*	**9** : 154
take out	1 : **62**	*eat*	1 : **40**	*in*	0 : **111**
eat up	1 : **40**	*get*	1 : **31**	*out*	3 : **95**
want on	0 : **34**	*have*	0 : **30**	*down*	**6** : 57
pick up	**11** : 19	*pick*	11 : 19	*away*	**2** : 25
put down	1 : **29**	*knock*	0 : **26**	*back on*	0 : **22**
have on	0 : **27**	*wear*	0 : **23**	*back in*	0 : **19**
wear on	0 : **23**	*wake*	0 : **18**	*over*	**1** : 10
114 more types	23 : 337	57 more types	20 : 150	8 more types	1 : 23

Several observations are obvious: First and unsurprisingly, children's VPCs are largely concerned with concrete actions, often involving movement in space and resulting end states. Second and more relevantly and reassuringly, the children are similar to each other. For example, the phrasal verbs *put in, put on, take off, take out, pick up,* and *eat up* are among the most frequent for each child, and often their preferences for a construction are identical; the same is true of just the verbs and just the particles. Third, all children support Browman's observation of *pick up*'s strong preference for V-Prt-DirObj, which is astonishing since, in Gries and Stefanowitsch's (2004) study of adult-only data, *pick up* was the most frequent phrasal verb, but had absolutely no preference for either construction.

While these tables provide some summary information, they do not speak to the role of FREQUENCY, which Browman merely stipulated and that Schnoebelen incorporated in his approach. Consider, therefore, Figure 10.6, Figure 10.7, and Figure 10.8, which plot the proportions of V-Prt-DirObj for each phrasal verb against that phrasal verb's frequency in the child language. In each graph, the dashed horizontal line indicates the proportion of V-Prt-DirObj for a child, and the dashed curve is a non-parametric smoother summarizing the correlation for all phrasal verbs attested in both constructions.

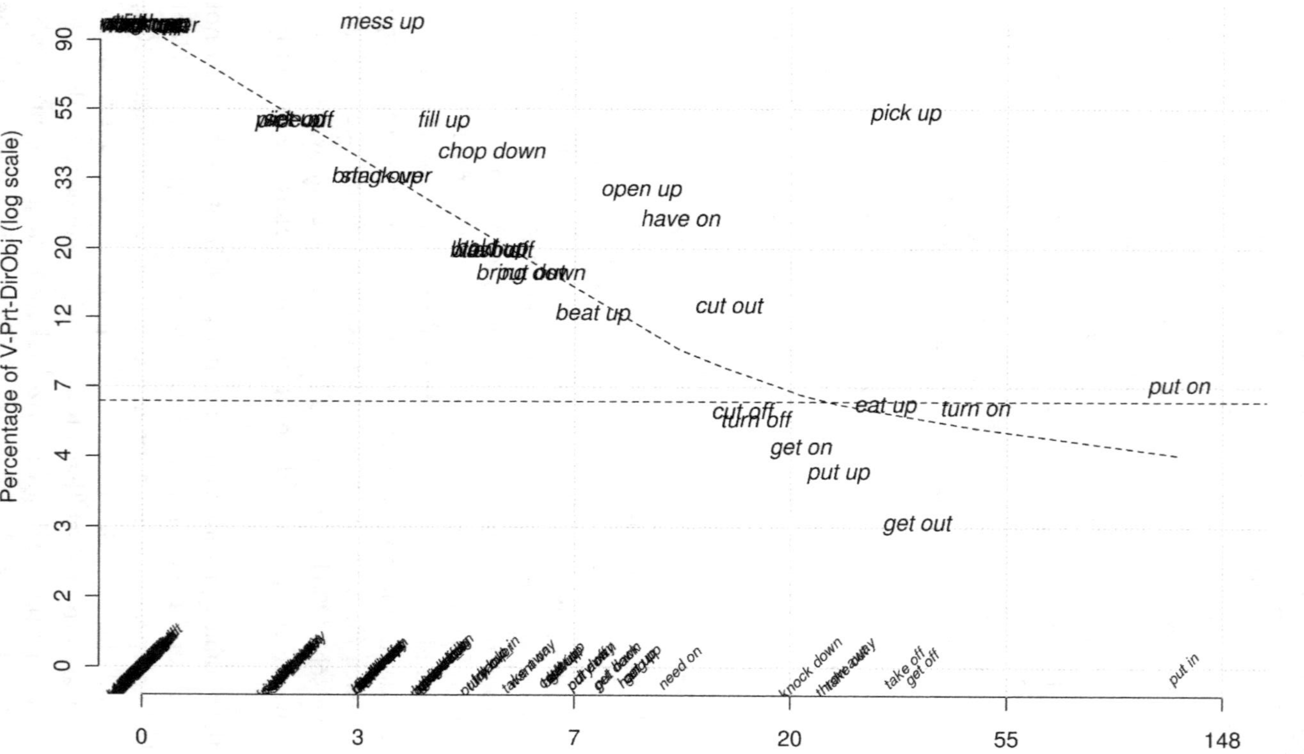

Figure 10.6. The relation of the percentage of V-Prt-DirObj out of all constructions of a phrasal verb to that phrasal verb's frequency in Abe's speech

Editor's Note: The type of overplotting illustrated in Figures10.6 to 10.8 is common in statistical graphs. The position of the words is meaningful on both axes and indicates more populated areas.

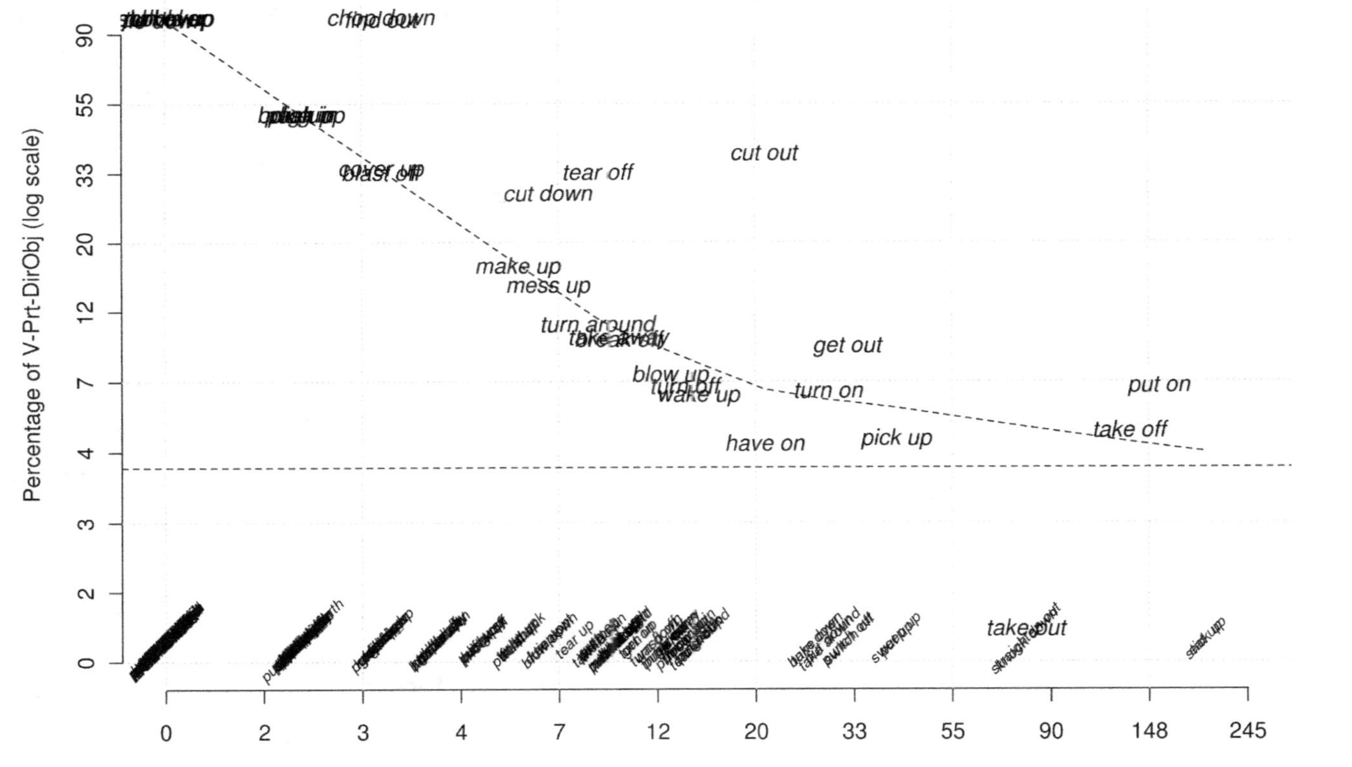

Figure 10.7. The relation of the percentage of V-Prt-DirObj out of all constructions of a phrasal verb to that phrasal verb's frequency in Adam's speech

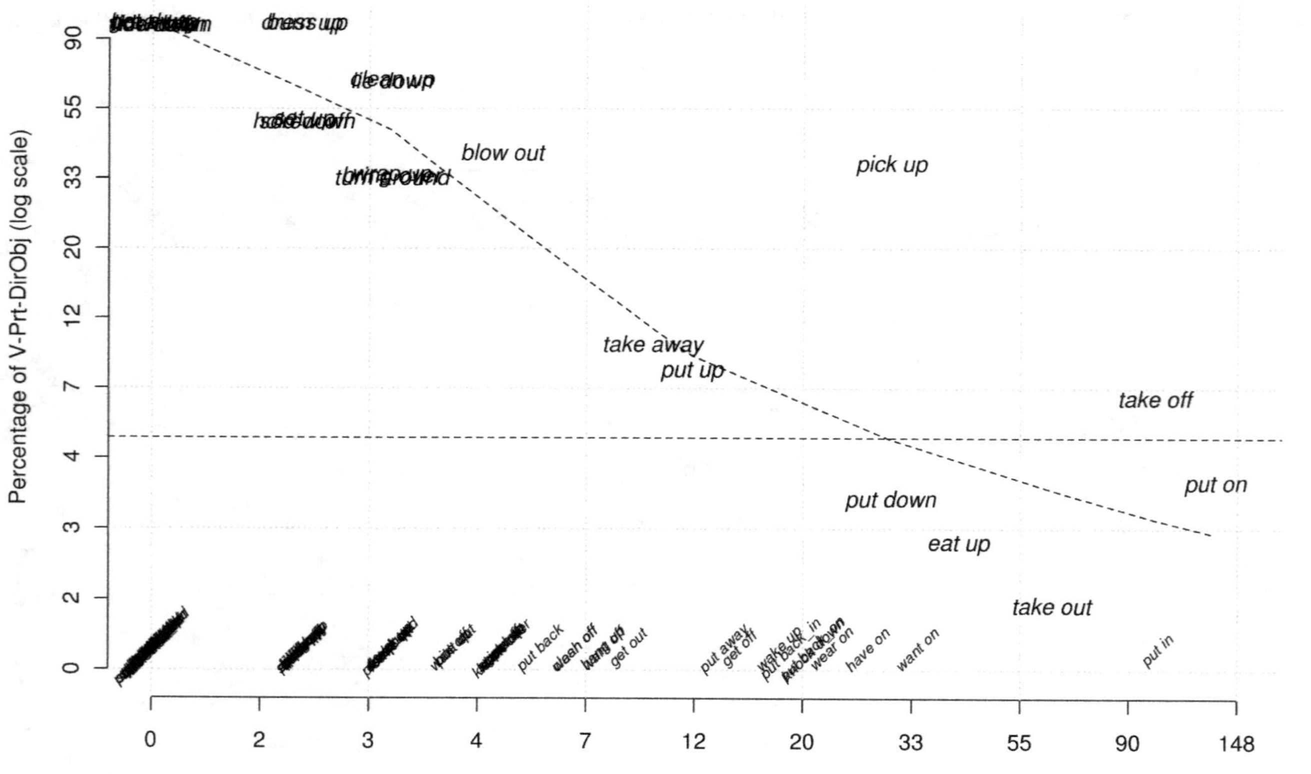

Figure 10.8. The relation of the percentage of V-Prt-DirObj out of all constructions of a phrasal verb to that phrasal verb's frequency in Nina's speech

Obviously, Frequency is correlated with Construction even when its impact is neither measured in Schnoebelen's sophisticated way nor in Browman's somewhat problematic way (cf. again note 1). However, the relation between Construction and Frequency is not the one discussed in Browman – it is the opposite: as the smoother and its negative slope indicate, higher phrasal-verb frequency is correlated with (higher percentages of) V-DirObj-Prt, and in some sense this is not surprising, given the frequency of talk about spatial movement and accessible referents in children's speech.

Finally, a potential objection must be anticipated. These data shed some doubt on Broihier *et al.*'s (1994) and Diessel and Tomasello's (2005) remarks regarding the productivity of the alternation. On the one hand, there are obviously phrasal verbs that occur in both constructions, but on the other hand, it is just as obvious that the vast majority of phrasal verbs does not: only $^{26}/_{196}$ of Abe's phrasal verb types are attested in both constructions, as are only $^{25}/_{239}$ of Adam's and $^{17}/_{124}$ of Nina's, and this is not "extensive variation" that Diessel and Tomasello simply "believe[d]" makes rote-learned VPCs very unlikely. (Their only evidence for this was a list of nine phrasal verbs that did alternate, and given the size of their corpus there was in fact little else they could do.) In fact, the proverbial devil's advocate might even say that both Diessel and Tomasello's findings as well as mine reported above could all be completely epiphenomenal in the sense that they only arise from properties of the approximately 90% of the verb types that do *not* alternate. The larger database of the present study, however, allows to address this threat by: (a) removing the potentially confounding non-alternating phrasal verbs and the way they enter into the analysis; and (b) repeating all statistical analyses from §3.2 to §3.5 for each child only with those phrasal verbs that a child uses in both constructions.[3] Space does not permit an exhaustive discussion of the results, but most results regarding the "traditional variables" prove to be robust (cf. the appendix for summary graphs):

- Length: the objects of V-Prt-DirObj are longer than those of V-DirObj-Prt (all children);
- ObjType: empty cells notwithstanding, all three children's data exhibit the same tendencies as before;
- Semantics: all three children's data exhibit the same tendencies as before.

More surprising are the results for Segment and CV alternation, which stand in exact opposition to the ones obtained earlier. When only alternating phrasal verbs are studied, Browman's hypothesized tendency of particles beginning with a vowel to occur in V-Prt-DirObj is not supported. The same holds for the hypothesized tendency of a preference for CV alternating patterns. Both of these latter results point to the need for more comprehensive and precise studies of the variables for only the alternating cases – such particulars are hard to predict – and some possibilities for further study will be outlined below.

4 Concluding remarks

Diessel and Tomasello (2005) and the present study have shown that, just like in adult speech, children's PrtPlc is governed by many interrelated variables from different levels of linguistic analysis. With regard to the sample of VPCs, children's VPCs are less variable than those of adults because children talk about what is relevant to them and cognitively manageable:

- they use a more restricted set of phrasal verbs, which is on the whole more concerned with concrete objects and motion through space to a final position;
- they exhibit a much more biased distribution of constructions, with V-DirObj-Prt accounting for 95% of all VPCs.

These effects can be explained straightforwardly. V-DirObj-Prt is used mainly for the scenario of a human agent causing an object to move, and this scenario is cognitively basic and highly salient for children, whose earliest single word-utterances already use particles such as *up* and *down* to refer to (resultant) locations of concrete objects (including themselves). Correspondingly, children disprefer this construction for more aspectual/completive and idiomatic meanings (e.g., *He eated up the meat* or *You find out where my piece goes*; cf. also Fischer 1971: 144). Also, V-DirObj-Prt is also more often used in spoken language and thus more likely to constitute a significant portion of the children's input.

With regard to the variables investigated here, I tried to go replicate and also go beyond Diessel and Tomasello (2005):

- rather than conflating the data, children were studied separately, and there were a few cases where a conflation would have masked individual differences;
- Diessel and Tomasello's monofactorial findings were confirmed both by replicating their methods but also by removing potentially

confounding lexical effects and checking only the phrasal verbs that alternate;
- some of the traditionally-studied variables exhibit different effect sizes (e.g., LENGTH);
- some traditionally-studied variables exhibit slightly different effects (e.g., OBJTYPE);
- the present study provided a more comprehensive overview of lexically-specific preferences;
- the present study investigated new variables that have rarely been studied: SEGMENT, CV ALTERNATION, FREQUENCY, and the special role of *(pick) up*.

Crucially, when all phrasal verbs are studied – not just the ones that alternate – then the effects known from adult data and from Diessel and Tomasello as well as the new phonological variables studied here for the first time are fully compatible with the psycholinguistically-motivated approach advocated by Gries (2003a) and adopted by Diessel and Tomasello and Schnoebelen. However, apart from the obvious need for a multifactorial study, several next steps suggest themselves.

First, some of the present results in turn require further scrutiny. For instance, there is the more general methodological question of whether to include in one's statistical analysis only those phrasal verbs that alternate (a common practice in sociolinguistic circles) or all phrasal verbs (as in Diessel and Tomasello). Abstractly speaking, the former approach appears methodologically more desirable in spite of the "damage" it does to sample sizes. The present study does not provide a clear-cut answer, however. On the one hand, the traditional determinants of PrtPlc, which are also the ones that are largely independent of particular lexical items, exhibited the same tendencies in both approaches. On the other hand, the new phonological determinants, which are much more tied to individual lexical items, did not yield the same results in both approaches, which may well mean that these variables' connections to individual lexical items is so strong that, once non-alternating phrasal verbs are disregarded, no effect remains. This may indeed be what is going on, and if it is, it would support the notion of preferably studying only alternating verbs, but further study is required, both of more, and more diverse, variables and more precise study of the CV alternation: rather than studying only the transition from the verb-final segment to the particle-initial segment, all possible transitions could be studied (end-of-verb to beginning-of-particle, end-of-particle to beginning-of-object for V-Prt-DirObj as well as end-of-verb to beginning-of-object and end-of object to beginning-of-particle for V-DirObj-Prt) and maybe restricted to short objects (because the kind of phonological planning giving rise to CV ALTERNATION may not operate across longer objects).

More research is also needed regarding the impact of definiteness. Like adults, children prefer V-Prt-DirObj with lexical direct objects, but unlike adults, (in)definiteness plays no role.[4] This may either be due to the fact that children indeed do not yet grasp the more subtle way in which determiners reflect information structure on top of the choice of lexical vs. pronominal objects, or it may mean that pointing gestures and other contextual clues facilitate referent identification and, thus, blur the role of definiteness; more study, maybe on the basis of video recordings, etc. can answer this question (cf. Allen *et al.* 2008 for an overview of related work).

Then, we need more detailed knowledge about individual phrasal verbs, verbs, and particles and their relation to more general determinants. For example, we have seen that *pick up* behaves very differently from all other verbs – why is that so, when does it begin, and how does it change over time? For example, the present data set contained something that, to my knowledge has hardly been mentioned or studied before with regard to adult PrtPlc and not at all for children, namely: (a) many bipartite particles of the types exemplified in (7) and (8) (i.e., *back in, back on,* etc.); and (b) modified particles as in *they eat the whole taco all up* or *you'll have to fix that all up* or *chop it right down*. While all these examples occur in V-DirObj-Prt (cf. Fraser 1974: 573), we know nothing about how and why this is so. Lastly in the area of lexically-specific constructional preferences, it would be useful to be able to carry out fine-grained *and* longitudinal studies where one identifies for a particular phrasal verb its first use in V-Prt-DirObj and then tracks back how the phrasal verb, but also just the verb and just the particle, is used over time by the child and in the ambient language, to gain a better understanding of what drives children's realization that a phrasal verb can be used in both constructions.

Finally, the question with maybe the largest scope of all: how does the acquisition of PrtPlc relate to the acquisition of other alternations, such as the dative alternation. Snyder and Stromswold (1997) have shown that children begin to acquire several alternations all around the same time (at approximately age 2;2) and since PrtPlc and the dative alternation are governed by similar determinants (cf. Gries 2003b and Bresnan *et al.* 2007), the holy grail is to develop a unified account of the acquisition of constituent order alternations, and the present study adds another piece of evidence to the claim that such an approach *must* be multifactorial. The present study does obviously not do all that, but if it helps stimulate research in this important area, one of its main objectives has been attained.

Notes

* I thank Stefanie Wulff for comments. The usual disclaimers apply.

1. Two things are worth pointing out with regard to these variables. First, although Browman does not explore this, the variable vowel-initial vs. consonant-initial particle is of course highly correlated with the particle as such and its other phonological properties. First, in the present data set, there were only two particles beginning with /ʌ/, one of which is the most frequent particle *up*, the other being the extremely rare *under*. Since *up* on its own is correlated with the order V-Prt-DirObj, it is difficult to estimate how much of the initial-segment variable is due to other correlated variables. Second, there were three particles beginning with /ə/, and these are of course all from the very small group of particles with more than one syllable (*along*, *around*, and *away*), which may affect PrtPlc, too. Third, especially in V-Prt-DirObj, the initial segment of the particle may interact with the final segment of the verb such that speakers may unconsciously prefer a CV alternation pattern. While Gries (2003a: 120f) could not find such an effect, he only looked at one small sample of adult data and further systematic study of this is required and will be reported on below. The exact nature of this effect is, therefore, not clear yet, and awaits a larger and multifactorial study.

   Second, Browman does not explain why there should be a correlation between the frequency of a phrasal verb and its constructional preference. Schnoebelen's approach, in which frequency of occurrence figures in his entropy calculations, fares much better in that regard. Also, the way in which Browman operationalized the frequency of the phrasal verb may not be optimal since she did not only use the frequency of the phrasal verb proper, but added to that the frequencies of the verb and the particle. This may be problematic because, in adult language, *in* and *on* are not particularly frequent as particles in transitive phrasal verbs, but they are of course rather frequent everywhere else, which will distort the frequencies that are intended to only represent phrasal verb frequencies.

2. The coding of the final segment of the verb was based on the form produced by the child. That is, when the child used *blowed* as the past tense of *blow*, then this was coded as /d/ or C (for consonant).

3. Figures 10.6 to 10.8 already provide that kind of information because the smoothers are based on the alternating verbs only.

4. This is even so when the first two rows of Figure 10.2 are tested with a chi-square test for sub-tables (χ^2 for contingency within a sub-table = 0.06; df = 1; p = 0.8; cf. Gries, to appear, for details on, and the implementation of, this test).

References

Allen, S., Skarabela, B. and Hughes, M. (2008) Using corpora to examine discourse effects in syntax. In H. Behrens (ed.) *Corpora in Language Acquisition Research: History, methods, perspectives* 99–137. Amsterdam: Benjamins.

Bloom, L. (1973) *One Word at a Time: The use of single-word utterances.* The Hague: Mouton.

Bolinger, D. L. (1971) *The Phrasal Verb in English.* Cambridge, MA: Harvard University Press.

Bresnan, J., Cueni, A., Nikitina, T. and Baayen, R. H. (2007) Predicting the dative alternation. In G. Boume, I. Kraemer and J. Zwarts (eds) *Cognitive Foundations of Interpretation* 69–94. Amsterdam: Royal Netherlands Academy of Science.

Broihier, K., Hyams, N., Johnson, K. B., Pesetsky, D., Poeppel, D., Schaeffer, J. and Wexler, K. (1994) The acquisition of the Germanic VPC. Paper delivered at the Eighteenth Boston University Conference on Language Development, Boston.

Browman, C. P. (1986) The hunting of the quark: The particle in English. *Language and Speech* 29(4): 311–334.

Brown, R. (1973) *A First Language: The early stages.* Cambridge, MA: Harvard University Press.

Couper-Kuhlen, E. (1986) *An Introduction to English Prosody.* Tübingen: Niemeyer.

Dehé, N. (1999) On particle verbs in English: More evidence from information structure. In N. M. Antrim, G. Goddall, M. Schulte-Nafeh and V. Samian (eds) *Proceedings of the Twenty-eighth Western Conference on Linguistics* 92–105. Fresno, CA: California State University.

Diessel, H. and Tomasello, M. (2005) Particle placement in early child language: A multifactorial analysis. *Corpus Linguistics and Linguistic Theory* 1(1): 89–112.

Fischer, S. D. (1971) *The Acquisition of Verb-particle and Dative Constructions.* Unpublished doctoral dissertation. Cambridge, MA: MIT.

Fraser, B. (1974) The phrasal verb in English, by Dwight L. Bolinger. *Language* 50(3): 568–575.

Gries, St. Th. (2003a) *Multifactorial Analysis in Corpus Linguistics: The case of particle placement.* London: Continuum.

Gries, St. Th. (2003b) Towards a corpus-based identification of prototypical instances of constructions. *Annual Review of Cognitive Linguistics* 1: 1–27.

Gries, St. Th. (2005) Syntactic priming: A corpus-based approach. *Journal of Psycholinguistic Research* 34(4): 365–399.

Gries, St. Th. (2007) New perspectives on old alternations. In J. E. Cihlar, A. L. Franklin and D. W. Kaiser (eds) *Papers from the Thirty-ninth Regional Meeting of the Chicago Linguistics Society, Vol. II: The panels* 274–292. Chicago, IL: Chicago Linguistics Society.

Gries, St. Th. (to appear) Frequency tables, effect sizes, and explorations. In D. Glynn and J. Robinson (eds) *Polysemy and Synonymy: Corpus methods and application in Cognitive Linguistics.* Amsterdam: Benjamins.

Gries, St. Th. and Stefanowitsch, A. (2004) Extending collostructional analysis: A corpus-based perspective on "alternations". *International Journal of Corpus Linguistics* 9(1): 97–129.

Hopper, P. J. and Thompson, S. A. (1980) Transitivity in grammar and discourse. *Language* 56(2): 251–299.

Hyams, N., Schaeffer, J. and Johnson, K. B. (1993) *On the Acquisition of VPCs.* Manuscript, University of California at Los Angeles and University of Amherst.

Kuczaj, S. (1976) -Ing, -s *and* -ed: *A study of the acquisition of certain verb inflections.* Unpublished doctoral dissertation. University of Minnesota.

MacKay, D. G. (1987) *The Organization of Perception and Action.* Berlin: Springer.

Peters, J. (2001) Given vs. new information influencing constituent ordering in the VPC. In R. Brend, A. K. Melby and A. Lommel (eds) *LACUS Forum XXVII: Speaking and Comprehending* 133–140. Fullerton, CA: LACUS.

Quirk, R, Greenbaum, S., Leech, G. and Svartvik, J. (1985) *A Comprehensive Grammar of the English Language.* London: Longman.

Rohdenburg, G. (2003) Cognitive complexity and horror aequi as factors determining the use of interrogative clause linkers in English. In G. Rohdenburg and B. Mondorf (eds) *Determinants of Grammatical Variation in English* 205–249. Berlin: Mouton de Gruyter.

Sawyer, J. (2001) Bifurcating the verb-particle construction: Evidence from child language. *Annual Review of Language Acquisition* 1: 119–156.

Schlüter, J. (2003) Chomsky's worst possible case: phonological determinants of grammatical variation. In G. Rohdenburg and B. Mondorf (eds) *Determinants of Grammatical Variation in English* 69–118. Berlin: Mouton de Gruyter.

Schnoebelen, T. (2008) Measuring compositionality in phrasal verbs. Unpublished ms dated 3/4/2008, Stanford University.

Selkirk, E. O. (1984) *Phonology and Syntax: The relation between sound and structure.* Cambridge, MA: The MIT Press.

Snyder, W. and Stromswold, K. (1997) The structure and acquisition of English Dative constructions. *Linguistic Inquiry* 28(2): 281–317.

Suppes, P. (1974) The semantics of children's languages. *American Psychologist* 29(2): 103–114.

Appendix: the effect of the variables studied with alternating phrasal verbs only

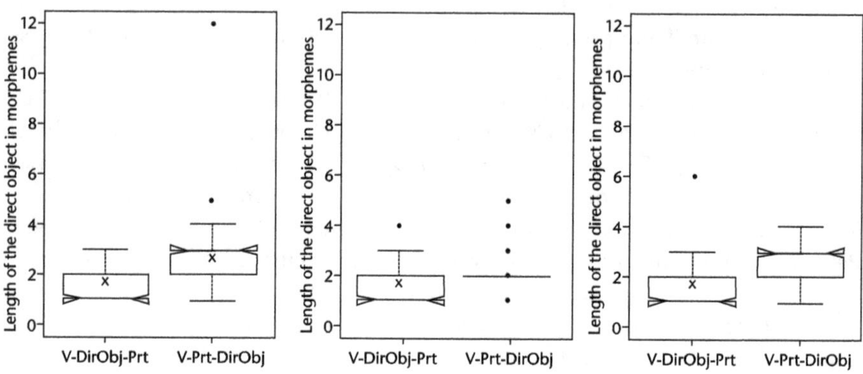

Figure (i): CONSTRUCTION × LENGTH (left: Abe; center: Adam; right: Nina)

Abe:

Obj Type	V-DirObj-Prt	V-Prt-DirObj
definite	18 (-)	22 (+)
indefinite	5 (-)	9 (+)
name	0 (NA)	0 (NA)
no mod	1 (-)	4 (+)
pass. pron.	9 (-)	21 (+)
pronoun	43 (-)	5 (+)

Adam:

Obj Type	V-DirObj-Prt	V-Prt-DirObj
definite	15 (-)	25 (+)
indefinite	1 (-)	5 (+)
name	0 (NA)	0 (NA)
no mod	6 (-)	10 (+)
pass. pron.	2 (-)	8 (+)
pronoun	27 (-)	6 (+)

Nina:

Obj Type	V-DirObj-Prt	V-Prt-DirObj
definite	8 (-)	20 (+)
indefinite	1 (-)	3 (+)
name	0 (-)	3 (+)
no mod	6 (-)	5 (+)
pass. pron.	5 (-)	4 (+)
pronoun	20 (-)	3 (-)

Construction

Figure (ii): CONSTRUCTION × OBJTYPE (left: Abe; center: Adam; right: Nina) ("(NA)" indicates that the residuals could not be computed given division by 0)

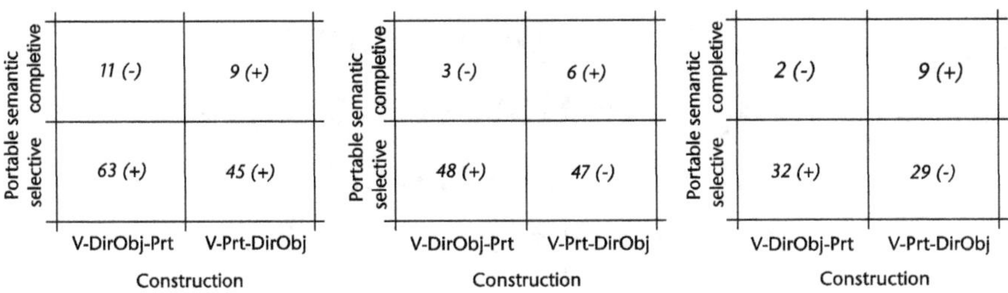

Figure (iii): Construction × Semantics (left: Abe; center: Adam; right: Nina)

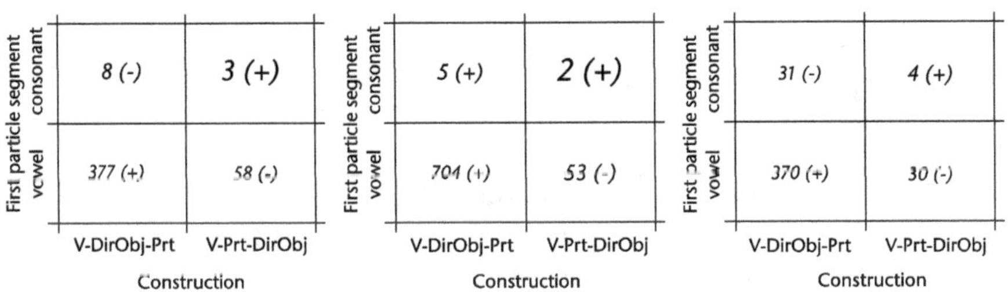

Figure (iv): Construction × Segment (left: Abe; center: Adam; right: Nina)

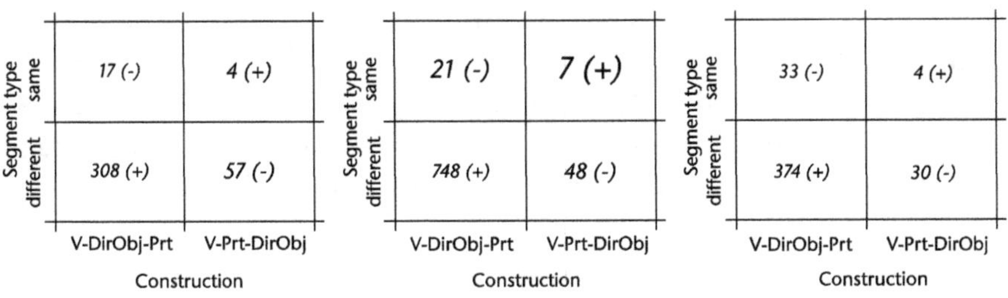

Figure (v): Construction × CV alternation (left: Abe; center: Adam; right: Nina)

11 Looks, appearances and judgements: Towards a unified constructionist analysis of predicative complement alternations in English and Spanish*

Francisco Gonzálvez-García[a]

1 Introduction

Drawing on data extracted from corpora (e.g. the original edition of the British National Corpus (BNC henceforth), the Great Britain component of the International Corpus of English (ICE-GB henceforth), the Lancaster-Oslo-Bergen Corpus (LOB henceforth), the *Corpus de Referencia del Español Actual* (CREA henceforth)) in conjunction with examples found in Google and the literature on the topic (previously approved by native informants), this paper is a first step towards a unitary analysis of attributive sentences in English and Spanish. Specifically, a defence is provided for a Goldbergian constructionist account (Goldberg 1995, 2006) of the semantico-pragmatic restrictions impinging on the alternation of predicative complements (Levin 1993) or, alternatively, small clauses (SCs henceforth) in the sense of e.g. Aarts (1992) and Demonte and Masullo (1999). The focus of this paper is on alternations between predicative complements with a phrasal realization (as in (1a)–(2a)) and with an infinitival one (as in (1b)–(1d)) after *seem*-type verbs (e.g. *look, seem, look, appear, sound,* etc.) in English and *parecer*-type verbs (e.g. *parecer* 'seem', *resultar* 'turn out', etc.) in Spanish, exemplified in (2) below.[1]

a Francisco Gonzálvez-García is Lecturer in English Language and Linguistics at the University of Almería, Spain. E-mail: fgonza@ual.es

(1) (a) Peter seems agitated.
Example taken from Aijmer (2009: 72).
(b) Harry looked/sounded (to be) the best.
Example taken from Newman (1981: 146).
(c) Obispal sounded (to be) on the verge of deducing the truth. (BNC, CM4 565)
(d) Plymouth looked *(to be) cruising to victory. (BNC, CBG 8091)
(e) This analysis appeared *(to be) substantiated by the small size of the proletariat in most Latin American countries, [...]. (BNC, G1R 376)

(2) (a)

Pedro	parec-e	algo	alter-ad-o.[2]
Peter	seem-PRS.3SG	somewhat	agitate-PTCP-M.SG

"Peter seems agitated".

(b)

[...] todo	parec-ía	(est-ar)	en	calma.
[...] everything	seem-IMPPRET.3SG	be-INF	in	calm

(CREA, El Mundo, 23/08/1995)
"Everything seemed to be calm".

(c)

La	bola	era	tan	cercan-o
DEF.F.SG	ball	be.IMPPRET.3SG	so	close-M.SG

que	parec-ía	*(est-ar)	suced-iendo	en	casa.
that	seem-IMPPRET.3SG	be-INF	happen-GER	at	home

(CREA, El País, 09/05/2003)
"The ball [TV show] was so familiar that it seemed *(to be) taking place at home".

(d)

El	evento	parec-ía	?(est-ar)	organiz-ad-o
DEF.M.SG	event	seem-IMPPRET.3SG	be-INF	organize-PTCP-M.SG

por	Christopher	Cannan [...].
by	Christopher	Cannan

(CREA, El Mundo, 03/01/2003)
"The event seemed ?(to be) organized by Christopher Cannan [...]".

This paper argues the case for the following claims: First, the complementation strategy choice after *seem* and *parecer* ('seem'), including the otherwise puzzling asymmetries noted in (1)–(2) above, are motivated by a number of semantico-pragmatic and information structure differences which can be aptly described and explained under a (Goldbergian) constructional account (Goldberg 1995, 2006). Second, rather than proposing two different types of *seem/parecer*, an epistemic one and a sensory one, we submit that both senses can be more parsimoniously captured under the rubric of the *subjective-attributive* construction, whose general constructional meaning is modulated by the construction's components as having a perceptual or cognitive interpretation. Third, the unitary analysis of predicative complements after *seem* and *parecer* can also be duplicated for predicative complements after verbs of sensory and/

or cognitive perception (e.g. *consider, find, see, considerar* 'consider', *encontrar* 'find', *ver* 'see', etc.) in English and Spanish.

(3) (a) I find him very funny. (BNC, HJG 954)
(b) In the years I have trained Rottweilers, I have always found there to be a barrier at a certain stage where the dog becomes stubborn. (BNC, AR5 1535)
(c) Es-o lo encuentr-o evidente. (CREA, Oral, GC-7)
DIST-M.SG 3SG.ACC find-PRS.1SG evident
"That I find evident".
(d) Yo cre-o que hay una gran
1SG believe-PRS.1SG COMP there.be.PRS INDF.SG.F great
posibilidad de acuerdo.
possibility of agreement
(CREA, La Vanguardia, 02/06/1995).
"I believe that there is a great chance of agreement".

Third, the SC after verbs of cognition/perception (or, alternatively, the *evaluative subjective-transitive* construction) displays a number of interesting similarities with the SC after *seem* and *parecer* concerning: (a) the core constructional meaning; (b) the semantico-pragmatic profile of the subject/experiencer; (c) the semantico-pragmatic profile of the direct object/subject-theme; (d) the semantico-pragmatic profile of the predicative phrase (or, alternatively, attribute); and (e) the feasibility of coercion, especially in relation to scalarity (or, more generally, subjectivity), progressive modification and, to some extent, occurrence with an imperative verb form.

Fourth, a partial (rather than complete) inheritance system of the type invoked in the Goldbergian strand of Construction Grammar (CxG henceforth) (Goldberg 1995, 2006) enables us to capture the similarities between the SC after cognition and perception verbs in English and Spanish, on the one hand, and the SC after *seem* and *parecer* on the other, while also taking on board the asymmetries between these constructions, especially those concerning the choice of the main clause subject, and the feasibility of reflexive arguments.

This paper is structured as follows: §2 outlines some of the basic claims impinging on the distinction between epistemic and perception *seem/parecer*-type verbs. §3 outlines the main semantico-pragmatic features of SCs after verbs of cognition and/or perception, referred to here as the *evaluative subjective-transitive* construction, in English and Spanish. §4 singles out the main properties of SCs after *seem/parecer*-type of verbs, regarded as the *subjective-attributive* construction and then goes on to pinpoint a number of crucial analogies as well as some differences between these two constructions, thus providing evidence that a unitary analysis is feasible on constructionist grounds *à la* Goldberg (1995, 2006). §5 explores the role of information structure in shaping the non-equivalence of predicative complement alternations involving *seem/parecer* with and without an infinitival form (e.g. *He seems* (*to be*) *angry, Parece* (*estar*) *enfadado*). Finally, §6 summarizes the main findings in relation to earlier discussion and highlights some important avenues for future research into this topic.

2 Epistemic vs. perception *seem/parecer* revisited from a constructionist perspective

A twofold distinction between an epistemic sense and a perception sense has been posited in the literature for *seem/parecer*-type verbs (see Matushansky 2002; Aijmer 2009; Fernández Leborans 1999 and references therein, *inter alios*). This distinction is sensitive to at least two main parameters: (a) the choice of the *seem*-type verb; and (b) the complementation strategy with which the verb in question combines.

With respect to the first parameter, Austin (1962: 36–37, 43) provides a most illuminating discussion with special focus on *look, seem,* and *appear* in the following terms:

> Consider, then:
> (1) He looks guilty.
> (2) He appears guilty.
> (3) He seems guilty.
> We would say that the first of these things simply by way of commenting on his looks – he has the look of a guilty person. The second, I suggest, would typically be used with reference to certain special circumstances [...] And the third, fairly clearly, makes an implicit reference to certain evidence – evidence bearing, of course, on the question whether he is guilty, though not such as to settle that question conclusively – "On the evidence we've heard so far, he certainly seems guilty." (quoted in Newman 1981: 136; emphasis in original).

The second parameter proceeds on the assumption that there appears to be a strong correlation between the meanings or functions of the verb and the syntactic frames in which it can occur. Thus, *seem* and *parecer* can for instance have the meaning 'appearance' and hedge possibility or indicate hearsay depending on the construction it occurs in. As Mithun (1986) has put it:

> Consider English *seem*. It can indicate that a statement is based on appearance ("Sam seems tired"). This specification of source can hedge probability. I should not be surprised, or held to be lying if in fact Sam is not tired at all, but rather dislikes his companions. With a slightly different construction, "seem" can indicate hearsay. ("It seems that Sam's in the hospital".) (Mithun 1986: 90; quoted in Aijmer 2009: 64)

For our purposes here, English *seem* takes three main complementation strategies (see Aijmer 2009: 72 for a more detailed inventory):[3]

(4) (a) The squire seems *sick*. **(SC = direct perception)**
(b) The squire seems *to be sick*.
(non-finite clause = epistemic perception)
(c) It seems *that the squire is sick*.
(finite clause = epistemic perception)
Examples taken from Matushansky (2002: 225).

According to Matushansky (2002: 225), (4a) implies a perception of the subject's condition by the experiencer (*I perceive that P holds*), whereas (4b) is an epistemic deduction (*from what I see I conclude that P holds*). Thus, according to Matushansky, (4b) is truth-conditionally and pragmatically identical to (4c), but (4a) is not. However, as noted by Aijmer (2009: 72), *seem* can add an experiencer to each of the three complementation strategies exemplified above, thus signalling an epistemic perception usually with an evaluative colouring. Interestingly enough, a similar semantico-pragmatic contrast is observable in the distribution of *parecer* ('seem') in Spanish (see Fernández Leborans 1999: 2442).[4]

(5) (a) Pedro parec-e (un-a) *buen-a* *persona.*
Pedro seem-PRS.3SG INDEF-F.SG good-F.SG person
(SC = direct perception)
"Pedro seems a nice person".
(b) Pedro *me* parec-e (una) *buen-a* *persona.*
Pedro 1SG.DAT seem-PRS.3SG INDEF-F.SG good-F.SG person
(SC + dative = epistemic/evaluative perception)
"Pedro seems to me a nice person".
Examples taken from Fernández Leborans (1999: 2443).

(c) Pedro parec-e *ser* *(un-a)* *buen-a* *persona.*
Pedro seem-PRS.3SG be.INF INDEF-F.SG good-F.SG person
(non-finite clause = epistemic perception)
"Pedro seems to be a nice person".

(d) [...], Pedro, quien *me* parec-e *ser* *(un-a)*
[...], Pedro, REL.SG 1SG.DAT seem-PRS.3SG be.INF INDEF-F.SG
buen-a *persona,* trabaj-a ahí.
good-F.SG person work-PRS.3SG there
(non-finite clause + dative = epistemic/evaluative perception)
"Pedro, who(m) I consider to be a good person, works there".

(e) Parec-e *que* *Pedro* *es* *un-a* *buen-a*
seem-PRS.3SG COMP Pedro be-PRS.3SG INDEF-F.SG good-F.SG
persona.
person
(finite (*que*-) clause = epistemic perception)
"It seems that Pedro is a nice person".

(f) Me parec-e que Pedro es un-a
1SG.DAT seem-PRS.3SG COMP Pedro be-PRS.3SG INDEF-F.SG
buena persona.
good-F.SG person
(finite (*que*-) clause + dative = epistemic/evaluative perception)
"It seems to me that Pedro is a good person".

However, it should be emphasized that in the case of the SC with a dative-experiencer argument, predicative elements denoting states of affairs amenable to a direct perception interpretation are barred from this environment:[5]

(6) (a) Ana me parec-e *tímid-a.*
Ana 1SG.DAT SEEM-PRS.3SG shy-F.SG
"Ana seems shy to me".

(b) Luis nos parec-e *seri-o* *y* *trabajador.*
Luis 1PL.DAT SEEM-PRS.3SG serious-M.SG and hardworking
"Luis seems to us a serious, hardworking person".

(7) (a) * ?Ana me parec-e *enferm-a.*
Ana 1SG.DAT seem-PRS.3SG sick-F.SG
"Ana seems to me sick".

(b) *María me parec-e *enfad-ad-a.*
María 1SG.DAT seem-PRS.3SG make.angry-PTCP-F.SG
"María seems to me angry".

(c) *Antonio nos parec-e *content-o.*
Antonio 1SG.DAT seem-PRS.3SG happy-M.SG
"Antonio seems to us happy".

Examples taken from Fernández Leborans (1999: 2444; my emphasis, FGG).

In order to arrive at a finer-grained characterization of the perception type of *seem/parecer* in SCs, the scalarity-related restriction must be taken into account. In this respect, Bolinger (1972a) argues that if the SC complement of *seem* is adjectival, the adjective must be scalar (or, alternatively, gradable):

(8) (a) The music seems nice/*choral.
(b) The problem seems insoluble/*mathematical.
Examples taken from Bolinger (1972a: 77).

However, as noted by Bolinger (1972a: 77), degree modifiers renders the starred examples in (8) perfect:

(9) (a) The music seems *almost* choral.
(b) The problem seems *pretty much* mathematical.

Phenomena of the type illustrated in (9) above are handled in CxG as instances of coercion, understood as the resolution of a conflict between constructional and lexical denotata (Michaelis 2003: 264), in which the former invariably wins over the latter (Michaelis 2003: 268). Thus, the modifiers *almost* and *pretty* in (9) coerce *prima facie* nongradable adjectives into a having a gradable interpretation. It should nonetheless be emphasized that not anything goes (see Duffley and Larrivée 2010 for further discussion). Thus, for instance, some adjectives cannot be coerced, as shown in (10).

(10) (a) This number seems large.
(b) *This number seems third (in a sequence).
(c) This number seems to be third (in a sequence).
Examples taken from Matushansky (2002: 231).

Nominal realizations of the predicative element (or, alternatively, the XPCOMP) also exhibit scalarity-related restrictions. Thus, by way of illustration, Bolinger (1972a: 78) demonstrates that only "predicative degree nouns" are permitted in the complement of *seem*. Compare (11) and (12):

(11) (a) What he writes seems nonsense.
(b) *What he writes seems adventure.
(c) What he writes seems to be adventure.

(12) (a) Merlin seems a fool/a bastard.
(b) *Merlin seems a wizard/a man/Arthur's friend.
(c) Merlin seems to be a wizard/a man/Arthur's friend.
(c') *Merlin seems quite/an utter wizard/man/Arthur's friend.
(d) You'd seem such a linguist!

However, this restriction is not (fully) operational in Romance languages such as Italian and Spanish, where non-scalar (bare) NPs are acceptable with the proviso that these are construable as conveying an evaluative stance by the subject/speaker in an adequate supporting context.

(13) (a) (Me) sembr-a un dottore/idiota.
1SG.DAT seem-PRS.3SG INDF.M.SG doctor/idiot
"S/he seems (to me) to be a doctor/idiot".

(b) Sab-iendo lo que ha hecho, no me
know-GER DEF.N.SG REL AUXPFV.3SG do.PTCP NEG 1SG.DAT
parec-e *ni siquiera* persona.
seem-PRS.3SG not even person
"Knowing what s/he has done, s/he does not even seem (to me) to be a person".

As a matter of fact, languages differ with respect to possible complements of their equivalents of *seem*. In English, *seem* can appear with an (extended) adjectival Phrase (AP henceforth), a prepositional phrase (PP henceforth), or a nominal phrase (NP henceforth), as in (14)–(15), with a non-finite infinitival clause, as in (16)–(17), or with two types of finite clauses, as in (18)–(19).

(14) (a) Yolanda seems *stupid.* **(AP)**
(b) Belinda seems *out of her mind.* **(PP)**
(c) Orlando seems *an idiot.* **(NP)**
Examples taken from Matushansky (2002: 220).

(15) (a) Yolanda parec-e *estúpid-a.* **(AP)**
Yolanda seem-PRS.3SG stupid-F.SG
"Yolanda seems stupid".

(b) ??Belinda parec-e *fuera de su-s cabales.* **(PP)**
Belinda seem-PRS.3SG outside of POSS-3PL mind
"Belinda seems out of her mind".

(c) Orlando parec-e *un idiota.* **(NP)**
Orlando seem-PRS.3SG INDF.M.SG idiot
"Orlando seems an idiot".

Examples taken from Matushansky (2002: 220).

(16) Miranda seems *to be stupid/an idiot/out of her mind.*
(non-finite *to*-infinitive clause)
Example taken from Matushansky (2002: 220).

(17) Miranda parec-e *ser estúpida/ un-a idiota/*
Miranda seem-PRS.3SG be.INF stupid-F.SG INDF-F.SG idiot
est-ar fuera de su-s cabales.
be-INF outside of POSS-3PL mind
"Miranda seems to be stupid/an idiot/out of her mind".
(non-finite infinitive clause)

(18) (a) Clarinda seems *like she is in a bad mood.*
(b) It seems *that Fernando is sick.*
(finite clause).
Examples taken from Matushansky (2002: 221).

(19) (a) # Clara parec-e como si estuviera
Clara seem-PRS.3SG as if be.IMPPRET.SUBJV.3SG
de mal humor.
of bad humour
"Clara it seems as if she was in a bad mood".
(b) Parec-e como si Clara estuviera
seem-PRS.3SG as if Clara be.IMPPRET.SUBJV.3SG
de mal humor.
of bad humour
(finite clause)
"It seems as if Clara was in a bad mood".

In this connection, Moro (1997: 205) brings to the foreground the existence of language-specific asymmetries regarding the realization of the predicates selected by SCs:

(20) (a) *Jan schijn-t *ziek.*
Jan seem-PRS.3SG ill
"Jan seems ill".
(b) John seems *ill.*
(c) Gianni sembr-a *il re di Francia.*
Gianni seem-PRS.3SG DEF.M.SG king of France
"Gianni seems the king of France".
(d) *Gianni seems *the King of France.*
Examples taken from Moro (1997: 205).
(e) Juan parec-e *el rey de Francia.*
Juan seem-PRS.3SG DEF.M.SG king of France
"Juan seems the king of France".
(f) *John seems *in the room.*
(g) John seems *in deep water.*

Moro (1997: 2005), however, takes the above asymmetries to show "these rather scattered patterns suggest that they are all rather idiosyncratic and language specific [...]." While acknowledging that these language-specific idiosyncrasies exist, it is my claim that they do not undermine the crucial role of subjectivity, as defined above, in general and scalarity in particular in shaping the dynamic, though nevertheless motivated, interaction between the inherent meaning and form properties of the construction and its individual components. Therefore, the main emphasis in this paper is on robust generalizations (i.e. a unitary analysis of attributive sentences of the type under scrutiny here), while this should not taken to preclude the existence of lower-level (language-specific and construction-specific) constructions at varying levels of granularity (cf. Croft's 2003 verb-class and verb-specific constructions and Boas' 2008 mini-constructions; see also Iwata 2008).

With these observations in mind, I will now go on to briefly illustrate how a number of restrictions exhibited *seem* and *parecer* in the SC can be explained in the light of subjectivity in general and feasibility of scalarity coercion in particular. Consider (21)–(22) below:

(21) (a) The singer seems ?out of luck/out of synch.
(b) The picture seems out of focus.
(c) The wheels seem ?out of alignment/*in alignment.
(d) *Marvin seemed out of the room/off the spaceship.
Examples taken from Matushansky (2002: 261).
(e) Marvin seemed in good shape/in the pink of health.

Although the SC tends to favour PPs encoding emotional states which can be construed by the subject/speaker in gradable and, therefore, evaluative terms (cf. 21e), some PPs with a literal meaning are also possible depending on how detectable the property is (cf. 21b). However, the PP must encode a property, not a location, as shown in (22), since locations cannot under normal circumstances be construed in gradable, subjective terms.

(22) *He seems in London/in the house/out of the room.

By the same token, a number of categories such as bare infinitives, gerunds, and passive participles encoding an overwhelmingly dynamic state of affairs/process or action are barred from the SC environment with *seem*, as these clash in principle with the requirement that the attribute should encode a stative process/state of affairs amenable to a gradable and evaluative interpretation by the subject/speaker.

(23) (a) *He seems work.
(b) *He seems working.
(c) *The child seems born in LA.
(d) #The book seems written by Shakespeare.
(e) This book *almost* seems written by Shakespeare.

An important observation emerges from the picture sketched so far. While examples (23a)–(23c) feature barely coercible elements in terms of scalarity, and thus yield an ungrammatical result with *seem* in SCs, certain categories such as e.g. *-ed* participles may be rescued from a marginally acceptable result if coerced *via* a scalarity-inducing element. This is the case of (23e), where *almost* renders a *prima facie* non-gradable property as a gradable one (i.e. "of an outstanding literary quality similar to that found in the works of Shakespeare").

To conclude this section, let us dwell on how the ongoing discussion so far is reconcilable or not with a unitary analysis of the constructions examined here. In this connection, although Fernández Leborans (1999: 2443ff) invokes a distinction between a perception sense of *parecer* and an opinion sense of *parecer* in the SC environment, she nonetheless claims that both senses can be subsumed under the common meaning of *psychological experience*: "something manifests itself or appears (to someone) as an object of perception, or opinion or belief".

However, before further pursuing the viability of such a unitary analysis for the English data and its translatability into constructionist terms, we need to examine the advantages of invoking a unitary analysis of SCs especially after cognition and perception verbs in English and Spanish under the rubric of the *subjective-transitive* construction (§3). This discussion will serve as the basis on which the defence of a unitary constructionist analysis for SCs with attributes, as in (1)–(2) above, will be grounded (§4).

3 The *subjective-transitive* construction in English and Spanish

Before going into the specifics of the *subjective-transitive* construction in English and Spanish, a number of preliminary observations are in order. The first concerns the sense(s) in which the term "construction" is understood here. An updated operational definition of this term runs as follows:

> *Any linguistic pattern* is recognized as a construction as long as some aspect of its form or function is not strictly predictable from its component parts of from other constructions recognized to exist. In addition, patterns are stored as constructions even if they are fully predictable as long as they occur with sufficient frequency [...]. (Goldberg, 2006: 5; my emphasis, FGG).

Second, and more crucially for our purposes here, when the labels SC or, alternatively, *subjective-transitive* (and *subjective-attributive*) construction, are invoked in this paper, these should not be taken to detract from Croft's (2003) observation that much of argument structure is construction-specific and language-specific. The labels are shorthand for expository convenience. Our position in this respect is in agreement with Goldberg (2006: 226), who opts for retaining "the more traditional emphasis on trying to capture and motivate generalizations, imperfect though we recognize them to be".

The term "subjective" should be understood here in at least a three-fold sense (see Englebretson 2007 and references therein for an overview of the connections between subjectivity, evaluation and evidentiality): (a) as referring to the main clause subject/speaker and the degree of involvement implicit in his/her stance towards the proposition (see also Lyons 1982: 102); and (b) as being connected with evidentiality as in e.g. Chafe and Nichols (1986), in particular with the distinction between direct and hearsay evidence, respectively.

The general meaning of the *subjective-transitive* construction can for current purposes be summarized as follows:

X (NP$_1$) expresses a high degree of direct/personal commitment towards proposition Y (NP$_2$ XPCOMP).

The anatomy of this construction sense is reproduced in Figure 11.1, following the Goldberg-style of annotation, while also introducing some

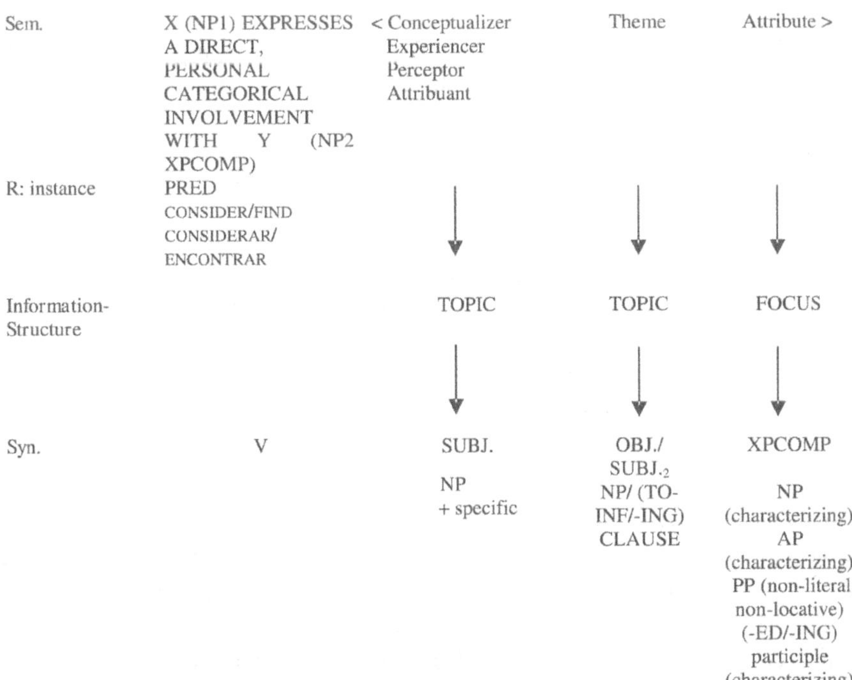

Figure 11.1. The anatomy of the *(evaluative) subjective-transitive* construction.

modifications to maximize its explanatory power (see Gonzálvez-García 2006, 2009 for further discussion).

In Figure 11.1, the top line of the construction represents the semantic relations of the participants of the construction. The second line indicates some of the verbs that may felicitously fuse with the constructional semantics of the SC, thus modulating its abstract sense and yielding the *evaluative subjective-transitive* sense of the construction. The next line captures information-structure information about the participants of the construction. The following line reproduces relevant syntactic information about the construction's arguments. SUBJ. stands for subject, OBJ./SUBJ.$_2$ is meant to capture the dual syntactico-semantic status of the postverbal NP as direct object of the main verb and/or subject of the XPCOMP, while XPCOMP stands for an attribute that may take a wide range of morphosyntactic realizations (NP, AP, PP, AdvP). The last line in the anatomy, which introduces a variation in the Goldbergian-style format, spells out additional morphological information paired with pertinent semantico-pragmatic information. Solid lines between the semantic roles, the pragmatic roles and the syntactic functions indicate that the semantic role must be fused with an independently existing verbal participant role.

For the purposes of this paper and for expository convenience, I will restrict myself to the sense of the construction that fuses with cognition verbs (e.g. *consider, think, find, considerar* ("consider"), *encontrar* ("find"), *creer* ("think"), etc.), namely, the *evaluative subjective-transitive* construction. This constructional sense encodes a decidedly subjective, personal *assessment* on the part of the subject/speaker (a person) about an entity (a thing or a person) on the basis of first-hand evidence, as shown in (24).

(24) I find her so sweet. (BNC, HGK 2426)
- (a) (#but in fact I do not personally think that she is sweet at all.)
- (b) (#although I haven't actually had any direct experience with her, nor have I met her in person – this is just an inference that I have drawn on the basis of what people say about her.)
- (c) (although some of her colleagues think that she is a bit of an old dragon.)

Having provided a brief constructionist characterization of the *evaluative subjective-transitive* construction, the next section examines in some detail the *subjective-attributive* construction and closes with the most significant analogies and differences between these two constructions. The main point of this comparison is to argue the descriptive and explanatory convenience of a non-monotonic or partial inheritance system of the type advocated in

Goldberg (1995, 2006) and adds a further twist to the focus on generalizations within and across constructions.

4 The *evaluative subjective-transitive* and the *subjective-attributive* constructions: Towards a unitary constructionist analysis

Let us start off with the constructional characterization of SCs with *seem*-type (and *parecer*-type) verbs, which will be referred to here as instances of the *subjective-attributive* construction. The general skeletal meaning of this construction can be glossed as follows, and its formalization (with similar modifications to those introduced in Figure 11.1) is presented in Figure 11.2.

The *subjective-attributive* construction: X (DAT) EXPRESSES A DIRECT, PERSONAL, CATEGORICAL INVOLVEMENT WITH Y (SUBJ + XPCOMP).

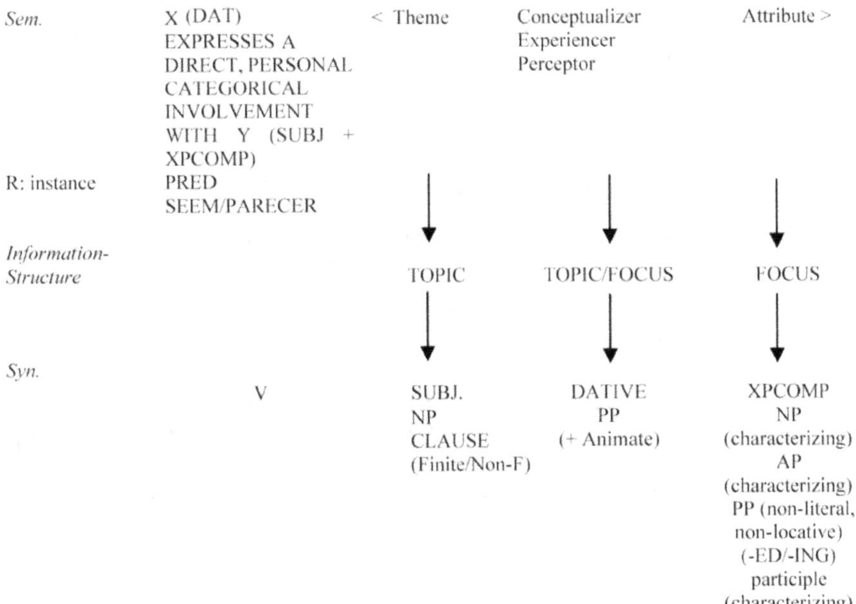

Figure 11.2. The anatomy of the *subjective-attributive* construction.

The most significant analogies and asymmetries between the constructions under scrutiny here can for current purposes be summarized as follows.

First, in much the same vein as the *evaluative subjective-transitive* construction, the *subjective attributive* construction with *seem/parecer* encodes a direct, personal and forceful stance by the implicit or explicit experiencer towards the proposition envisioned in the clause.

(25) (a) This seems (to me)(quite) difficult.
(#but in fact I do not personally think that this is difficult at all.)
(#although I have no first-hand evidence to think so.)
(although other people may indeed think otherwise.)

(b) (Me) parec-es (un-a) buen-a persona.
1SG.DAT seem-PRS.2SG INDF-F.SG good-F.SG person
"You seem to me a good person".
(#pero realmente no cre-o que
but really NEG think-PRS.1SG COMP
lo seas.)
DEF.N be.PRS.SUBJV.2SG
"but I really do not think that you are so".
(#pero realmente no tengo evidencia de primer-a mano para
but really NEG have evidence of first-F.SG hand PURP
pens-ar es-o).
think-INF DIST-SG
"but I really do not have any first-hand evidence to think that".
(aunque otr-o-s piens-en que no lo
although other-M.PL think-PRS.SUBJV.3PL COMP NEG DEF.N
eres en absoluto).
be.PRS.2SG in absolute
"although others may think that you are far from that".

Second, the experiencer of the *subjective-attributive* construction after *seem/parecer* must be human or at least likely to be construable as such (e.g. *via* metonymy). The same restriction holds for the *evaluative subjective-transitive* construction.

(26) (a) The BBC considers this alternative inappropriate.
(b) *The Arts Faculty building considers this alternative inappropriate.
(c) This alternative seems inappropriate to the BBC.
(d) *This alternative seems inappropriate to the Arts Faculty building.

(27) (a) La RAE consider-a est-a construcción
DEF.F.SG RAE consider-PRS.3SG PROX-F.SG construction
incorrect-a.
incorrect-F.SG
"The RAE considers this construction incorrect".

(b) *El edificio de la RAE consider-a
DEF.M.SG building of DEF.F.SG RAE consider-PRS.3SG
est-a construcción incorrect-a.
PROX-F.SG construction incorrect-F.SG
*"The RAE building considers this construction incorrect".

(c) Est-a construcción a la RAE le
PROX-F.SG construction DAT DEF.F.SG RAE 3SG.DAT
parec-e incorrect-a.
seem-PRS.3SG incorrect-F.SG
"This construction seems incorrect to the RAE".

(d) *Est-a construcción es para el
PROX-F.SG construction be.PRS.3SG for DEF.M.SG
edificio de la RAE incorrect-a.
building of DEF.F.SG RAE incorrect-F.SG
*"This construction is incorrect to the RAE building".

Third, the subject of the *subjective-attributive* construction after *seem*/*parecer* and the direct object in the *evaluative subjective-transitive* construction cannot be a dummy element such as e.g. existential *there*. This is so because, as noted by Langacker (1991: 352f), existential *there* designates an abstract setting. Therefore, under the constructional analysis invoked here, these abstract settings cannot be construed as stimuli of the vision/evaluation by the experiencer/subject, thus yielding an ungrammatical result in the constructions under investigation here.

(28) He believed there *(*to be*) four components of emotion that in varying relationships and quantities cause our subjective experience of emotion. (ICE-GB, W1A-017-5)

(29) There seems *(*to be*) much less interaction between the cells. (BNC, ASL 702)

(30) Parec-e *(*hab-er*) un consenso general
seem-PRS.3SG there.be-INF INDF.M.SG consensus general
entre los estudios-o-s de est-a materia [...]
among DEF.M.PL scholar-M-PL of DIST-F.SG subject
(CREA, 1995, S. Cervera Enguix, B. Quintanilla Madero, Anorexia nerviosa. Manifestaciones psicopatológicas fundamentales, Eunsa, Pamplona)
"There seems *(to be) a general consensus among the experts on this subject".

A fourth important similarity is that the semantico-pragmatic profiles of the attribute (i.e. the XPCOMP) in these two types of construction in English and Spanish exhibit a number of similar restrictions which can be explained under the general umbrella of subjectivity, broadly construed (i.e. direct sensory/cognitive perception by the experiencer/subject of the state of affairs envisioned in the clause).

The NPs yielding a felicitous result in the predicative complement slot must be amenable to a characterizing construal by the experiencer/subject argument. Thus, for instance, referential expressions yield an invariable ungrammatical result.

(31) (a) I believe Peter *(to be) *the man who is just sitting over there.*
(b) *Consider-o a Pedro *el hombre que*
consider-PRS.1SG OBJ Pedro DEF.M.SG man REL
est-á sent-ad-o justo ahí.
be-PRS.3SG sit-PTCP-M.SG just there
"I consider Peter the man who is sitting right over there".

(32) (a) Peter seems *(to be) *the man who is just sitting over there.*
(b) Pedro parec-e *(ser) *el hombre que est-á*
Pedro seem-PRS.3SG be.INF DEF.M.SG man REL be-PRS.3SG
sent-ad-o justo ahí.
sit-PTCP-M.SG just there
"Pedro seems *(to be) the man who is sitting right over there".

At a higher level of granularity, a further asymmetry can be detected between *be/ser*-type verbs and *seem/parecer*-type verbs. Thus, while the former type of verb allows for inverse copular constructions (cf. 33b and 33b'), *seem/parecer*-type verbs and *consider*-type verbs (in the passive) yield an unfelicitous result in that environment in English, as shown in (35b)–(36b) in contrast to their acceptability or marginal acceptability in Spanish (35a')–(35b').

(33) (a) John is the culprit.
(a') John es el culpable.
John be.PRS.3SG DEF.M.SG culprit
(b) The culprit is John.
(b') El culpable es John.
DEF.M.SG culprit be.PRS.3SG John

(34) (a) What to do next remains the real problem.
(a') Qué hac-er después sigue siendo el
REL do-INF afterwards go.on.PRS.3SG be.GER DEF.M.SG
verdader-o problema.
true-M.SG problem
(b) The real problem remains what to do next.
(b') El verdader-o problema sigue siendo
DEF.M.SG true-M.SG problem go.on.PRS.3SG be.GER
qué hac-er después.
REL do-INF afterwards

(35) (a) His attitude seems the worst problem.
(a') Su actitud parec-e el problema
3SG.POSS attitude seem-PRS.3SG DEF.M.SG problem
más grave.
more grave
(b) *The worst problem seems his attitude.
(b') El problema más grave parece
DEF.M.SG problem more grave seem-PRS.3SG
su actitud.
3SG.POSS attitude

(36) (a) His attitude was considered the worst problem.
(b) *The worst problem was considered his attitude.
Examples taken from Arche García-Valdecasas (2004: 38; my translation, FGG).

Ed- and *-ing* participles (and their counterparts in Spanish) are allowed in the *evaluative subjective-transitive* construction and the *subjective-attributive* construction with *seem/parecer* with the proviso that they can be construable as expressing a gradable property/state of affairs/event and thus as subject to a personal stance on the part of the subject/speaker.

(37) (a) Nor did he heed the fools who believed these waters *haunted by ghost ships with the earth-bound spirits of their crews* [...] (LOB, N27:38)
(b) Algun-o-s cre-ían la casa
some-M-PL believe-IMPPRET.3PL DEF.F.SG house
habitada por un fantasma.
inhabit-PTCP-F.SG by INDF.M.SG ghost
"Some people believed the house haunted by a ghost."

(38) (a) Jacob Manor seemed [to be] *unaffected by this fact.* (BNC, ANU 879; material in square brackets inserted by the author, FGG).
(b) Jacob Manor no parec-ía en modo algun-o
Jacob Manor NEG seem-IMPPRET.3SG in way INDF-M.SG
(est-ar) *preocup-ad-o por est-e hecho.*
be-INF worry-PTCP-M.SG by PROX-M.SG fact

However, those cases in which the *ed-* and *-ing* forms have an unambiguous dynamic interpretation, as in passives and progressive verb forms, are not acceptable in these two constructions:

(39) (a) Hamlet believed his father *(*to be*) *murdered* (?*by Claudius*).
Example taken from May (1987: 32).
(b) Numbers are thought *(*to be*) *declining.* (ICE-GB, W2C-001-36)

(40) (a) *Hamlet's father seemed *murdered by Claudius.*
(b) *They seemed *following the correct route.*

(c) *El padre de Hamlet parec-ía
DEF.M.SG father of Hamlet seem-IMPPRET.3SG
asesin-ad-o por Claudius.
murder-PTCP-M.SG by Claudius
(c) *"Hamlet's father seemed murdered by Claudius".
(d) *Ellos parec-ían *siguiendo la ruta*
3PL seem-IMPPRET.3PL follow.GER DEF.F.SG route
correct-a.
correct-F.SG
(d') *"They seemed following the correct route".

In the case of Spanish, Fernández Leborans (1999: 2444) argues that passive participles are acceptable with perceptual *parecer* ("seem"), but not with cognitive *parecer*. However, upon closer inspection, it seems that this generalization is also sensitive to the scalarity-coercion or, alternatively, to subjectivity in the sense of e.g. Lyons (1982).

(41) (a) *?El discurso me parec-e escrito
DEF.M.SG discourse 1SG.DAT seem-PRS.3SG write.PTCP
por su secretari-o particular.
by 3SG.POSS secretary-M.SG personal
"The discourse seems to me written by his personal secretary".
(b) *Es-e niño me parec-e nac-id-o
DIST-M.SG child 1SG.DAT seem-PRS.3SG be.born-PTCP-M.SG
en un país del Este.
en INDF.M.SG country of.DEF.M.SG East.
*"That child seems to me born in an Eastern country".
Examples and acceptability judgements from Fernández Leborans (1999: 2444; my translation, FGG)
(a') El discurso me parece más bien
DEF.M.SG discourse 1SG.DAT seem-PRS.3SG more well
escrito por su secretari-o particular
write.PTCP by 3SG.POSS secretary-M.SG personal
(que por él mism-o).
than by 3SG.M same-M.SG
"The discourse seemed more as if it had been written by his/her personal secretary rather than himself/herself".
(b') Es-e niño me parec-e *más bien*
DIST-M.SG child-M.SG 1SG.DAT seem-PRS.3SG more well
nac-id-o en un país del Este.
be.born-PTCP-M.SG in INDF.M.SG country of.DEF.M.SG East
"That child seems to me as if he had been born in an Eastern country".

Moreover, PPs and adverbial phrases with a literal, locative meaning are incompatible on semantico-pragmatic grounds with the psychological, evaluative stance inherent to the meaning of the *subjective-attributive* construction.

(42) (a) *Marvin seemed *out of the room/off the spaceship/over there.*
(b) Marvin seemed *in the pink of health.*
(c) *Marvin parec-ía *fuera de la habitación/*
Marvin seem-IMPPRET.3SG out of DEF.F.SG room
fuera de la nave espacial/ por allí.
out of DEF.F.SG ship by there
"Marvin seemed *out of the room/out of the spacecraft/over there*".
(d) Marvin parec-ía *en la flor*
Marvin seem-IMPPRET.3SG in DEF.F.SG flower
de la vida.
of DEF.F.SG life
"Marvin seemed in the pink of health".

In addition, because both types of constructions convey a *tout court* assessment/perception rather than one extending through time (see further Newman 1981; Langacker 1991: 450–451), that is, a fairly stable stance in the experiencer/subject's universe of perceptions, aspectual modifications are expected to be highly restricted in these two constructions. However, as in the case of the *evaluative subjective-transitive* construction, the *subjective-attributive* construction with *seem/parecer* may be coerced into the progressive construction, especially when a cognitive-evaluative interpretation is involved. In both types of constructions, the progressive modification implies that "the situation is conceived as changing in some way" (Langacker 1991: 208, Williams 2002: 87, *inter alios*).

(43) (a) The kind of betrayal she'd *been believing him guilty* of was mean, petty minded, and he was none of those things. (BNC, HA9 3460)
(b) El Partido Laborista *est-á encontr-ando* tan sólo
DEF.M.SG Party Labour AUX-PRS.3SG find-GER so only
un candidato alarmante para el liderazgo,
INDF.M.SG candidate alarming for DEF.M.SG leadership
y no es otr-o que Tony Blair.
and NEG be.PRS.3SG another-M.SG than Tony Blair
(CREA, La Vanguardia, 17/06/199)
"The Labour Party is finding only one candidate alarming for leadership, and this is none other than Tony Blair".

(44) (a) Su propuesta *me sigue parec-iendo*
3SG.POSS proposal 1SG.DAT go.on.PRS.3SG seem-GER
inmejorable.
superb
"His proposal still seems to me superb".

(b) ??Su propuesta *sigue* *parec-iendo* inmejorable.
3SG.POSS proposal go.on.PRS.3SG seem-GER superb
"His proposal still seems superb".
Examples from Fernández Leborans (1999: 2445; my translation).

(45) (a) Grantham is still seeming a bit small tonight [...].
http://katemillerphotography.blogspot.com/2009/03/grantham-is-seeming-bit-small-tonight.html.
Accessed on 3 March 2009.
(b) The world is looking very different.
http://blogs.worldbank.org/meetings/es/node/568.
Accessed on 5 December 2009.

So far we have been concerned with the main analogies. Two important differences can nonetheless be pinpointed between the *subjective-transitive* construction and the *subjective-attributive* in English and Spanish. These can for current purposes be stated as follows:

First, the *evaluative subjective-transitive* construction readily admits coercion *via* reflexive pronouns in the object slot (see further Gonzálvez-García 2007, 2009), which are systematically disallowed in the *subjective-attributive* construction in English and Spanish.

(46) (a) [...] dinner guests could know *themselves* safe from distasteful anecdotes about carving knives or missing kidneys. (BNC, CJF 1867)
(b) Te sab-es mí-a.
2SG.ACC know-PRS.2SG 1SG.POSS
(Café Quijano, Dame de esa boca)
"You know yourself to be mine".
(c) *I seem insane to myself.
Example taken from Postal (1971: 258).
(d) *Me parezco (a mí mism-o)
1SG.DAT seem-PRS.1SG DAT 1SG.DAT same-M.SG
bastante extrovertid-o.[6]
quite extroverted-M.SG
*"I seem (to myself) quite extroverted".

Second, some verbs may be coerced into the imperative form in the *evaluative subjective-transitive* construction and the *subjective-attributive* construction in English. However, this type of coercion is not possible with *parecer*-type verbs in Spanish (see Gonzálvez-García 2007, 2009 for further discussion).

(47) (a) Consider/#believe/#find yourself lucky.
(b) Consid-éra-te/ *piéns-a-te/ *encuéntr-a-te
consider-IMP-REFL.2SG think-IMP-REFL.2SG find-IMP-REFL.2SG
afortunad-o.
lucky-M.SG
"Consider/think/#find yourself lucky".

(48) (a) (Just) Appear crazy/*seem crazy.
Examples and acceptability judgements taken from Bolinger (1972b: 76, n10).
(b) Look sexy, sound sexy, smell sexy, dress sexy ...
http://www.democraticunderground.com/discuss/duboard.php?az=view_all&address=105x3395457.
Accessed on 5 December 2009.

(49) (a) *¡Parec-e loc-o!
seem-IMP.2SG crazy-M.
"Seem crazy".
(b) *¡Parec-e educad-o (con Pablo)!
seem-IMP.2SG polite-M.SG with Pablo
"Seem polite (to Pablo)".
Example taken from Arche García-Valdecasas (2004: 163).

Last but not least, the *evaluative subjective-transitive* construction seems to favour first person subjects (see Borkin 1973: 45–46). However, the *subjective-attributive* construction is highly restricted regarding the occurrence of first-person pronouns as subjects or experiencers. Bolinger (1974b: 74) notes that the oddity of *parezco* stems primarily from the fact that "I don't have to rely on opinions where my own states and sensations are concerned; I experience them directly". However, if "we can rig a context so that the person whose views are reflected is clearly someone other than the first, then a *parezco* gets by more easily". Thus, a sentence like *Yo parezco vivir bien* is acceptable if understood along the following lines: "I only seem, in your eyes, to live well; actually my taxes are eating up practically all my income" (Bolinger 1974b: 74).

In line with Bolinger's observation, it seems that modals, for instance, have an ameliorating effect in the corresponding acceptability results in English and Spanish.

(50) In your bedroom. I'm not as naïve as I may seem. (BNC, HA5 1843)

(51) A primer-a vista, pued-o parec-er dur-a.
to first-F.SG sight, can-PRS.1SG seem-INF tough-F.SG
Sin embargo sient-o muchísimo que Ulises
not.withstanding be.sorry-PRS.1SG quite.a.lot COMP Ulysses
ya no viv-a.
already NEG live-PRS.SUBJV.3SG
(CREA, 1975, Antonio Gala, ¿Por qué corres Ulises?, Madrid, Espasa Calpe)
"At first sight, I may seem tough. However, I'm terribly sorry that Ulysses is no longer alive".

An important observation emerging from Bolinger's argumentation and the examples in (50)–(51) above is that the occurrence of *seem* and *parecer* with a first-person subject is felicitous given an adequate supporting discourse context building up e.g. a semantic relation of contrast between, say, appearances, the impression subjects may make on other people, etc., and the subjects' introspective views of themselves. Considerations of this kind take us to the realm of discourse structure, the impact of which on the constructions under analysis here is dealt with in the following section.

5 On the role of information structure

As will be recalled from the anatomies of the *evaluative subjective-transitive* and *subjective-attributive* constructions in Figures 11.1 and 11.2 above, the function pole of the construction captures information structure and discourse-functional properties. In this connection, the (semantico-pragmatic) non-equivalence of the complement-taking possibilities of Spanish *parecer* ("seem") has been extensively argued for in Porroche (1990). Drawing on Kirparsky's (1970) notion of factivity, Porroche (1990) claims that the finite clause can be felicitously followed by plain statements, while this is not so true in the case of the *evaluative subjective-transitive* construction:

(52) (a)

Parec-e	*que*	*es*	*muy*	*cruel,*	golpe-a
seem-PRS.3SG	COMP	be.PRS.3SG	very	cruel	beat-PRS.3SG

tod-o-s	los	día-s	a	los	niñ-o-s	y
all-M-PL	DEF.M.PL	day-PL	OBJ	DEF.M.PL	child-M-PL	and

los	at-a	a	la	cama	cuando
ACC.3PL	tie-PRS.3SG	to	DEF.F.SG	bed	when

se	va.
PRONOM.CLITIC	go.PRS.3SG

"It seems s/he is very cruel, s/he beats his kids every day and s/he ties them to their beds when s/he leaves home".

(b)

?Parec-e	*muy*	*cruel,*	golpe-a	tod-o-s	los
seem-PRS.3SG	very	cruel	beat-PRS.3SG	all-M-PL	DEF.M.PL

día-s	a	los	niñ-o-s	y	los	at-a
day-PL	OBJ	DEF.M.PL	child-M-PL	and	ACC.3PL	tie-PRS.3SG

a	la	cama	cuando	se	va.
to	DEF.F.SG	bed	when	PRONOM.CLITIC	go.PRS.3SG

"S/he seems very cruel, s/he beats his kids every day and s/he ties them to their beds when s/he leaves home".

Examples and acceptability judgements taken from Porroche (1990: 136).

Moreover, Porroche (1990: 137) notes that given the scenario in which a person enters a hospital and sees that somebody is really sick, the variant with the finite clause (cf. 53b) is preferred over the one in (53a).

(53) (a) Parec-e *muy* *enferm-o.*
seem-PRS.3SG very sick-M.SG
"He seems very sick".
(b) Parec-e *que* *est-á* *muy* *enferm-o.*
seem-PRS.3SG COMP be-PRS.3SG very sick-M.SG
"It seems that he is very sick".

Two short questionnaires were designed, one featuring the Spanish sentences in (53a)–(53b) as well as (54a)–(54b) with some distractors, and another with their corresponding counterparts in English. The questionnaires were answered by 19 Spanish University students and 19 British University students (aged between 22 and 24), respectively. The informants were asked to rate the situation described in the sentences as: (a) highly likely; (b) likely; (c) not particularly likely; and (d) I'm not sure/ I don't know.

(54) (a) Parec-e *muy* *enfadad-o.*
seem-PRS.3SG very angry-M.SG
"He seems very angry".
(b) Parec-e *que* *est-á* *muy* *enfadad-o.*
seem-PRS.3SG COMP be-PRS.3SG very angry-M.SG
"It seems that he is very angry".

A number of considerations provisionally emerge from this small-scale questionnaire. First, English appears to differ from Spanish in favouring the use of the *evaluative subjective-transitive* construction to express the experiencer's certainty about a given situation on the basis of first-hand evidence. Second, in the case of Spanish, native speakers appear to be divided on the most felicitous choice, *pace* Porroche (1990). Third, while the English informants provided fairly homogeneous answers regardless of the nature of the XPCOMP, the Spanish informants were by contrast divided on their judgements. The most striking disparity in the judgements by native Spanish speakers can be observed in the pair involving e.g. *enfadado* "angry" as XPCOMP.

The results displayed in Figure 11.3 need, however, to be taken with caution and therefore as provisional, as a larger-scale elicitation experiment needs to be carried out to arrive at more conclusive results, paying especial attention to the role of specific item-based combinations (e.g. those involving *enfadado* 'angry' as XPCOMP), among other factors.

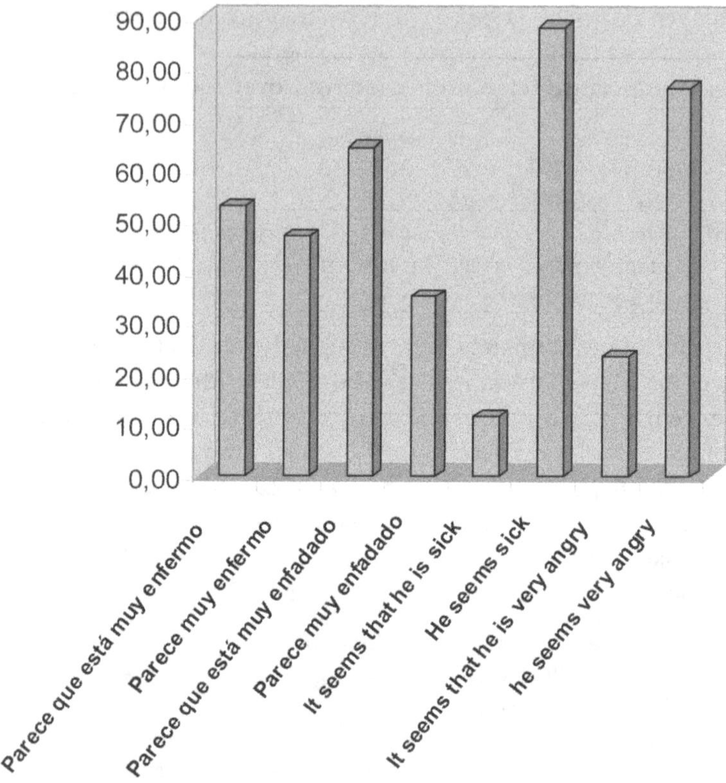

Figure 11.3. Acceptability judgements of *seem* and *parecer* with a finite clause and a SC

6 Closing remarks and outlook

In the spirit of Goldberg (2006), the main focus of this paper has been on elucidating whether a unitary analysis of SCs after *consider*-type verbs and *seem*-type verbs in English and Spanish, referred to respectively as the *evaluative subjective-transitive* and the *subjective-attributive* constructions, is viable. In view of the evidence presented here, the answer seems to be affirmative. These two constructions have been shown to share a number of important similarities impinging not only on the constructional meaning but also on the semantico-pragmatic profile of the construction's components, most notably, the subject/the dative-experiencer, the direct object (or the grammatical subject) and the attribute encoded in the XPCOMP. It has been argued that subjectivity in general and scalarity in particular emerge as the two overall determinants of the interpretation and acceptability of the two constructions examined here. At a higher level of resolution, these two constructions can be seen to be subject to coercion effects *via* progressive modification. However, some asymmetries between these two constructions have also been detected. These can be summarized as follows: the *evaluative subjective transitive* construction allows for coercion *via* a reflexive pronoun in the direct object as well as coercion *via* an imperative form. The former type of coercion is systematically disallowed in the *subjective-attributive* construction in English and Spanish, while the latter is acceptable with some members of the *seem*-type class, but yields an unacceptable result with *parecer*-type verbs. Last but not least, the *evaluative subjective-transitive* construction shows an overriding preference for first-person singular subjects, which does not find parallel in the *subjective-attributive* construction.

However, it should be immediately emphasized that the unitary analysis proposed here is relative to a particular level of resolution in the *constructicon*. The question now arises as to whether other broader-scale (or, conversely, slightly more fine-grained) unitary analyses are viable for the constructions under analysis here. As Boas reminds us,

> when analyzing a syntactic surface pattern, we should first attempt to pair form with meaning at the most abstract level. Only when we do not arrive at any proper interpretation do we need to look into discovering other types of constructions that are semantically more specific. (Boas, 2008: 33)

In the light of Boas' suggestion, the question can now be recast as follows: is the analysis proposed here a unitary analysis at the most abstract level? In other words, to which degree language users would take these two constructions (i.e. the evaluative subjective-transitive construction and the subjective-attributive construction) to belong to the same construction at a more abstract level? In this connection, at least two alternative analyses must be mentioned. The first one is that proposed by Gisborne (2008), who drawing on Word Grammar (Hudson 1999) and the Goldbergian strand of CxG, argues for a unitary analysis for the following four predicative complementation patterns (which, in his terminology, includes raising and control, infinitival SCs and non-verbal SCs): result, potential outcome, modal evaluation and deontic modal (Gisborne 2008: 226). This author provides an extremely detailed hierarchy of predicative complements, although he acknowledges that "there is still plenty of research that can be done which would affect the final outcomes of this hierarchy" (Gisborne 2008: 250).

The second unitary analysis that I will briefly present here is that of Yoon (2004), who is concerned with infinitival complement constructions in Spanish. Drawing on the Goldbergian formulation of CxG, Yoon posits two distinct, yet related, constructions: (a) the DESIRE-BECOME construction, which fuses with volition verbs (i.e. verbs of desideration, intention, and attempt); and (b) the ASSESS-STATE construction, which combines with emotion, cognition and communication verbs (see Yoon 2004: 383–384). Interestingly enough, Yoon's (2004) proposal displays a closer affinity with our analysis, because, following the Goldbergian version of CxG, she posits a core constructional meaning for these two constructions. Specifically, the central sense of the first construction is that a subject desires/intends to accomplish an action or to achieve a certain state, while the second conveys that one assesses and evaluates one's situation or state.

In this final section, we have briefly outlined two alternative unitary analyses of predicative complements which differ from the one proposed here in allowing for broader-scale generalizations. These analyses not only lend further credence to the viability of a unitary analysis of predicative complements in English and Spanish but also enable us to catch a glimpse of the connections among constructions at different levels of abstraction (or, conversely, of granularity) which lie at the heart of the *constructicon*, understood as a "a highly structured lattice of interrelated information" (Goldberg 1995: 5). Whether these three analyses (or aspects of them) can be fruitfully combined or not only future research will tell.

Notes

* Financial support for the research presented in this article has been provided by the DGI, Spanish Ministry of Education and Science and the FEDER funds, grants HUM2007-65755/FILO, HUM2007-62220FILO as well as the Xunta de Galicia PGDIT-INCITE09 204 155PR. I am grateful to Chris Butler and Jiyoung Yoon for most helpful comments and advice. Any remaining errors are solely my own.

1. The label "small clause" (SC) is employed throughout this paper only for expository convenience. No endorsement of this analysis, as practised within the formalist camp – especially the Chomskyan framework – (see Aarts 1992; Demonte and Masullo 1999 and references therein), is implied here.
2. From now on interlinear morpheme-by-morpheme glosses will be provided for the Spanish examples following the Leipzig Glossing Rules (http://www.eva.mpg.de/lingua/files/morpheme.html). The gloss PRONOM.CLITIC has been added to refer to a pronominal clitic. The examples reproduced in this

paper without a source have been created by the author and approved by native informants.

3. *Seem* and its correspondences in other languages have received a great deal of attention (see Aijmer 2009: 64 and Cornillie 2007: 9–13 for further discussion and references). However, I concur with Aijmer (2009: 64) that "it does not follow that the constructions and their functions are the same in all languages which have verbs of the *seem*-class".
4. Similar differences to the ones attested with *seem* have been noted for *sound* (Iatridou 1990: 560) and other verbs such as *smell, taste, feel,* etc.
5. Arche García-Valdecasas (2004: 160 n86) observes that the presence or absence of the dative-experiencer leads to important acceptability differences which cannot be exclusively attributed to the choice of the predicative phrase, but are also due to the liability to occur with specific tense and aspectual modifications. Thus, by way of illustration, the combinations with the dative-experiencer of the type in (a) can freely combine with past and present perfect forms. However, these yield at best a marginally acceptable result if the the dative-experiencer is omitted.

   (a) María ?(me) parec-e/ parec-ió/ ha parec-ido
   María 1SG.DAT seem-PRS.3SG seem-INDEFPRET.3SG AUXPFV.3SG seem-PTCP
   cruel con Juan.
   cruel with Juan
   "María seems/seemed/has seemed to me cruel with Juan".

   Arche García-Valdecasas (2004) contends that the restrictions regarding tense and aspect exhibited by the combinations without the dative-experiencer can be taken to point to a modal-like status for this construction.
6. It must be emphasized that this asymmetry between these two constructions cannot be properly accounted for irrespective of an important difference in their syntax, as shown in Figures 11.1 and 11.2. In Spanish, the pronoun *me* can be interpreted either as a direct object (as in a reflexive pronoun) or as a dative experiencer, which causes an ambiguity in some contexts. As shown in Figure 11.2, the verb *parecer* would normally allow for a dative experiencer, thus blocking the feasibility of having *me* as a direct object instead of *me* as a dative experiencer. I owe this observation to Jiyoung Yoon.

References

Aarts, B. (1992) *Small Clauses in English: The nonverbal types.* Berlin: Mouton de Gruyter.

Aijmer, K. (2009) *Seem* and evidentiality. *Functions of Language* 16(1): 63–88.

Arche García-Valdecasas, M. J. (2004) *Propiedades aspectuales y temporales de los predicados de individuo.* Ph.D. dissertation. Instituto Universitario Ortega y Gasset, Universidad Complutense de Madrid.

Austin, J. L. (1962) *Sense and Sensibilia.* London: Oxford University Press.

Boas, H. C. (2008) Determining the structure of lexical entries and grammatical constructions in Construction Grammar. *Annual Review of Cognitive Linguistics* 6: 113–144.

Bolinger, D. (1972a) *Degree Words.* The Hague: Mouton.

Bolinger, D. (1972b) The syntax of *parecer.* In A. Valdman (ed.) *Papers in Linguistics and Phonetics to the Memory of Pierre Delattre* 65–76. The Hague: Mouton.

Borkin, A. (1973) To be or not to be. In C. Corum, T. C. Smith-Stark and A. Weiser (eds) *Proceedings of the Ninth Regional Meeting of the Chicago Linguistic Society* 44–56. Chicago, IL: Chicago Linguistics Society.

Chafe, W. and Nichols, J. (eds) (1986) *Evidentiality: The linguistic coding of epistemology.* Norwood, MA: Ablex Publishing Corporation. [Advances in discourse processes 20].

Cornillie, B. (2007) *Evidentiality and Epistemic Modality in Spanish (Semi-) Auxiliaries: A cognitive-functional approach.* Berlin: Mouton de Gruyter.

Croft, W. (2001) *Radical Construction Grammar.* Oxford: Oxford University Press.

Croft, W. (2003) Lexical rules vs. constructions: A false dichotomy. In H. Cuyckens, T. Berg, R. Dirven and K. Panther (eds) *Motivation in Language: Studies in honour of Günter Radden* 49–68. Amsterdam: Benjamins.

Demonte, V. and P. Masullo (1999) La predicación: Los complementos predicativos. In I. Bosque and V. Demonte (eds) *Gramática descriptiva de la lengua española. Vol. 2: Las construcciones sintácticas fundamentales. Relaciones temporales, aspectuales y modales* 2461–2523. Madrid: Espasa Calpe.

Duffley, P. J. and P. Larrivée (2010). Anyone for non-scalarity?. *English Language and Linguistics* 14(1): 1–17.

Englebretson, R. (2007) Stancetaking in discourse: An introduction. In R. Englebretson (ed.) *Stancetaking in Discourse* 1–25. Amsterdam: Benjamins.

Fernández Leborans, M. J. (1999) La predicación: Las oraciones copulativas. In I. Bosque and V. Demonte (eds) *Gramática descriptiva de la lengua española, Vol. 1: Sintaxis básica de las clases de palabras* 2357–2460. Madrid: Espasa Calpe.

Gisborne, N. (2008) Dependencies are constructions. In G. Trousdale and N. Gisborne (eds) *Constructional Approaches to English Grammar* 219–255. Berlin: Mouton de Gruyter.

Goldberg, A. E. (1995) *Constructions: A construction grammar approach to argument structure.* Chicago, IL: University of Chicago Press.

Goldberg, A. E. (2006) *Constructions at Work: The nature of generalization in language.* Oxford: Oxford University Press.

Gonzálvez-García, F. (2006) Passives without actives: Evidence from verbless complement constructions in Spanish. *Constructions* SV1-5/2006: 1–63.

Gonzálvez-García, F. (2007) "Saved by the reflexive": Evidence from coercion via reflexives in verbless complement clauses in English and Spanish. *Annual Review of Cognitive Linguistics* 5: 193–238.

Gonzálvez-García, F. (2009) The family of object-related depictives in English and Spanish: Towards a usage-based, constructionist analysis. *Language Sciences* 31(5): 663–723.

Hudson, R. (1990) *Word Grammar*. Oxford: Blackwell.

Iatridou, S. (1990) About Agr(P). *Linguistic Inquiry* 21(4): 551–577.

Iwata, S. (2008) *Locative Alternation: A lexical-constructional approach*. Amsterdam: Benjamins.

Kirparsky, P. and C. Kiparsky (1970) Fact. In D. D. Steinberg and L. A. Jakobovits (eds) *Semantics* 345–369. Cambridge: Cambridge University Press.

Langacker, R. W. (1991) *Foundations of Cognitive Grammar, Vol. 2: Descriptive Application*. Stanford, CA: Stanford University Press.

Levin, B. (1993) *English Verb Classes and Alternations: A preliminary investigation*. Chicago, IL: University of Chicago Press.

Lyons, J. (1982) Deixis and subjectivity: Loquor, ergo sum? In R. J. Jarvella and W. Klein (eds) *Speech, Place and Action: Studies in deixis and related topics* 101–124. New York: Wiley.

Matushansky, O. (2002) Tipping the scales: The syntax of scalarity in the complement of *seem*. *Syntax* 5(3): 219–276.

May, T. (1987) Verbs of result in the complements of raising constructions. *Australian Journal of Linguistics* 7: 25–42.

Michaelis, L. A. (2003) Word meaning, sentence meaning, and syntactic meaning. In H. Cuyckens, R. Dirven and J. Taylor (eds) *Cognitive Approaches to Lexical Semantics* 163–209. Berlin: Mouton de Gruyter.

Mithun, M. (1986) Evidential diachrony in Northern Iroquoian. In W. Chafe and J. Nichols (eds) *Evidentiality: The linguistic coding of epistemology* 89–112. Norwood, MA: Ablex Publishing Corporation. [Advances in discourse processes 20].

Moro, A. (1997) *The Raising of Predicates: Predicative noun phrases and the theory of clause structure*. Cambridge: Cambridge University Press. [Cambridge Studies in Linguistics 80].

Newman, J. (1981) *The Semantics of Raising*. Ph.D. dissertation. University of California at San Diego.

Postal, P. (1971) *Cross-over Phenomena*. New York: Holt, Rhinehart and Winston.

Porroche, M. (1990) *Aspectos de la atribución en español*. Pórtico: Zaragoza.

Williams, C. (2002) *Non-Progressive and Progressive Aspect in English*. Schena: Fasano.

Yoon, J. (2004) Infinitival complement constructions in Spanish: A construction grammar approach. In J. Auger, J. Clancy Clements and B. Vance (eds) *Contemporary Approaches to Romance Linguistics. Selected papers from the Thirty-third linguistic symposium on Romance languages (LSRL)* 381–397. Amsterdam: Benjamins. [Current Issues in Linguistic Theory 258].

12 Metonymy-motivated morphosyntactic alternations*

Antonio Barcelona[a]

1 Introduction

The goal of this paper is to argue, from the perspective of cognitive linguistics, for the role of conceptual metonymy in the motivation of certain types of morphosyntactic alternations. In §2, I will specify the notion of "morphosyntactic alternation" that I will be adhering to throughout this discussion, and I will present the main types of morphosyntactic alternations that, in my view, can be discerned. §3 offers a few examples of the alternations which have been argued by cognitive linguists to be cognitively motivated. §4 directly addresses the topic of the paper, namely metonymy-motivated morphosyntactic alternations. Finally §5 presents the conclusions.

2 My notion of "morphosyntactic alternation"

2.1 Terminological prerequisites

2.1.1 The term "construction" and other basic notions ("frame", "ICM", metaphor, metonymy) in cognitive linguistics

In cognitive linguistics (CL henceforth), a **grammatical construction** is a conventional pairing of form (including such formal parameters as prosody and the sequential order and combinatory patterns of phonemes and higher

a Antonio Barcelona is Full Professor of English Language and Linguistics at the University of Córdoba, Spain. E-mail: antonio.barcelona@uco.es units) and meaning, including pragmatic and social meaning (Lakoff 1987: 462–586; Langacker 1987, 1991a; Fillmore 1988; Fillmore *et al.* 1988; Goldberg 1995).

Grammatical constructions include lexemes as well as phrases, clauses, or sentences, since all of these structures are arrangements of form conventionally paired to one or more meanings (Langacker 1987: 58). Langacker (1987) reserves the term "constructional schema" for an abstraction or schematization of the formal and semantic commonalities ranging over a number of "usage events", or particular, individual expressions.

A controversial issue is whether or not morphemes are also grammatical constructions. To Langacker they are not (Langacker 1987: 58, 82, especially 409). Following Goldberg (2006), however, in what follows I will also treat morphemes as grammatical constructions because of their essential similarity to other grammatical constructions, since morphemes are also conventional symbolic units resulting from the pairing of a formal structure with a semantic structure, like lexemes, phrases, clauses or sentences.

My notions of frame/ICM, metaphor and metonymy correspond in general to those prevalent in CL. See e.g. Barcelona (2002a), Barcelona (2002b), and Panther and Thornburg (2003).

2.1.2 "Basic form" and "basic meaning"

In my characterization of the notion of "morphosyntactic alternation", I will be making reference to these two notions. By "basic form" I mean:

(a) The **uninflected full** (i.e. nonabbreviated) **form** of lexemes; or
(b) The **full** (i.e. **nonelliptical** or **nondefective**) **form of syntactic constructions**.

The form *gasoline* (and its corresponding spoken form) is the basic form of the lexeme "gasoline". And neither the form *gas* (the clipped uninflected form of the same lexeme), nor the form *gasolines* (the inflected form of the lexeme, resulting from the combination of the lexical morpheme with the plural inflectional morpheme) constitute basic forms of the lexeme.

Similarly, *fast* is the basic form shared by the adjective and the adverb lexemes "fast" and by the noun and the verb lexemes "fast", whereas the inflected forms *faster* and *fasts* are not basic forms of, respectively, the adjective (or the adverb) and the noun (or the verb).

The reason why inflected forms are not regarded as "basic forms" is, obviously, that they constitute a modification of the corresponding uninflected form due to the presence of an inflectional morpheme, this modification consisting, in English, in the addition of some phonological material (suffixal morphs), in an internal change of the form (e.g. the vocalic alternations of irregular verbs), or in other changes.

The basic form is the full (i.e. nonabbreviated) and uninflected form of the lexeme; for example, the citation form of the verb *speak*, rather than the inflected forms *speaks, spoke, spoken, speaking*. Due in part to the fact that it is often morphologically simpler than the inflected forms and that the latter constitute modifications of it, the basic form often has prototypical status within the small cognitive category constituted by the various forms of a lexeme: Its role in the cohesiveness and distinctiveness of that category is reflected in the fact that the average English speaker (doubtless also due to schooling) uses the basic form as the cognitive reference point from which to conceptualize the category consisting of the various forms of the lexeme ("*speaks* is a form of the verb *(to) speak*"). On the prototypical forms of lexemes, see Barcelona (2009: 366–369).

As for the basic form of syntactic constructions, let us consider the sentences in italics in these two examples:

(1) MARY (*smiles affectionately*): [...]

(2) MARY (*she smiles affectionately*): [...]

Example (1) includes a brief stage direction in O'Neill's *Long Day's Journey into Night*. The sentence in italics is elliptical; hence it is not the basic form of the generic declarative clause construction. In Example (2) we find the basic form of this clausal construction.

We will later see that in some cases the alternation in form may also be regarded as an alternation in the choice of constructions as form-meaning pairings.

In what follows, by "basic meaning" I will mean the combination of the **profile** of a construction and the **base** on which this profile is selected (the notions of profile and base are due to Langacker, e.g. 1987, 1999). The profile of a construction is the conceptual entity (the set of "things" and their relations) obligatorily accessed as part of the meaning of the construction. This conceptual entity is understood against its **base** (the conceptual content presupposed by the profile of a construction). Two constructions may share the same base and differ in profile. *Aunt* and *uncle* share the same base, namely a partial kinship network related to one reference individual. But whereas *aunt* profiles a female sibling of one of the parent's of the reference individual (*Mary* in (3) and (4)), *uncle* profiles a male sibling (see e.g. Langacker 1999: 9).

(3) Mary's aunt is ill.

(4) Mary's uncle is old.

Two constructions may share the same profile but differ in terms of the base evoked (Langacker 1999: 11–12):

(5) The yellow paper.

(6) The yellowed paper.

The adjective in (5) and the participial adjective in (6) profile the same relation (i.e. one between a "thing" – *the paper* – and a region in color space), but they differ in the conceptual content, i.e. the **base** they evoke: Whereas the participle presupposes a prior process along the time axis leading to the state profiled, the adjective does not presuppose such a process.

2.2 The common notion of "morphosyntactic alternation" in linguistics

The notion of grammatical or morphosyntactic alternation is normally used to refer to cases in which a given grammatical structure (usually a clause or sentence type) regularly admits of formal variations without (so at least is usually claimed)[1] changing its meaning. A typical example, intensely debated in generative linguistics, is the so-called "dative alternation" (*John gave me a book – John gave a book to me*). As a cognitive linguist, I should in principle be inclined to reject even the notion of morphosyntactic alternation, which to most cognitive linguists is simply the descendant of the generative notions of lexical rules and transformations (see Michaelis and Ruppenhofer 2001 or Goldberg 2002).

The strategy followed by most cognitive linguists is to regard alternations (for example, the two syntactic presentations of the recipient semantic role in the dative alternation) as two different constructions included in the same family of constructions (the ditransitive construction), which are distinguished (in this case minimally) in terms of syntactic form, but also in terms of meaning (even if this meaning difference is only of a purely pragmatic nature – the two constructions seem to be differentiated in terms of assignment of information focus). The reason is that, as stated above, in CL a construction is a conventional pairing of meaning and form, so that a difference in form should in principle correspond to a difference in meaning (Langacker 1987, 1991a; Lakoff 1987).

However, Cappelle (n.d.) suggests a different (and controversial) strategy for construction grammar, namely that of regarding the alternative patterns as **allostructions** (on the model of such terms as "allophone" or "allomorph"). He claims that there are no clear semantic differences between the options and that, like allophones or allomorphs, these alternations occur in something similar to complementary distribution. However, in my view there *are* semantic differences between the alternates. Cappelle's example is the particle placement alternation in phrasal verbs i.e. *take off your shoes/take your shoes off.* The simple fact that the two options can be distinguished in terms of information structure and other factors is already a difference in overall meaning.

2.3 My loose use of the term "morphosyntactic alternation" in this article

In a way, the notion of morphosyntactic alternation that I will be applying in this article is not too distant from the standard notion, but it extends and modifies it. I will assume that we have morphosyntactic alternation in any of the three following situations (or in a combination of them):

Type 1: The conventional pairing of a **basic** form with more than one **basic** constructional meaning; the meanings can be related or unrelated to each other. In other words, this alternation consists in the coding of more than one construction by the same basic form.

Type 2: The conventional pairing of a **basic** constructional meaning with more than one uninflected form, independently of the degree of relatedness of the forms to each other. In other words, this alternation consists in the **sharing** of the same basic meaning by two or more closely connected constructions.

Type 3: Two or more constructions stand in a model-variant relationship to each other within the same family or network of constructions and **the basic form and/or meaning of the variant construction are relatively "distant" variants of those of the model construction**. In other words, the alternation consists in the **contrast** between a model and a variant.

Type 1 often results in homonymy or polysemy at the morphemic and lexical level, depending on the relatedness of the meanings involved, and is often the outcome of a derivational process (typically conversion, though other processes may be involved). We will comment on some morphemic or lexical examples in §4.

At the level of syntactic constructions, this type of morphosyntactic alternation often results in syntactic and semantic ambiguity: i.e. in what might be called **syntactic polysemy** if the meanings are extensionally related, or **syntactic homonymy**, if they are not.

The syntactic construction instantiated by Example (8) is an extension of the syntactic construction instantiated by Example (7):

(7) The engineer looked into the tunnel.

(8) The engineer looked into the problem.

In (7) the syntactic form "NP-*look into*-NP" is paired to a dynamic meaning that might be described as an action consisting of the visual examination of the interior of a container, whereas in (8) the same syntactic form is paired to a meaning that might be described as an action consisting of the nonvisual mental examination of the complexities of a problem. The same basic form is used to code two different yet related meanings, which are connected by metaphor (UNDERSTANDING IS SEEING).

Example (9) is an instance of syntactic homonymy, where the same form is paired to different meanings which are not related to each other:

(9) The chicken is ready to eat.

Depending on the context, the basic form "NP-*be ready-to*-Infinitive of transitive verb" will code a construction where *eat* is a transitive verb with an implicit subject (the chicken) and an unspecified object, and whose basic meaning could be approximately paraphrased as "The chicken is ready to eat X". Or a construction where *eat* is a transitive verb with an unspecified subject (probably some of the speech participants) and an implicit object (the chicken), and whose basic meaning could be approximately paraphrased as "The chicken is ready to be eaten by X".

Type 2 alternations normally occur when a morphosyntactic construction (typically a lexeme, but sometimes also a phrase or a clause) develops one or more nonprototypical forms (i.e. "weak" or "clipped", abbreviated forms in lexemes as in the *gasoline-gas* alternation, or elliptical forms in phrases or clauses).

Postulating this type of alternation does not amount to defending claims that perfect synonymy or paraphrase are frequent or even possible; these claims contradict the default assumption in CL that a difference in form tends to correspond to a difference, no matter how small, in meaning. Therefore, even if the same **basic** constructional meaning is paired to the two forms, the nonprototypical form inevitably involves at least a subtle distinction in meaning (often of a social, attitudinal or stylistic nature). For example, the apparent synonymy between the (written) form *'ve* and the (written) form *have* of the perfective auxiliary in English is far from perfect, given stylistic connotation (greater formality and/or emphasis is attributed to the full form).

In these cases, we have two analytical options, which are not mutually exclusive:

(a) To regard the canonical, prototypical forms and the nonprototypical forms as alternative forms of the same construction (in the previous example, the construction would be the lexical construction "Auxiliary have") sharing the same **basic** meaning and not other aspects of their overall meaning. In other words, to regard them with their meaning, as "allostructions" (but using the term in a slightly different sense from Cappelle's).
(b) To be blindly consistent with the spirit of construction grammar in general and with Goldberg's model in particular and regard, e.g. the pairing of (auxiliary) *have* with its meaning and the pairing of *'ve* with its meaning as two *distinct* though closely connected constructions (two different lexemes, *'ve* and *have* in this case). This option looks counterintuitive.

As Cappelle points out, Langacker's Cognitive Grammar is equipped to admit option (a) via the notion of "categorizing relations" (Langacker 1987: 379), and even Goldberg's notion of "inheritance links" (e.g. Goldberg 1995: 72–100) might be used to accommodate certain "allostructions". Therefore I advocate option (a), which, by the way, is the one that has been traditionally followed.

In type 3 alternations, the basic meaning and/or form of the variant construction is different, though related, to those of a construction having prototype or model status with respect to that variant in the network.

In type 1 the same basic form is shared by various constructions and in type 2 the same basic meaning is shared by various "allostructions". What distinguishes both types 1 and 2 from type 3 is, first, that in type 3 the contrast does not operate only on the formal or on the semantic plane because it may operate on both; and, second, that the form and/or meaning of model and variant are relatively distant to each other. In a way, type 3 can be regarded in some cases as an extension of type 1 or 2 or in other cases as a hybrid between them. A detailed example of type 3 will be presented in §4.

3 Cognitively motivated alternations in CL

A large number of the instances of metaphor-motivated or metonymy-motivated extensions of grammatical constructions which have been discussed in the CL literature can be regarded as alternations of any of the three types proposed above. For the sake of brevity, I will present just a few examples:

An example of type 1 alternation is the metonymy-motivated conversion of proper names into common nouns (Barcelona 2004), as in *He is a Shakespeare.* Another example is constituted by some metonymy-motivated active zone constructions. Langacker (2009) discusses examples like *The swan in the water* (where only part of the "trajector", *the swan*, is included in the landmark, *the water*), which can be regarded as instances of the polysemy of *in* (compare the prototypical sense of *in* illustrated by *The cake in the oven,* where the cake is fully included in the oven).

An example of type 3 alternation is the metaphor-motivated extension of the caused motion construction into the resultative construction (Goldberg 1995), as *She sent me into a fury.* Further examples are constituted by the inheritance links in Goldberg's grammar between a larger construction and a proper subpart of it (e.g. between the caused motion and the intransitive motion construction), and certain inheritance links between a construction whose sense is considered central to a family of constructions and the various constructions in the family whose senses form a polysemy network with that central sense (e.g. the links between the ditransitive construction designating actual "giving" and other kinds of ditransitives, such as those designating "promising", "refusal", etc.). We can also include in type 3 the many constructions related (in Langacker's CG) in terms of construal shifts (Langacker 1987).

For the reasons stated in §2, very few examples of type 2 alternations have been recognized in CL. Among them, the instances of metonymy-motivated formal variants of constructions discussed by Barcelona (2009) and Bierwiaczwonek (2005) can be mentioned (see §4).[2]

4 Some metonymy-motivated morphosyntactic alternations

In the course of my research on metonymy in constructional meaning and form (see e.g. Barcelona 2005, 2009, in preparation), I have been able to identify a large number of metonymy-motivated phenomena, which constitute instances of the three types of morphosyntactic alternations proposed above, and which belong to the following linguistic domains, among others: Suffixal derivation, conversion, compounding, ellipsis, and syntactic constructions.

4.1 Type 1 morphosyntactic alternations: The conventional pairing of a basic form with more than one basic constructional meaning

A large number of the metonymy-motivated grammatical phenomena just referred to above are instances of this type of morphosyntactic alternation. Below I will only be able to describe in some detail three of the many findings in my own recent research.

(a) Suffixal derivation: {ful}, in *armful,* as in (10):

(10) Tyrone's arm is around his wife's waist as they appear from the back parlor. Entering the living room he gives her a playful hug.
TYRONE: *You're a fine armful now, Mary, with those twenty pounds you've gained.*
(*Act 1 of Eugene O'Neill's play* Long Day's Journey into Night)

I take morphemes to be borderline instances of constructions, as stated above. In cases like *armful,* {ful} is a derivational morpheme deriving nouns from nouns. It originates in the adjective *full.* Its meaning is "the quantity of X that fills or would fill Y (Y being coded by the lexical morpheme)"; description adapted from the definitions in the *Webster's* (McKechnie 1978) and the two Oxford dictionaries consulted: the *Oxford English Dictionary* (OED; Benbow 2002) and the *Oxford Advanced Learner's Dictionary* (Hornby 1984). In (10), *armful* is used to designate a certain amount of body size, one that would fill somebody else's arm completely (in a hug).

We are commenting here on the historical alternation between the two senses developed in Germanic by noun phrases headed by a noun denoting anything that could be regarded as a receptacle, and modified by the adjective *full* modified in turn by a genitive or an *of*-phrase. In the first, basic sense *full* and its modifier was a description of the container, as in *a spoon full of soup*; in the transferred sense, the *full* sequence was a description of the quantity that fills or would fill the container, as if the modern form *a spoon full of soup* were interpreted today as meaning "the amount of soup that fills or would fill a spoon". This historical alternation is of type 1 because when it took place the form of the polysemous noun phrase was identical for both senses, although each of them later led to a slightly different form. In OE the phrases in the second sense became near compounds like *handfull* and later on the adjective *full* eventually got grammaticalized into the modern derivational morpheme. (The alternation, the grammaticalization and consequent conversion of *full* as suffix *–ful* are implicit in the discussion in OED entry 2 for suffix *–ful* and in OED entry A, 1.b for *full.*)

The standard sense of the derivational morpheme seems to have been historically motivated, among other factors, by the metonymy DEGREE OF FILLING OF THE CONTAINER FOR QUANTITY OF CONTENT FILLING IT (a submetonymy of CONTAINER FOR CONTENT). That is, the domain of quantity is activated not directly by the domain of containers, but by the domain of the **degree to which the container has been or can be filled** by the content, within the ICM of FILLING. In this morpheme (as in the original adjective), the content reaches the maximum possible degree of filling and the container (a metaphorical one in this case, namely Mary's arms) is "full" as a result. This metonymy also motivates other present-day conventional linguistic expressions in which a measure of the capacity of a container is a metonymic source activating a certain quantity of the content: *Give me* half a glass *of beer* i.e. the amount of beer that can fill half a glass of beer, *She just drank* two inches, etc.

The "container" (sometimes a metaphorical one) is specified by the lexical morpheme, {arm} in this case, in the derived noun. Other examples of the use of this morpheme are (*a*) *bottleful,* (*a*) *boxful,* (*a*) *canful,* (*a*) *worldful,* (*a*) *churchful,* etc. That is, a *churchful* denotes "as many (people, benches, etc.) as a church can hold", the meaning of *bottleful* is "as much as a bottle can hold", etc. (both definitions taken from the OED).

This morpheme should not be confused with the one operating in *playful hug* (an adjective-forming morpheme meaning "full of", "having", "characterized by"). The meaning of this other morpheme is metaphorically motivated, since an abstract notion, typically a process ("play", "joy", etc.) is understood as a physical "content", and a person, a behavior (a hug), etc. is understood as a metaphorical container.

(b) Conversion: The noun *interstate,* as in (11):

(11) *If you have ever driven west on Interstate 70 from Denver to the Continental Divide, you have seen Mount Bethel.*

Interstate means "interstate highway" in this sentence, as can be seen from the text where it appears.[3] The use of the lexeme *interstate* as a noun (even in plural) in the sense "interstate freeway" is quite conventional in American English, and it arises by conversion from its adjectival use, according to the dictionaries mentioned above.

The original sense of the adjective lexeme *interstate* in American English was "between (US) States", as in *interstate commerce* or in *interstate border,* and, in this sense, it functions almost exclusively as a syntactic modifier and it never takes the plural morpheme. These grammatical constraints, and the semantic fact that the lexeme designates a relation rather than an entity, probably leads most standard dictionaries (like the *Webster's* and the two Oxford dictionaries mentioned above) to class the lexeme as an adjective. This is the only class which is registered for the word in the *Webster's*; the Oxford dictionaries also register its noun use, though they do not reserve a separate entry for it.

In (11), the lexeme *interstate* does not change its form, but its meaning is different from the adjectival meaning, since it does not simply denote a relation but a type of entity characterized by being involved in a relation, i.e. a typical nominal meaning. In any case, the key factor to decide whether we have one lexeme with two meanings (polysemy) or two different lexemes with the same basic form (homonymy) is whether or not the difference in meaning also brings about a change in grammatical class. With the relational sense "between states", the basic written form *interstate* and its corresponding spoken form code at best a nonprototypical adjective, since it is nongradable (**interstater*, **more interstate*, **very interstate*) and cannot be used predicatively (**This problem is interstate*). On the other hand, when the same basic forms denote a type of entity ("a highway between states"), they code a prototypical or near-prototypical noun, since they can take the plural morpheme, they can be the head of an NP with typical nominal syntactic functions, and they may occasionally take the genitive morpheme: *All interstates are necessary; The federal government is building an expensive new interstate; The interstate's length is 2000 miles; The new interstates increased the mobility of the American people.* I thus assume the existence of two homonymous lexemes, each one coding a different though related meaning and belonging to a different grammatical class: *interstate*-adjective (a nonprototypical adjective) and *interstate*-noun (a prototypical noun). Since the latter lexeme arises from the adjective, this process is an instance of adjective-noun **conversion**.

This conversion is due, among other factors, to a semantic shift motivated by the metonymy DISTINCTIVE POLITICAL-GEOGRAPHICAL PROPERTY ("LINKING TWO STATES") OF AN INTERSTATE HIGHWAY FOR THE INTERSTATE HIGHWAY, which is a manifestation of the higher level metonymy DISTINCTIVE PROPERTY OF A CATEGORY FOR THE CATEGORY. We find the same metonymy underlying the use of the form *black* for "black person" (Kövecses and Radden 1998).

The lexeme *interstate*-noun is a recent addition to the lexicon (dated 1968 by the OED, 2nd edn), and the homonymous adjective preceded it historically and is still the lexeme most frequently associated with the written form *interstate* or its corresponding spoken form.

(c) *The Continental Divide* as a phrasal name, as in Example (11) above.

The OED (s.v. *continental*) describes the meaning of this phrase, which it terms a "special collocation" of the adjective *continental*, as "a divide separating two river systems of a continent; *spec.* the divide in North America separating rivers flowing into the Atlantic from those flowing into the Pacific". The same dictionary registers s.v. *divide* this meaning for the phrasal name *the (Great) Continental Divide*: "that of the Rocky Mountains". That is, we find here an instance of syntactic ambiguity that results in syntactic polysemy-based homonymy of the spoken form.

The conventionalization of this phrase as an alternative **name** for the Rocky Mountains ridge can be regarded as the result of, among other factors, the choice of one of the roles performed by the Rockies within the ROCKY MOUNTAINS frame (a part of the cognitive domain of NORTH AMERICAN GEOGRAPHY) as a metonymic source activating the whole frame; that role is that of CONTINENTAL BASIN DIVIDE. This would be a PART FOR WHOLE metonymy: SALIENT PROPERTY OF AN ENTITY (ROLE AS CONTINENTAL BASIN DIVIDE) FOR THE ENTITY (THE ROCKY MOUNTAINS). The knowledge about the Rockies shared by most speakers includes their role as a divide separating rivers flowing into the Atlantic from rivers flowing into the Pacific, apart from other salient properties such as their size or their location. This role is used to activate the whole conceptual frame.

This metonymy motivated the conventional meaning of the phrasal construction *The (Great) Continental Divide*, so that once the construction has been mastered, the metonymy normally plays no role in guiding inference to its meaning. However, in ambiguous contexts or with speakers not familiar with the construction, the metonymy would again be instrumental in arriving at the conventional prototypical meaning of the expression.

4.2 Type 2 morphosyntactic alternations: The conventional pairing of a basic constructional meaning with more than one uninflected form

An important idea that should be borne in mind to understand why metonymy can motivate constructional form is that each conventional constructional form constitutes a concept, because the *schematization* (Langacker 1987: 68–75) of linguistic form provides it with a conceptual dimension. If the schematized forms of a construction are concepts, then they can constitute conceptual categories, organized around one or more prototypical members by means of various types of links. One of these links is the PART-WHOLE link, which often gives rise to a metonymic connection between certain forms, especially when a certain form constitutes a salient part of another (Bierwiaczonek 2005; Barcelona 2009: 366–369). Three instances are presented below.

(a) The abbreviated form *gas* of the noun *gasoline,* as in (12), slightly adapted from Radden (2000: 94–95):

(12) *John: How much gas did you buy?*
Mary: I filled 'er up.

The form *gas* is, according to standard dictionaries, the colloquial US abbreviation, also quite common in British English, of the standard forms *gasoline* or *gasolene* of the lexeme *gasoline.* This nonprototypical form is licensed by the metonymy SALIENT PART OF FORM FOR WHOLE FORM (see Barcelona 2005, 2009, in preparation). The written segment <*gas*> and the corresponding spoken segment are the most prominent segments of their respective full forms, given their initial position and given that in the spoken canonical form the initial syllable bears primary stress. To these purely formal factors we should add a semantic factor: Both segments are capable of evoking the basic meaning of the lexeme readily, whereas segments such as <*line*>, or <*lene*> in the written form and the corresponding segments in the spoken forms would not be as efficient for that purpose.

(b) The elliptical form *table* for the noun phrase *the table,* in *by the right of table* and *at right rear of table,* as in (13), taken from the same play as (10):

(13) *TYRONE: [...] But thank God, I've kept my appetite and I've the digestion of a young man of twenty, if I am sixty-five.*
MARY: You surely have, James. No one could deny that.
(She laughs and sits in the wicker armchair at right rear of table [...]).

Singular noun phrases with a count nominal head normally require a determinative element in English. And when the noun phrase referent is definite, the determinative element must be a definite determinative element like the article *the,* a demonstrative (*this, that*), *whose,* etc.

The head *table* stands in this example for *the table,* which instantiates one of the canonical forms of singular definite noun phrases with a count nominal head; this form could informally be described as "definite determinative + singular count nominal".[4] The connection between the form of the NP lacking the definite determinative and the full form of the NP is, once more, one of part to whole. As used in this text, the nominal segment *table* can activate the full noun phrase *the table*, of which it is interpreted as an abbreviation. The factors responsible for this activation are:

First, the context, which makes the referent of the NP definite. The table is definite for the reader, thanks to the information, given in the initial stage direction of this first scene of the play, that there is a (round) table with several chairs in the center of the room where the scene takes place, and it is definite for the play audience, who can see the table.

Second, the metonymic part-whole connection between a SALIENT PART OF A CONSTRUCTIONAL FORM and the WHOLE CONSTRUCTIONAL FORM. The head nominal is the element bearing the main conceptual content in a noun phrase. In this sense, it is **normally** more salient than the determinative: it is the "profile determinant" of the whole construction.

Third, the text genre. This reduced form of the NP is normally acceptable only in certain genres often using certain abbreviatory conventions, like drama, where stage directions include some of those conventions.

Therefore, metonymy, together with other factors, both motivates the development and conventionality of this nonprototypical form of definite count NPs, and guides inferencing to its morphosyntactic categorization.

The same factors, including the same metonymy, account for the occurrence of *right rear* for *the right rear* in (13).

(c) The elliptical form of a complex sentence/clause: Matrix clause ellipsis as in (14):

(14) *Speaker A: Do you believe in clubs for young men?*
Speaker B: Only when kindness fails.[5]

The abstract canonical form of the complex sentence/clause realized in the Speaker B's reply can informally be represented as *Matrix part of the main clause + when clause.* The part of the main clause remaining once the subordinate clause is excluded can be called the **matrix** part of the main clause, or simply the "matrix clause".

The ellipsis occurring in this text is **formally** possible because a subordinate clause introduced by a subordinator (*when*) can act as a metonymic source for the whole complex clause/sentence. Thus we find once more the metonymy SALIENT PART OF CONSTRUCTIONAL FORM FOR WHOLE CONSTRUCTIONAL FORM at work.

This metonymy would help us reconstruct an elliptical clause/sentence even in nonsense sequences like (15):

(15) *Speaker A: Does it often rain here?*
Speaker B: Only when kindness fails.

Of course, it would be very difficult to arrive at any coherent inferences on the basis of this reply (other than B is trying to be funny, or that he has gone mad), but in any case the reply would automatically be understood as elliptical for *It often rains here only when kindness fails*. This shows that speakers have internalized an abstract formal schema for the construction and that the elliptical variant of this schema that we find in this text can be recognized as such thanks in part to the above metonymy.

Ellipsis is different from active zone phenomena (Langacker 1987, 1999, 2009). Though many active zones are often motivated by metonymy, their target is sometimes quite variable and depends on context and background knowledge: *Clubs* activates in (14) the active zone "the convenience/usefulness of building/establishing/having clubs". In strict ellipsis, on the other hand, the missing part of the form is uniquely recoverable; that is, in the previous nonsense dialogue, the ellipted part can only be *It often rains here*; in weak ellipsis the eligible elements for recoverability belong to a finite set (see Quirk *et al.* 1985, for the distinction between strict and weak ellipsis).

In all of the instances of abbreviation and ellipsis examined in §4.2, the full and the shorter forms share the same basic meaning, but they differ in their overall meaning. The shorter form differs from the full form in terms of style (it tends to be more informal, whereas the full form is often more formal) and genre (cf. the stage direction convention discussed above) or attitude, among other dimensions. If speaker B had replied in (14) *I believe in clubs for young men only when kindness fails*, his reply would be interpreted as more formal and as additionally organizing the information into a "given" section (the matrix clause *I believe in clubs for young men*) which would constitute a build-up stage preparing the hearer for the section conveying the new information – the punchline (on word order in the organization of given-new information, see Barcelona (1986) and Quirk *et al.* (1985), *inter alia*). All of these are facts showing that the nonprototypical forms of a construction, though having the same basic meaning as the prototypical form, have a different overall meaning.

4.3 Type 3 morphosyntactic alternations: The formal and/or semantic contrast between two or more constructions standing in a model-variant (i.e. inheritance) relationship to each other within the same family of constructions

Due to lack of space only one example of this type of alternation can be discussed, namely the epistemic conditional construction in (11), here repeated as (16):

(16) If you have ever driven west on Interstate 70 from Denver to the Continental Divide, you have seen Mount Bethel.

The sentence under scrutiny here consists of a complex clause, which in turn includes a subordinate conditional *if* clause. The meaning we are concerned with here is the **overall constructional meaning** of the whole complex clause.

The meaning of the type of conditional construction represented by this complex clause is "epistemic necessity". In its most obvious interpretation, it can be glossed this way: "If I can assume it to be a true fact that you have ever driven west on Interstate 70 from Denver to the Continental Divide then I necessarily have to conclude that you have seen Mt Bethel". These conditional constructions are called **epistemic conditionals** by Sweetser (1990: 116–117; 1996), who claims that they are a metaphorical extension from what she calls **content conditionals**, also called **predictive conditionals** by Dancygier (1993). "Content"/"predictive" conditionals are the "normal", prototypical conditionals like *If it is sunny, she'll go out.*

In the semantic structure of content or predictive conditionals, according to Sweetser (1990: 115), there is a causal or at least a (positive or negative) "enablement" relationship, between protasis and apodosis: The most likely interpretation of *If it is sunny, she'll go out* is that the occurrence of sunny weather will cause or enable her to (decide to) go out (and conversely, that the absence of sunny weather will cause or enable her to (decide) not to go out).

There is not enough space in this paper to discuss Sweetser's claim that the extension from content to epistemic conditionals is motivated by metaphor. As I have argued elsewhere in detail (Barcelona 2006), there are powerful grounds for claiming either that metonymy underlies the metaphor motivating the extension or that it motivated the extension directly, therefore making a metaphorical account unnecessary. In this section I will only discuss the second of these two alternative metonymic accounts, i.e. the exclusively metonymic motivation for the extension.

Before this it is necessary to explore in some greater depth the role of epistemicity in conditional constructions. In a predictive conditional, the speaker as conceptualizer (the speaker is normally also the conceptualizer or reasoner) is not normally in the "scope of predication", and is simply in the "ground", to use Langacker's terms (Langacker 1999: 5–7, 22, 49–53), whereas the connection between protasis and apodosis is in profile, and thus included in the scope of predication. The construal of the situation is thus "objective" rather than "subjective", again using Langacker's terminology (1999: 6; 1987; 1991a, 1991b: Chapter 12); that is, the situation is not primarily **presented** as conceptualized by the speaker. However, the speaker/conceptualizer, as part of the ground, is always present, and he/she necessarily takes a stance toward the validity of the causal or enabling connection between protasis and apodosis. Such a stance is, in Fillmore's (1990a, 1990b) terms, an "epistemic stance", and it simply remains implicit in the normal understanding of these constructions. This stance is, however, presented as being in the conceptual foreground (which Langacker calls the "objective scene" or "immediate scope") by epistemic conditionals, in whose interpretation it figures prominently

Since the epistemic domain is prominent in the meaning of an epistemic conditional, its sequence of verb forms is free from the constraints required by a predictive meaning. This greater freedom brings about the conventionalization of a number of special morphosyntactic forms for epistemic conditional constructions, which exhibit a variety of verb phrase form sequences that would normally be inadequate to symbolize a predictive meaning: future–future, past-present, present-present, perfect-perfect, etc. (Sweetser 1996; Fillmore 1990a, 1990b). The sentence under analysis exhibits one of those forms (perfect-perfect). This variety of forms results in a network of **conventional epistemic-conditional constructions**.

The highlighting and consequent prominence of the speaker's epistemic stance can be claimed to be due to metonymy. That is, the relation or proposition consisting in a CAUSAL CONNECTION BETWEEN A HYPOTHETICALLY SATISFIED CONDITION AND A RESULT activates its SALIENT CONCOMITANT SUBRELATION, namely the built-in epistemic connection between satisfied condition and result. This is a WHOLE FOR PART metonymy, because the assertion of the causal link between the satisfaction of a hypothetical condition and the production of the result implicitly includes a premise-conclusion connection between condition and result. Let us examine again the content conditional *If it is sunny, she'll go out.* A possible paraphrase capturing the speaker's implicit epistemic stance would be (with the words reflecting the epistemic stance in brackets) "If (it is a true fact that) the weather is sunny, then (I can conclude that) this fact will cause or enable her to decide to go out". In the adequate context, this internal metonymic mapping might guide in part the reading of even that example as an epistemic conditional if that had been the speaker's intent.

This metonymic explanation also accounts for the structural parallelism between predictive and epistemic conditionals, because in both types of constructions the basic elements are the same (speaker/conceptualizer and causal connection between condition and result). The metonymy simply activates the **roles** of premise and conclusion that are respectively implicit in every condition and every result in a conditional construction.

This metonymic explanation also helps us to understand the nondiscrete nature of the distinction between content or predictive conditionals and epistemic conditionals. The sentence under analysis in this section is a partial blend of prototypical predictive and prototypical epistemic conditionals. The presence of *ever* (*If you have ever driven*) adds a tinge of hypotheticality to the clause that approximates it to predictive conditionals, even though the sequence of verb forms decidedly favors an epistemic reading. A metonymic account is better suited to accommodate these cases, as it helps us to view the source (hypothetical condition-result in this case) and the target (premise-conclusion) as conceptually contiguous.

The role of metonymy in the meaning of the epistemic conditional construction is, thus, twofold: **to motivate** constructional meaning (it motivates the conventional epistemic meaning of the construction), and **to guide the inference** to this meaning. The inference is fairly routinized in most cases, but given that sometimes an epistemic conditional construction can be formally identical to a predictive conditional construction, especially in the protasis, some inferential work may occasionally be necessary. This inferential work would then be guided again by the same metonymy that gave rise to this meaning. Take the above epistemic reading of *If it is sunny, she'll go out.* The words in brackets represent the epistemic intent of the speaker. The metonymy would facilitate the recognition by the hearer/reader of this intent.

5 Summary and conclusions

Once reformulated so as to avoid having to assume the "perfect synonymy view", and in a way that also includes polysemy, inheritance and other sorts of connections across constructions, the notion of morphosyntactic alternation can become acceptable from a cognitivist-linguistic perspective.

Conceptual metonymy has been shown to be a crucial motivating factor in some instances of the three types of alternations discussed in this paper. Type 1 alternations motivated by metonymy seem to be normally instances of conversion or recategorization giving rise to polysemy-based homonymy (*interstate* adjective/noun; the historical alternation involved in the *–ful* suffix discussed above; and *the continental divide* as a descriptive NP vs. *The Continental Divide* as a phrasal name).

Metonymy-motivated type 2 alternations normally consist in certain types of lexical abbreviatory forms and ellipsis, like those discussed in this paper (see also Barcelona 2009).

For lack of space, only one detailed example of metonymy-motivated type 3 alternations has been presented in this paper (predictive/epistemic conditionals). Other metonymy-based instances of this type of alternation are the alternation descriptive noun phrase/bahuvrihi nouns (Spanish *cara dura* 'hard face' vs. *caradura* 'cheeky person'; Barcelona 2008) or the conversion of prototypical cardinal numeral determiners into cardinal numeral pronouns denoting age, as in *He was a young man of twenty* (Barcelona 2009). Type 3 alternations are not restricted to re-categorization, abbreviation or ellipsis: All types of extensional processes may be involved in it.

Notes

* The research reported in this paper has been funded in part by two grants awarded to projects BFF2003-07300 and FFI2008-04585/FILO by the Spanish government, Ministry of Science and Technology. I was the head researcher in both projects.

1. An exception are lexically-based approaches to alternations such as the one proposed by Levin (1993: 2), who claims that "diathesis alternations" are sometimes accompanied by changes of meaning. I am grateful to one of the reviewers for pointing out this fact to me.
2. Three excellent recent papers discussing the role of metaphor and metonymy in constructional alternations are Ruiz de Mendoza and Pérez Hernandez (2001) and Ruiz de Mendoza and Mairal (2007, this volume).
3. Taken from http://hikingincolorado.org/beth.html, last retrieved on 12 April 2010. The whole text is not reproduced here for lack of space.

4. "Nominal" designates here any noun-headed construction embedded in the overall NP. Cf. *The* [*man*] and *The* [*intelligent man*]. Both *man* and *intelligent man* are "nominals" in this sense.
5. For a full analysis of the role of metonymy in this joke, including the implicatures guiding its comprehension, see Barcelona (2003) and Barcelona (in preparation).

References

Barcelona, A. (1986) *El orden de constituyentes en inglés y en español.* Microfiche edition. Granada: University of Granada Press.

Barcelona, A. (2002a) Clarifying and applying the notions of metaphor and metonymy within cognitive linguistics: an update. In R. Dirven and R. Pörings (eds) *Metaphor and Metonymy in Comparison and Contrast* 207–277. Berlin: Mouton de Gruyter.

Barcelona, A. (2002b) On the ubiquity and multiple-level operation of metonymy. In B. Lewandowska-Tomaszczyk and K. Turewicz (eds) *Cognitive Linguistics Today* 207–224. Frankfurt: Peter Lang. [Lódz Studies in Language 6].

Barcelona, A. (2003) The case for a metonymic basis of pragmatic inferencing: Evidence from jokes and funny anecdotes. In K. Panther and L. Thornburg (eds) *Metonymy and Pragmatic Inferencing* 81–102. Amsterdam: Benjamins. [Pragmatics and Beyond New Series 113].

Barcelona, A. (2004) Metonymy behind grammar: The motivation of the seemingly "irregular" grammatical behavior of English paragon names. In G. Radden and K. Panther (eds) *Studies in Linguistic Motivation* 357–374. Berlin: Mouton de Gruyter.

Barcelona, A. (2005). The multilevel operation of metonymy in grammar and discourse, with particular attention to metonymic chains. In F. Ruiz de Mendoza Ibáñez and S. Peña Cervel (eds) *Cognitive Linguistics: Internal dynamics and interdisciplinary interaction* 313–352. Berlin: Mouton de Gruyter. [Cognitive Linguistics Research 32].

Barcelona, A. (2006). On the conceptual motivation of epistemic conditionals: metonymy or metaphor? In R. Benczes and S. Csabi (eds) *The Metaphors of Sixty Papers Presented on the Occasion of the 60th Birthday of Zoltán Kövecses*, 39–47. Budapest: School of English and American Studies, Eötvos Loránd University,

Barcelona, A. (2008). The interaction of metonymy and metaphor in the meaning and form of "bahuvrihi" compounds. *Annual Review of Cognitive Linguistics* 6: 208–281.

Barcelona, A. (2009) Motivation of construction meaning and form: The roles of metonymy and inference. In K. Panther, L. Thornburg and A. Barcelona (eds) *Metonymy and Metaphor in Grammar* 363–401. Amsterdam: Benjamins [Human Cognitive Processing 25].

Barcelona, A. (in preparation) *On the Pervasive Role of Metonymy in Constructional Meaning and Structure and in Discourse Comprehension: An empirical study from a cognitive-linguistic perspective.* (Provisional title.) Berlin: Mouton de Gruyter. [Cognitive Linguistics Research].

Benbow, T. J. (ed.) (2002) *Oxford English Dictionary.* Oxford: Oxford University Press. CD-ROM edition of Second Edition (1989), and of Additions Series (1993–1997)

Bierwiaczwonek, B. (2005) On formal metonymy. In K. Kosecki (ed.) *Perspectives on Metonymy: Proceedings of the international conference "Perspectives on Metonymy", held in Lódz, Poland, May 6–7, 2005* 43–67. Berlin: Peter Lang. [Lódz Studies in Language 14].

Cappelle, B. (n.d.) Particle placement and the case for "allostructions". Retrieved on 12 April 2010 from http://www.constructions-online.de/articles/specvol1/683/index_html.

Dancygier, B. (1993) Interpreting conditionals: time, knowledge and causation. *Journal of Pragmatics* 19(1): 403–404.

Fillmore, C. (1988) The mechanisms of construction grammar. In S. Axmaker, A. Jaisser and H. Singmaster (eds) *Proceedings of the Fourteenth Annual Meeting of the Berkeley Linguistics Society. General session and parasession on grammaticalization* 35–55. Berkeley, CA: Berkeley Linguistics Society.

Fillmore, C. (1990a) Epistemic stance and grammatical form in English conditional sentences. In M. Ziolkowski, M. Noske and K. Deaton (eds) *Papers from the Twenty-sixth Regional Meeting of the Chicago Linguistics Society* 137–162. Chicago, IL: Chicago Linguistics Society.

Fillmore, C. (1990b) The contribution of linguistics to language understanding. In A. Bocaz (ed.) *Proceedings of the First Symposium on Cognition, Language and Culture* 109–128. Santiago: Universidad de Chile.

Fillmore, C., Kay, P. and O'Connor, M. C. (1988). Regularity and idiomaticity in grammatical constructions: The case of *let alone. Language* 64(3): 501–538.

Goldberg, A. (1995) *Constructions: A construction grammar approach to argument structure.* Chicago, IL: University of Chicago Press.

Goldberg, A. (2002) Surface generalizations: An alternative to alternations. *Cognitive Linguistics* 13(4): 327–356.

Goldberg, A. (2006) *Constructions at Work: The nature of generalization in language.* Oxford: Oxford University Press.

Hornby, A. S (assisted by A. P. Cowie and A. C. Gimson) (1982) *Oxford Advanced Learner's Dictionary of Current English.* (16th revised impression of 3rd edition, 1974.) Oxford: Oxford University Press.

Kövecses, Z. and Radden, G. (1998) Metonymy: Developing a cognitive linguistic view. *Cognitive Linguistics* 9(1): 37–77.

Lakoff, G. (1987) *Women, Fire and Dangerous Things: What categories reveal about the mind.* Chicago, IL: University of Chicago Press.

Langacker, R. W. (1987) *Foundations of Cognitive Grammar, Vol. I: Theoretical prerequisites.* Stanford, CA: Stanford University Press.

Langacker, R. W. (1991a) *Foundations of Cognitive Grammar, Vol. II: Descriptive application.* Stanford, CA: Stanford University Press.

Langacker, R. W. (1991b) *Concept, Image and Symbol: The cognitive basis of grammar.* Berlin: Mouton de Gruyter.

Langacker, R. W. (1999) *Grammar and Conceptualization.* Berlin: Mouton de Gruyter.

Langacker, R. W. (2009). Metonymic grammar. In K Panther, L. Thornburg and A. Barcelona (eds) *Metonymy and Metaphor in Grammar* 45–71. Amsterdam: Benjamins [Human Cognitive Processing 25].

Levin, B. (1993) *English Verb Classes and Alternations: A preliminary investigation.* Chicago, IL: University of Chicago Press.

McKechnie, J. L. (ed.) (1978) *Webster's New Twentieth Century Dictionary of the English Language* (Second edition). Collins and World.

Michaelis, L. A. and Ruppenhofer, J. (2001) *Beyond Alternations: A constructional model of the German applicative pattern.* Stanford, CA: CSLI Publications.

Panther, K. and Thornburg, L. (2003) Introduction: On the nature of conceptual metonymy. In K. Panther and L. Thornburg (2003) (eds) *Metonymy and Pragmatic Inferencing* 1–20. Amsterdam: Benjamins. [Pragmatics and Beyond New Series 113].

Quirk, R., Greenbaum, S., Leech, E. and Svartvik, J. (1985) *A Comprehensive Grammar of the English Language.* London: Longman.

Radden, G. (2000) How metonymic are metaphors? In A. Barcelona (ed.) *Metaphor and Metonymy at the Crossroads: A cognitive perspective* 93–108. Berlin: Mouton de Gruyter. Reprinted with additions in R. Dirven and R. Pörings (eds) *Metaphor and Metonymy in Comparison and Contrast* 407–434. Berlin: Mouton de Gruyter.

Ruiz de Mendoza Ibáñez, F. J. and Pérez Hernández, L. (2001) Metonymy and the grammar: Motivation, constraints and interaction. *Language and Communication* 21(4): 321–357.

Ruiz de Mendoza Ibáñez, F. J. and Mairal Usón, R. (2007) High-level metaphor and metonymy in meaning construction. In G. Radden, K. M. Koepcke, Th. Berg and P. Siemund (eds) *Aspects of Meaning Construction* 33–49. Amsterdam: Benjamins.

Ruiz de Mendoza Ibáñez, F. J. and Mairal Usón, R. (this volume) Constraints on syntactic alternation: Lexical-constructional subsumption in the Lexical-Constructional Model.

Sweetser, E. (1990) *From Etymology to Pragmatics: Metaphorical and cultural aspects of semantic structure.* Cambridge: Cambridge University Press.

Sweetser, E. (1996). Mental spaces and the grammar of conditional constructions. In G. Fauconnier and E. Sweetser (eds) *Spaces, Worlds and Grammars* 318–333. Chicago, IL: University of Chicago Press.

13 A Functional Discourse Grammar approach to the *Swarm*-alternation as a case of conversion*

Carmen Portero Muñoz[a]

1 Introduction

In this paper I will deal with the *Swarm*-alternation as a case of conversion. I will contend that a functional approach of the kind proposed by García Velasco (2007, 2009) within the Functional Discourse Grammar framework (henceforth FDG; Hengeveld and Mackenzie 2008) may solve some of the shortcomings of former accounts of the locative alternation (of which the *Swarm*-alternation is regarded as a specific case).

This paper is organized as follows. In §2, after outlining the process of conversion in English, I will introduce the *Swarm*-alternation, showing that this type of verbal alternation can be treated as a case of conversion on semantic and syntactic grounds. In §3 I will first revise the traditional lexico-semantic account of the *Swarm*-alternation and then propose an alternative analysis using the FDG framework. In §4 I will summarize the main conclusions of this study.

2 The *Swarm*-alternation: A case of conversion

In this section the *Swarm*-alternation will be treated as a case of conversion. In §2.1 I will offer a brief outline of the process of conversion in English.

a Carmen Portero Muñoz is Lecturer in English Language and Linguistics at the University of Córdoba, Spain. E-mail: ff1pomuc@uco.es

In §2.2 I will introduce the *Swarm*-alternation. In §2.3 the semantic effects associated with this alternation will be summarized. Finally, in §2.4 I will show that the *Swarm*-alternation does not behave very differently from canonical cases of conversion as regards syntactic shift.

2.1 Conversion in English: A brief outline

Different definitions have been given of what conversion is. For Quirk *et al.* (1985: 1558), conversion is "a derivational process whereby an item is adapted or converted to a new word class without the addition of an affix". Thus, the verb *bottle* in (1a) is regarded as derived from the noun *bottle* in (1b) by a process of conversion.

(1) (a) I must *bottle* the wine.
    (b) I must put the wine in the *bottle.*

On the other hand, Bauer (1983: 227) defines conversion as "the use of a form which is regarded as being basically of one form class as though it were a member of a different form class, without any concomitant change of form".

Both Quirk *et al.* and Bauer mention the lack of morphological modification characterizing conversion, though Quirk *et al.* consider it as a "derivational process" while Bauer speaks of a different "use of a form". In both cases, however, reference is made to the syntactic shift process that takes place in cases of conversion.

Quirk *et al.* (1985: 1563–1565) point out that the notion of conversion can be extended to cases in which there is a change of secondary word class within the same major word category, for example, when non-gradable adjectives are used as gradable (e.g. He's more *English* than the English), when uncountable nouns are used as countable (e.g. two *coffees*), or when transitive verbs are used as intransitive (e.g. The door *closed* behind him). The use of some verbs in alternative constructions is, therefore, regarded as parallel to the major conversion processes. In spite of this, most scholars are reluctant to treat cases of secondary word class as conversion processes since the lack of syntactic shift tilts the scales in favour of a syntactic rather than derivational approach. Huddleston and Bauer (2002: 1640), for example, explicitly exclude verbal alternations from conversion:

> We do not, however, take a change of secondary class as a matter of conversion. Consider the verb *frighten,* for example: this is primarily a transitive verb (*I don't want to frighten you*), but it can also appear in intransitive constructions (*I don't frighten easily*). There is nevertheless

> no reason to say that intransitive *frighten* is a different word from transitive *frighten,* and hence no reason to say that this extension in the use of *frighten* is a matter of lexical word-formation, more specifically of conversion.

In the following section, contrary to most approaches that exclude verbal alternations from this process, the *Swarm*-alternation will be regarded as a case of conversion.

2.2 What is the *Swarm*-alternation?

The *Swarm*-alternation is illustrated by Levin's (1993: 54) examples in (2):

(2) (a) Bees are swarming in the garden. (Locative construction)
(b) The garden is swarming with bees. (*with*-variant)

This alternation is regarded as the intransitive version of the "locative alternation" with *spray/load* verbs, which can be seen in (3) (see Levin 1993: 50–55):[1]

(3) (a) Jack sprayed paint on the wall.
(b) Jack sprayed the wall with paint.

The *Swarm*-alternation involves the possible expression of the "*locatum* argument" (Clark and Clark 1979) or theme, i.e. the entity whose location changes (e.g. *bees* in (2)), and the "location argument" (e.g. *the garden* in (2)). The Locative construction expresses an activity or event located within an area. On the other hand, in the alternative *with*-variant,[2] the Location is promoted to subject position while the *Locatum* is expressed as a Displaced Theme in a prepositional phrase headed by *with.*

There is a high degree of consensus about the classes of verbs that undergo this alternation. There are three main classifications, by Salkoff (1983), Levin (1993) and Dowty (2000, 2001). In spite of some differences among their classes, at least they all seem to agree on a number of semantic sets. The main classes are summarized in (4):

(4) (a) **Motion verbs**
To move to/into/over a place in large quantities: *swarm, throng,* etc.
To flow (quickly) in large quantities: *teem, flow, overflow, pour, brim (over), stream,* etc.
To move in different specific ways (repeatedly, quickly, unsteadily...): *crawl, reel, bustle,* etc.
(b) **Light emission verbs:** *shine, blaze, twinkle, sparkle, glow, gleam,* etc.
(c) **Sound emission verbs:** *buzz, hum, bubble, burst,* etc.

There appear to be two semantically differentiated macro groups, denoting motion on the one hand, and some type of emission (of light or sound) on the other. This suggests the existence of some general property that the different sets share and which serves as a trigger to participate in the alternation. In this connection, Dowty (2000: 116) observes that there are features of a cognitive nature that alternating verbs share, like the fact that they all denote a type of action or process that is easy and quick to perceive. Thus, according to Dowty (2001: 177), it is easier to perceive a table crawling with ants than a cow grazing, and this difference is used to explain the difference between examples (a) and (b) in (5):

(5) (a) The table is crawling with ants.
(b) *The field is grazing with cattle.

This observation is corroborated by Fried (2005: 488–489) in his study of the *Swarm*-alternation in Czech. He points out that verbs participating in the alternation in Czech can all be classified as verbs of appearance in the sense of "appealing to the perceptual capacity of sentient beings".

2.3 Semantic change: The *with*-construction and the holistic effect

One of the aspects that has attracted most attention about this alternation is the holistic effect associated with the *with*-construction: whereas the Locative sentence implies simply that there are some entities in a place and they are moving about (in the case of motion verbs), in the *with*-variant the Location subject is described as "completely filled" with large numbers of the entities expressed in the *with*-phrase.

Anderson (1971), cited in Dowty (2001: 173), already noted this semantic difference and illustrated this observation with the examples in (6):

(6) (a) Bees are swarming in the garden, but most of the garden has no bees in it.
(b) # The garden is swarming with bees, but most of the garden has no bees in it.

In general, the Locative construction denotes an action (with verbs denoting movement) or activity (with verbs of light or sound emission), whereas the *with*-construction describes a state which is attributed to a place.

In Dowty's (2000: 122) view, what the *with*-construction does is to indicate that in view of the activity taking place in the location functioning as subject, we assign this location to some kind of category. Dowty (2001:

176) notes that the sentences in the alternative *with*-construction describe a situation where the perception of a certain kind of movement occurring simultaneously and repetitively throughout all parts of a place or space, is more salient than the perception of the individuals, which he refers to as "the Dynamic Texture Hypothesis" following Ray Jackendoff's suggestion (Dowty 2000: 123, 2001: 175): the *with*-variant "ascribes a texture to a location, cognitively analogous to visual or tactile textures of surfaces".

However, Dowty's Dynamic Texture Hypothesis does not capture the meaning of the *with*-construction completely. For example, Hoeksema (2009: 70) notes that in a sentence like *The book was littered with typos* the correct interpretation would be that "the book had a very high number of typos, regardless of their distribution across the book", rather than "the typos form an even pattern across the book, e.g. because there are ten on every page".

There are also examples of verbs which denote situations easy and quick to perceive and which do not participate in the alternation. Thus, Hoeksema (2009: 56) observes that it may be easier and faster in a real-world setting to perceive that cows are grazing than it is to find out whether a place is bubbling with cultural activities, though we still cannot say that **The meadow is grazing with cows.*

In view of these facts, Hoeksema (2009: 69) proposes a different core meaning for the *Swarm*-construction, and he points out that it can be regarded as a causative degree construction, in which "the object of *with* causes the subject to exhibit a high degree of some property by completely affecting it".

Hoeksema's observation is not quite satisfactory, however, since the completive feature is not the cause but rather the consequence of a high degree of some property that the meanings of all verbs participating in the alternation share. Thus, although most of these verbs are included in different semantic domains, the salience of some property related to these verbs (quantity of involved participants, repetition of the action, intensity of sound or light) makes them likely candidates to participate in the alternation. In fact, Dowty is aware of this when he says:

> the LS-form ascribes an abstract property (expressed by the predicate) to a Location (denoted by the subject NP): the property a place or space has when it is "characterized" by an activity taking place within it – that is, *when the extent, intensity, frequency and/or perceptual salience of this activity (which?) takes place there is sufficient* to categorize the Location in a way that is relevant for some purpose in the current discourse. (Dowty, 2000: 122; emphasis mine)

Therefore, the holistic meaning could just be explained as a consequence of a specific property of these verbs.

As there appear to be cognitive grounds for participation in the alternation, it is not surprising that the alternation is found in other languages as well. In the literature on the *Swarm*-alternation it has been reported that constructions parallel to the English Locative-Subject form are found in a number of Indo-European languages and, at least, some non-Indo-European languages (Dowty 2001: 175). For example, they have been noted in French (Boons *et al.* 1976), Czech (Fried 2005), Serbo-Croatian (Vasina 1995, cited in Dowty 2000), or Dutch (Hoeksema 2009).[3]

2.4 Syntactic shift: Adjectivization

In the previous section, I have revised the common assumption that the *with*-construction is semantically different. This semantic change can be seen in typical cases of conversion. However, as mentioned in §2.1, the difficulty in including verbal alternations among cases of conversion is in part due to the fact that no change of grammatical category is involved in going from the basic to the derived form. In this section, I will show that verbs participating in the *Swarm*-alternation are not very different from canonical cases of conversion as regards the syntactic shift process characterizing typical cases. More specifically, I will provide evidence to show that verbs in the *with*-construction display a similar behaviour to classical examples of conversion of verbs into adjectives, as those illustrated in (7) and (8):[4]

(7) An *escaped* prisoner.

(8) The *falling* prices.

In order to illustrate this point the focus will be on examples in which the alternating verbs are suffixed by *-ing* or *-ed.*[5] Salkoff (1983: 302, n. 7) points out that many of the alternating verbs in these cases may be considered adjectives and that they are listed as such in many dictionaries: *bustling, choking, flaming, glaring, teeming,* etc. However, he points out that it is still unclear whether a given *-ing* form should be considered as an adjective or a participle in these cases.

My suggestion is that verbs in the *with*-construction might be compared to adjectival forms. As mentioned in §2.3, verbs in the *with*-variant suffer a semantic change so that they denote a state attributed to a place instead of an action or activity. In short, verbs appear to suffer a process of deverbalization by losing some of their verbal properties. This process is made more evident in those cases in which the verb is suffixed with *-ing* or *-ed* since their adjectivization is formally manifested through the presence of suffixes used in the creation of adjectives and through the new possibilities of distribution, which are adjective-like. A number of findings resulting from the analysis of the BNC examples support this hypothesis.

First, the corpus search has revealed the attributive use of those *-ing* forms as adjectives premodifying nouns denoting either moving entities or a location, in correspondence with the use of the verb in the two constructions, as examples in (9) show:

(9) (a) Sometimes you heard a soft splash as a fish jumped for one of the **swarming insects**. (BNC, CDB 1831)
(b) Unnoticed in the corridors of that crowded and **swarming inn** sat three young people. (BNC, ANK 2041)

The possible use of these forms in predicative and attributive position can be taken as evidence of their adjectival nature (Quirk *et al.* 1985: 168–171; Pullum and Huddleston 2002: 540–541).

In addition to the *-ing* forms, in some verbs, like *throng,* most of the examples are passive (or semi-passive) participle forms following any form of *be* (example (10)):

(10) The canals are **thronged** with tour buses, the bridges festooned with banners. (BNC, CJA 126)

Though the grammatical category of these forms is not clear, at least it is clear that they are not active forms of the verb and they can be compared to adjectives.

A further indication of this is the possibility of these *-ed* and *-ing* forms to be combined with other adjectives, as the examples in (11) show:

(11) (a) The river was **fast-flowing, crystal-clear and swarming** with catfish and barbell. (BNC, H0A 1671)
(b) The streets are quite **narrow, and thronged** with people. (BNC, KAL 533)

The adjectival character of these forms is most clearly seen in examples like those in (12), in which they are coordinated with an adjective that is also postmodified by a prepositional phrase headed by *with,* showing semantic and syntactic parallelism:

(12) (a) A gorgeously dressed footman inspected her ticket, then bowed her into the hallway which was **brilliant with** candles **and thronged with** people. (BNC, CMP 1869)

(b) It is a city **alive with** an indefatigable passion for life in all its splendour –; **bustling with** cafés, shops and restaurants. (BNC, ECF 3974)

In addition, there are also examples where the *-ing/-ed* forms followed by *with* are premodified by a degree adverb, as (13) shows:

(13) Agnes waited for George, but when he stayed quiet, she said: "Harry, Neptune Court and its purlieus will be **absolutely crawling** with cops." (BNC, H86 1241)

It should also be noticed that with most of these cases it is possible to replace the copular verb with a lexical copular verb such as *seem*, which makes the *-ing* and *-ed* forms look more like adjectives than as passive participles, as shown in (14):

(14) The river **seemed** fast-flowing, crystal-clear and **swarming** with catfish and barbell. (BNC, H0A 1671)

Summing up, the data show that verbs in the *with*-construction of the *Swarm*-alternation have adjectival properties. The adjectival properties include the possibility of:

(a) Appearing in attributive and predicative position;
(b) Coordinating the participle with an adjective;
(c) Premodifying the participle with an intensifier;
(d) Replacing *be* by a lexical copular verb such as *seem.*

The closeness of alternating verbs to adjectival forms is made even more evident in the fact that Salkoff (1983: 298) introduced deverbal adjectives with copula *be* and pure un-derived adjectives in his study of the *Swarm*-alternation, as examples in (15) and (16) show:
Derived adjectives:

(15) The sky was **ablaze** with stars. (Salkoff 1983: 304)

Pure non-derived adjectives:

(16) The story is **rich** with humour. (Salkoff 1983: 298)

Therefore, it can be seen that these adjectival uses of both the *-ing* and the *-ed* forms are parallel to clear cases of adjectives, both deverbal and basic, which are used in the same construction. These varied forms share a central feature: they all denote a property predicated of a Location (Rowlands 2002).

In view of these facts, it would appear that verbs in the alternating construction have lost (some of) their verbal properties. In fact, in some cases (for example, motion verbs) no action or activity is denoted but rather what is denoted is a state which is attributed to a place. This semantic process of deverbalization also exists when the verb appears in the simple form, though it is more clearly manifested when the verb is suffixed by *-ing* or *-ed,* since in these cases the loss of verbal properties is formally manifested in their adjective-like behaviour. Therefore, these cases are at least partially comparable to typical cases of conversion where a change of grammatical category is produced.

3 Theoretical approaches to the *Swarm*-alternation

Traditional approaches to the *Swarm*-alternation have focused on the semantic change that verbs participating in the alternation undergo and have explained it as a morphological process by means of lexical rules (Dowty 2000, 2001). An example of this derivational view is provided by Levin and Rappaport Hovav's (1998) semantic decomposition approach within lexical semantics. This derivational approach will be revised in §3.1.

However, if we consider the partial syntactic shift process that alternating verbs undergo, the *Swarm*-alternation might be characterized as a syntactic, though semantically constrained, process, that is, as "the use of a word with a given syntactic category in a syntactic position that it normally does not occupy, taking on the properties of those items that usually occupy that position" (Plag 2003: 214). A functional approach of the kind proposed by García Velasco (2007, 2009) within the FDG framework may solve some of the shortcomings of former accounts of the locative alternation (of which the *swarm*-form is regarded as the intransitive variant). This is possible in the context of FDG given the separation of frames and lexemes which the theory proposes (García Velasco and Hengeveld 2002). This alternative approach will be the topic of §3.2.

3.1 Derivational approach

Dowty (2000: 121; 2001: 176) regards forms in the *with*-variant as cases of lexical derivation captured by means of a lexical rule, which he informally states as follows:

> For any verb input *A*, the rule yields a new verb (or "new verbal construction") with the same phonological form as before, with new

> syntactic subcategorization "*y A* with *x*" (i.e. subject and *with*-phrase complement), and with a new meaning, which describes the property a location *y* has when the kind of activity denoted by the original *A* is being performed in most/all (very small) subparts of location *y*, by some instance of *x* in each case; that is, the original property *A* is distributed throughout all small regions of *y*. (Dowty, 2001: 176)

Following this rule, verbs in the Agent-Subject form would be the input and the corresponding verbs in the Location-Subject form, suffering both syntactic valence and meaning change, would be the output.

In spite of mentioning the syntactic valence change, Dowty relies on the semantic side of the process to draw his own conclusion on the treatment of the *Swarm*-alternation. He does not, however, use any specific theory but only makes a theoretical claim. A theoretical framework which has been used to account for the locative alternation is the theory of lexical-semantics.

Within lexical semantics the relation between the different uses of some verbs illustrating the change of secondary word class can be explained by drawing a distinction between two sorts of operation in the lexico-semantic/syntax interface: "morpholexical operations" and "morphosyntactic operations" (Sadler and Spencer 1998: 208–212).

"Morpholexical operations" are meaning-changing operations and semantically constrained, while "morphosyntactic operations" are meaning-preserving and semantically unconstrained operations. Morpholexical operations are said to create new Lexico-Conceptual Structures (henceforth LCSs), new semantic representations, each associated with its own Predicate Argument Structure (PAS). On the other hand, morphosyntactic operations intervene between PASs and syntactic structures, resulting in a multiplicity of syntactic realizations for one and the same argument structure.

This distinction allows us to tell cases of word-formation apart from cases which must be accounted for within syntax, like the passive construction. As shown in §2.3, the *Swarm*-alternation is an example of a meaning-changing and semantically constrained operation. Therefore, it is a morpholexical operation. In this approach, the verb in the *with*-construction should be described by means of a word-formation rule that takes an intransitive verb as input and alters its LCS. Since the LCS of verbs in the *with*-construction contains that of verbs in the Locative construction, verbs found in the Locative construction would be the input to this rule while those found in the *with*-construction would be the output.

Possible LCSs representations for the two variants of the verb *swarm* are given in (17) in a similar fashion to Levin and Rappaport Hovav's (1998: 261) proposal for the *Load*-alternation within lexical semantics:

(17) (a) Locative [x ACT at y] [*SWARM*]
(b) *With* [y BE]$_{\text{STATE}}$ BY MEANS OF [x ACT at y] [*SWARM*]

Crucially, this approach implies that there are two verbs, one of which is derived from the other by means of a lexical rule: the *with*-variant is an extension of the locative variant, since (a) is embedded under BY MEANS OF in (b). As in Dowty's proposal, emphasis is put on the semantic change suffered in the LCS of these verbs, which involves different lexical semantic templates with a shared constant.

However, there are some problems with this approach as, in general, with derivational accounts of the *Swarm*-alternation. As noted by Dowty, the process is relatively arbitrary as there are many lexical gaps and the existence of more than one pattern for these verbs is rather unpredictable. This makes the use of rules rather questionable. In addition, derivational approaches like Levin and Rappaport Hovav's semantic decomposition approach only focus on the description of the semantic change in the output of the rule, either in terms of a change in LCS or making reference to the completion feature of derived verbs. However, they do not provide a characterization of the semantic or pragmatic constraints licensing the alternation with some verbs but not others, which is key in determining participation in this alternation. In connection with this, since the constraints affecting this alternation are not the type of semantic information that is usually represented in LCS but are cognitive in nature, it is difficult to see how such constraints could be formalized in conventional word formation rules. Dowty (2000: 121) is implicitly aware of this problem when he acknowledges that the process could be compared to processes of lexical semantic extension (Numberg 1995) and metaphor.

The last problem is related to the direction of derivation. It is simply assumed that the direction of derivation goes from the Locative construction to the *with*-construction since the LCS of verbs in this construction presupposes that of verbs in the first construction, and also maybe by analogy with the *Load*-alternation, which is marked in some languages in the second construction. However, there is no mark on the verb in the *Swarm*-alternation to corroborate this hypothesis. In addition to this, the *with*-construction appears to be more frequent with some verbs. Thus, metaphorical cases seem to occur only in the *with*-construction (e.g. *John's voice was dripping with sarcasm* vs **Sarcasm was dripping from John's voice*).

3.2 Non-derivational approach: Functional Discourse Grammar

As a case of conversion, the *Swarm*-alternation is subjected to the two opposite views (derivational or syntactic) used to deal with this process. For those focusing on the syntactic side of the alternation, the process would rather be treated as conventionalized grammatical patterns that accommodate the "use of existing words in syntactic environments where they have not previously entered" (Salkoff 1983: 288), therefore modifying their syntactic and semantic features in systematic ways. This means that no derivation takes place and that there are no basic and derived lexemes but only a unique lexeme used in two different constructions. Consequently, the process will be dealt with within syntax.

In this section, I will show how a functionalist theory like FDG, as developed in García Velasco (2007, 2009), provides an adequate framework for this syntactic approach to the *Swarm*-alternation.

The FDG model is a structural-functional theory of language that is designed as the Grammatical Component of a wider theory of verbal interaction. Its defining characteristics can be summarized as follows: (a) FDG has a top-down organization; (b) FDG takes the Discourse Act rather than the sentence as its basic unit of analysis; (c) FDG contains an Interpersonal Level, which captures all distinctions related to the interaction between Speaker and Addressee, a Representational Level, which deals with the semantic aspects of a linguistic unit, a Morphosyntactic Level, which is concerned with the structural aspects of a linguistic unit, and a Phonological Level, which contains both the segmental and the suprasegmental phonological representation of an Utterance; and (d) FDG is connected to Conceptual, Contextual, and Output Components.

Within the top-down organization of the grammar, pragmatics governs semantics, pragmatics and semantics govern morphosyntax, and pragmatics, semantics and morphosyntax govern phonology. Thus, in the prelinguistic Conceptual Component a communicative intention and the corresponding mental representations are relevant. The operation of Formulation translates these conceptual representations into pragmatic and semantic representations at the Interpersonal and the Representational Levels respectively. The configurations at the Interpersonal and the Representational Levels are translated into a morphosyntactic structure at the Morphosyntactic Level through the operation of Morphosyntactic Encoding. The structures at the Interpersonal, Representational and Morphosyntactic Levels are translated into a phonological structure at the Phonological Level.

Due to space limitations I will only refer to those aspects of the model which are specifically involved in the topic under analysis. More specifically, I will introduce the distinction between the operations of Formulation and Encoding, which take place at the Representational and Morphosyntactic Levels, respectively, in order to deal with a relevant aspect of the Representational Level, namely the separation between frames and lexemes. In addition, I will refer to the distinction between Lexemes and Words, which are located in each of these levels, respectively. For a thorough exposition of FDG I refer the reader to Hengeveld and Mackenzie (2008).

As regards the functions of Formulation and Encoding, Formulation concerns the rules that determine what constitute valid underlying pragmatic and semantic representations in a language. On the other hand, Encoding concerns the rules that convert these pragmatic and semantic representations into morphosyntactic and phonological ones. The operation of Formulation involves the selection of appropriate frames for the Interpersonal and Representational Levels, the insertion of appropriate lexemes into these frames, and the application of operators which represent the grammatical distinctions required. On the other hand, Encoding involves the selection of appropriate templates for the Morphosyntactic and Phonological Levels, the insertion of grammatical morphemes, and the application of operators in order to articulate the output of the grammar.

At the Representational Level frames capture such aspects as quantitative and qualitative valency, the combinations of semantic categories allowed (like Properties (f_2), Individuals (x), Locations (l), Times (t), etc.), and possible modification structures. Lexemes are independent units that have to be associated with the aforementioned frames. This separation of lexemes and frames is a key feature of FDG offering a possible solution to some of the shortcomings of the lexical semantics approach (see García Velasco and Hengeveld 2002).

As lexemes are separated from their frames, they are linked to (or inserted into) predication frames via abstract meaning definitions with which they are provided. Abstract meaning definitions specify the syntactically relevant information accounting for the lexeme's distributional properties. Therefore, they should contain the information necessary to link the lexeme to an appropriate predication frame. These definitions use basic ontological categories of a conceptual nature, in a similar way to Jackendoff (1990). The abstract meaning definitions of lexemes should specify the ontological category they designate and the number of participants required. The role of each participant in the predication can also be extracted from the lexeme's abstract meaning definition since semantic functions can be defined on the basis of the position which a variable takes in a given abstract meaning definition.

Different predication frames are proposed corresponding roughly to the different syntactic categories. Thus, García Velasco and Hengeveld (2002: 109) point out that the general inventory of predication frames potentially relevant to languages should contain at least frames for heads and modifiers of predicate phrases and for heads and modifiers of term phrases, frames for modifiers of predications and propositions, and frames for term predicates.

By way of illustration, the authors consider the lexeme *open.* A possible abstract meaning definition of this lexeme is shown in (18):

(18) *Open* [V]
$[f_1$: [CAUSE (x_1) [BECOME **open'** (x_2)]]]

This definition expresses the fact that the lexeme *open* designates a relation (as represented by the "f" variable) between two entities (represented by the "x" variables). On the basis of the information contained in this definition, the lexeme *open* may be linked to the predication frame proposed for heads of predicate phrases, more specifically one for transitive, [+control], [+dynamic] predicates, with the result shown in (19):[6]

(19) $(T_1$: $(f_1$: open [V] $(f_1))$ $(T_1))$ $(R_1$: $(x_1)_{Ag}$ $(R_1))$ $(R_2$: $(x_2)_{Go}$ $(R_2))$[7]

This frame would be used to account for sentences like (20):

(20) Sheila opened the door.

In the implementation of the grammar the frames are selected first and then lexemes are inserted. However, García Velasco and Hengeveld contend that the linking of lexemes to frames cannot be developed on a one-to-one basis, but that lexemes may take different frames if they have more than one meaning definition. For Hengeveld and Mackenzie (2008: 19), this provides a natural framework for understanding the phenomenon of coercion, through which lexemes that are strongly associated with a given frame can be forced into a frame that is usually associated with lexemes of a different meaning class. Thus, the lexeme *open* has another meaning definition, given in (21):

(21) *Open* [V]
$[f_1$: [BECOME (x_1) **open'** (x_1)]]

In this case, the information contained in this definition motivates the linking of this lexeme to an intransitive frame, more specifically one for [–control], [+dynamic] States of Affairs, as in (22):

(22) (T_1: (f_1: *open* [V] (f_1)) (T_1)) (R_1: $(x_1)_{Pat}$ (R_1))

This would account for sentences like (23):

(23) The door opened.

In the case of *swarm* and similar verbs an abstract meaning definition like (24) could be postulated:

(24) *Swarm* [V]
[f_1: [DO (x_1) at y **swarm'** (x_1)]]

This definition expresses that the lexeme *swarm* designates a relation (as represented by the "f" variable") such that an entity (represented by x_1) moves in a place (represented by y).

The fact that *swarm* is characterized as "event-denoting" and the presence of these variables will guide towards the linking of this lexeme to an eventive frame, more specifically an intransitive one, with the result shown in (25):[8]

(25) (T_1: (f_1: *swarm* [V] (f_1)) (T_1)) (R_1: $(x_1)_{Mover}$ (R_1))

This would explain the use of *swarm* in sentences like (26):

(26) The flies swarmed (in the room).

On the other hand, as mentioned in §2.4, verbs in the alternating construction have lost (some of) their verbal properties. In fact, in some cases (for example, motion verbs) no action or activity is denoted but rather what is denoted is a state which is attributed to a place. Therefore, I suggested that verbs in the alternative *with*-construction might be compared to adjectival forms. In these cases, a possible abstract meaning definition would be (27):

(27) [f_1: [[y BE]$_{STATE}$ BY MEANS OF [DO (x_1) at y **swarm'** (x_1)]]

The information available in this definition motivates the selection of the predication frame proposed for modifiers of a term phrase, as (28) shows:

(28) (R_1: (t_1: – $(t_1)_ø$: (f_1: ♦ (f_1)) $(t_1)_ø$ (R_1))

The sentence in (29) would illustrate this use of *swarm*:

(29) The river seemed crystal-clear and swarming with catfish.

In spite of the fact that verbs are not only found in the *be* + *-ed* or *-ing* forms (that is, there are also examples like *The river swarmed with catfish*), it could be argued that there are different degrees of adjectivization of these verbs and cases in the *-ed* or *-ing* forms show the highest degree, being adapted formally to fit in an adjective slot, as shown in §2.4.

At this point comes into play the second relevant FDG distinction mentioned above, that between Lexemes and Words (Hengeveld and Mackenzie 2008). Lexemes are operative at the Representational Level, while Words are operative at the Morphosyntactic Level. Processes of derivation within FDG can produce new lexemes in some cases and new words in others. On the one hand, operations that adapt the form of a lexeme that has been inserted into an underlying semantic slot it was not designed to occupy will result in new word forms rather than new lexemes. Some of the examples that the authors mention are participle formation to show embedding as a modifier, nominalization to show embedding in a referential slot or the use of transitive verbs as intransitive. They point out that, as long as these processes are productive and predictable, they will be dealt with in the morphosyntactic encoder as processes of preparing lexemes for morphosyntax. On the other hand, operations that do more than just adapt a lexeme to an environment it was not designed for, but add independent aspects of meaning are dealt with in the lexicon, as processes extending the set of primitives, and not in the grammar.

However, the dividing line between processes that only adapt existing lexemes and those that create new ones is not clear cut. Thus, later on in the book, when the authors explain the function of dummies, they give the example in (30) (Hengeveld and Mackenzie 2008: 413):

(30) They American-ize-d Belgium.

The authors suggest that examples like this one can be dealt with in the morphosyntactic encoder as processes that apply when lexemes by themselves are not suitable for use in certain underlying functions to acquire the word form required for that function. However, in this specific case, the adjective *American* is causativized as a result of being introduced in a two-place predication frame. Therefore, if semantic import is to be taken as a relevant feature for the distinction between word-creating and lexeme-creating processes, it is not clear whether cases like this one should be considered as processes just adapting existing lexemes (see also García Velasco, this volume).

It could be argued that the distinction between lexeme-creating and word-creating processes is gradual: the more productive and predictable a process is the more likely it is to be regarded as the creation of a new word, while completely idiosyncratic or isolated processes will be dealt with within the lexicon. However, there are processes in a middle grey area, that is, processes that are partially productive or predictable but that are subjected to regularities. In my view, *swarm* and similar verbs are among these cases and they could also be regarded as lexemes adapted to appear in alternative distributions. The semantic import of the *swarm* cases goes beyond the adaptation of the lexeme to a new slot. However, they are not very different from example (30).

Therefore, it could be stated that it is not a new lexeme that is created but a different word, which appears in a new slot and which in some cases is further adapted for this purpose by acquiring adjectival properties.

The postulation of the separation between lexemes and predication frames which makes it possible the lexeme's insertion in two different predication frames overcomes one of the most serious problems concerning this alternation that derivational approaches are unable to account for. As pointed out before, though there are acknowledged regularities, the process is relatively arbitrary. Therefore, the postulation of rules seems an inadequate solution to account for this process. By explaining alternations as the insertion of a lexeme in different predication frames, resorting to lexical rules is avoided.

However, the postulation of abstract meaning definitions which trigger the lexeme's insertion in different frames poses some problems. For one thing, a problem is related to the type of information represented in these definitions and the type of information required to account for verbal alternations. These definitions are supposed to capture only those semantic aspects responsible for the syntactic behaviour of lexemes, basic specifications like the fact that a given lexical item denotes an event or a thing, or the number of participants involved. However, it appears that other types of knowledge are required. For example, in the case of the *swarm* verbs, Dowty (2000: 116) observes that there are features of a cognitive nature that alternating verbs share, as mentioned in §2.2. He notes that motion verbs like *move, fly, walk, swim* fail to alternate because they are "bland" verbs, that is, they are the most semantically "unmarked" of motion verbs, which contribute hardly any information about the manner of movement. This claim is also advanced by Iwata (2005: 380) in his study of the locative alternation. (See also García Velasco, this volume, for a similar conclusion as regards the causative/inchoative alternation.)

Summing up, if abstract meaning definitions should contain syntactically relevant information, and if pragmatic information is responsible for the participation of verbs in alternative constructions, the unavoidable consequence of this is that pragmatic information should be incorporated into abstract meaning definitions, as García Velasco (2007: 183) contends. More specifically for the purpose of the present paper, as part of the information required to decide whether a verb participates in the *Swarm*-

alternation is pragmatic in nature, the abstract meaning definition for *swarm* and similar verbs would have to include specifications of a pragmatic nature.

However, García Velasco (2007) does not make explicit whether this pragmatic information should be part of a revised version of FDG abstract meaning definitions or just accessed somehow from the Conceptual component. My suggestion is that we should have *enriched* (complex) abstract meaning definitions, which would include different aspects of a verb meaning responsible for its use in different constructions, depending on which aspect of the meaning is profiled. Following a proposal by Boas (2000: 284–285, cited in Iwata 2005: 381), abstract meaning definitions would include two types of information: "on-stage information", accounting for the type of the event denoted or the number of participants involved, which is the information generally regarded as encoded verb meanings, and "off-stage" information, inferred from "on-stage" information thanks to our world knowledge, which is accessible from the Conceptual component. Thus, the "on-stage" information of *swarm* specifies movement in a location alone, but the "off-stage" information tells us that the swarming activity is likely to lead to the location being full. This could be represented as shown in (31):

(31) [DO ($^{q}x_1$) at y **swarm'**]
↓
Conceptual information: if a large amount of entities (represented by $^{q}x_1$) move in a place the movement is perceptually salient, causing the place to be full.
↓
thereby [y BE full]$_{STATE}$

These definitions would be similar to Fillmore's frame semantic scenes. The meaning of *swarm* would be represented as shown in (32):

(32) [f_1: [DO ($^{q}x_1$) at y **swarm'** (x_1)] *whereby* [y BE full]$_{STATE}$]

Abstract meaning definitions would then be complex structures which contain different aspects represented by different thematic cores: a thematic core representing the ontological category the lexeme designates and the number of participants required and a different thematic core inferred from the basic one thanks to information of a pragmatic nature. These thematic cores could be profiled separately resulting in compatibility with different predication frames. Verbs participating in the alternation can thus be regarded as verbs with a complex meaning which can be used in different predication frames depending on the thematic core which is profiled. It could be argued that the new meaning acquired is just the result of profiling a different facet of the meaning of one and the same lexeme. Therefore, a different word is created, displaying new distributional properties and, in some cases, adapted for this purpose by acquiring adjectival features.

The proposal of enriched abstract meaning definitions overcomes the second serious problem related to FDG's abstract meaning definitions: the postulation of *two* different abstract meaning definitions for one lexeme. If each lexeme is provided with its own abstract meaning definition, this would imply accepting the existence of two different (though related) lexemes in alternative constructions, one of which has been derived from the most basic one. Therefore, the suggestion that abstract meaning definitions should be enriched so as to incorporate pragmatic information not only is adequate to account for the pragmatic constraints on participation in verbal alternations but also to avoid an implicit derivational view of the process.

As compared with lexical semantics, no lexical rules are postulated since FDG does not presuppose any kind of derivation from a basic form. In this way, FDG can avoid the difficulties posed by the existence of lexical gaps and the problem of the direction of derivation. On the other hand, the postulation of enriched abstract meaning definitions represents an attempt to handle the pragmatic constraints that alternating verbs are subjected to.

Summing up, FDG offers a possible way out of some of the traditional problems concerning the approaches to verbal alternations. This model postulates a separation between lexemes and the predication frames where they are used. It proposes a linking mechanism by means of abstract meaning definitions associated to each lexeme. The proposal presented in this paper is that the meaning of verbs participating in the *Swarm*-alternation can be represented by using enriched abstract meaning definitions which contain a thematic core representing the ontological category they designate and the number of participants required and a different thematic core inferred from the basic one thanks to information of a pragmatic nature. Verbs participating in the alternation can thus be regarded as verbs with a complex meaning which can be used in different predication frames depending on the thematic core which is profiled.

4 Conclusion

In this paper I have argued that the *Swarm*-alternation can be treated as a case of conversion on both semantic and syntactic grounds. It has been shown that, similarly to typical cases, lexemes participating in this alternation exhibit semantic change and different distributional properties in the two constructions involved, i.e. the Locative construction and the *with*-variant.

In the second part of this paper I have outlined the traditional derivational account of the *Swarm*-alternation by means of a word-formation rule that takes an intransitive verb as input and alters its LCS within lexical semantics. On the other hand, I have contended that a theory like FDG can more adequately handle the *Swarm*-alternation without resorting to lexical rules. FDG can focus on the syntactic side of the alternation, i.e. the flexibility of lexemes appearing in two different constructions, by postulating a separation of predication frames and lexemes. Thanks to this separation and to the inclusion of a Conceptual component, FDG offers some advantages over lexical semantics, being able as it is to account for a dynamic conception of lexical meaning.

Notes

* The present research has been conducted within the framework of the project FFI 2008-04585/FILO, funded by the Spanish Ministry of Education and Innovation. I wish to thank two anonymous reviewers, and especially Christopher Butler and Daniel García Velasco for their valuable comments on an earlier version of this paper.

1. The *Swarm*-alternation has been explicitly linked to the *Spray/Load*-alternation by a number of different researchers, who suggest that they are aspects of the same Locative alternation (see, for example, Levin 1993: 53–55). In this kind of analysis the *swarm* verbs are treated as unaccusatives, meaning that their Locative subject is an underlying object which corresponds to the *spray/load* object in the *with*-variant.
2. Dowty (2000, 2001) refers to the Locative construction and the *with*-variant as the "A(gent)-Subject form" and the "L(ocation)-Subject" form, respectively.
3. An interesting fact of Dutch is that there is a large number of verbs ending in *-eren, -elen,* which are traditionally referred to as frequentatives and intensives (Hoeksema 2008: 60), which corroborates the hypothesis that

verbs participating in the alternation share a salient property which makes them likely candidates not only in English but also in Dutch.

4. For a discussion of this topic see Quirk *et al.* (1985: 168) and Pullum and Huddleston (2002: 540–541).
5. The examples provided are taken from the World Edition of the British National Corpus (henceforth BNC). In order to limit the scope of the analysis, I have used the free online version, which provides a maximum of 50 examples. It is important to emphasize that no extensive use will be made of statistical data to describe the behaviour of alternating verbs. Instead, relevant examples have been chosen to illustrate the points made.
6. Ideas and formalism have moved on considerably in the six years between the publication of García Velasco and Hengeveld (2002) and Hengeveld and Mackenzie (2008). Nevertheless, I have drawn on García Velasco and Hengeveld (2002) for the present discussion since the linking of lexemes to frames via abstract meaning definitions is not specifically dealt with in Hengeveld and Mackenzie (2008). In fact, the authors refer to García Velasco and Hengeveld (2002) for a discussion of this topic (Hengeveld and Mackenzie 2008: 19). For an update of predication frames, see Hengeveld and Mackenzie (2008: 181–215).
7. The formalism used in defining these predication frames shows a basic distinction between units at the interpersonal level, which are defined in terms of their function in communication (represented by variables in capitals), and units at the representational level, which are defined in terms of the entity type they represent (represented by variables in lower case) (García Velasco and Hengeveld 2002: 109). The variables T and R represent the communicative functions of ascription and reference, respectively, whereas the variables x_1 and x_2 represent individuals.
8. The role of each participant in the predication can be obtained from the lexeme's abstract definition. Thus, the argument of a BE function will be assigned the role of Mover, L-Emitter (i.e. Light Emitter) and S-Emitter (i.e. Sound Emitter) in the case of verbs like *swarm, sparkle* and *buzz,* respectively (see Van Valin and LaPolla 1997: 115).

References

Anderson, S. (1971) The role of deep structure in semantic interpretation. *Foundations of Language* 7(3): 387–396.

Bauer, L. (1983) *English Word-formation.* Cambridge: Cambridge University Press.

Boas, H. C. (2000) *Resultative Constructions in English and German.* Ph.D. dissertation. University of North Carolina at Chapel Hill.

Boons, J. P., Guillet, A. and Leclère, C. (1976) *La structure des phrases simples en francais: Constructions intransitives.* Genève: Droz.
Clark, E. and Clark, H. (1979) When nouns surface as verbs. *Language* 55(4): 767–811.
Dowty, D. R. (2000) "The garden swarms with bees" and the fallacy of "argument alternation". In Y. Ravin and C. Leacock (eds) *Polysemy: theoretical and computational approaches* 111–128. Oxford: Oxford University Press.
Dowty, D. R. (2001) The semantic asymmetry of "argument alternations" (and why it matters). In G. van der Meer and A. G. ter Meulen (eds) *Making Sense: from lexeme to discourse* 171–186. Groningen: Centre for Language and Cognition. [Groninger Arbeiten zur germanistischen Linguistik 44].
Fried, M. (2005) A frame-based approach to case alternations: The *swarm*-class verbs in Czech. *Cognitive Linguistics* 16(3): 475–512.
García Velasco, D. and Hengeveld, K. (2002) Do we need predicate frames? In R. Mairal Usón and M. J. Pérez Quintero (eds) *New Perspectives on Argument Structure in Functional Grammar* 95–123. Berlin: Mouton de Gruyter.
García Velasco, D. (2007) Lexical competence and Functional Discourse Grammar. *Alfa. Revista de Lingüística* 51(2): 165–187.
García Velasco, D. (2009) Conversion in English and its implications for Functional Discourse Grammar. *Lingua* 119(8): 1164–1185.
García Velasco, D. (this volume) The causative/inchoative alternation in Functional Discourse Grammar.
Hengeveld, K. and Mackenzie, J. L. (2008) *Functional Discourse Grammar: A typologically-oriented theory of language structure.* Oxford: Oxford University Press.
Hoeksema, J. (2009) The *swarm* alternation revisited. In E. Hinrichs and J. Nerbonne (eds) *Theory and Evidence in Semantics* 53–81. Chicago, IL: University of Chicago Press.
Huddleston, R. and Bauer, L. (2002) Lexical Word formation. In R. Huddleston and G. K. Pullum (eds) *The Cambridge Grammar of the English Language* 1621–1721. Cambridge: Cambridge University Press.
Iwata, S. (2005) Locative alternation and two levels of verb meaning. *Cognitive Linguistics* 16(2): 355–407.
Jackendoff, R. (1990) *Semantic Structures.* Cambridge, MA: The MIT Press.
Levin, B. (1993) *English Verb Classes and Alternations: A preliminary investigation.* Chicago, IL: University of Chicago Press.
Levin, B. and Rappaport Hovav, M. (1998) Morphology and lexical semantics. In A. Spencer and A. M. Zwicky (eds) (1998) *Handbook of Morphology* 248–271. Oxford: Blackwell.
Numberg, G. (1995) Transfers of meaning. *Journal of Semantics* 12(2): 109–32.
Plag, I. (2003) *Word-formation in English.* Cambridge: Cambridge University Press.
Pullum, G. K. and Huddleston, R. (2002) Adjectives and adverbs. In R. Huddleston and G. K. Pullum (eds) *The Cambridge Grammar of the English Language* 525–595. Cambridge: Cambridge University Press.

Quirk, R., Greenbaum, S., Leech, G. and Svartvik, J. (1985) *A Comprehensive Grammar of the English Language*. London: Longman.

Rowlands, R. C. (2002) *Swarming with Bees: Property predication and the* swarm *alternation*. Ph.D. dissertation. University of Canterbury.

Sadler, L. and Spencer, A. (1998) Morphology and argument structure. In A. Spencer and A. M. Zwicky (eds) (1998) *Handbook of Morphology* 206–212. Oxford: Blackwell.

Salkoff, M. (1983) The bees are swarming in the garden: A systematic synchronic study of productivity. *Language* 59(2): 288–346.

Van Valin, R. D. and LaPolla, R. (1997) *Syntax: Structure, meaning and function*. Cambridge: Cambridge University Press.

Vasina, S. (1995) The *Swarm*-alternation and argument structure in Serbo-Croatian. Unpublished paper: Ohio State University.

14 Morphological relatedness and zero alternation in Old English*

Javier Martín Arista[a]

1 Introduction

The function of derivational morphology is to enlarge the lexicon in order to meet communicative needs (Štekauer 2005a: 207; 2005b: 45). As a general rule, word-formation changes, restricts or enlarges the meaning of the base of derivation by means of some sort of formal modification, in such a way that the change of meaning undergone by the base has a formal counterpart and, conversely, the difference in form between base and derivative motivates the variation of meaning existing between the original lexeme and the newly coined one. There are two areas, however, in which an irregular association or *mismatch* (Francis and Michaelis 2003: 2) appears between form and meaning, in the sense that either the change of meaning results from no change of form or the change of form triggers no meaning change. This article engages with this mismatch, that is, it is concerned with morphological contrast or, more specifically, with the presence and the absence of formal contrast between morphologically related words. The topic has been and still is at the heart of the linguistic debate, both at the theoretical and the descriptive levels. Theoretically speaking, for the structural and the structural-functional traditions the relationship between form and function, mediated by the notion of motivation, has been of paramount importance for linguistic organization and description.[1] On the descriptive side, as Beard and Volpe (2005: 190) point out, "for centuries linguists struggled with a set of morphological enigmas: [...] zero morphemes [...] empty morphemes [...] and morphological asymmetry".

For this aim, I have chosen Old English as the language of analysis and discussion, in the belief that morphological theory requires rich and varied

a Javier Martín Arista is Senior Lecturer in English at the University of La Rioja, Spain. E-mail: javier.martin@unirioja.es morphological data. Although Present-day English also has instances of zero derivation, such as *book* (noun) > *book* (verb), and empty morph, like *lexicographic* > *lexicographical,* Old English has been preferred for this piece of research for two reasons. First, its morphology is more generalized than that of Present-day English. Old English displays full inflection in the major lexical classes of the noun, adjective and verb, as well as in the minor lexical class of the pronoun (while the adverb has comparative and superlative grade forms). And, second, in Old English, as in the other old Germanic languages, there is a strong tendency to create new lexemes by derivational means rather than borrowing them from other languages, as Present-day English often does. This homogeneous nature of the Old English lexicon, which is purely Germanic, has an important consequence for word-formation, which Kastovsky explains in the following terms:

> The vocabulary [of Old English-JMA] is characterized by large morphologically related word-families, where the relationship is transparent not only formally but most often also semantically. Put differently, much of the OE [Old English-JMA] vocabulary is derivationally related by productive word-formation patterns. (1992: 294)

Having made it clear that Old English has been chosen as the language of analysis because of the pervasiveness and transparency of its morphology, the remainder of this work will shed light on the question of how transparent Old English word-formation is. The phenomena under scrutiny do not add to the alleged transparency of the derivational morphology of Old English. On the contrary, they undermine it, either for reasons of formal opaqueness (arising if there is no difference of form between base and derivative) or for reasons of semantic opaqueness (when no difference of meaning can be identified between the input and the output of a word-formation process). Against this background, the main aims of this article are to clarify a number of terminological questions relating to the distinction between zero derivation and conversion and to offer a general account of these phenomena, along with empty morphs, in Old English derivational morphology. The analysis that is carried out in the following sections shows that zero derivation and redundant derivation with empty morphs are related phenomena if word-formation is considered in its syntagmatic and paradigmatic dimensions. Moreover, the discussion of the zero alternation yields conclusions relevant for the organization of the Old English lexicon.

2 A typology of affixless derivation in Old English

When the phenomenon of word-formation is considered in its paradigmatic dimension, recurrent pairings of meaning and form arise, which I have termed elsewhere (Martín Arista 2006) *morphological alternations*, after Bloomfield's classical definition of an alternation as a recurrent contrast of form and meaning. As illustration, consider the following derivatives of the Old English diminutive suffix *-incel*:

(1) *Bo:gincel* "small bough", *byrðincel* "a little burden", *cofincel* "little chamber", *ðe:owincel* "little servant", *liðincel* "little joint", *ra:pincel* "small rope", *scipincel* "little ship", *sta:nincel* "little stone", *su:lincel* "small furrow", *tu:nincel* "small property", *wilnincel* "a little female servant".

Although there arise instances of lexicalization (in the sense of lack of analysability) such as *do:cincel* "bastard", *hæftincel* "slave" and *hu:sincel* "habitation", in general there is a recurrent meaning contrast between bases like *scip* "ship" and diminutives like *scipincel* "little ship". The examples above raise the question from the perspective of the affix. From the angle of the base of derivation, it is very frequently the case that the combination of a given base with different affixes creates clearly distinguishable meanings, as in (2):

(2) *Bro:ðorli:cnes* "brotherliness", *bro:ðorli:c* "brotherly", *bro:ðorræ:den* "fellowship", *bro:ðorscipe* "brotherhood", *bro:ðorle:as* "brotherless".

The derivatives in (2) focus on the main function of derivational morphology, namely to produce new meanings by modifying the already existing ones. Paradigmatic alternations such as *ø/-incel* give rise to the derivational paradigm of Old English, which is realized by the paradigms of individual lexical items, often strong verbs, as is the case with the one of *bacan* "bake" given in (3):

(3) *A:bacan* "to bake", *ascbacen* "baked on ashes", *bacan* "to bake", *bæcere* "baker", *bæcering* "gridiron", *bæcern* "bakery", *bæcestre* "baker", *ealdbacen* "stale", *elebacen* "cooked in oil", *gebæc* "bakemeats", *heorðbacen* "baked on the hearth", *ni:wbacen* "newly baked", *ofenbacen* "baked in an oven".

While an alternation can frequently be identified, in the sense of a recurrent and predictable contrast of meaning between the output of a derivational process and its input, it is also true that there are instances in which no formal or functional contrast exists between the derivative and its base. As I have remarked above, these instances constitute mismatches because there is no explicit form that performs a function or because no obvious function is served by an explicit form. As for the former question, the phenomena at stake are zero derivation and conversion; regarding the latter question, the phenomenon under scrutiny is the zero morph. I subsume zero derivation and conversion, on the one hand, and zero morph, on the other hand, under the label of zero alternation and, for the time being, do not distinguish between zero derivation and conversion. Consider, as a point of departure for discussion, the following instances:

(4) (a) *A:ngenga* "solitary goer, isolated one".
A:ngenga "solitary, isolated".
(b) *Eorðstyren* "earthquake".
Eorðstyrennes "earthquake".

The noun *a:ngenga* "solitary goer, isolated one" in (4a), which qualifies as a compound with base from the paradigm of the strong verb *gangan* "go", takes on a new adjectival function in such a way that there is no formal difference between the two citation forms (nominative singular masculine) and, more importantly, no derivational affix is attached to the derived form. Turning to (4b), no change of meaning results from the attachment of the suffix *-nes* to the already suffixal form *eorðstyr-en* "earthquake". No change of gender is triggered, either, by the suffix *-nes*, given that both nouns are inflected for the feminine.

In general, word-formation involves the external or internal modification of derivation bases to convey new meanings. External modification attaches lexical or grammatical forms to bases of derivation, whereas internal modification changes one or more segments of the base, rather than attaching alien material to the base of derivation, as external modification does. This difference is shown by Example (5), which displays, respectively, an instance of suffixation with *-ung* and ablaut strong verb > adjective:

(5) (a) *Hand* "hand" > *handlung* "handling".
(b) *Bli:can* "shine" > *blæ:c* "bright".

Affixation, as illustrated by (5a) is the main means of external modification in Old English, while ablaut, as shown by (5b), is the most usual exponent of internal modification. Leaving aside compounding, there are two types of affixless derivation in Old English: zero derivation and conversion. Zero derivation is derivation without derivational morphemes, which calls for a new subdivision: zero derivation proper (which constitutes external modification) when inflectional morphemes are used for derivational purposes, thus performing two functions because they do not lose their inflectional character; and zero derivation by ablaut, which takes place when the base of derivation undergoes internal modification. This subdivision is illustrated by (6):

(6) (a) *Bindan* "to bind" > *binde* "headband".
(b) *Faran* "go" > *fær* "movement".

In (6a) the verbal inflection for the infinitive *-an* is replaced by the nominal inflection for the nominative feminine singular *-e*, while in (6b) the infinitival ending is lost and the root vowel is changed. Zero derivation proper and zero derivation by ablaut are not mutually exclusive: there are instances in which zero derivation makes use of ablaut along with an inflectional ending, as can be seen in the following examples:

(7) (a) *Helm* "protection" ~ *gehilmed* "helmeted".
(b) *Muð* "mouth" ~ *gemy:ðe* "junction of two streams".

To the modern eye, the process that turns out the adjective *a:ngenga* "solitary, isolated" in (4a) from the noun *a:ngenga* "solitary goer, isolated one" is zero derivation *or* conversion. In general, the distinction between these phenomena is unclear and rather controversial in the literature. Although it is acknowledged that conversion is more related to lexical class whereas zero derivation falls rather on the morphological side, it is often the case that no strict separation is postulated between the two, thus, for instance, Bauer (1988), Štekauer (1996) and Manova and Dressler (2005), who deny the existence of zero derivation.[3] Other authors, like Bauer and Varela (2005: 12) accept zero derivation, but consider it *out of favour* with respect to conversion. I concur with Kastovsky (2005: 33) that zero derivation is intimately related to the notion of motivation, which is central to the structural-functional tradition. I also agree with Kastovsky (2005) on the relevance of zero derivation for a diachronic study of English word-formation, although I part company with this author as regards the one-to-one relationship between form and function.

In an analysis aimed at avoiding the proliferation of zeros in Old English inflectional morphology, Kastovsky remarks:

> In the absence of overt derivational suffixes, all we are left with are case/number endings, which produce word-forms and have no derivational function. This means [...] that in those instances where the stem-formatives originally acting as derivational exponents were lost or reinterpreted (e.g. *spring, cuma, hunta*) we have to assume their replacement by a zero morpheme in order to keep up the binary interpretation of word-formation syntagmas. (Kastovsky, 2005: 44)

In the proposal that I advance below the emphasis is not put on the units, but on the processes of word-formation without explicit derivational material. If, on the one hand, the focus shifts from the nature (derivational vs. inflectional) of the units to the process of zero derivation as involving some sub-phenomena, and, on the other, the double function of certain morphemes is not excluded, an overall analysis can be offered which rests basically on the concept of zero derivation without zero morphemes, thus the term zero alternation: when considered in the whole derivational paradigm, two morphologically related lexical items show a mismatch of form because the derivative is derivationally unmarked.

This definition allows for the inclusion of the following typology of zero derivation processes in the word-formation of Old English: (a) zero derivation with explicit inflectional morphemes and without explicit derivational morphemes, as in *ri:dan* "to ride" > *ri:da* "rider"; (b) zero derivation without explicit or implicit morphemes, either inflectional or derivational, as in *bi:dan* "to delay" > *bi:d* "delay"; (c) zero derivation without inflectional or derivational morphemes but displaying ablaut, as in *dri:fan* "to drive" > *dra:f* "action of driving"; and (d) zero derivation with ablaut and formatives that can no longer be considered productive affixes, such as *-m* in *fle:on* "to fly" > *fle:am* "flight". Given this typology, the derivation of *me:os* "mossy" from *me:os* "moss" falls under type (b) whereas the one of *nearu* "constricted" from *nearu* "strait" belongs to type (a).

When dealing with the lack of a biunivocal correspondence between content and expression in this particular area of word-formation, I benefit from the insights of the structural-functional tradition, which, unlike classical structuralism, finds no problem in accepting form-function incongruences. For Kastovsky (1968), *ri:da* "rider" is a product of inflection, which overlooks the morphological relationship holding between the noun *ri:da* "rider" and the strong verb *ri:dan* "ride" as well as the Effector role, in the terminology of Van Valin and LaPolla (1997) and Van Valin (2005), performed by the nominal argument of the verb in the semantic-syntactic correlate. I consider, therefore, *ri:da* a zero derivative of *ri:dan,* thus a derivational product, even though it resorts to inflectional means, namely the morpheme *-a*. This proposal is also different from Kastovsky's (2005: 37), for whom zero is a *place-holder for overt affixes having a similar function*. Although this analysis has an important advantage over Kastovsky's earlier (1968) proposal, namely that of stating morphological relatedness, it restricts zeros to inflection and, in spite of admitting that there are *formal means to derive one lexical item from another* (Kastovsky

2005: 37), excludes or, at least, does not engage with types (b), (c) and (d) of my typology.

Kastovsky's (2005) approach to the question follows from a series of publications that have demonstrated the existence of a shift in the type of Old English morphology from variable base morphology to invariable base morphology (Kastovsky 1986, 1989, 1990, 1992). This shift blurrs the effects of ablaut, which is purely morphological at the end of the period (Kastovsky 2006). Pesquera Fernández (2009) has found a significant number of alternations that lack phonological motivation in the derivation from strong verbs in Old English, which is in accordance with Kastovsky's shift. On the other hand, González Torres (2009) has convincingly shown that the bases of derivation of affixal nouns are harder to identify than Kastovsky's (2005) strict separation of inflectional and derivational morphology predicts: approximately 1000 affixal nouns out of a total of ca. 3300 have more than one base of derivation, typically a verb and a noun or a verb and an adjective. That is, derivational morphology is more variable in Old English than Kastovsky (2006) considers it to be, at least in nouns. Or, in other words, Kastovsky's (1992, 2006) shift from variable to invariable morphology probably takes place later than this author claims and, consequently, there is no problem in considering the suffix *-a* in *ri:da* "rider" inflectional and derivational while analyzing the process of building *ri:da* on the strong verb *ri:dan* "to ride" as zero derivation. In the struggle to state morphological relatedness, zero derivation stands as the last line of defence.

Summarizing, zero derivation in Old English can be broken down into zero derivation with explicit inflectional morphemes, zero derivation without explicit or implicit morphemes, zero derivation without morphemes but displaying ablaut, and zero derivation with ablaut and former affixes that constitute unproductive formatives in synchronic analysis. To this typology of zero derivation, which is restricted to variable lexical categories, the derivation of lexical items belonging to invariable classes must be added. In this proposal, this is done under the label of *conversion*. Having proposed the basics of the typology of affixless word-formation in Old English, the remainder of this section addresses some pending questions concerning conversion and zero derivation at this stage of the English language.

Conversion is category extension without external or internal modification. Two instances of conversion, from pronoun to adverb and from adverb to adposition, respectively, follow in (8):

(8) (a) *Æ:nig* (pronoun) "any, any one" > *æ:nig* (adverb) "only".
(b) *Æ:r* (adverb) "before" > *æ:r* (adposition) "before".

The analysis of the previous examples is based on the existence of modification as well as the presence and nature of affixes. When a derivational affix turns up, affixation proper is at work. If no derivational affix is attached, the next step involves deciding whether there is formal modification or not. If, given the whole inflectional paradigm, there is no modification between the base and the derivative, the morphological process in point is conversion. If there is modification, there remains to decide if an inflectional affix or ablaut is used for derivational purposes. That is, whereas zero derivation requires ablaut or the attachment of an inflectional affix, conversion is category extension without affixes or ablaut. This classification revolves around lexical class in a significant way. When affixless derivation holds between variable lexical classes, the phenomenon at stake is zero derivation, while conversion has an output that belongs to an invariable lexical class. Put differently, if the output of derivation bears an inflectional ending (thus belonging to a variable lexical class) the phenomenon under scrutiny is zero derivation; if the output of the derivational process shows no inflectional ending (which makes it a member of an invariable lexical class), the derivational process at work is conversion. In Old English zero derivation is strongly associated with the strong verb with its inflectional forms, whereas conversion affects grammatical classes, whose members produced by conversion do not have verbal bases but adjectival, adverbial and adpositional ones.

After settling the terminological question, the following section delves into zero derivation in Old English and opens by considering the basic status of strong verbs in word-formation.

3 Zero derivation

The Germanic strong verb with its present, preterite and past participle stems is central to lexical formation, as is shown by Bammesberger (1965) and Seebold (1970), among others. Focusing on Old English, Kastovsky (1992), following Hinderling (1967), considers strong verbs the starting point of word-formation processes. Take, as illustration, the derivational paradigm of the verb *(ge) drifan* "drive":

(9) *(Ge)dri:fan* (strong I) pret. sing. *dra:f*, pret. plur. *drifon, dreofon*, past part. *drifen* "to drive, force, hunt, follow up, pursue; drive away, expel; practise, carry on; rush against, impel, drive forwards or backwards; undergo".

Noun, feminine: *dra:f* "action of driving", *(ge)drif* "fever", *fordrifnes* "opposition", *onwega:drifennes* "a driving away", *to:dræ:fednes* "dispersion", underdrifennes "subjection", *u:tdræ:f* "decree of expulsion".
Noun, masculine: *dræ:fend* "hunter", *u:tdræ:fere* "driver out".
Noun, neuter: *gedri:f* "a drive".
Verb, strong (I): *a:dri:fan* "to drive", *bedri:fan* "to beat", *efta:dri:fan* "to reject", *eftfordri:fan* "to drive away", *fordri:fan* "to sweep away", *frama:dri:fan* "to remove", *frama:dry:fan* "to drive away", *indri:fan* "to ejaculate", *oferdri:fan* "to overcome", *onwega:dri:fan* "to drive away", *to:dri:fan* "to scatter", *ðurhdri:fan* "to drive through", *u:ta:dri:fan* "to drive out", *u:tdri:fan* "to expel", *wiðdri:fan* "to repel."
Verb, weak (1): *a:dræ:fan* "to drive away", *dry:fan* "to stir up", *fordræ:fan* "to compel", *(ge)dræ:fan* "to drive", *to:dræ:fan* "to scatter", *u:ta:dræ:fan* "to drive out".
Adjective: *fullgedrifen* "full of wild beasts", *undrifen* "not driven or tossed".

As can be seen in (9), strong verbs such as *bedri:fan* "to beat" derive from the infinitive of the basic strong verb. The noun *dra:f* "action of driving" derives from the preterite form of the strong verb, while the adjective *undrifen* "not driven or tossed" derives from the past participle. Diachronically, the derivatives with *æ* like *u:tdræ:f* "decree of expulsion" derive from the Germanic weak verb **draibjanan* > Old English *(ge)dræ:fan* "to drive" (Holthausen 1963: 75; Seebold 1970: 163; Orel 2003: 74), although the weak verb can be traced back to the strong one in Germanic (Hinderling 1967: 37). Synchronically, *dræ:f* holds a vocalic alternation with the preterite singular form of the strong verb *dra:f* of the seventh vocalic type (A7) identified by Kastovsky (1968: 67), which is due to i-mutation and involves the back vowel *a* and the front vowel *æ*. Strong verbs are the spine of Old English word-formation, not only because they produce derivatives belonging to other lexical classes but also because they constitute the base of derivation of other strong verbs (*dri:fan* "drive" > *efta:dri:fan* "to reject", *frama:dry:fan* "to drive away", *ðurhdri:fan* "to drive through", etc.), which, in turn, give rise to new derivations, as in *dri:fan* "drive" > *fordri:fan* "to sweep away" > *fordrifnes* "opposition". In the context of the whole lexicon of Old English, the lexical database *Nerthus* yields 12764 lexemes that belong to the derivational paradigms of strong verbs, out of a total of 30157 in *Nerthus,* which amounts to 42.3% of the lexicon.

Extensive lexical analysis of Old English word-formation has shown that whenever there is a strong verb in a series of morphologically related words, the strong verb is likely to qualify as the base of derivation of the paradigm. It is hard to find exceptions to this generalization, which is supported by the information provided by etymological dictionaries of

Germanic such as Seebold (1970) and Orel (2003), but consider the derivational paradigm *swe:g-/swo:-*:

(10) *A:nswe:ge* "harmonious", *a:swe:gan* "to thunder", *a:swo:gan* "to cover over", *bencswe:g* "bench-rejoicing", *(ge)swe:ge* "harmonious", *geswe:gsumli:ce* "unanimously", *geswo:gung* "swooning", *ha:sswe:ge* "sounding hoarsely", *hearpswe:g* "sound of the harp", *hereswe:g* "martial sound", *hlu:dswe:ge* "loudly", *inswo:gan* "to invade", *inswo:gennes* "onrush", *midswe:gan* "to cover, choke", *ona:swe:gan* "to sound forth", *samodswe:gende* "consonantal", *samswe:ge* "sounding in unison", *selfswe:gend* "vowel", *swe:g* "sound", *swe:gan* "to make a noise", *swe:gcræft* "music", *swe:gdynn* "noise", *swe:gendlic* "vocal", *swe:ghle:oðor* "sound", *swe:ging* "sound", *swe:glic* "sonorous", *swe:tswe:ge* "agreeable", *swi:ðswe:ge* "strong-sounding", *swo:gan* "to sound", *ungeswe:ge* "inharmonious", *ðurhswo:gan* "to penetrate", *welswe:gende* "melodious".

Seebold (1970) does not provide a strong verb etymology in Germanic. Holthausen (1963: 334) and Orel (2003: 393) give the noun **swegl* "music", whereas Heidermanns (1993: 576) opts for the adjective **sweiga* "still". Kastovsky (1968: 109) analyzes the morphological relation between the strong verb (VIIf) *swo:gan* "to sound" and the noun *swe:g* "sound" and identifies a vocalic alternation (A8) and a consonantal one (C4) caused, respectively, by i-mutation and palatalization. This reasoning reinforces the basic character of the strong verb, with the corresponding derived status of the noun. However, morphonological analysis does not help when the paradigm under scrutiny is one like *teld-*, given below:

(11) *Beteldan* "to cover", *bu:rgeteld* "pavilion", *ganggeteld* "portable tent", *(ge)teld* "tent", *(ge)teldan* "to spread a covering", *geteldung* "tabernacle", *geteldwurðung* "feast of tabernacles", *oferteldan* "to cover over", *teldgehli:wung* "tabernacle", *teldian* "to spread (net)", *teldsticca* "tent-peg", *teldtre:ow* "tent-peg", *teldwyrhta* "tent-maker", *tyldsyle* "tent".

Holthausen (1963: 344) gives the noun *teld* "tent" as the source of *(ge)teldan* "to spread a covering" (strong IIIb) and *teldian* "to spread (net)" (weak). Taking a similar line, Seebold (1970: 501) provides Germanic *teldam* and *teldo:* for, respectively, Old English *teld* and *teldian.* If no morphonological alternation holds, a case may be made for the noun as base of the strong verb, but if the direction of i-mutation goes from the noun to the verb, as in *sta:n* "stone" > *ofstæ:nan* "to stone" (strong I), the case for the basic noun and the derived strong verb is more convincing. The same situation holds with respect to the adjective *bra:d* "broad" and the strong verbs *(ge)bræ:dan* "to make broad", *forebræ:dan* "to prolong" and *oferbræ:dan* "to spread over" (strong VIIe). Heidermanns (1993: 40) lists the Germanic primary adjective *breida-* "broad" while Orel (2003: 53) offers both the Germanic adjective and weak verb, namely _*braidaz_ "broad" and _*braidjanan_ > Old English *bræ:dan* "to make broad".

Pilch (1970) and Orel (2003), while acknowledging the decisive role played by the strong verb in the formation of words in the old Germanic languages, also list a few members of other lexical categories from which strong verbs are derived. Pilch (1970: 132) finds six instances of denominal strong verbs of the seventh class. Those without i-umlaut are given in (12a) and those showing i-umlaut in (12b):

(12) (a) *Ræ:dan* "to advise" (< *ræ:d*), *slæ:pan* "sleep" (< *slæ:p*), *blandan* "blend" (< *gebland*), *hro:pan* "to shout" (< *hro:p*).
(b) *We:pan* "weep" (< *wo:p*), *spæ:tan* "spit" (< *sp:tl*).

Additional evidence of denominal strong verbs formed by zero derivation is scarce, probably restricted to the ones that can be seen in (13):

(13) (a) *Sceððan* "to hurt, crush, oppress, disturb" (< *sceaða*).
(b) *Plegian* "to move rapidly" (< *plega*).

Deverbal (strong) and deadjectival strong verbs produced by zero derivation are more frequent, but still constitute an exceptional phenomenon. Some illustrations of each class follow in (14):

(14) (a) *Glæ:dan* "to cause to slip" (< *gli:dan*), *onbrinnan* "to set fire to" (< *onbeornan*).
(b) *Grimman to rage* (< *grimm*), *manigfealdan* "to multiply" (< *manigfeald*).

The examples reinforce the exceptional character of strong verbs as a target of zero derivation. Regarding strong verbs as a source of zero derivation, the literature has paid some attention to the formation of nouns from strong verbs, thus Kastovsky (1968), whereas the other major lexical categories require more research in this respect.[4] Kastovsky (1968) lists around 700 nouns zero derived from strong verbs (mainly of classes III, V and VII) and another 500 derived from weak verbs. Given that this author deals with the nominal class only and, moreover, is concerned with morphophonological alternations such as *fe:dan* "feed" ~ *fo:da* "food" and restricts his analysis to the major lexical classes, I offer an overall account of this area of Old English word-formation below.

Beginning with nouns, there are around 1700 zero derived members of this category in the lexicon, 750 of which qualify as masculine, 450 as feminine and another 450 as neuter (the figures are approximate). Some illustrations follow in (15): the nouns in (15a) are masculine, those in (15b) feminine and the ones in (15c) are inflected for the neuter gender.

(15) (a) *Belg* "bag" (< *belgan*), *for∂cyme* "coming forth" (< *for∂cuman*).
(b) *Gra:p* "grip" (< *gri:pan*), *u:tdræ:f* "decree of expulsion" (< *u:tdri:fan*).
(c) *Gehweorf* "a turning" (< *hweorfan*), *gesprec* "speech" (< *sprecan*).

These instances show, to begin with, that the presence of ablaut, as has been remarked above, is not a requirement for the existence of zero derivation. In (15a), for instance, there is no morphonological contrast between *belg* and *belgan*, although both words are morphologically related to each other through the derivational process under scrutiny. Morphonological alternations hold mainly between strong verbs and their zero derivatives and, secondarily, between weak verbs and their derivatives by means of zero, morphonological alternations involving nouns and adjectives being exceptional. Another remarkable aspect of these examples concerns the prefix *ge-*: approximately one half of the neuter nouns derived by the zero morpheme display this prefix (the amount of *ge-* masculines is about one tenth, whereas that of feminine nouns containing *ge-* is negligible).

Zero derived nouns come from strong verbs, adjectives, weak verbs and other nouns, as is illustrated by (16a)–(16d) respectively:

(16) (a) *Bælc* "pride" (< *belgan*), *cuma* "stranger" (< *cuman*).
(b) *A:ngilde* "single payment for damage" (< *a:ngilde*), *hæ:st* "violence" (< *hæ:st*).
(c) *Cwild* "death" (< *cwelan*), *ge∂o:ht* "thought" (*ge∂encan*).
(d) *Æ:boda* "messenger" (*æ:bod*), *beswica* "deceiver" (< *beswic*).

Zero derived weak verbs come from nouns, as in (17a), adjectives, as in (17b) and strong verbs, as in (17c):

(17) (a) *Æ:cgan* "to set on edge" (< *ecg*), *hagolian* "to hail" (< *hagol*).
(b) *Ha:tian* "to be or get hot" (< *ha:t*), *hwi:tian* "to whiten" (< *hwi:t*)
(c) *Drencan* "to give to drink, drown" (*drincan*), *slæhtan* "to strike" (< *sle:an*)

Weak verbs, as is the case with neuter nouns, often display the prefix *-ge*: around 600 out of 1400 take this prefix. Weak verbs derived by zero derivation belong to the morphological classes 1, 2 and 3, as illustrated, respectively by (18a), (18b) and (18c):

(18) (a) *Befe:gan* "to join", *derian* "to damage".
(b) *Broccian* "to tremble", *forheardian* "to grow hard".
(c) *Æthabban* "to retain", *libban* "to live".

Zero derived nouns and weak verbs are far more frequent than the adjectives derived by the same means: there are around 1700 zero derived nouns and 1400 weak verbs, approximately, as opposed to around 500 adjectives produced by this morphological process. Most of these derive from verbs. The base is a strong verb, as in (19a), far more frequently than a weak verb, as in (19b):

(19) (a) *Inbyrde* "born on the estate" (< *inberan*), *onfunden* "experienced" (< *onfindan*).
(b) *A:fandod* "excellent" (< *a:fandian*), *besce:awod* "thoughtful" (< *besce:awian*)

The rest constitute zero derivatives of nouns, including, for instance, the ones given in (20). The adjectives in (20a) come from nouns and those in (20b) from strong verbs through nouns:

(20) (a) *Hre:ofl* "leprous" (< *hre:ofl*), *i:sen* "of iron" (< *i:sen*).
(b) *Crypel* "crippled" (< *cre:opan*), *hryre* "perishable" (< *hre:osan*).

Recapitulating, this section has offered an overview of zero derivation in which the following points have been stressed: (a) the main sources of zero derivation are strong verbs, although weak verbs, nouns and adjectives also perform the function of derivational bases; (b) all major lexical categories, including strong verbs, are targets of zero derivation; and (c) the phenomenon of zero derivation is quantitatively relevant. Apart from these aspects, in the following sections I raise the question of empty morphs in Old English and explain it on the grounds of the coexistence of zero derivation and affixal derivation in the Old English lexicon.

4 Redundant derivation and empty morphs

Whereas the previous section has focused on the zero expression of morphological relatedness, this one deals with the opposite phenomenon, that is, morphological relatedness which is explicitly marked by means of an affix that does not cause a net semantic effect.[5] I use the term *empty morph* to describe the latter situation. The empty morph in Old English can be found in instances like the following:

(21) (a) *Ðri:stlic/∂ri:stiglic* "daring".
(b) *So:∂fæst/so:∂fæstlic* "true".

Although no claim of absolute synonymy is made, it is possible to find a context in which the morphs *-ig-*, and *-lic*, in (21a) and (21b) respectively, do not produce a significant meaning change between the members of these pairs. Example (21a) illustrates the empty morph in intermediate position, while example (21b) shows a final empty morph. It must be noted from the beginning of this discussion that the empty morph thus defined is restricted to recursive word-formations like *∂ri:st-ig-lic* "daring" and *so:∂-fæst-lic* "true" whereas no empty morph formation is identified in a non-recursive suffixal derivative such as *onwealdig* "powerful" with respect to the zero derived adjective *onweald* "powerful" (<*gewealdan* "to rule"). In other words, internal modification is put aside in the analysis of empty morphs.

The empty morph is mainly an adjectival phenomenon in Old English for two reasons. First, it appears in derived adjectives far more often than in derived members of other lexical categories and, second, it involves adjectival suffixes in the vast majority of instances. In this line, no empty suffix has been found in the class of verbs. As for the categories noun and adverb as displaying empty morph formations, consider the following examples:

(22) (a) *Ma:nli:ce/ma:nfulli:ce* "wickedly".
(b) *Ofermo:dli:ce/ofermo:digli:ce* "proudly".
(c) *Oferflo:wednes/oferflo:wedli:cnes* "excess".
(d) *Gema:hnes/gema:hlicnes* "importunity".

As can be seen in the examples in (22), the suffixes involved in empty morph formations are adjectival, as is the case with *-ful*, in (22a), *-ig* in (22b), and *li:c* in (22c) and (22d), regardless of the fact that they appear in deadjectival derivatives such as the adverbs in (22a) and (22b) or the nouns in (22c) and (22d). This is seen more clearly if empty morph nominal formations are analysed in detail, as in (23):

(23) (a) *Ø/-ful*
∂e:ostornes/∂e:ostorfulnes "darkness".
(b) *Ø/-georn*
fyrwitnes/fyrwitgeornes "curiosity".
(c) *Ø/-ig*
ofermo:dignes/ofermo:dnes "pride".
(d) *Ø/-lic*
gne:a∂nes/gne:a∂licnes "frugality".
(e) *Ø/-mod*
meagolnes/meagolmo:dnes "earnestness".
(f) *Ø/-ræ:d*
hi:wcu:∂nes/hi:wcu:∂ræ:dnes "familiarity".
(g) *Ø/-sum*
gehealdnes/gehealdsumnes "keeping".

Empty morphs in intermediate position arise in abstract deadjectival nouns formed by means of the nominal suffix *-nes* and inflected for the feminine gender. It must be noted that the empty morph is kept all the way down the derivation. For instance, the empty morph *-ful* can be identified not only in the pair *∂e:ostornes/∂e:ostorfulnes* "darkness" but also in *∂e:ostor/∂e:ostorful* "dark", in such a way that the basic adjective *∂e:ostor* "dark" is the base of derivation of *∂e:ostorfulnes* "darkness" and the derived adjective *∂e:ostorful* "dark" constitutes the input to the derivational process of suffixation that produces *∂e:ostorfulnes* "darkness". In other words, the empty morph appears first and foremost in the contrast between the basic and the derived adjective, which is established by means of the suffix *-ful*. A similar analysis can be carried out of the other instances presented in (23).

Empty morphs in intermediate position can be found in deadjectival adverbs of manner derived by means of the suffix *-li:ce*. The combinations include the affixes given in (24):

(24) (a) *-li:ce/-fæstli:ce*
so:∂li:ce/so:∂fæstli:ce "truly".
(b) *-li:ce/-fulli:ce*
fa:cenli:ce/fa:cenfulli:ce "deceitfully".
(c) *-li:ce/-sumli:ce*
lufli:ce/lufsumli:ce "kindly".

As has been pointed out with respect to nouns, adverbs such as *so:∂fæstli:ce* "truly" display an empty morph in intermediate position as a result of a previous step of their derivation. In this case, the basic adjective *so:∂* "true" is the base of derivation of *so:∂li:ce* "truly" while the derived adverb *so:∂fæstli:ce* "truly" is formed recursively from the previously derived adjective *so:∂fæst* "true", which displays an empty morph with respect to *so:∂* "true". A similar analysis is applicable to (24b) and (24c).

An important consequence of the morphological relationship just described with reference to Examples (23) and (24) is that no instances can be found of empty morphs in the final position of derived nouns or derived adverbs, whereas derived adjectives can display empty morphs both in intermediate and final positions. Beginning with the intermediate position, cases in point are the ones exemplified in (25), which contain empty morphs with the adjectival suffixes *-ig*, *-fæst*, *-ful* and *-e*, respectively:

(25) (a) *Ø/-ig*
gesundlic/gesundiglic "safe".
(b) *Ø/-fæst*
so:∂lic/so:∂fæstlic "true".

(c) *Ø/-ful*
andgietlic/andgietfullic "inteligible".

(d) *Ø/-e*
gede:flic/gede:felic "fit".

The pair *gesundlic/gesundiglic,* as is the case with *ðe:ostornes/ðe:ostorfulnes* in (25a), keeps the empty morph throughout the derivation (*gesund* >*gesundlic* "safe" and *gesund*>*gesundig*>*gesundiglic* "safe"). As in the pair *ðe:ostornes/ðe:ostorfulnes,* a basic adjective is the input to two derivational processes of suffixation, one in which the empty morph is the only suffix (*gesund* >*gesundlic*) and another one in which the empty morph attaches recursively to the previously derived *gesundig* to produce *gesundiglic.*

Whereas the empty morph can be identified in intermediate position as realized by four different suffixes, in final position it is associated basically with the suffix *-lic,* in combinations such as the ones in (26). It must be borne in mind, however, that the number of different affixes to which *-lic* attaches in empty morph adjectival formations is remarkable:

(26) (a) *-cund/-cundlic*
metcund/metcundlic "metrical".

(b) *-e/-elic*
ungefræ:ge/ungefræ:gelic "unusual".

(c) *-ed/-edlic*
una:ly:fed/una:ly:fedlic "illicit".

(d) *-en/-enlic*
una:meten/una:metenlic "unmeasured".

(e) *-end/-endlic*
oferflo:wend/oferflo:wendlic "excessive".

(f) *-fæst/-fæstlic*
gemetfæst/gemetfæstlic "moderate".

(g) *-feald/-fealdlic*
hundfeald/hundfealdlic "hundred-fold".

(h) *-ful/-fullic*
geflitful/geflitfullic "contentious".

(i) *-ic/-iclic*
canonic/canoniclic "canonical".

(j) *-ig/-iglic*
unmihtig/unmihtiglic "weak".

(k) *-isc/-isclic*
mennisc/mennisclic "human".

(l) *-le:as/-le:aslic*
scamle:as/scamle:aslic "shameless".

(m) *-od/-odlic*
ungehi:wod/ungehi:wodlic "unformed".

(n) *-ol/-ollic*
sme:aðancol/sme:a?ancollic "subtle".
(o) *-sum/-sumlic*
langsum/langsumlic "tedious".
(p) *-wi:s/-wi:slic*
gesce:adwi:s/gesce:adwi:slic "sagacious".

Other suffixes appearing in empty morph adjectival formations include *-mo:d* and *-ig,* illustrated, respectively, by (27a) and (27b):

(27) (a) *-ig/-igmo:d*
re:onig/re:onigmo:d "mournful".
(b) *-iht/ihtig*
hre:odiht/hre:odihtig "reedy".

In this section I have gathered evidence for an empty morph analysis of a significant number of adjectival suffixes which surface in derived adjectives and also in deadjectival nouns and adverbs. This is tantamount to saying that affixation is often meaningful and less frequently meaningless. Consequently, the question has been presented so far from the perspective of individual affixes that attach redundantly in some contexts, which differs from the line adopted in the previous section of focusing on processes rather than on units. Given that this approach has turned out more explanatory, to round off this discussion it is necessary, in the first place, to distinguish the empty morph phenomenon from the process of affix lexicalization and, second, to consider the empty morph with respect to the more general process of redundant derivation.

Beginning with lexicalization, the question that arises is whether the empty morph is independent of the process of lexical fading undergone by many Old English affixes, particularly prefixes, which eventually became interchangeable and disappeared or, at least, ceased to be used in a productive way. The phenomenon can be seen clearly in strong verbs derived by means of Germanic prefixes such as the following:

(28) (a) *A:-/be-/for-*
a:weorpan/beweorpan/forweorpan "to throw".
(b) *A:-/be-/ge-*
a:le:ogan/bele:ogan/gele:ogan "to lie".
(c) *A:-/be-/to:-*
a:brecan/bebrecan/to:brecan "to break to pieces".
(d) *A:-/ge-/for*
-a:bla:wan/gebla:wan/forbla:wan "to blow".
(e) *A:-/ge-/on-*
a:be:odan/gebe:odan/onbe:odan "to command"

(f) *A:-/ge-/to-*
a:helpan/gehelpan/to:helpan "to help".
(g) *Be-/on-/to-*
becuman/ancuman/to:cuman "to arrive".
(h) *Be-/for-/of-*
Beswelgan/forswelgan/ofswelgan "to swallow up".

Affix variation and lexicalization have been discussed with different degrees of detail by de la Cruz (1975), Horgan (1980), Hiltunen (1983), Kastovsky (1992) and Martín Arista (2010) in the wider setting of the decline of the Old English affixal system. As Hiltunen (1983: 54) remarks, "the fact that one and the same verb may occcur with two or more different prefixes [...] is often taken to indicate the lack of expressive content in the prefixes, and their incipient decline". In this respect, Kastovsky (1992: 377) notes that "in subsequent copies of one and the same text prefixes are often omitted, added or exchanged for other prefixes without any apparent semantic effect. This points to a considerable weakening of the meanings of these prefixes." For Brinton and Closs-Traugott (2005: 127) "the rise of prepositional verbs is concurrent with the loss of verbal prefixes, which over the OE [Old English-JMA] period had weakened, overextended, and lost information content".[6]

It is my contention that we are dealing with two different phenomena: on the one hand, the lexicalization (in the sense of semantic fading) of the prefixes, and the existence of empty morphs, on the other hand. Apart from the fact that the test of semantic fading is interchangeability, instead of morphological recursivity without semantic effect, as in empty morph formations, the significant difference lies in the fact that the Germanic prefixes have disappeared or are fully unproductive, whereas suffixes such as *-lic>-ly* are fully productive nowadays (Marchand 1969) and, moreover, have kept their meaning.

It remains to determine whether the empty morph phenomenon can be inserted into the more general realm of convergent derivation, which can be identified in instances like the following:

(29) (a) *Eorðstyren/eorðstyrennes/eorðstyrung* "earthquake".
(b) *Fiscfell/fisclacu/fiscmere/fiscpo:l/fiscwelle* "fishpond".

Unlike redundant derivations such as *gesce:adwi:s/gesce:adwi:slic* "wise", which have been explained as the result of empty morphs in recursive word-formation, in (29a) and (29b) there is not recursivity on a compulsory basis and, moreover, affix contrast can be found between suffixes which are fully distinctive in other contexts. The convergent derivation that results from the attachment of bound lexical items, as in (29a), or the compounding with free lexical items, as in (29b), represents a special case of partial synonymy, given that meaning similarity and morphological relatedness are present in instances like those in (29). In Old English, the phenomenon can be found in the major lexical classes of the noun, the adjective and the adverb, as is shown, respectively, by (30a), (30b), and (30c):

(30) (a) *A:li:esendnes/a:li:esing/a:li:esnes* "redemption".
(b) *Una:wend/una:wended/una:wendende/una:wendendlic* "unchangeable".
(c) *Orce:ape/orce:apes/orce:apunga/orce:apungum* "without cause".

The case with verbs is different. Convergent derivation is a suffixal phenomenon and involves, with the exception of the adverb, suffixes that have survived into Present-day English or even continue in use, whereas the semantic fading of verbal affixes illustrated by example (28) has resulted in the disappearance of the Germanic prefixes in question.

Convergent derivation is typical of triplets of a zero derived adjective and two suffixal derivatives that are morphologically related to the adjective through the shared base of derivation, as in (31a), (31b), and (31c):

(31) (a) *Hre:oh/hre:ohful/hre:ohlic* "stormy".
(b) *Torht/torhtlic/torhtmo:d* "glorious".
(c) *Wi:s/wi:sfæst/wi:slic* "wise".

In adverbs, convergent derivations often involve the suffixes *-e* and *-li:ce*:

(32) (a) *Gri:mme/grimli:ce* "fiercely".
(b) *Hæ:ste/hæ:stli:ce* "violently".
(c) *Hnesce/hnescli:ce* "softly".

The first lexical items in the triplets in (31) and the pairs in (32) display derivational means originating in ablaut and inflection, including bases and affixes. Thus, the strong verb *witan* "to know" provides the stem-formed base for the zero derived *wi:s* in (31c), which, in turn, is inputted to the suffixation processes that turn out *wis:fæst* and *wi:slic*. Similarly, the adjective *grimm* "grim" is inflected for *gri:mme* and derived by *-li:ce* to produce *grimli:ce* in (32a). An interesting aspect of the recursive suffixation of zero derived bases is that affixal derivatives often convey a more specific meaning, whereas zero derivatives are hyperonymic with respect to suffixed forms or, at least, display a wider array of senses. This is the case with nouns and adjectives, illustrated, respectively by (33a) and (33b):

(33) (a) *La:r* "lore, learning, science, art of teaching, preaching, doctrine, study, precept, exhortation, advice, instigation, history, story, cunning"; *la:rdo:m* "teaching, instruction".

(b) *I:del* "worthless, useless, vain; empty, desolate, bare, void, destitute, devoid (of); idle, unemployed"; *i:delgeorn* "slothful, idle, useless"; *i:dellic* "vain, idle".

Throughout this process of semantic differentiation the presence of affixes is not the only morphological feature that changes in nouns. The attachment of suffixes to the zero derived base modifies the gender of the noun, typically from the neuter to the masculine, as in (34a), or to the feminine, as in (34b):

(34) (a) *Bod* "command" n.; *bodscipe* "command" m.

(b) *Ealdor* "life" n.; *ealdnes* "old age" f.

Even this brief presentation of the phenomena at stake has shown that redundant derivation with empty morphs cannot be identified either with semantic fading or convergent derivation. It represents an independent phenomenon that deserves attention not only in its own terms but, above all, for its relation to zero derivation and, ultimately, for its explanatory character for the overall organization of the Old English lexicon. Some concluding remarks along these lines are offered in the next section.

5 Concluding remarks

This article has dealt with zero alternation in Old English as comprising two phenomena, zero derivation and the empty morph, both of which constitute a mismatch between form and function: while the derivational function is served by no explicit derivational form in zero derivation, an explicit affix plays no role in the configuration of the meaning of the derived lexical item. A typology of affixless derivation in Old English has been proposed that distinguishes zero derivation and conversion. Zero derivation, in turn, can be broken down into zero derivation with explicit inflectional morphemes, zero derivation without explicit or implicit morphemes, zero derivation without morphemes but displaying ablaut, and zero derivation with ablaut and unproductive formatives. A distinction has been drawn between the sort of redundant derivations produced by zero morphs and the semantic fading of prefixes on the one hand, and the convergent derivation that results from two or more derivational histories that proceed in the same direction, on the other. By way of conclusion, I should like to insist on the relationship among these phenomena and their implications for the organization of the Old English lexicon.

Assuming synchronic continuity in Old English, the evidence furnished in the previous sections indicates that there are, at least, two lexical layers in the Old English lexicon: one in which inflection (including ablaut) provides means for derivation and another one in which derivation makes use of lexical resources of its own. As I have remarked above, the change from variable to invariable base morphology probably takes place later than Kastovsky (2005, 2006) holds, at least in derivational morphology. More importantly, if no diachronic change is admitted in order to preserve the synchronic integrity of the Old English period, there cannot be type shift, as Kastovsky (1989, 1990, 1992) puts forward, either, because changes of linguistic type arise in the diachronic axis and result from linguistic evolution occurring throughout the history of the language. If the reasoning is correct, two layers coexist in the lexicon of Old English, namely the layer of zero derivation and the layer of affixation. I have proposed a typology of zero derivation phenomena that does justice to the quantitative and qualitative importance of the phenomenon in Old English and gathered evidence for the existence of empty morphs at this stage of the English language. I have the feeling that empty morph formations with affixes that are fully distinctive in other derivations represent the sort of inconsistencies and variations associated with the transition from a system of derivation by inflectional means to a new system of affixation (basically suffixation) proper. Moreover, the existence of convergent derivation demonstrates that the products of derivation by inflectional means and derivation proper coexist and often produce partial synonymy. To close this discussion, I must admit that redundant and convergent derivation as described in this work might be due in part to lack of semantic granularity in the definition of the meanings of the lexical items. For this reason I have referred to partial synonymy: at least a context can be found where the lexical items under scrutiny are synonyms, but more research is needed in this area.

Notes

* This research has been funded by the Ministry of Science and Innovation through the project FFI2008-04448/FILO. I should like to thank Christopher Butler and the referees for their comments and suggestions on an earlier version of this article. The usual disclaimers apply.

1. At this point, I should like to refer the reader to Dik's (1986) seminal work on functional explanations. On this question, see also Butler (2003a, 2003b).
2. On conversion in English and directionality, see also Balteiro (2007a, 2007b).
3. But see Bammesberger (1965), Hinderling (1967), Pilch (1970) and Stark (1982).
4. See Lieber (2004) on redundant affixation and semantic compatibility.
5. On the prefix *ge-* see also Hinderling (1967), Lindemann (1970) and Martín Arista (2006, 2008).

References

Balteiro, I. (2007a) *A Contribution to the Study of Conversion in English*. Münster: Waxmann.

Balteiro, I. (2007b) *The Directionality of Conversion in English: A dia-synchronic study*. Frankfurt am Mein: Peter Lang.

Bammesberger, A. (1965) *Deverbative jan-Verba des Altenglischen, vergleichend mit den übrigen altgermanischen Sprachen dargestellt*. München: Ludwig-Maximilians Universität.

Bauer, L. (1988) *Introducing Linguistic Morphology*. Edinburgh: Edinburgh University Press.

Bauer, L. and Varela, S. (2005) Conversion and zero-derivation: An introduction. In L. Bauer and S. Varela (eds) *Approaches to Conversion/Zero Derivation* 1–17. Münster: Waxmann.

Beard, R. and Volpe, M. (2005) Lexeme-morpheme base morphology. In P. Štekauer and R. Lieber (eds) *Handbook of Word-formation* 189–205. Dordrecht: Springer.

Brinton, L. and Closs Traugott, E. (2005) *Lexicalization and Language Change*. Cambridge: Cambridge University Press.

Butler, C. (2003a) *Structure and Function: A guide to the three major structural-functional theories, Part 1: Approaches to the simplex clause*. Amsterdam: Benjamins.

Butler, C. (2003b) *Structure and Function: A guide to the three major structural-functional theories, Part 2: From clause to discourse and beyond*. Amsterdam: Benjamins.

Cruz, J. de la (1975) Old English pure prefixes: Structure and function. *Linguistics* 13(145): 47–81.

Dik, S. (1986) On the notion "functional explanation". *Belgian Journal of Linguistics* 1: 11–52.

Francis, E. and Michaelis, L. (2003) Mismatch: A crucible for linguistic theory. In E. Francis and L. Michaelis (eds) *Mismatch: Form-function incongruity and the architecture of grammar* 1–27. Stanford, CA: CSLI Publications.

González Torres, E. (2009) *Affixal Nouns in Old English: Morphological description, multiple bases and recursivity.* Unpublished Ph.D. dissertation. University of La Rioja.

Heidermanns, F. (1993) *Etymologisches Wörterbuch der germanischen Primäradjective.* Berlin: Walter de Gruyter.

Hiltunen, R. (1983) *The Decline of the Prefixes and the Beginnings of the English Phrasal Verb.* Turku: Turun Yliopisto.

Hinderling, R. (1967) *Studien zu den starken Verbalabstrakten des Germanischen.* Berlin: Walter de Gruyter.

Holthausen, F. (1963) *Altenglisches etymologysches Wörterbuch.* Heidelberg: Winter.

Horgan, D. (1980) Patterns of variation and interchangability in some Old English prefixes. *Neuphilologische Mitteilungen* 91: 127–130.

Kastovsky, D. (1968) *Old English Deverbal Substantives Derived by means of a Zero Morpheme.* Ph.D. Dissertation. Tübingen: Eberhard-Karls-Universität.

Kastovsky, D (1986) Deverbal nouns in Old and Modern English: From stem-formation to word-formation. In J. Fisiak (ed.) *Historical Semantics-Historical Word Formation* 221–261. Berlin: Mouton de Gruyter.

Kastovsky, D. (1989) Typological changes in the history of English morphology. In U. Fries and M. Heusser (eds) *Meaning and Beyond* 281–293. Tübingen: Niemeyer.

Kastovsky, D. (1990) The typological status of Old English Word Formation. *Papers from the Fifth International Conference on English Historical Linguistics.* In S. Adamson, V. Law, N. Vincent and S. Wright (eds) 205–224. Amsterdam: Benjamins.

Kastovsky, D. (1992) Semantics and vocabulary. In R. Hogg (ed.) *The Cambridge History of the English Language I: The beginnings to 1066* 290–408. Cambridge: Cambridge University Press.

Kastovsky, D. (2005) Conversion and/on zero: Word-formation theory, historical linguistics, and typology. In L. Bauer and S. Varela (eds) *Approaches to Conversion/Zero Derivation* 31–50. Münster: Waxmann.

Kastovsky, D. (2006) Typological changes in derivational morphology. In A. van Kemenade and B. Los (eds) *The Handbook of The History of English* 151–177. Oxford: Blackwell.

Lieber, R. (2004) *Morphology and Lexical Semantics.* Cambridge: Cambridge University Press.

Lindemann, J. W. R. (1970) *Old English Preverbal Ge-: Its meaning.* Charlottesville, VA: Virginia University Press.

Manova, S. and Dressler, W. (2005) The morphological technique of conversion in the inflecting-fusional type. In L. Bauer and S. Varela (eds) *Approaches to Conversion/Zero Derivation* 67–101. Münster: Waxmann.

Marchand, H. (1969) *The Categories and Types of Present-day English Word-formation.* München: C.H. Beck'sche.

Martín Arista, J. (2006) Alternations, relatedness and motivation: Old English *A-*. In P. Guerrero Medina and E. Martínez Jurado (eds) *Where Grammar*

Meets Discourse: Functional and cognitive perspectives 113–132. Córdoba: Servicio de Publicaciones de la Universidad de Córdoba.

Martín Arista, J. (2008) *Ge-* and the descriptive power of *Nerthus*. *Journal of English Studies* 5(6): 209–231.

Martín Arista, J. (2010) Strong verbs derived from strong verbs: Affix variation, grammaticalisation and recursivity. *SKASE Journal of Theoretical Linguistics* 7(1): 36–56.

Orel, V. (2003) *A Handbook of Germanic Etymology*. Leiden: Brill.

Pesquera Fernández, L. (2009) *Transparent and Opaque Word-formation in the Derivational Paradigms of Old English Strong Verbs*. Unpublished Ph.D. dissertation. University of La Rioja.

Pilch, H. (1970) *Altenglische Grammatik: Dialektologie, Phonologie, Morphologie, Syntax*. München: Max Hueber.

Seebold, E. (1970) *Vergleichendes und Etymologisches Wörterbuch der Germanischen Starken Verben*. The Hague: Mouton.

Stark, D. (1982) *The Old English Weak Verbs: A diachronic and synchronic analysis*. Tübingen: Niemeyer.

Štekauer, P. (1996) *A Theory of Conversion in English*. Frankfurt am Mein: Peter Lang.

Štekauer, P. (2005a) *Meaning Predictability in Word Formation*. Amsterdam: Benjamins.

Štekauer, P. (2005b) Onomasiological approach to word-formation. In P. Štekauer and R. Lieber (eds) *Handbook of Word-formation* 207–232. Dordrecht: Springer.

Van Valin, R. (2005) *Exploring the Syntax-semantics Interface*. Cambridge: Cambridge University Press.

Van Valin, R. D. and LaPolla, R. J. (1997) *Syntax: Structure, meaning and function*. Cambridge: Cambridge University Press.

Index

1. Page numbers include the endnotes on that page.
2. Subject terms appearing in headings or in titles of books, articles and journals have not been indexed.

K

L

Q

R

www.ingramcontent.com/pod-product-compliance
Lightning Source LLC
LaVergne TN
LVHW021127110826
R19582500001B/R195825PG844660LVX00015B/27
* 9 7 8 1 8 4 5 5 3 7 4 4 9 *